DRONE OPERATIONS

RECREATIONAL AND COMMERCIAL PILOTING

RICHARD SKIBA

Copyright © 2024 by Richard Skiba

All rights reserved.

No portion of this book may be reproduced in any form without written permission from the publisher or author, except as permitted by copyright law.

This publication is designed to provide accurate and authoritative information in regard to the subject matter covered. While the publisher and author have used their best efforts in preparing this book, they make no representations or warranties with respect to the accuracy or completeness of the contents of this book and specifically disclaim any implied warranties of merchantability or fitness for a particular purpose. No warranty may be created or extended by sales representatives or written sales materials. The advice and strategies contained herein may not be suitable for your situation. You should consult with a professional when appropriate. Neither the publisher nor the author shall be liable for any loss of profit or any other commercial damages, including but not limited to special, incidental, consequential, personal, or other damages.

Skiba, Richard (author)

Drone Operations: Recreational and Commercial Piloting

ISBN 978-1-7635353-3-6 (paperback) 978-1-7635353-4-3 (eBook) 978-1-7635353-5-0 (Hardcover)

Non-fiction

Contents

Preface		1
1.	Introduction	5
2.	Types of Drones	24
3.	Drone Regulations	43
4.	Drone Regulations in the USA	48
5.	Drone Regulations in Australia	62
6.	Drone Regulations in the United Kingdom	75
7.	Drone Regulations in Europe	95
8.	Drone Regulations in India	102
9.	Perform Operational Inspections on Remote Operated Systems	111
10.	Impacts of Weather on Drone Flights	155
11.	Aircraft Loading	185
12.	Remote Pilot Aircraft and Their Components	195
13.	Launch, Control and Recover a Remotely Piloted Aircraft	223
14.	Hazardous Attitudes, Aeronautical Decision-Making and Judgment	260
15.	Communications	270
16.	Managing Human Factors in Remote Pilot Aircraft Systems Operations	301

17.	Multirotor Remote Pilot Aircraft Systems Operations	330
18.	Fixed Wing Remote Pilot Aircraft Systems Operations	363
19.	On Ground Control	401
20.	Navigating Remote Pilot Systems	418
21.	Managing Remote Pilot Aircraft Systems Energy Source Requirements	453
22.	Conducting Aerial Search Using Remote Piloted Aircraft	471
23.	Commercial and Industrial Applications	493
References		509
Index		514

Preface

A drone, also known as an unmanned aerial vehicle (UAV), is an aircraft that operates without a human pilot onboard. Drones can be remotely controlled by a human operator or can fly autonomously based on pre-programmed flight plans or dynamic inputs from onboard sensors. They come in various sizes and configurations, from small consumer models used for recreational purposes to larger, more sophisticated models used for tasks such as aerial photography, surveillance, agriculture, and even military operations.

Drones are known by various names depending on their specific purpose, design, or function. Here are some common names and terms used to refer to drones:

1. UAV (Unmanned Aerial Vehicle)

2. RPAS (Remotely Piloted Aircraft Systems)

3. UAS (Unmanned Aircraft System)

4. Quadcopter (a type of drone with four rotors)

5. Multirotor (a drone with multiple rotors, typically more than four)

6. Hexacopter (a drone with six rotors)

7. Octocopter (a drone with eight rotors)

8. Fixed-wing UAV (a drone with fixed wings, resembling traditional airplanes)

9. sUAS (Small Unmanned Aircraft System)

10. Microdrone (very small drones, often used for indoor or close-range operations)

11. Nano drone (extremely small drones, typically used for surveillance or research)

12. Aerial drone

13. Flying robot

14. Remotely operated aircraft

These are just a few examples, and there may be other specialized terms or names used in specific industries or contexts, and these will be used interchangeably throughout this book.

This book on drone operations offers aims to provide comprehensive knowledge by consolidating information on drone technology, regulations, safety protocols, and best practices. It provides readers with a comprehensive understanding that would otherwise be scattered across various sources. Whether catering to novices or seasoned operators, this book serves as an educational aid, offering valuable insights into drone operation techniques, flight planning strategies, maintenance procedures, and effective troubleshooting methods.

With drone regulations constantly evolving, this book can offer clarity on legal requirements, airspace restrictions, and compliance measures, helping operators navigate the intricate web of regulatory frameworks. A range of specific country regulations are covered within the book.

The book also aims to provide safety awareness relevant to drone operations. Emphasizing safety principles is crucial in drone operations to prevent accidents and mitigate risks. This book underscores the importance of safety protocols, encourages thorough risk assessments, outlines emergency procedures, and promotes responsible flying practices.

Many practical exercises, case studies, and real-world examples are incorporated in this book to enhance operational skills and foster sound decision-making abilities, facilitating the development of proficiency in piloting drones. Further, tailored to specific sectors such as photography, videography, agriculture, surveying, or public safety, this book offers professionals valuable insights into how drones are employed, including advanced techniques and emerging trends within their respective industries.

Overall, this book serves as a comprehensive reference guide, enabling operators to quickly access information on a wide range of topics, from equipment selection and maintenance to flight planning and data analysis. It is intended to provide readers with information and guidance on the operation of drones for recreational and commercial purposes. Before delving into the content of this book, it is important for readers to understand and acknowledge the following disclaimer:

1. Compliance with Local Laws and Regulations: The operation of drones, whether for recreational or commercial purposes, is subject to a myriad of local laws, regulations, and restrictions. Readers are advised to familiarize themselves with the applicable laws and regulations in their respective jurisdictions before engaging in any drone-related activities. This includes but is not limited to obtaining necessary permits, licenses, and authorizations from relevant authorities.

In the United States, for example, recreational drone operators must adhere to regulations set forth by the Federal Aviation Administration (FAA), including registration requirements for drones weighing over a certain threshold. Additionally, commercial drone operators are subject to Part 107 regulations, which govern the operation of small unmanned aircraft systems (sUAS) for commercial purposes.

1. Training and Practice are Essential: The safe and effective operation of drones requires proper training and consistent practice. Readers should understand that proficiency in piloting drones, understanding airspace regulations, and handling emergency situations are skills that must be developed over time through dedicated training and practice.

A novice drone pilot should undergo comprehensive training programs offered by reputable organizations or institutions to learn essential skills such as flight manoeuvres, emergency procedures, and airspace navigation. Additionally, regular practice sessions in controlled environments can help pilots improve their proficiency and confidence in operating drones safely.

1. Assumption of Risk: Engaging in drone operations involves inherent risks, including but not limited to collisions, equipment malfunctions, and regulatory violations. Readers should recognise these risks when participating in drone-related activities and should take appropriate precautions to mitigate them.

While drones offer exciting opportunities for aerial photography and videography, operators must be aware of the risk of collisions with obstacles or other aircraft, especially in congested airspace. Pilots should conduct pre-flight inspections, maintain visual line of sight with their drones, and adhere to altitude and distance limits to minimize the risk of accidents.

1. Consultation with Professionals: Readers are encouraged to seek guidance and advice from qualified professionals, such as aviation experts, legal advisors, and drone industry professionals, to address specific concerns or questions related to drone operations. Professional consultation can provide valuable insights and ensure compliance with applicable regulations and best practices.

Commercial drone operators may benefit from consulting with aviation attorneys or regulatory experts to navigate complex legal requirements and obtain necessary waivers or exemptions for specialized operations, such as night flights or flights over people.

Introduction

The term "drone" historically originated in the context of military intelligence, surveillance, and reconnaissance missions due to the advantage of not risking a pilot's life in combat zones [1]. While the US Federal Aviation Administration officially adopted the term "unmanned aircraft vehicle/system (UAV/UAS)" in 2005, the term "drone" continues to be preferred in peer-reviewed literature [2]. The historical association of drones with military applications is well-documented, with drones being extensively utilized in various military activities [3].

Figure 1: A U.S. Navy Grumman F7F-2D Tigercat drone control aircraft of Utility Suqdron VU-6 following a Radioplane KD2R drone in 1953. USN, Public domain, via Wikimedia Commons.

Figure 2: A RAF Reaper UAV (Unmanned Aerial Vehicle), taken in 2009. Photo: POA(Phot) Tam McDonald/MOD, OGL v1.0OGL v1.0, via Wikimedia Commons.

Over time, the use of drones has expanded beyond military applications to encompass a wide range of civilian uses [4]. Drones are now employed in diverse fields such as healthcare, where they show significant potential for applications like medical surveillance, disaster site monitoring, and epidemiological research [5, 6]. Additionally, drones have found utility in delivering emergency medical supplies like automated external defibrillators to aid in out-of-hospital cardiac arrest situations [7, 8].

The historical evolution of drone technology has seen a shift towards civilian applications, including cultural preservation through the use of drone-based orthophotos for restoring historical buildings [9]. Furthermore, the term "drone" has become the popular and dominant descriptor for unmanned aerial vehicles, reflecting its widespread usage and recognition [10].

A drone, also known as an Unmanned Aerial Vehicle (UAV), refers to an aircraft that operates without a human pilot on board. Drones have gained significant popularity in recent years due to their diverse applications in various fields, including wildlife monitoring, parcel delivery, urban mobility, disaster management, and healthcare supply chain [11-15]. These unmanned aircraft are equipped with sensors, cameras, and other technologies that enable them to perform tasks autonomously or under remote control [16].

The use of drones has expanded beyond military applications to include environmental research, conservation efforts, and even forensic investigations [13, 14]. Drones have been utilized to study wildlife behaviour, monitor ecosystems, and support conservation initiatives [11, 13]. Additionally, drones have been integrated into healthcare systems to transport medical supplies quickly and efficiently, especially in emergency situations like the COVID-19 pandemic [12].

Figure 3: Dron DJI Mini 4 Pro. Example of a civil drone. Jacek Halicki, CC BY-SA 4.0, via Wikimedia Commons.

Despite their numerous benefits, drones have raised concerns regarding their impact on wildlife, particularly in terms of disturbance and noise pollution [11, 13, 14]. Studies have shown that drones can affect the behaviour of animals such as kangaroos and sea turtles, highlighting the need to establish ethical operating thresholds when using drones in wildlife monitoring [11, 13]. Furthermore, the noise emissions from drones have been a subject of research, with efforts to understand the effects of drone noise on humans and wildlife [17].

Drone technology has seamlessly woven into the fabric of daily life, thanks to its ever-evolving complexity. Across various sectors, drones serve myriad contemporary applications:

- Photography and Videography: Drones have transformed the field of photography, offering photographers unparalleled aerial perspectives. Tailored to specific photography needs, these drones capture stunning vistas of city skylines, coastal landscapes, and architectural wonders. Additionally, they enhance video recording endeavours, enriching sports events, filmmaking projects, and virtual real estate tours with unique angles and immersive visuals.

- Delivery Services: Delivery drones have revolutionized logistics by efficiently transporting food, packages, and goods directly to consumers' doorsteps. These "last mile" delivery drones streamline operations for retailers and grocery chains, offering a swift and efficient alternative to traditional delivery methods.

- Search and Rescue: Drones play a vital role in rescue operations, particularly in hazardous environments where human intervention is perilous. Autonomous underwater vehicles assist in water-based rescues, while aerial drones aid in locating individuals stranded in avalanches or other emergencies, ensuring swift and effective responses to crises.

- Agriculture: In agriculture, drones optimize farm management practices by conducting field surveys, seeding operations, livestock monitoring, and crop yield estimation. These UAVs bolster efficiency, alleviate physical strain on farmers, and economize time in agricultural operations.

- Surveillance: Law enforcement agencies and military forces harness the power of drones for enhanced surveillance capabilities. Drones support police in monitoring events, gathering evidence of traffic violations, and reconstructing crime scenes. Similarly, military personnel employ drone technology for reconnaissance missions, target tracking, and strategic planning endeavours.

- Personal Use: As costs decline, drones have become accessible to the general public for recreational purposes. Enthusiasts engage in activities such as aerial photography and hobbyist flying. However, recreational drone pilots must adhere to regulations and obtain necessary certifications to ensure safe and responsible operation.

- Wildlife Monitoring: Drones offer a cost-effective solution for wildlife conservation efforts. Conservationists utilize drones to monitor wildlife populations, track animal movements, and assess ecosystem health from aerial perspectives, facilitating conservation initiatives and reforestation projects.

- 3D Modelling: LiDAR-equipped drones conduct landscape surveys and gather data for creating detailed 3D models. These drones provide precise data essential for urban planning, environmental monitoring, and infrastructure development projects.

- Military Operations: Modern military drones, equipped with advanced technologies like thermal imaging and laser range finders, play pivotal roles in intelligence gathering, reconnaissance missions, and targeted airstrikes for national defence purposes.

Photography and videography have undergone a remarkable transformation with the advent of drones. These aerial vehicles have revolutionized the way photographers and filmmakers capture images and footage, offering unprecedented perspectives that were previously inaccessible. Tailored to meet the diverse needs of photography enthusiasts and professionals alike, drones are equipped with advanced imaging capabilities that enable them to capture stunning vistas with clarity and precision.

One of the most significant advantages of drone photography is its ability to provide aerial views of landscapes and cityscapes. From towering city skylines to serene coastal vistas, drones offer photographers the opportunity to capture breathtaking scenes from above, revealing patterns, textures, and perspectives that are often overlooked from ground level. This aerial perspective adds a new dimension to photography, allowing photographers to showcase familiar landmarks and landscapes in a fresh and captivating way.

Figure 4: Aerial Photography Using Drones by Drone Reviews - Aerial View of Sydney, Australia. Drone Reviews, CC BY 2.0, via Wikimedia Commons.

Moreover, drones have become indispensable tools for videographers, enhancing video recording endeavours across various domains. Whether documenting sports events, filming cinematic sequences for movies, or creating virtual real estate tours, drones enable filmmakers to capture dynamic footage from unique angles and perspectives. By manoeuvring effortlessly through the air, drones provide filmmakers with the flexibility to explore creative compositions and perspectives, resulting in videos that are immersive and visually engaging.

Drones have transformed photography and videography by offering photographers and filmmakers unparalleled aerial perspectives. Tailored to meet specific photography needs, drones capture stunning vistas of cityscapes, coastal landscapes, and architectural wonders, while also enhancing video recording endeavours across various domains. With their ability to capture unique angles and perspectives, drones have revolutionized the way images and footage are captured, adding a new dimension to visual storytelling.

Delivery drones represent a groundbreaking innovation in the realm of logistics, fundamentally reshaping the landscape of last-mile delivery services. Traditionally, the final leg of the delivery process, known as the "last mile," has been a bottleneck for retailers and logistics companies, plagued by challenges such as traffic congestion, inefficient routing, and high costs. However, delivery drones offer a transformative solution to these long-standing issues by providing a fast and efficient means of transporting goods directly to consumers' doorsteps.

Figure 5: A Flirtey drone delivers an automated external defibrillator (AED) to treat cardiac arrest. Mollyrose89, CC BY-SA 4.0, via Wikimedia Commons.

By leveraging drone technology, retailers and grocery chains can bypass the constraints of traditional delivery methods, delivering packages with unprecedented speed and precision. These unmanned aerial vehicles are equipped with sophisticated navigation systems and autonomous flight capabilities, allowing them to navigate through urban environments and reach destinations quickly and efficiently. As a result, delivery drones offer a viable alternative to conventional delivery vehicles, particularly in densely populated areas where congestion and traffic congestion pose significant challenges to timely delivery.

Furthermore, delivery drones offer unparalleled flexibility and scalability, enabling retailers to adapt to fluctuating demand and respond rapidly to customer needs. With the ability to fly over traffic and obstacles, drones can cover distances more efficiently than ground-based vehicles, making them particularly well-suited for delivering small, time-sensitive items such as groceries, medication, and consumer electronics.

As an example of drone utilisation for delivery, Zipline International Inc. is an American firm specializing in the design, production, and operation of delivery drones. The company maintains distribution hubs across several countries including Rwanda, Ghana, Japan, the United States, Nigeria, Cote d'Ivoire, and Kenya. As of November 2023, Zipline's drones have completed over 800,000 commercial deliveries and flown more than 40 million miles autonomously [18].

Zipline's drones are primarily utilized for transporting essential medical supplies such as whole blood, platelets, frozen plasma, and cryoprecipitate, as well as medical products like vaccines, infusions, and common medical commodities. Notably, in Rwanda, Zipline's drones handle more than 75 percent of blood deliveries outside of the capital city, Kigali. In Ghana, the company began drone deliveries of vaccines, blood, and medicines in April 2019. Additionally, during the COVID-19 pandemic in 2020, Zipline's partner organization, Novant Health, received a Part 107 aviation waiver from the US Federal Aviation Administration (FAA) to use Zipline's drones for delivering medical supplies and personal protective equipment (PPE) to healthcare facilities in North Carolina.

Beyond medical deliveries, Zipline also offers delivery services for non-medical products. This includes partnerships with retail giants like Walmart, initiated in 2021, and with food service provider Sweetgreen, announced in 2023. Zipline's website showcases a range of potential applications for their drone delivery services, including restaurant deliveries, grocery deliveries, convenience shopping, and e-commerce fulfillment.

Figure 6: A Zipline drone flying and delivering a package. Roksenhorn, CC BY-SA 4.0, via Wikimedia Commons.

Moreover, delivery drones have the potential to reduce carbon emissions and environmental impact associated with traditional delivery methods. By operating on electric power and flying directly to their destinations, drones minimize the need for large fleets of delivery trucks and vans, thereby decreasing traffic congestion and air pollution in urban areas.

Overall, delivery drones represent a game-changing innovation in the field of logistics, offering retailers and businesses a cost-effective, efficient, and environmentally friendly solution for last-mile delivery. As technology continues to advance and regulatory frameworks evolve, delivery drones are poised to play an increasingly prominent role in shaping the future of e-commerce and supply chain management.

Search and rescue missions often involve perilous environments where human intervention poses significant risks. In these challenging situations, drones emerge as indispensable tools, playing a pivotal role in facilitating rescue operations. Whether deployed in remote wilderness areas or amidst natural disasters, drones offer unique capabilities that enhance the effectiveness and efficiency of search and rescue efforts.

Figure 7: A member of "Serve On" holds up a flying drone - used to help identify areas that are worst-hit by the earthquake in Nepal. DFID - UK Department for International Development, CC BY 2.0, via Wikimedia Commons.

One area where drones excel is in water-based rescues, where traditional methods may be impractical or unsafe. Autonomous underwater vehicles (AUVs) equipped with specialized sensors and imaging technology can navigate underwater environments with precision, assisting in the search for missing persons or submerged objects. These AUVs can survey large areas of water quickly and efficiently, providing invaluable assistance to search and rescue teams in locating individuals in distress.

Similarly, aerial drones are instrumental in locating and rescuing individuals stranded in hazardous environments such as avalanches or inaccessible terrain. Equipped with high-resolution cameras, thermal imaging sensors, and other advanced technologies, aerial drones can survey vast areas from above, quickly identifying potential hazards and locating individuals in need of assistance. By providing real-time aerial reconnaissance, drones enable search and rescue teams to assess the situation rapidly and deploy resources effectively, ensuring swift and coordinated responses to emergencies.

Overall, drones play a vital role in search and rescue operations by offering unparalleled capabilities for navigating hazardous environments and locating individuals in distress. Whether deployed underwater or in the air, drones enhance the efficiency and effectiveness of rescue efforts, helping to save lives and mitigate the impact of disasters and emergencies.

In the realm of agriculture, drones have emerged as transformative tools, revolutionizing traditional farm management practices. By harnessing the capabilities of unmanned aerial vehicles (UAVs), farmers can optimize various aspects of their operations, leading to increased efficiency and productivity across the agricultural sector.

One of the key applications of drones in agriculture is conducting field surveys. Equipped with advanced sensors and imaging technology, drones can capture high-resolution aerial imagery of farmland, providing farmers with valuable insights into crop health, soil moisture levels, and pest infestations. This aerial data enables farmers to make informed decisions about irrigation, fertilization, and pest control, ultimately improving crop yields and reducing resource wastage.

Moreover, drones play a crucial role in seeding operations, particularly in large-scale farming operations. By deploying drones equipped with precision seeding systems, farmers can accurately distribute seeds across vast tracts of land, ensuring optimal spacing and coverage for maximum crop growth. This automated seeding process not only saves time and labour but also improves planting efficiency and crop uniformity, leading to higher yields and reduced input costs.

Figure 8: A drone intended for agricultural use. Agridrones Solutions Israel, CC BY-SA 4.0, via Wikimedia Commons.

In addition to field surveys and seeding operations, drones are also utilized for livestock monitoring in agriculture. With the ability to cover large areas of pastureland quickly and efficiently, drones enable farmers to track the health and behaviour of their livestock, identify sick or injured animals, and detect potential predators or intruders. This real-time monitoring capability allows farmers to respond promptly to livestock-related issues, improving animal welfare and overall farm management practices.

Furthermore, drones are invaluable tools for estimating crop yields and assessing crop health throughout the growing season. By analysing aerial imagery captured by drones, farmers can accurately quantify crop yields, predict harvest times, and identify areas of the field that may require additional attention or intervention. This data-driven approach to crop management enables farmers to optimize their resources, maximize yields, and minimize waste, ultimately enhancing the sustainability and profitability of their operations.

Figure 9: Onyxstar HYDRA-12 UAV with embedded hyperspectral camera for agricultural research. Cargyrak, CC BY-SA 4.0, via Wikimedia Commons.

Drones have revolutionized agriculture by optimizing farm management practices and enhancing productivity across the agricultural sector. From conducting field surveys and seeding operations to monitoring livestock and estimating crop yields, drones offer farmers powerful tools for improving efficiency, reducing costs, and achieving sustainable agricultural practices. As technology continues to advance, the role of drones in agriculture is expected to expand further, driving innovation and driving the future of farming.

In both law enforcement and military contexts, drones have become indispensable tools for enhancing surveillance capabilities, offering a range of benefits in monitoring, evidence gathering, and strategic planning.

Law enforcement agencies rely on drones to monitor events and gather evidence, providing a bird's-eye view of activities from above. Drones equipped with high-resolution cameras and live-streaming capabilities enable police to surveil large areas efficiently and discreetly, aiding in crime prevention and response efforts. Additionally, drones are valuable tools for gathering evidence of traffic violations, allowing authorities to monitor roadways and capture footage of speeding vehicles or other infractions. In the event of a crime, drones can also be deployed to reconstruct crime scenes, providing investigators with valuable insights into the sequence of events and the spatial relationships between various elements.

Similarly, military forces leverage drone technology for reconnaissance missions and strategic planning endeavours. Equipped with advanced sensors and imaging systems, military drones can conduct aerial reconnaissance over enemy territory, gathering intelligence on enemy positions, movements, and infrastructure. This real-time surveillance capability enables military commanders to make informed decisions about troop deployments, target prioritization, and operational planning, enhancing the effectiveness and efficiency of military operations. Additionally, drones are used for target tracking, enabling military personnel to monitor and follow high-value targets or potential threats with precision and accuracy.

Overall, drones play a vital role in surveillance operations for both law enforcement and military purposes, providing valuable capabilities for monitoring, evidence gathering, and strategic planning. By offering aerial perspectives and real-time surveillance capabilities, drones enhance situational awareness and decision-making capabilities, ultimately contributing to the safety and security of communities and the success of military missions. As drone technology continues to advance, the role of drones in surveillance is expected to expand further, driving innovation and enhancing capabilities in both civilian and military contexts.

Firefighters utilize drones in various ways to enhance their firefighting efforts and improve overall safety during emergency response operations. Here are some common applications of drones in firefighting:

Aerial Reconnaissance: Drones equipped with cameras and thermal imaging sensors provide firefighters with valuable aerial perspectives of fire scenes. By capturing high-resolution imagery and thermal data from above, drones enable firefighters to assess the extent of the fire, identify hot spots, and detect potential hazards such as structural weaknesses or hazardous materials. This aerial reconnaissance allows firefighters to develop effective firefighting strategies and prioritize resource allocation based on real-time situational awareness.

Search and Rescue: Drones equipped with high-resolution cameras and infrared sensors are valuable tools for search and rescue operations in firefighting scenarios. These drones can quickly scan large areas, including hard-to-reach or hazardous terrain, to locate missing persons or trapped victims. By providing aerial support to ground-based rescue teams, drones help expedite search efforts and improve the chances of locating and rescuing individuals in distress.

Fire Mapping and Monitoring: Drones equipped with GPS technology and mapping software are used to create detailed maps of fire-affected areas, including fire spread patterns and evacuation routes. By monitoring fire behaviour and progression in real-time, drones enable firefighters to anticipate changes in fire conditions, adjust firefighting tactics accordingly, and effectively communicate situational updates to incident commanders and emergency responders.

Figure 10: Grizzly Creek Fire Drone Flight at Hanging Lake. White River National Forest U.S. Forest Service, Public domain, via Wikimedia Commons.

Hazardous Material Detection: Drones equipped with gas sensors and other environmental monitoring tools can detect hazardous materials or chemical leaks in fire scenes. By conducting aerial surveys of the area, drones help identify potential hazards to firefighter safety and inform decision-making regarding evacuation procedures, containment measures, and appropriate protective equipment.

Post-Fire Assessment: After the fire has been extinguished, drones are used to conduct post-fire assessments and damage inspections. By capturing aerial imagery of the fire-affected area, drones assist firefighters in evaluating structural integrity, assessing damage to buildings and infrastructure, and identifying any remaining hot spots or smouldering debris that may pose a risk of re-ignition.

Overall, drones play a crucial role in enhancing firefighting operations by providing firefighters with valuable aerial perspectives, real-time data, and situational awareness during emergency response scenarios. By leveraging drone technology, firefighters can work more safely and effectively to mitigate fire hazards, protect lives and property, and ultimately save lives.

As the costs of drone technology decrease, it has become increasingly accessible to the general public for personal and recreational use. This accessibility has led to a surge in interest among enthusiasts who are eager to explore the capabilities of drones for various recreational activities. Among these activities, aerial photography stands out as a popular pursuit, allowing hobbyists to capture stunning aerial shots and videos from unique perspectives that were previously inaccessible. Additionally, hobbyist flying, which involves piloting drones for enjoyment and skill development, has gained traction as an engaging pastime for drone enthusiasts of all ages.

However, despite the recreational appeal of drone technology, it is essential for enthusiasts to operate their drones responsibly and in accordance with established regulations. Recreational drone pilots are required to adhere to airspace rules and safety guidelines set forth by aviation authorities to ensure the safety of airspace users and the general public. This includes obtaining necessary certifications or registrations, such as the Federal Aviation Administration's (FAA) Part 107 certification in the United States, which demonstrates competency in drone operation and knowledge of airspace regulations.

Figure 11: Drone used for personal use. Oregon Department of Transportation, CC BY 2.0 >, via Wikimedia Commons.

Furthermore, responsible drone operation involves a commitment to safety and awareness of potential risks associated with flying drones in different environments. Recreational drone pilots must exercise caution when operating their drones near populated areas, airports, or other restricted zones to avoid potential accidents or conflicts with other airspace users. Additionally, being mindful of privacy concerns and respecting the privacy of others is crucial when capturing aerial footage or images in public spaces.

While drones offer exciting opportunities for recreational use and creative expression, it is essential for enthusiasts to approach drone flying with a sense of responsibility and awareness of regulatory requirements. By adhering to safety guidelines, obtaining necessary certifications, and respecting airspace regulations and privacy considerations, recreational drone pilots can enjoy the benefits of drone technology while minimizing risks and ensuring a positive experience for themselves and others.

In the realm of 3D modelling, drones equipped with Light Detection and Ranging (LiDAR) technology have revolutionized the process of capturing accurate spatial data for various applications. LiDAR-equipped drones conduct aerial surveys of landscapes, gathering detailed information about surface topography, vegetation, and structures with remarkable precision. This data is then used to create highly accurate 3D models of the surveyed area, providing valuable insights for a range of industries and disciplines.

One of the primary applications of LiDAR-equipped drones is in urban planning and development projects. By capturing detailed 3D models of urban environments, including buildings, roads, and infrastructure, drones equipped with LiDAR technology enable urban planners and architects to visualize proposed developments and assess their impact on the surrounding landscape. This data-driven approach to urban planning allows for more informed decision-making and better integration of new developments into existing urban environments.

Figure 12: Quad propeller drone with Lidar technology. Jonte, CC BY-SA 4.0, via Wikimedia Commons.

Furthermore, LiDAR-equipped drones play a crucial role in environmental monitoring and conservation efforts. By conducting aerial surveys of natural landscapes, such as forests, wetlands, and coastal areas, drones can capture detailed data about vegetation density, terrain elevation, and habitat characteristics. This information is essential for monitoring changes in ecosystems over time, identifying areas of ecological significance, and informing conservation strategies aimed at preserving biodiversity and mitigating environmental degradation.

In addition to urban planning and environmental monitoring, LiDAR-equipped drones are also used in infrastructure development projects such as road construction, pipeline monitoring, and utility management. By providing accurate 3D models of terrain and infrastructure assets, drones enable engineers and project managers to plan and execute construction projects more efficiently, minimize environmental impacts, and optimize resource allocation.

LiDAR-equipped drones play a vital role in 3D modelling applications, providing precise spatial data that is essential for urban planning, environmental monitoring, and infrastructure development projects. By leveraging the capabilities of LiDAR technology, drones enable professionals across various industries to make informed decisions, optimize resources, and achieve better outcomes in their respective fields.

TYPES OF DRONES

Unmanned Aerial Vehicles (UAVs) can be classified based on various criteria. One common classification is based on the type of UAV, which includes fixed-wing and rotary-wing UAVs [19]. Another classification criterion is based on the propulsion system used, which categorizes UAVs into fuel-based, hybrid fuel-electric, and pure electric propulsion systems [20]. Additionally, UAVs can be classified based on their applications, such as in agriculture, urban vegetation mapping, surveillance, disaster management, and more [21-23].

Furthermore, UAVs can be classified based on their capabilities and features. For instance, UAVs can be classified based on their ability to fly autonomously or be remotely piloted [24]. Moreover, the classification of UAVs can also be related to their detection and identification methods. RF-based techniques have been employed for UAV detection and identification, leading to hierarchical classification approaches for RF-based UAV detection systems [25, 26].

In the context of UAV networks, classifications can be made at different levels, such as cell level, system level, and system of system level, to understand how different components contribute to overall system performance [27]. Moreover, the use of machine learning algorithms has enabled the classification of benign or malicious packets in UAV networks for enhanced security [28].

General Types

Drones come in various types, each designed for specific purposes and applications including:

1. Fixed-Wing Drones: Fixed-wing drones resemble traditional airplanes and feature wings that generate lift as they move forward. These drones are well-suited for long-distance flights and aerial mapping missions due to their efficient design and extended flight times. Fixed-wing drones are commonly used in agriculture, surveying, and aerial photography.

2. Multirotor Drones: Multirotor drones, such as quadcopters and hexacopters, feature multiple rotors arranged in a symmetrical configuration. These drones are highly manoeuvrable and capable of hovering in place, making them ideal for tasks that require precise positioning or aerial photography and videography. Multirotor drones are popular among hobbyists, filmmakers, and commercial operators.

3. Single-Rotor Helicopters: Single-rotor helicopters, also known as rotary-wing drones, feature a single large rotor mounted on top of the aircraft. These drones offer greater lifting capacity and stability compared to multirotor drones, making them suitable for heavy-lift applications such as aerial crane operations or transporting cargo in challenging environments.

4. Hybrid Drones: Hybrid drones combine features of fixed-wing and multirotor designs, allowing them to take off and land vertically like a multirotor drone while also benefiting from the efficiency of fixed-wing flight for long-distance travel. These drones offer versatility for applications that require both vertical take-off and long-endurance flight, such as surveillance or aerial mapping.

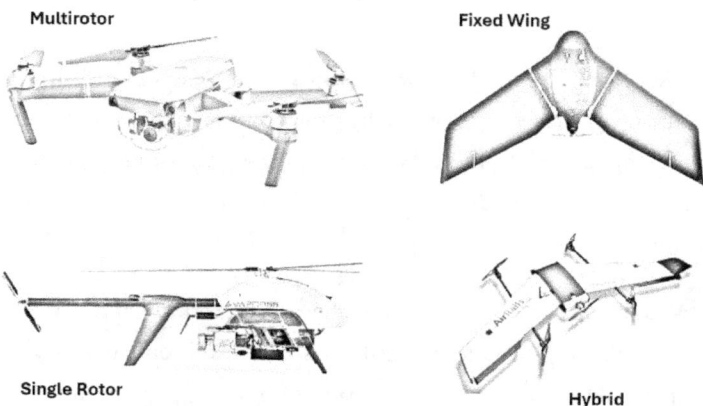

Figure 13: General drone types.

Fixed Wing Drones

Fixed-wing drones utilize aerodynamics to generate lift and remain airborne, similar to traditional aircraft. They are commonly employed for mapping large areas due to their extended autonomy and efficiency. Unlike multi-rotor drones, fixed-wing drones rely on their aerodynamic design for sustained flight, resulting in longer endurance and faster flight speeds.

However, fixed-wing drones tend to be more expensive than multi-rotor drones and require ample space for take-off and landing, akin to airplanes. Some larger models necessitate specialized ground equipment for launching and recovery. Additionally, fixed-wing drones lack the vertical take-off and landing capabilities of multi-rotor drones, limiting their manoeuvrability and suitability for certain applications.

Figure 14: Fixed wing drone used by USGS. Bureau of Land Management Oregon and Washington from Portland, America, Public domain, via Wikimedia Commons.

Fixed wing drone used by USGS. Bureau of Land Management Oregon and Washington from Portland, America, Public domain, via Wikimedia Commons.

Despite these limitations, fixed-wing drones offer several advantages. They can cover longer distances, map larger areas, and remain airborne for extended periods, making them ideal for tasks such as aerial mapping, surveying, agriculture, and inspection. Their high altitude capabilities and ability to carry heavier payloads further enhance their utility in various technical applications.

However, operating fixed-wing drones requires training and proficiency due to their unique flight characteristics and landing requirements. Launching and controlling a fixed-wing drone necessitate confidence and skill, as they are always moving forward and typically require a launcher for take-off. Additionally, processing and analysing the vast amount of data captured by fixed-wing drones can be complex and time-consuming, requiring specialized software and expertise.

Overall, fixed-wing drones are valued for their efficiency, range, and endurance, making them indispensable tools for a wide range of technical applications, including aerial mapping, surveying, agriculture, inspection, construction, and security. Despite their challenges, their capabilities make them indispensable assets in various industries.

Multirotor Drones

Multi-rotor drones present an accessible and cost-effective solution for aerial surveillance and photography, offering precise control over positioning and framing. Named for their multiple rotors, these drones commonly come in configurations such as tricopters, quadcopters, hexacopters, and octocopters, with quadcopters being the most prevalent variant. Unlike fixed-wing drones, multi-rotor drones feature multiple vertically rotating motors, enabling them to take off, land, fly, and hover with agility akin to traditional helicopters.

Figure 15: Quadrocopter DJI Mavic Pro additionally equipped with spectrophotometer Ocean Insight STS-VIS and supplementary equipment. Taras Kazantsev, CC BY 4.0, via Wikimedia Commons.

Renowned for their versatility, multi-rotor drones are widely favoured for both recreational and professional applications, particularly in aerial photography. Their compact size and manoeuvrability make them an ideal choice for capturing dynamic shots from various perspectives. Additionally, multi-rotor drones offer the flexibility to mount different types of cameras for diverse tasks, further enhancing their utility.

However, multi-rotor drones are accompanied by limitations, primarily concerning flight autonomy and efficiency. Their reliance on multiple rotors consumes more energy, resulting in shorter flight times compared to fixed-wing counterparts. Typically, multi-rotor drones offer flight durations of less than an hour, necessitating the use of multiple batteries for prolonged operations, thus incurring additional costs.

Advantages of multi-rotor drones include enhanced control during flight, enabling precise movements in various directions, including vertical ascent and descent, lateral motion, and rotation. Their agility allows for close proximity flights to structures and facilitates efficient payload delivery and inspections. Additionally, some designs feature redundant components to ensure continued operation in the event of motor failure.

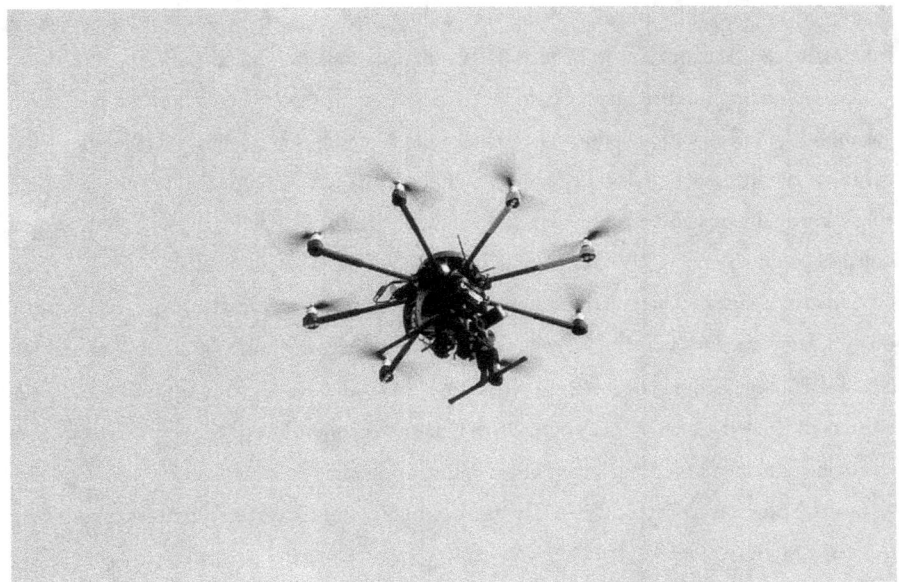

Figure 16: Unmanned aerial vehicle multirotor (A Tyges FV8 Thermodrone). David Perez, CC BY-SA 3.0, via Wikimedia Commons.

Despite their advantages, multi-rotor drones are unsuitable for certain tasks requiring extended endurance and high-speed flights, such as large-scale aerial mapping and long-distance inspections. Their inherent inefficiency and reliance on electric motors limit their flight times, typically ranging from 20 to 30 minutes with lightweight payloads. Moreover, the reliance on computer-controlled flight systems renders them vulnerable to failure, necessitating redundancy in components to mitigate risks.

In technical applications, multi-rotor drones find utility in visual inspections, thermal imaging, aerial photography and videography, and 3D scanning. While they excel in tasks requiring precise manoeuvrability and close-quarters operations, their limitations must be considered when selecting the appropriate drone for specific applications.

Single-Rotor Helicopters

Helicopters aren't limited to large, manned aircraft; they also manifest in smaller, unmanned drone forms. These drones come in a range of sizes, from tiny toys to sizable drones equipped with cameras, with prices scaling up accordingly. While some single-rotor drones can be found for as little as $20 in stores, others fetch thousands online.

An interesting feature of professional single-rotor drones is their potential to run on gas instead of electricity, depending on their size. While they boast greater efficiency than multi-rotor drones, they don't match the efficiency of fixed-wing counterparts. Flying a single-rotor drone can be nearly as challenging as piloting a fixed-wing one, requiring a delicate balance.

Although single-rotor drones may not offer as many applications as multi-rotor drones, they excel at carrying heavier payloads. Typically favoured by hobbyists seeking a new challenge, single-rotor drone types are robust and sturdy, resembling actual helicopters in their structure and design. With just one rotor and a tail rotor for stability and control, they offer a blend of multi-rotor agility and single-rotor efficiency.

Single-rotor drones typically utilize gas/petrol engines rather than batteries, resulting in longer flight times. However, their larger size and complexity compared to other UAVs make them pricier and more challenging to operate, with larger blades posing increased safety risks.

Advantages of single-rotor helicopters include their superior efficiency, especially when gas-powered, allowing for extended flight times. Their long blades, resembling spinning wings, contribute to this efficiency, making them suitable for hovering with heavy payloads or achieving a balance between hovering and forward flight.

However, single-rotor drone types have their drawbacks. They are complex, expensive, and less stable than multi-rotor counterparts, requiring meticulous maintenance due to their mechanical intricacy. Additionally, the presence of large spinning blades increases safety risks, especially in the event of component failure.

In technical applications, single-rotor drones find utility in tasks such as aerial LIDAR laser scanning, drone surveying, and carrying heavy payloads. While they offer unique capabilities, their complexity and safety considerations make them a specialized choice for specific operations. In he example shown as Figure 17, the unmanned helicopter is used for spatial dose measurement developed by the Japan Atomic Energy Agency, a national research and development institution. Equipped with a dedicated radiation measurement system on Yamaha Motor's autonomous flying unmanned helicopter RMAX G1, it measures direct gamma rays from the ground and scattered rays from the air.

Figure 17: JAEA Yamaha RMAX G1. Cp9asngf, CC BY-SA 4.0, via Wikimedia Commons.

Hybrid Drones

This innovative category of professional drones melds the extended flight duration characteristic of fixed-wing drones with the vertical take-off and landing capabilities of single-rotor or multi-rotor drones. A notable example of this hybridization is exemplified in the drone developed for Prime Air.

VTOL, an acronym for vertical take-off and landing, serves as the primary rationale behind the creation of this hybrid model. While fixed-wing drones boast significant differences in flight duration compared to other drone types, they encounter challenges with landing. The hybrid model adeptly integrates the strengths of both, despite being a relatively recent concept, it's swiftly gaining traction and recognition.

Hybrid VTOL drones blend the advantages of fixed-wing and rotor-based designs. These drones feature rotors affixed to fixed wings, enabling them to hover, take off, and land vertically. Although currently limited in availability, advancements in technology suggest that this option may witness increased popularity in the years ahead. Notable examples include Amazon's Prime Air delivery drone, showcasing a fixed-wing hybrid VTOL design.

Introduced as the latest frontier in drone technology, fixed-wing hybrid VTOL drones refer to fixed-wing aircraft modified for vertical take-off and landing. They amalgamate the endurance and range of fixed-wing UAVs with the vertical take-off capability of rotary-wing devices, addressing the space constraints inherent in traditional fixed-wing UAV operations. These drones find applications in mapping, power line inspection, surveillance, agriculture, and rescue operations.

However, the complexity of this VTOL drone renders it less suitable for novice operators, and its advanced technology positions it at the upper echelon of the fixed-wing drone market in terms of cost.

Figure 18: Hybrid drone. Tilo Ronschke, CC BY-SA 4.0, via Wikimedia Commons.

Hybrid VTOL drones present several advantages: the autopilot system handles stability, freeing up the pilot to concentrate on navigation, while leveraging the strengths of both fixed-wing and rotor-based designs, excelling in both hovering and forward flight capabilities. However, their availability in the market is currently limited, with only a few models accessible, and the technology supporting these drones is still in the evolutionary stages. In terms of technical applications, they find utility in drone delivery services.

Other variations

Various drone types beyond those previously discussed offer diverse functionalities:

Mini Drones: Designed primarily for recreational purposes, mini drones lack the robustness required for commercial tasks due to their lightweight build, which compromises image stability.

Nano Drones: Despite their diminutive size, nano drones are equipped with micro cameras, exemplified by models like the Black Hornet utilized by the British military. With flight durations of up to 25 minutes and a range of one mile, they enhance reconnaissance capabilities significantly.

Tactical Drones: Combining compact dimensions with agility, tactical drones feature GPS technology and infrared cameras, rendering them well-suited for surveillance missions despite their modest size of 4.5 feet and weight of 4.2 lbs.

Reconnaissance Drones: These drones, measuring approximately 16 feet in length and weighing over 2200 pounds, boast extended flight durations of up to 52 hours at altitudes of 35,000 feet. Known as High Altitude Long Endurance drones (HALE) and Medium Altitude Long Endurance drones (MALE), they facilitate comprehensive reconnaissance operations, launched from the ground.

Large Combat Drones: With lengths averaging around 36 feet, large combat drones are primarily employed for deploying laser-guided bombs or air-to-surface missiles. Featuring ranges exceeding 1000 miles and operational durations of up to 14 hours, they excel in combat scenarios.

Non-Combat Large Drones: Although sizable, non-combat large drones are not intended for combat applications. More advanced than nano drones, they are utilized for large-scale reconnaissance tasks.

Target and Decoy Drones: Serving roles in monitoring and engaging targets, target and decoy drones are tailored in appearance to meet specific mission requirements.

GPS Drones: Establishing connections with satellites via GPS technology, GPS drones accurately plot flight paths, collecting data crucial for informed decision-making.

Photography Drones: Equipped with professional-grade cameras, photography drones, including those with 4K capabilities, capture high-resolution images. Employing automated flight modes and precision stability, they excel in capturing expansive aerial photography.

Uses by Type

In various industries and applications, different types of drones are employed for specific tasks. These tasks range from aerial photography and film production to critical functions such as search and rescue. Multirotor drones are versatile, commonly used for a wide array of activities including roof and solar inspections, real estate photography, mapping, surveying, and power line inspections. They excel in tasks requiring close-range manoeuvrability and precise hovering. Fixed-wing drones, on the other hand, are preferred for tasks involving extensive mapping, surveying, and large-scale inspections due to their longer flight endurance and faster speeds.

Powered lift drones, a newer category, offer a hybrid solution combining the benefits of both multirotor and fixed-wing designs. These drones are suitable for various applications including aerial photography, mapping, surveying, and inspections. They provide the agility and vertical take-off capabilities of multirotors along with the efficiency and endurance of fixed-wing aircraft. Finally, helicopters, though less common in civilian applications, are indispensable for certain tasks such as aerial weed spraying, wildlife tracking, and search and rescue operations due to their vertical take-off and landing capabilities and manoeuvrability in challenging terrain. Each type of drone is tailored to specific needs, ensuring efficient and effective performance across diverse industries and tasks.

Figure 19 shows what aircraft types are in common use for different commercial drone applications.

	Multirotor	Fixed Wing	Powered Lift/Hybrid	Helicopter
Photography, Film and TV	✓			✓
Roof and solar inspection	✓	✓	✓	✓
Real Estate	✓			✓
Drones for mapping	✓	✓	✓	✓
Drones for surveying	✓	✓	✓	✓
Bridge and building inspection	✓			✓
Power line inspection	✓	✓	✓	✓
Drones in mining	✓	✓	✓	✓
Stockpile assessment	✓	✓	✓	✓
Vegetation crop mapping	✓	✓	✓	✓
Wildlife tracking and stock inspection	✓	✓	✓	✓
Aerial weed spraying	✓	✓	✓	✓
Search and rescue	✓	✓	✓	✓

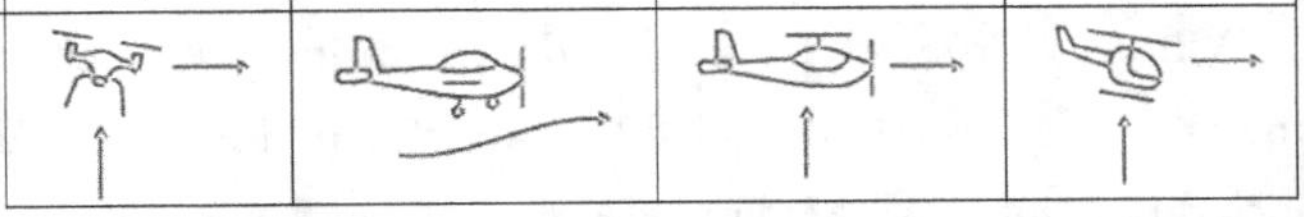

Figure 19: Drone types in common use for different commercial drone applications.

Drones categorised by weight/size

Drones can be categorized based on their size, ranging from very small nano drones to large drones, although this varies with jurisdictions. Typically, very small drones, also known as nano drones, measure 1 to 50 cm and are used for military surveillance due to their inconspicuous size. Small drones, slightly larger than nano drones, are typically between 50 cm and 2 meters and are utilized for recreational purposes like photography and indoor equipment inspections [29]. Medium drones, exceeding 2 meters in size and weighing up to 200 kilograms, find applications in both professional and amateur photography. Large drones, comparable to smaller aircraft, serve military purposes such as surveillance and combat, as well as civilian applications like drone deliveries and film-making [29].

Drones can also be classified based on their payload capacity into four categories: featherweight drones, lightweight drones, middleweight drones, and heavy-lift drones. Featherweight drones, weighing less than 11 grams, are used for military surveillance and can carry payloads ranging from 4 to 100 grams. Lightweight drones, weighing between

200 and 1000 grams, are employed for recreation and photography, with a payload capacity of 150 to 270 grams. Middleweight drones, ranging from 1 to 600 kg, are utilized for professional applications and aerial photography, carrying payloads averaging between 400 and 1460 grams. Finally, heavy-lift drones, weighing more than 160 kg, are primarily used for military purposes and civil applications such as drone deliveries, with payload capacities exceeding 1000 kg [29].

There is not a universal standard for classifying Unmanned Aircraft Systems (UAS), often referred to interchangeably as UAVs in this context. Different entities, such as defense agencies and civilians, have their own distinct criteria for categorizing UAS, with civilians often employing flexible classifications based on factors like size, range, and endurance, akin to the tier system used by the military [30]. The US National Aviation Intelligence Integration Office website offers a comprehensive overview of global UAS classification categories.

Within a US context, For size-based classification, UAS can be further subdivided into the following classes: Very small UAVs, including Micro or Nano UAVs; Small UAVs, including Mini UAVs; Medium UAVs; and Large UAVs [30].

Moreover, UAS can be classified based on their travel range and airborne endurance, utilizing subclasses delineated by the US military, such as Very low-cost close-range UAVs, Close-range UAVs, Short-range UAVs, Mid-range UAVs, and Endurance UAVs.

According to the US Department of Defense, UAVs are categorized into five groups, each distinguished by Size, Maximum Gross Take-off Weight (MGTW) in pounds, Normal Operating Altitude in feet, and Airspeed in knots. Group 1 encompasses Small UAVs weighing between 0-20 lbs, operating at altitudes below 1,200 AGL (Above Ground Level), and achieving speeds below 100 knots, while Group 5 includes the Largest UAVs with a weight exceeding 1320 lbs, capable of operating at altitudes above 18,000 feet and any airspeed. If a UAS possesses characteristics of a higher group, it is classified accordingly [30].

As a further example of jurisdictional variation, in Australia drone weight categories are determined based on the Maximum Take Off Weight (MTOW), which includes the weight of the aircraft, fuel/batteries, and payload. Officially, there are two weight categories, but in practice, there are three [31].

The first category encompasses aircraft weighing less than 25kg. However, the Civil Aviation Safety Authority may impose further restrictions, limiting it to less than 7kg if the Remote Pilot Licence training was conducted on an aircraft weighing less than 7kg.

This weight category is not influenced by the manufacturer or payload. Remote Pilot Licence holders can operate any drone within the specified weight range for which they hold a license.

For drones with MTOW exceeding 25kg, licensing is specific to each individual aircraft type. This means that the Remote Pilot Licence is issued for a particular manufacturer and aircraft design, rather than a general category.

The Drone Rules 2021, introduced by the Directorate General of Civil Aviation (DGCA) in India, classify drones based on their total maximum weight, which encompasses both the drone's weight and any payload it carries [32]. These weight categories play a crucial role in determining the applicable regulations and requirements for each drone type.

Outlined in the Drone Rules 2021, the general weight categories include [32]:

1. Nano Drones: Drones with a total maximum weight of up to 250 grams (approximately).

2. Micro Drones: Drones with a total maximum weight ranging from 251 grams to 2 kilograms (approximately).

3. Small Drones: Drones with a total maximum weight ranging from 2.01 kilograms to 25 kilograms (approximately).

4. Medium Drones: Drones with a total maximum weight ranging from 25.01 kilograms to 150 kilograms (approximately).

5. Large Drones: Drones with a total maximum weight exceeding 150 kilograms (approximately).

Each weight category is associated with specific regulations and requirements concerning registration, licensing, permissions, and more. For instance, commercial operations involving drones in the "Micro," "Small," "Medium," and "Large" categories often necessitate Remote Pilot Licenses (RPLs) and explicit permissions from the DGCA.

The classification of drones according to AESA regulations introduces six distinct categories based on their Maximum Take-Off Mass (MTOW) or weight, each accompanied by specific criteria to define inclusion within these categories.

Outlined in Regulations (EU) 2019/947 and (EU) 2019/945, the six drone classes, denoted from C0 to C6, have been established. The latest inclusion of the last two classes in Delegated Regulation (EU) 2020/1058 marks their adoption as standard categories for European scenarios.

Class C0 pertains to drones with a MTOW not exceeding 250g, adhering to defined specifications such as maximum speed, design for injury prevention, and inclusion of manufacturer instructions.

Drones categorized as C1 must meet criteria including a weight between 250g and 900g, with features like geo-awareness, remote identification, and safe recovery systems mandated for this class.

Class C2 encompasses drones weighing up to 4kg, requiring additional functionalities such as low-speed operation, interference-protected data links, and lighting systems for night visibility.

Class C3 involves drones with a MTOW limit of 25kg, necessitating features like geo-awareness, flight termination systems, and unique serial numbers for identification.

Drones classified as C4 must be safely controllable, have no automatic flight mode except for stabilization, and be accompanied by manufacturer instruction manuals.

For Class C5, drones with MTOW below 25kg must meet requirements like clear altitude information, low-speed capabilities, and systems for stall recovery and safe landing.

Class C6 drones, also capped at 25kg MTOW, require systems for altitude data management, secure data links, and remote identification, among other specifications.

Drones by Range

Drones can be categorized based on their range into very close range, close range, short range, mid-range, and long range.

Very close-range drones are capable of flying within a radius of 5 km from the controller, maintaining flight for an average duration of 1 hour, primarily utilized for recreational activities [29].

Close-range drones extend their reach up to 50 km from the controller and can sustain flight for 1-6 hours, often deployed in military surveillance operations due to their ability to achieve higher altitudes.

Short-range drones expand the flight radius to up to 150 km, boasting powerful batteries enabling flight durations of 8-12 hours, commonly employed in combat and surveillance missions [29].

Mid-range drones possess impressive capabilities, capable of covering 400 miles (644 km) and maintaining flight at altitudes of 12,000 to 30,000 feet for over 24 hours, typically utilized in combat and surveillance operations [29].

Long-range drones, also known as endurance drones, surpass other categories in terms of flight time and range, with capabilities to travel well over 400 miles (644 km) without signal loss. Primarily employed in military surveillance and espionage, they find applications in tracking weather patterns, geological surveys, and geographic mapping by professionals [29].

Classification by Power Source

Drones rely on various power sources to operate, including batteries, gasoline, hydrogen fuel cells, and solar energy. These different power sources offer distinct advantages and drawbacks, leading to the classification of drones into different types based on their power sources.

Battery-powered drones are favoured for their lightweight construction, ability to store significant energy, and high discharge rates. However, they are limited by their short lifespan, susceptibility to fire if mishandled, and rapid energy consumption [29].

Gasoline-powered drones, typically larger in size, carry highly combustible fuels, posing potential safety risks and emitting more noise compared to battery-operated counterparts. Despite these drawbacks, they offer benefits such as the absence of expensive battery backup and charging stations, quicker refuelling times, higher flight speeds, capacity for heavier payloads, longer flight times, and smoother flight characteristics [29].

Hydrogen fuel cell drones represent a renewable and environmentally friendly option with higher energy density than batteries, resulting in longer flight times and quick refuelling capabilities. However, they generate considerable heat and currently exhibit lower efficiency levels [29].

Solar drones leverage sunlight to charge their batteries, reducing operating costs and extending operating hours. While they are lightweight and environmentally friendly, their flight time is limited to periods when sunlight is available.

The primary power source for most drones is the battery, with common types including lithium polymer (LiPo), nickel-metal hydride (NiMH), and nickel-cadmium (NiCd) batteries. Gasoline/petrol is typically utilized for large-sized drones due to its lightness and affordability. Hydrogen-powered drones offer efficiency benefits at high altitudes but are still evolving in terms of efficiency and heat generation. An example of a hydrogen-powered drone is the CW-25H, capable of carrying payloads up to 4 kg and recognized for its innovation at CES 2022. Solar-powered drones capitalize on sunlight conversion into electricity for prolonged flights [29].

Types of drones according to motors

Based on the motor type, drones can be categorized into brushed motor drones and brushless motor drones [29].

Brushed drone motors are known for their affordability and compact size, making them suitable for various applications. They excel in extreme environments due to their lack of electronics and feature replaceable brushes for extended longevity. With simple two-wire control and no requirement for a speed controller at fixed speeds, they offer straightforward operation. However, they exhibit drawbacks such as uncomplicated wiring, lower energy efficiency, and faster wear of commutators and brushes.

On the other hand, brushless drone motors offer several advantages over brushed motors. Their brushless design requires minimal maintenance and ensures longer durability. They are more efficient, resulting in less energy wasted as heat, and provide better speed and torque due to the absence of brushes. With a wider speed range and superior heat dissipation, they are suitable for high-speed and high-power operations, albeit at a higher cost [29].

Brushed motors are commonly found in recreational drones, offering cost-effectiveness but requiring more maintenance compared to brushless counterparts. While their power remains consistent across models, their size varies, influencing performance. These motors are typically connected to a speed reducer system, reducing strain on the motor and extending its lifespan [29].

In contrast, brushless motors stand out for their maintenance-free operation and higher power output. Their design eliminates brush friction, allowing for more efficient performance and greater speeds. However, each brushless motor requires its own electronic speed controller (ESC) to regulate rotation speed, as they primarily operate with alternating current.

Relevance of Drone Classification to Operations

Understanding drone classifications in your jurisdiction is crucial for several reasons:

1. Regulatory Compliance: Different jurisdictions have varying regulations regarding the operation, registration, and licensing requirements for drones. Knowing the classifications ensures compliance with local laws and regulations, helping to avoid legal issues and potential penalties.

2. Safety: Drone classifications often correspond to different operational limitations and requirements, such as altitude restrictions, flight range, and payload capacity. Understanding these classifications helps ensure safe operation, reducing the risk of accidents, collisions, and injury to people or property.

3. Operational Limitations: Certain classifications may have specific operational limitations or prohibited areas, such as flying near airports, government buildings, or crowded events. Knowing these limitations helps drone operators plan their flights effectively and avoid restricted areas.

4. Insurance Requirements: Insurance policies for drones may vary based on their classifications. Some insurance providers may offer different coverage options or premiums depending on the type of drone and its intended use. Understanding drone classifications ensures that adequate insurance coverage is obtained to protect against potential liabilities.

5. Professional Use: For commercial or professional drone operations, knowing the classifications is essential for determining the appropriate licensing, certification, or training requirements. It also helps in selecting the right equipment and understanding the capabilities and limitations of different drone types for specific applications.

6. Data Privacy: In some jurisdictions, drone classifications may have implications for data privacy and security, particularly when drones are equipped with cameras or sensors. Understanding these classifications helps ensure compliance with privacy laws and regulations governing the collection and use of data obtained through drone operations.

Overall, knowing drone classifications in your jurisdiction is fundamental for operating drones safely, legally, and responsibly, whether for recreational or commercial purposes. It enables drone operators to navigate regulatory requirements, mitigate risks, and uphold standards of professionalism and accountability in their operations.

Drone Regulations

Drone regulations, established by government agencies, serve as comprehensive guidelines governing the operation, registration, and usage of unmanned aerial vehicles (UAVs), more commonly known as drones. The primary objective of these regulations is to ensure safety, privacy, and security within the airspace where drones operate. These regulations encompass several key aspects to achieve these goals.

Firstly, registration requirements are prevalent across many countries, mandating that drones be registered with a government agency before they are allowed to operate. This process aids authorities in tracking drone ownership and holding operators accountable for their actions.

Secondly, licensing and certification are essential for commercial drone operators, necessitating specific permits or qualifications to legally conduct business activities involving drones. These licenses often entail passing exams or completing training programs to demonstrate proficiency in drone operation.

Operational restrictions form another crucial component of drone regulations, delineating the permissible locations, timings, and manner of drone flights. This may include restrictions on flying near airports, over crowds, or in sensitive areas such as government buildings or national parks, with altitude and speed limitations often imposed.

Payload restrictions are also addressed in regulations, particularly concerning the types of payloads drones are permitted to carry. This is especially pertinent for drones equipped with cameras or sensors, where privacy concerns may arise from the collection of images or data.

Additionally, safety features are mandated to minimize the risk of accidents or collisions. These may include fail-safe mechanisms, geo-fencing technology to prevent drones from entering restricted airspace, or lighting systems for visibility during nighttime operations.

Privacy protection measures are integrated into drone regulations to address concerns regarding the collection and use of images or data obtained through drone operations. This may involve restrictions on surveillance activities or requirements for obtaining consent when capturing images of individuals or private property.

Finally, enforcement mechanisms and penalties are outlined in regulations to deter violations. Operators found breaching drone regulations may face fines, license revocation, or other disciplinary actions.

Drone regulations play a vital role in promoting responsible and safe drone operation while mitigating potential risks to public safety, privacy, and security. Compliance with these regulations is imperative for drone operators to avoid legal repercussions and facilitate the safe integration of drones into airspace.

Drone regulations vary significantly from country to country, leading to a lack of harmonization globally [33]. International collaborators must adhere to the specific rules and regulations of each country to ensure compliance [34]. For instance, in Europe, regulations are overseen by the European Aviation Safety Agency (EASA), while Australia follows the Civil Aviation Safety Authority Regulations (CASR-101) [35].

In Africa, the regulatory landscape for drones in agriculture is challenging, with many countries having either very restrictive regulations or no proper regulations in place, making it cumbersome to acquire licenses for drone operations [36]. Similarly, Kenya faced issues with high tariffs on imported drones, prompting a re-evaluation of its drone regulations [37].

Different countries and regions, such as the USA, EU, China, and Turkey, have distinct regulations governing drone use [38]. The European Union directly regulates drones over 150 kg through the International Civil Aviation Organization (ICAO), while regulations for drones under 150 kg are determined by individual countries [39].

Several countries have implemented strong and current drone regulations to ensure safety, security, and responsible drone use. Here are some examples:

1. United States: The Federal Aviation Administration (FAA) regulates drone operations through Part 107 of the Federal Aviation Regulations (FARs), which outlines rules for commercial drone operations. Additionally, the FAA has es-

tablished various airspace restrictions and registration requirements for recreational drone users.

2. United Kingdom: The Civil Aviation Authority (CAA) governs drone operations in the UK, with regulations categorized under the Air Navigation Order. The UK has strict rules regarding drone registration, pilot certification, and airspace restrictions. Drone users must adhere to the Drone Code, which outlines guidelines for safe and legal drone use.

3. Canada: Transport Canada regulates drone operations through the Canadian Aviation Regulations (CARs) and the Canadian Drone Safety website. Drone pilots must obtain a Special Flight Operations Certificate (SFOC) for certain types of operations, and recreational users must follow safety guidelines outlined by Transport Canada.

4. Australia: The Civil Aviation Safety Authority (CASA) oversees drone operations in Australia, with regulations outlined in the Civil Aviation Safety Regulations (CASR) Part 101. Drone pilots must obtain a Remote Pilot Licence (RePL) for commercial operations and adhere to strict safety standards and airspace restrictions.

5. Germany: The German Aviation Authority (Luftfahrt-Bundesamt) regulates drone operations in Germany, with rules outlined in the Luftverkehrsgesetz (Air Traffic Act) and the Drohnenverordnung (Drone Regulation). Drone pilots must obtain a license for certain types of operations and adhere to strict safety and privacy regulations.

6. France: The Directorate General of Civil Aviation (DGAC) regulates drone operations in France, with rules outlined in the Code de l'aviation civile (Civil Aviation Code) and the Arrêté du 17 décembre 2015 (Decree of December 17, 2015) regarding drone flights. Drone pilots must obtain a permit for certain types of operations and follow strict safety and privacy guidelines.

7. Japan: The Ministry of Land, Infrastructure, Transport and Tourism (MLIT) regulates drone operations in Japan, with rules outlined in the Civil Aeronautics Act and the Civil Aviation Bureau's drone regulations. Drone pilots must obtain a license for certain types of operations and adhere to strict safety and privacy

regulations.

These countries have comprehensive drone regulations in place to ensure safe and responsible drone use while addressing security and privacy concerns.

Despite the common goal of minimizing risks to airspace users and property, there are notable variations in drone regulations across countries [40]. The lack of standardization in regulations poses challenges for the industry's development, with divergent approaches observed in countries like New Zealand, the United States, and Singapore [41].

Drone regulations exhibit significant variation across countries due to differences in legal structures, airspace management systems, safety considerations, privacy norms, and cultural attitudes towards drones. Several factors contribute to this diversity in regulations:

- Firstly, there are differences in registration and licensing requirements. Some nations mandate drone operators to register their aircraft with aviation authorities or acquire specific licenses or permits for commercial operations. The prerequisites for registration and licensing, such as age criteria, training obligations, and application procedures, vary across jurisdictions.

- Secondly, operational restrictions dictate where and when drones can be flown, varying between countries. These restrictions encompass flying near airports, over populous regions, or sensitive sites like governmental establishments, military bases, or natural reserves. Limits on altitude, flight speed, and requirements for maintaining line-of-sight during operation also differ.

- Thirdly, drone categories and classifications diverge based on factors like weight, size, and intended usage. These classifications often determine the applicable regulations for different types of drones. While some countries categorize drones based on weight classes, others categorize them based on capabilities or intended operations.

- Furthermore, regulations concerning payload and equipment vary. Some jurisdictions impose limitations on the types of payloads drones can carry, especially regarding cameras or sensors, citing privacy or security concerns. Conversely, other regions have more lenient rules in this regard.

- Privacy and data protection laws also differ significantly. Some nations enforce stringent privacy regulations, necessitating drone operators to obtain consent before capturing images or recording video footage of individuals or private property. Conversely, other countries have more permissive regulations or are still formulating legislation to address evolving privacy concerns.

- Additionally, regulations regarding safety and security measures exhibit disparities. These include requirements for safety features like geo-fencing technology, automatic return-to-home functions, or anti-collision systems, which vary across jurisdictions. Moreover, some nations have specific rules concerning data encryption to prevent unauthorized access or interference.

- Lastly, enforcement mechanisms and penalties for violating drone regulations vary. While some countries impose fines, license suspensions, or criminal charges for serious infractions, others prioritize education and awareness campaigns to foster compliance.

Overall, the variation in drone regulations underscores the diverse regulatory strategies adopted by different countries to manage the opportunities and challenges posed by the rapid proliferation of drone technology. As the drone industry evolves, countries may revise and update their regulations to align with evolving technological, operational, and societal dynamics.

Drone Regulations in the USA

In the United States, drone regulations are primarily governed by the Federal Aviation Administration (FAA), which has established rules and guidelines to ensure safe and responsible drone operation. Some key aspects of drone regulations in the USA include:

1. Registration: The FAA requires all drones weighing between 0.55 pounds (250 grams) and 55 pounds (25 kilograms) to be registered with the agency. This applies to both recreational and commercial drone operators, and registration must be renewed every three years.

2. Remote Pilot Certification: Commercial drone operators are required to obtain a Remote Pilot Certificate by passing the FAA's Part 107 exam. This certification demonstrates the operator's knowledge of airspace regulations, safety procedures, and operational best practices.

3. Operational Limitations: The FAA imposes several operational limitations on drone flights, including restrictions on flying near airports, over people, and above certain altitudes. Drones must also remain within the operator's visual line of sight during flight, unless a waiver is obtained.

4. Airspace Authorization: Drone operators must obtain authorization from the FAA or use designated apps like LAANC (Low Altitude Authorization and Notification Capability) to fly in controlled airspace or near airports.

5. No-Fly Zones: Certain areas, such as national parks, military installations, and sensitive government facilities, are designated as no-fly zones for drones. Flying

in these areas is strictly prohibited.

6. Safety Measures: The FAA mandates certain safety features for drones, such as anti-collision lights for nighttime operations and geo-fencing technology to prevent drones from entering restricted airspace.

7. Privacy Protection: While the FAA primarily focuses on safety regulations, privacy concerns related to drone operations are typically addressed at the state and local levels. Some states have enacted laws restricting drone surveillance and data collection to protect individual privacy rights.

8. Enforcement and Penalties: Violations of FAA regulations can result in civil penalties, fines, or legal action. Enforcement is carried out by the FAA, local law enforcement agencies, and other authorized entities.

Drone regulations in the USA are designed to promote the safe and responsible integration of drones into the national airspace system while addressing concerns related to privacy, security, and public safety. The FAA continues to update and refine its regulations to keep pace with advancements in drone technology and changes in operational practices.

Determining whether you're flying for leisure or commercial purposes is crucial in understanding which rules apply to your drone usage. If your intention is recreational, simply paying a nominal registration fee and passing a basic knowledge test suffices. However, engaging in commercial activities with your unmanned aerial vehicle (UAV) requires a more comprehensive exam and obtaining Part 107 certification. With this certification, you gain the ability to utilize your drone for various commercial endeavours, such as selling stock imagery, participating in film productions, capturing aerial footage at events like weddings or in real estate ventures [42-44].

Regarding drone laws in the USA, understanding your status as a drone user is paramount to researching and adhering to the relevant regulations. For recreational drone flyers, taking the Drone Safety Test is mandatory. Conversely, for those flying drones for commercial, governmental, or other non-recreational purposes, acquiring a Remote Pilot Certificate from the FAA is imperative. Additionally, any drone weighing more than 250 grams (0.55 lbs) requires registration through the FAA's Drone Zone, with each registration valid for three years ventures [42-44].

Operating a UAV entails abiding by general rules and guidelines set forth by the FAA, including maintaining visual line-of-sight, adhering to altitude restrictions, and avoiding controlled airspace without proper authorization. Additionally, all drone operators should download the B4UFLY app, which provides real-time information on airspace restrictions and flying requirements based on their GPS location ventures [42-44].

Commercial drone operators must possess a current Remote Pilot Certificate issued by the FAA and ensure that each drone is registered on the FAADroneZone website. Furthermore, several key requirements, such as maintaining visual line-of-sight, complying with altitude limits, and yielding right-of-way to manned aircraft, must be met while conducting aerial surveys or inspections for work purposes ventures [42-44].

To fly a drone recreationally, passing The Recreational UAS Safety Test (TRUST) is necessary, while obtaining a Remote Pilot Certificate from the FAA is mandatory for commercial drone operations. Certification requirements include being proficient in English, possessing physical and mental capabilities to operate a drone safely, being at least 16 years old, passing the Part 107 test at an FAA-approved testing centre, and undergoing TSA security screening ventures [42-44].

The United States airspace is classified into different categories based on the level of control and management required for air traffic. These classifications help ensure the safe and efficient operation of aircraft within the national airspace system.

Airspace is categorized into regulatory and nonregulatory, with four types falling under these categories: controlled, uncontrolled, special use, and other airspace.

Controlled airspace encompasses various classifications within which air traffic control (ATC) services are provided. Of particular relevance to remote pilots are Class B, Class C, Class D, and Class E airspace. Class B airspace typically extends from the surface to 10,000 feet mean sea level (MSL) and surrounds the busiest airports, requiring authorization from ATC for operation. Class C airspace, spanning from the surface to 4,000 feet above airport elevation, surrounds airports with control towers and radar approach controls, necessitating authorization for operation. Class D airspace, extending from the surface to 2,500 feet above airport elevation, surrounds airports with operational control towers, also requiring ATC authorization. Class E airspace, not falling under Class A, B, C, or D airspace, encompasses a significant portion of airspace in the United States, facilitating safe control of aircraft during instrument flight rules (IFR) operations.

Uncontrolled airspace, or Class G airspace, extends from the surface to the base of overlying Class E airspace. Remote pilots do not require ATC authorization to operate in Class G airspace.

Special use airspace designates areas where specific activities are confined or where limitations may be imposed on aircraft operations. This includes prohibited areas, restricted areas, warning areas, military operation areas (MOAs), alert areas, and controlled firing areas (CFAs). Information about special use airspace is depicted on instrument charts, detailing effective altitude, operational conditions, controlling agencies, and chart panel locations.

The primary classifications of US airspace include:

1. Class A:

   - Class A airspace extends from 18,000 feet above mean sea level (MSL) up to and including flight level (FL) 600 (60,000 feet MSL).

   - It is typically found above the flight levels used for most commercial and general aviation operations.

   - All aircraft operating in Class A airspace must be under instrument flight rules (IFR) and are subject to air traffic control (ATC) clearance.

2. Class B:

   - Class B airspace surrounds the busiest airports in the United States.

   - It extends from the surface to typically 10,000 feet MSL and is shaped like an inverted wedding cake, with successive layers of airspace expanding outward from the airport.

   - Air traffic control clearance is required for all aircraft to enter Class B airspace, and aircraft must be equipped with a two-way radio and an operating transponder.

3. Class C:

   - Class C airspace surrounds airports with a moderate level of air traffic activity.

- It extends from the surface to typically 4,000 feet above the airport elevation and within a radius of 5 nautical miles.

- Similar to Class B airspace, air traffic control clearance is required for entry, and aircraft must have a two-way radio and an operating transponder.

4. Class D:

- Class D airspace surrounds airports with operational control towers but lower levels of air traffic compared to Class B and Class C airports.

- It typically extends from the surface to 2,500 feet above the airport elevation and within a radius of 4 nautical miles.

- Pilots must establish two-way communication with the air traffic control tower before entering Class D airspace.

5. Class E:

- Class E airspace encompasses controlled airspace that is not classified as Class A, B, C, or D.

- It extends from either the surface or a designated altitude to the base of Class A airspace.

- Class E airspace is typically found in areas where instrument procedures are established, such as airways, off-route airspace, and terminal areas.

6. Class G:

- Class G airspace is uncontrolled airspace that lies below Class E airspace.

- It extends from the surface up to the base of Class E airspace or 14,500 feet MSL, whichever is lower, in most areas.

- Pilots operating in Class G airspace are not required to communicate with air traffic control but must adhere to visual flight rules (VFR) minimums.

These airspace classifications help ensure safe separation between aircraft and facilitate the efficient flow of air traffic throughout the National Airspace System (NAS). Pilots must be familiar with the requirements and procedures associated with each class of airspace to operate safely and in compliance with federal regulations.

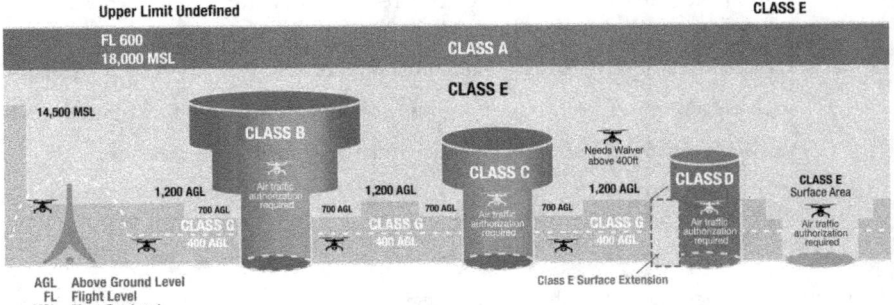

Figure 20: Airspace guidance for small UAS operators. Adapted from Department of Transportation, Airport Operators Guide to UAS.

Drones operating in US airspace are subject to various limitations and regulations to ensure safety and compliance. Some of the key limitations include:

1. Altitude Restrictions: Drones must generally operate below 400 feet above ground level (AGL) to avoid conflicts with manned aircraft.

2. Visual Line of Sight (VLOS): Operators must maintain visual contact with their drone at all times during flight, without the use of visual aids like binoculars or telescopes.

3. Restricted Areas: Drones are prohibited from flying in certain restricted areas, such as around airports, military installations, national parks, and other sensitive locations.

4. Prohibited Activities: Certain activities, such as flying over crowds of people, near emergency response efforts, or in controlled airspace without authorization, are prohibited.

5. No-Fly Zones: Drones are not allowed to fly in designated no-fly zones, which may include areas near airports, government facilities, and other restricted airspace.

6. Privacy Considerations: Operators must respect individuals' privacy rights and refrain from capturing images or recordings in violation of privacy laws.

7. Licensing and Registration: Commercial drone operators must obtain a Remote Pilot Certificate from the Federal Aviation Administration (FAA) and register their drones with the FAA before flying for commercial purposes.

8. Equipment Requirements: Drones must meet certain equipment requirements, such as having an FAA registration number displayed on the aircraft and broadcasting Remote ID information in accordance with FAA regulations.

Prohibited areas encompass designated airspace where aircraft flight is prohibited for reasons related to security or other national interests [45]. These areas are officially designated and documented in the Federal Register, as well as depicted on aeronautical charts. Identified by a "P" followed by a numerical designation (e.g., P-40), prohibited areas include locations like Camp David and the National Mall in Washington, D.C., housing the White House and Congressional buildings, respectively.

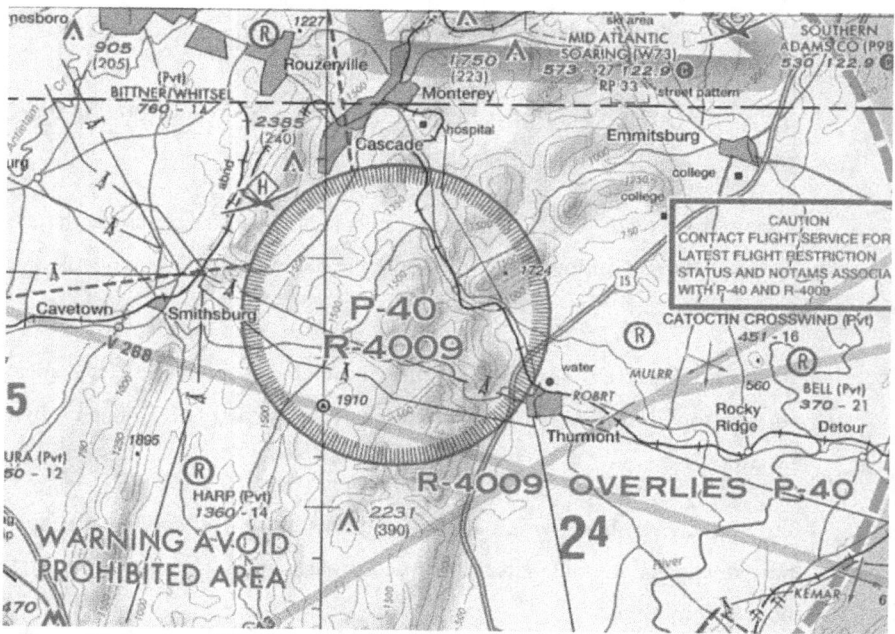

Figure 21: Section of VFR Terminal Area Raster Aeronautical Chart Baltimore/Washington, 84th edition, showing the prohibited area P-40 and restricted area R-4009 around Camp David. US Department of Transportation, Federal Aviation Administration, National Aeronautical Navigation Services, Public domain, via Wikimedia Commons.

Restricted areas are designated areas where aircraft operations pose potential hazards to nonparticipating aircraft [45]. While not entirely off-limits, these zones impose restrictions on aircraft flight due to safety concerns. Activities within controlled zones are constrained by their inherent risks, or limitations may be placed on aircraft operations that are not directly involved in these activities, or both. Such areas indicate the presence of uncommon, often unseen, hazards to aircraft, such as artillery firing, aerial gunnery, or guided missiles. Unauthorized entry into controlled zones without clearance from the relevant authority may pose significant risks to aircraft safety.

1. In cases where a restricted area is inactive and has been relinquished to the FAA, the air traffic control (ATC) facility permits aircraft to operate within the designated airspace without requiring explicit clearance.

2. Conversely, if the restricted area is active and has not been transferred to the FAA, the ATC facility issues specific clearance to ensure aircraft steer clear of the restricted airspace.

Restricted areas are marked on charts with an "R" followed by a numerical identifier (e.g., R-4401) and are depicted on the appropriate en-route chart corresponding to the altitude or flight level (FL) in use. Detailed information about restricted areas can be found on the reverse side of the chart.

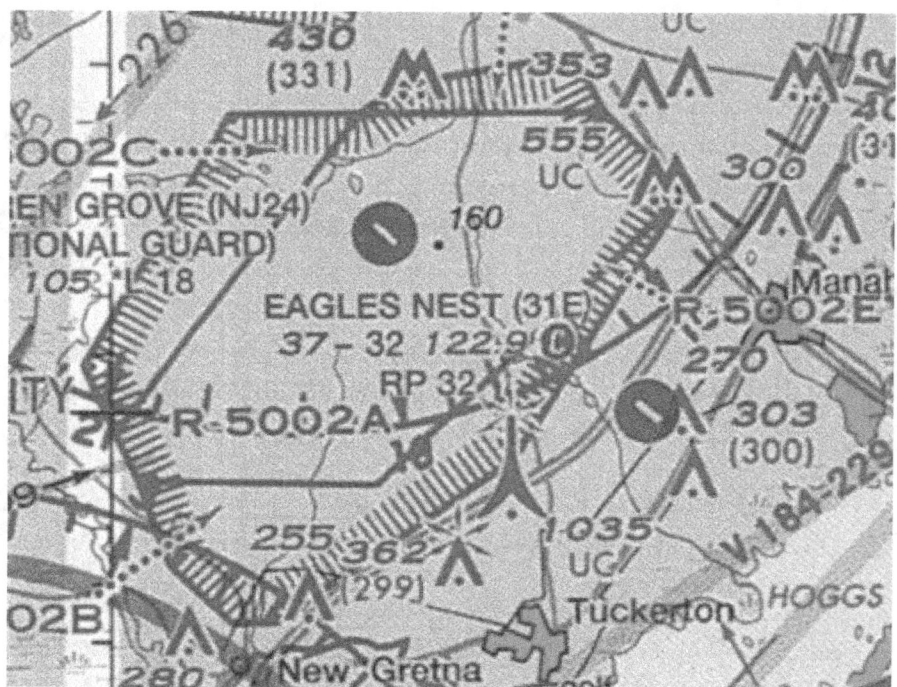

Figure 22: Section of the Sectional Aeronautical Chart for Washington, 90th edition, showing the restricted area R-5002 around Warren Grove, New Jersey. US Department of Transportation, Federal Aviation Administration, National Aeronautical Navigation Services, Public domain, via Wikimedia Commons.

Warning areas share similarities with restricted areas; however, they differ in terms of jurisdiction, as the United States government does not possess exclusive control over the airspace [45]. A warning area is airspace with specific dimensions, stretching outward from the United States coastline by 3 nautical miles (NM), and may feature activities that pose risks to aircraft not involved in said activities. The purpose of these areas is to alert pilots who are not participating in the activities to potential hazards. Warning areas can be situated over domestic waters, international waters, or both, and are designated with a "W" followed by a numerical identifier (e.g., W-237).

Figure 23: Chart showing warning area. US Department of Transportation, Federal Aviation Administration, National Aeronautical Navigation Services, Public domain, retrieved from Federal Aviation Administration (2016).

Military Operation Areas (MOAs): MOAs encompass airspace that has specific vertical and lateral boundaries established to segregate certain military training exercises from instrument flight rules (IFR) traffic. During the utilization of an MOA, nonparticipating IFR traffic may be permitted to transit through the area if air traffic control (ATC) can ensure IFR separation. If not feasible, ATC will divert or restrict nonparticipating IFR traffic. MOAs are depicted on sectional charts, visual flight rules (VFR) terminal area charts, and en route low altitude charts without numerical identification. However, detailed information about MOAs, including operational times, affected altitudes, and the controlling agency, can be found on the reverse side of sectional charts.

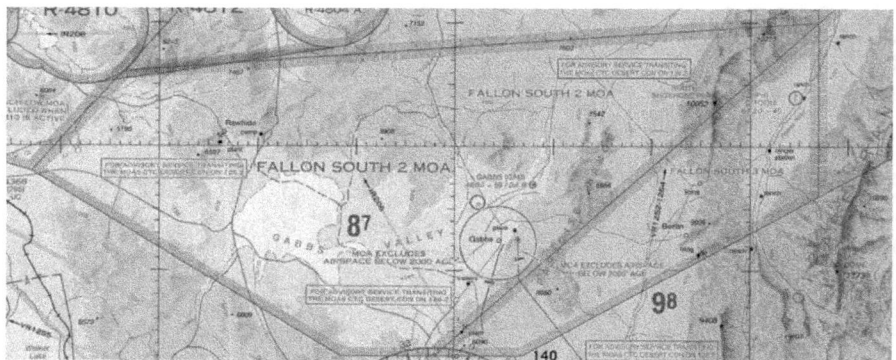

Figure 24: A depiction of the Fallon 2 South w:Millitary Operations Area, near w:Fallon Air Station, on a VFR map. FAA, Public domain, via Wikimedia Commons.

Alert areas are marked on aeronautical charts using an "A" followed by a numerical designation (e.g., A-211) to indicate regions where there might be a heightened concentration of pilot training or unconventional aerial activities. Pilots should exercise vigilance when navigating through alert areas. All operations within an alert area must comply with regulations, without exception, and both pilots of participating aircraft and those passing through the area share equal responsibility for avoiding collisions.

Figure 25: Example of an Alert Area (A-211). Federal Aviation Administration, National Aeronautical Navigation Services, Public domain, retrieved from Federal Aviation Administration (2016).

Controlled Firing Areas (CFAs): CFAs encompass operations that, if carried out outside a controlled setting, could pose risks to aircraft not involved in the activity. Unlike other types of special use airspace, CFAs require cessation of activities upon detection of an approaching aircraft by a spotter aircraft, radar, or ground lookout position. CFAs are not charted as they do not require alterations to the flight path of nonparticipating aircraft.

The term "Other airspace areas" refers to the vast majority of remaining airspace, encompassing various zones and routes, including:

- Local Airport Advisory (LAA)

- Military Training Routes (MTR)

- Temporary Flight Restrictions (TFR)

- Parachute Jump Aircraft Operations

- Published VFR Routes

- Terminal Radar Service Areas (TRSAs)

- National Security Areas (NSAs)

- Air Defense Identification Zones (ADIZ) land and water based, requiring Defense VFR (DVFR) flight plan for VFR operations

- Flight Restricted Zones (FRZ) near the Capitol and White House

- Wildlife Areas/Wilderness Areas/National Parks, with a request to operate above 2,000 AGL

- National Oceanic and Atmospheric Administration (NOAA) Marine Areas off the coast, requiring operation above 2,000 AGL

- Tethered Balloons for observation and weather recordings with cables extending up to 60,000 feet

Local Airport Advisory (LAA): LAA provides advisory services through Flight Service facilities situated at landing airports, utilizing ground-to-air frequencies or tower frequencies when the tower is closed. Services include local airport advisories, automated weather reporting, and continuous Automated Surface Observing System (ASOS)/Automated Weather Observing Station (AWOS) data display.

Military Training Routes (MTRs): MTRs are designated routes for military aircraft to conduct tactical flying exercises. These routes are typically below 10,000 feet MSL for operations exceeding 250 knots. IFR (IR) and VFR (VR) routes are identified by numbers and depicted on appropriate charts.

Temporary Flight Restrictions (TFR): TFRs are issued through Notices to Airmen (NOTAMs) to designate restricted airspace for specific periods. TFRs aim to protect persons and property, support disaster relief operations, manage airspace congestion, safeguard public figures, ensure space agency operations safety, and more.

Parachute Jump Aircraft Operations: These operations are listed in the Chart Supplement U.S. and frequently depicted on sectional charts.

Published VFR Routes: VFR routes facilitate navigation around or through complex airspace and are found on VFR terminal area planning charts.

Terminal Radar Service Areas (TRSAs): TRSAs offer additional radar services to participating pilots to enhance separation between IFR operations and VFR aircraft. The primary airport(s) within TRSAs become(s) Class D airspace, with the remaining area typically Class E airspace.

National Security Areas (NSAs): NSAs are designated airspace areas established for increased security around ground facilities. Flight within NSAs may be temporarily prohibited, with regulations disseminated via NOTAMs, and pilots encouraged to avoid these areas voluntarily.

Local laws may also prohibit use of drones and operators must be astutely aware of applicable laws and regulations relevant to their area.

Figure 26: Drone prohibition sign, Hawaii beach. Kris Arnold from New York, USA, CC BY 2.0, via Wikimedia Commons.

DRONE REGULATIONS IN AUSTRALIA

In Australia, the regulations governing the operation of unmanned aerial vehicles (UAVs), commonly known as drones, are overseen by the Civil Aviation Safety Authority (CASA). These regulations aim to ensure the safe operation of drones while protecting the privacy and safety of individuals and property. Here's an overview of UAV regulations in Australia [46]:

1. Registration and Accreditation: If you intend to fly a drone weighing 250 grams or more for recreational or commercial purposes, you must register the drone with CASA and obtain accreditation. However, drones used solely for sport or recreational activities within a model aircraft association may be exempt from registration.

2. Safety Regulations: Drone operators must adhere to safety regulations, including maintaining visual line-of-sight with the drone, flying below 120 meters (400 feet) above ground level, and not flying near aircraft, airports, or emergency operations.

3. No-Fly Zones: Certain areas are designated as no-fly zones, such as airports, helipads, emergency scenes, and areas with high population density. Flying drones in these restricted areas is prohibited without authorization.

4. Distance from People and Property: Operators must maintain a safe distance from people, property, and vehicles not under their control. This includes respecting the privacy of individuals and refraining from flying over private property without permission.

5. Licensing for Commercial Use: Pilots operating drones commercially or for hire must obtain a Remote Pilot License (RePL) or Remote Operator Certificate (ReOC) from CASA. These licenses require passing a knowledge test and demonstrating competency in drone operation.

6. Safety Precautions: Pilots must conduct pre-flight safety checks, including assessing weather conditions, ensuring the drone's battery is adequately charged, and verifying GPS signal strength.

7. Compliance with CASA Regulations: Drone operators are responsible for familiarizing themselves with CASA regulations and adhering to them at all times. Failure to comply with regulations can result in fines or penalties.

These regulations are periodically updated to address emerging safety concerns and technological advancements in drone technology. It's essential for drone operators in Australia to stay informed about the latest regulations and guidelines to ensure safe and legal drone operation.

Guidelines for recreational drone operators:

1. Altitude Limit: Keep your drone below 120 meters (400 feet) above ground level.

2. Distance from People: Maintain a minimum distance of 30 meters from individuals.

3. Single Drone Operation: Operate only one drone at a time.

4. Visual Line-of-Sight: Always ensure your drone remains within your visual line-of-sight, meaning you can see it directly with your eyes at all times.

5. Avoiding Crowded Areas: Do not fly your drone over or near people, crowded areas, beaches, parks, events, or sports fields where games are being played.

6. Privacy Respect: Respect individuals' privacy and refrain from recording or photographing people without their consent.

7. Distance from Aerodromes: If your drone weighs over 250 grams, maintain a distance of at least 5.5 kilometres from controlled airports using a drone safety app to identify restricted areas.

8. Hazard Avoidance: Operate your drone in a manner that does not pose a hazard to other aircraft, people, or property.

9. Daytime Operation Only: Fly your drone exclusively during daylight hours and avoid flying in cloudy or foggy conditions.

10. Emergency Avoidance: Refrain from flying your drone over or near areas where public safety is at risk or emergency operations are ongoing, such as car crashes, police activities, fires, or search and rescue efforts.

11. Helicopter Landing Sites and Small Aerodromes: When near helicopter landing sites or small aerodromes without control towers, you can fly your drone within 5.5 kilometres. However, if crewed aircraft are detected nearby, promptly manoeuvre away and land your drone safely.

12. Commercial Drone Operations: If you plan to use your drone for work or commercial purposes, additional regulations apply. Registration of the drone and obtaining a license or accreditation is necessary. However, if you fly your drone purely for recreational purposes, registration and accreditation are not required.

Regardless of personal opinions regarding the legislation, drones, irrespective of their size or purpose, are classified as "aircraft" under Australia's Civil Aviation Act. The Act defines aircraft as any machine or craft capable of deriving support in the atmosphere from air reactions, excluding those from the earth's surface. Consequently, all drones fall under the regulatory purview of the Civil Aviation Safety Authority (CASA). The primary regulations governing drones are outlined in Civil Aviation Safety Regulation (CASR) Part 101. The key rules include:

1. Avoid Creating Hazards: Operators must not fly drones in a manner that poses hazards to other aircraft, individuals, or property, even if compliant with other regulations.

2. Restricted Zones Around Aerodromes: Operating drones within 3nm (5.5km) of an active controlled aerodrome's movement area is prohibited. This includes taxiways, aprons, and areas used for aircraft take-off and landing.

3. Caution Near Non-Controlled Aerodromes: Launching drones within 3nm

(5.5km) of a non-controlled aerodrome's movement area is restricted if manned aircraft are operating there. Operators must manoeuvre away safely if aircraft activity is detected.

4. Avoiding Approach and Departure Paths: Guidance from CASA directs operators to avoid flying drones in approach and departure paths at non-controlled aerodromes and helicopter sites.

5. Prohibition on Flying in Restricted Areas: Drone operations in restricted or prohibited airspace areas without authority approval are prohibited due to potential hazards to aircraft.

6. Altitude Limit: Drones cannot fly above 400 feet (120 meters) above ground level unless approved by CASA.

7. Visual Line of Sight: Operators must maintain visual line of sight with the drone, without using binoculars or similar devices, ensuring continuous monitoring and control.

8. Night and Cloud Flying Restrictions: Drone flights are prohibited during civil dusk to dawn, and flying into clouds or fog is also prohibited.

9. Avoiding Emergency Services Operations: Operating drones over areas where emergency operations are conducted is prohibited unless authorized by the person in charge of the operation.

10. Distance from People: Operators must ensure drones are operated at least 30 meters away from individuals, except when essential to the control of the aircraft.

11. Restrictions on Flying Over Populous Areas: Drones must not fly over areas with sufficient population density to pose unreasonable risks to life, safety, or property of individuals not involved in the operation.

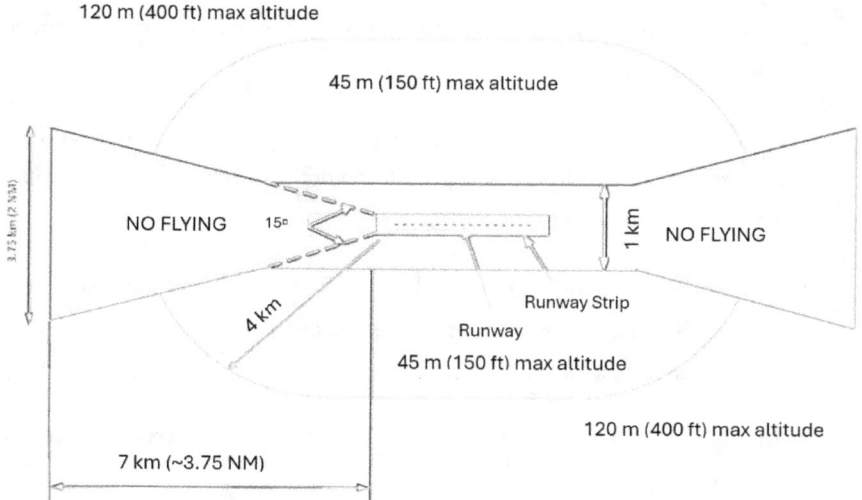

Figure 27: RPA is not to be flown in approach or departure paths.

Regarding FPV (first person view) flying, while it introduces exciting possibilities, it also poses safety risks due to reduced situational awareness. CASA provides exemptions for FPV flying under specific conditions, primarily applicable to members of recognized associations complying with specified policies.

Local drone laws, in addition to CASA regulations, govern drone operations. State governments and local councils may enforce restrictions on drone use, such as bans on operating in national parks or council property. Furthermore, specific regulations exist for operating drones near marine wildlife, requiring adherence to altitude and distance restrictions and obtaining permits in some cases.

Overall, navigating drone regulations requires thorough understanding and adherence to various rules, emphasizing safety and responsible operation. Conducting additional research on relevant laws and regulations is advised to ensure compliance during drone operations.

The primary legislation governing drone operations is the Civil Aviation Safety Regulations (CASR) Part 101.

Now, let's delve into the specifics of drone sizes for commercial purposes [47]:
Weight Categories:
- Micro: Less than 250g

- Very small: 250g-2kg

- Small: 2kg-25kg

- Medium: 25kg-150kg

- Large: Over 150kg

For a spatial company, focusing on the "very small" and "small" categories is ideal. However, if considering drones in the "medium" and "large" categories, it indicates a higher level of expertise and complexity.

Drone Specifications:

- Very Small (250g-2kg): These drones are commonly used for domestic purposes, equipped with features like a 4k stabilized camera for photography, GNSS capability, and sometimes thermal cameras. They're suitable for small photogrammetry missions, photography, or reconnaissance/flight planning.

- Small (2kg-25kg): Drones in this category can handle cinema-grade cameras, LiDAR payloads, and other specialized equipment. Operating such drones commercially requires a clear business strategy and program due to the increased complexity involved.

Legislative Requirements:

For the "Very Small" Category (250g-2kg):

- Obtain an Aviation Reference Number (ARN) from CASA.

- Complete the RPA Operator Accreditation, confirming understanding of basic rules.

- Register the drone with CASA.

For the "Small" Category (2kg-25kg):

- Obtain a Remote Pilot's License (RePL) for the pilot.

- The company needs a Remote Operator's Certificate (ReOC).

- Employ a Chief Pilot responsible for drone operations.

- Develop policies and undergo audits to maintain compliance with regulations.

Flight Conditions:
- Restrictions apply to all categories, including altitude limits, distance from people, and proximity to controlled aerodromes.
- Operations at night, in fog, or beyond visual line of sight require specific permissions and training, such as Beyond Visual Line of Sight (BVLOS) and Specific Operational Risk Assessment (SORA).

Navigating the legislative framework for drone usage in Australia requires adherence to these regulations, proper training, and compliance with safety measures outlined by CASA.

CASA has recently introduced a timeline detailing deadlines for UAV registration and accreditation for UAV operators [48].

Effective from 28 January 2021, individuals flying UAVs for purposes other than sport or recreation must [48]:
- Be at least 16 years old.
- Register their UAV via the myCASA website.
- Obtain either a remotely piloted aircraft (RPA) operator accreditation, a remote pilot licence (RePL), or a remotely piloted aircraft operator's certificate (ReOC).

Registration and RPA operator accreditation are mandatory for UAVs weighing:
- 250g or less (classified as a micro RPA).
- More than 250g but no more than 2kg (classified as a very small RPA).
- More than 2kg but no more than 25kg, and used exclusively over one's own land (classified as a small RPA).

Flying for business purposes encompasses activities such as photography, video production, equipment inspection, monitoring, research, or any duties assigned by an employer. Operator accreditation is not required for recreational use.

A RePL is necessary for individuals aiming to act as remote pilots for businesses holding a ReOC, or for flying UAVs or RPAs weighing over 25kg but under 150kg over their own property.

ReOCs are granted to government entities or individuals/businesses with an Australian Company Number (ACN) or Australian Business Number (ABN) seeking financial gain through drone services. They must employ RePL holders and operate outside standard conditions.

From 28 January 2021, flying unregistered UAVs for business or employment purposes can result in fines up to $11,100. However, recreational UAVs or model aircraft weighing more than 250g will also require accreditation and registration in the next registration phase, scheduled for March 2022. Presently, there is no age restriction for recreational UAV use.

As of 30 September 2021, the Transport Safety Investigation Regulations 2003 have been replaced by the new Transport Safety Investigation Regulations Act 2021. These regulations necessitate certain RPA operators to submit safety and occurrence reports to the Australian Transport Safety Bureau (ATSB), categorizing drones as Type 1 RPAs or Type 2 RPAs.

Type 1 RPAs include drones certified against airworthiness standards, medium drones over 25kg, and large drones over 150kg. Type 2 RPAs, weighing over 250g, have fewer reporting requirements, generally necessitating immediate reporting for incidents involving death or serious injury.

Mandatory UAV registration and reporting aim to enhance accountability and responsibility, ensuring compliance with regulations, and facilitating improved safety outcomes through ATSB investigations.

Distinguishing Between RPAs and Model Aircraft: For many years, people have enjoyed flying model aircraft, but how do these differ from the remotely piloted 'drones' that are frequently discussed? According to CASA, the differentiation between RPAs and model aircraft lies in their usage: RPAs are utilized for commercial, governmental, or research purposes, whereas model aircraft are flown purely for recreational enjoyment, such as sport and leisure activities. In essence, CASA categorizes unmanned aircraft based on their intended application.

Licensing Requirements: Model Aircraft: Operating a radio-controlled model aircraft does not necessitate formal piloting qualifications. However, adherence to specific regulations is mandatory (refer to 'What's allowed' below). Commercial operation of model aircraft is prohibited unless the operator holds an unmanned operator's certificate pertinent to that type of activity. Enthusiasts wishing to join an association or club may consider the Model Aeronautical Association of Australia (MAAA), boasting approximately 11,000 members. The MAAA provides a 'wings rating' system, comprising bronze, gold, and instructor levels.

RPAs: CASA maintains that UAS (Unmanned Aircraft Systems) pilots should possess general aviation knowledge equivalent to that of a private pilot's license, alongside specialized unmanned aircraft skills. For commercial operation of any-sized RPA, individuals must obtain a UAV (Unmanned Aerial Vehicle) controller's certificate and a business-specific unmanned operator's certificate (UOC). Additional certifications may include a flight radio operator's license and proficiency with the type of UAS employed.

Permitted Activities: RPAs:

- Approval is granted for unmanned aircraft activities conducted over unpopulated areas, up to 400 feet AGL (above ground level), or higher with special permissions.

- Special approvals are also mandated for operations in other areas.

- Operations within controlled airspace necessitate CASA authorization and coordination with Airservices Australia.

- RPAs can be operated under visual meteorological conditions (VMC) and/or instrument meteorological conditions (IMC) with appropriate approvals.

Model Aircraft:

- Model aircraft should only be flown within visual line-of-sight, during daylight visual meteorological conditions (VMC).

- Night flying and operation in or through cloud or fog are prohibited.

- The aircraft must remain visible to the operator at all times, without reliance on its point-of-view camera.

- Flying within 30 meters of vehicles, boats, buildings, or people is prohibited.

- Over populous areas, such as beaches, crowded parks, or sports ovals during events, model aircraft should not be flown.

- In controlled airspace, typically encompassing major cities, model aircraft must not exceed 400 feet (120 meters) in altitude.

- Maintaining a minimum distance of 5.5 kilometres from airfields is required.

These distinctions and regulations aim to ensure safe and responsible operation of both RPAs and model aircraft within Australian airspace.

Airservices Australia provides a comprehensive array of documents and publications essential for safe and efficient air navigation within Australia and its Territories.

Aeronautical Information Publication (AIP): The AIP Australia comprises a collection of documents offering operational information crucial for national (civil) and international air navigation. It encompasses details necessary for ensuring the safety and efficacy of air travel across the designated regions.

AIP Supplements (SUPS)/Aeronautical Information Circulars (AICs): SUPS supplement the AIP with operational information tailored to its requirements. Issued when temporary data is pertinent, SUPS are accompanied by advanced notification. Major changes impacting air operations are often disseminated through SUPS in compliance with the ICAO Aeronautical Information Regulation and Control (AIRAC) requirement. AICs, meanwhile, contain technical information and serve an educational purpose, providing advance notice of new facilities, services, procedures, etc.

Enroute Supplement Australia (ERSA): The ERSA is an indispensable publication for flight planning and in-flight navigation. It includes detailed pictorial representations of all licensed aerodromes, updated every 12 weeks. Other crucial information encompasses aerodrome physical characteristics, operational hours, visual ground aids, air traffic services, navigation aids, lighting, CTAF frequency, aerodrome operators' details, and any pertinent changes. Available in spiral bound or loose leaf format, ERSA can be obtained with or without the Runway Distance Supplement.

Runway Distance Supplement (RDS): This supplement furnishes data on take-off and landing distances along with supplementary information for all licensed aerodromes. Amendments are synchronized with ERSA updates.

Civil Aviation Act and Regulations (CARs): The Civil Aviation Act serves as the primary legislative framework for air safety control in Australia, containing crucial regulatory provisions. The accompanying Regulations delineate mandatory regulatory requirements pertaining to airworthiness, operational matters, licensing, enforcement powers, and air traffic control.

Civil Aviation Orders (CAOs): Provisioned under the Regulations, Civil Aviation Orders provide information on technical standards and specifications. They contain detailed mandatory operational, airworthiness, and safety requirements, including design criteria, standards, specifications, operational procedures, and safety directives.

Civil Aviation Advisory Publications (CAAPs): CAAPs serve as advisory documents, elucidating the purpose of Regulations/Orders and offering guidance on compliance with mandatory requirements. Organized into Blue (Operational), Green (Airworthiness), and Yellow (Aerodrome) sections, CAAPs simplify regulatory concepts for stakeholders.

Departure and Approach Procedures (DAP): DAPs encompass charts related to all instrument departure and approach procedures, categorized into DAP East and DAP West packages. Additionally, DAPs include information on Noise Abatement Procedures applicable to all locations.

Visual Terminal Charts (VTC): VTCs provide both aeronautical and topographical information at a scale of 1:250,000, aiding Visual Flight Rules (VFR) operations near major aerodromes. These charts often highlight tracks to be flown and significant landmarks, facilitating VFR pilots in avoiding inadvertent penetration of controlled airspace.

Enroute Charts (ERC) High and Low: ERC (L) charts are designed at various scales to accommodate significant air traffic route areas, depicting controlled airspace, prohibited, restricted, and danger areas, air routes, Air Traffic Services (ATS), and radio-navigation services. On the other hand, ERC (H) charts offer selected information similar to ERC (L) series, primarily catering to aircraft operating at higher altitudes on transcontinental and intercapital routes, typically at FL200 and above.

Terminal Area Charts (TAC): These charts are tailored for terminal areas, offering detailed airspace information, air routes, prohibited, restricted, and danger areas, navigation aids, and radio frequencies. TACs are designed at a larger scale, enhancing usability in congested areas, with scale variations depending on specific charts.

Visual Navigation Charts (VNC): VNCs aid in flight planning in relation to controlled airspace, facilitating transition from World Aeronautical Charts (WAC) to Visual Terminal Charts (VTC) around terminal areas, and providing navigation assistance near controlled airspace or restricted and danger areas. These charts offer topographical information at a scale of 1:500,000.

Planning Chart Australia (PCA): PCA includes meteorological Area Forecast boundaries and locations, communication coverage outside controlled airspace, and coverage provided by WACs. It serves as a valuable resource for flight planning and pre-flight preparations.

World Aeronautical Charts (WAC): Part of the ICAO 1:1,000,000 international series, Australian WACs are designed for pre-flight planning and pilotage. Constructed using Lambert's conformal conic projection and adhering to ICAO specifications, these charts offer essential information for safe and efficient air navigation.

Starting from April 5, 2020, you are required to maintain records of your drone operations to demonstrate compliance with the drone safety regulations. However, if you are solely flying for recreational purposes or operating a very small remotely piloted aircraft (RPA) falling under the Sub 2 kg excluded category, record-keeping is not mandatory. These obligations pertain to both small (2-25 kg) and medium (25-150 kg) RPAs when flown over your own property. The following documentation must be upheld:

- An operational log for each operation

- A technical log for each medium RPA

- A remote pilot log detailing flight time and specifics for each medium RPA operation. These records must be maintained by the remote pilot and preserved for a minimum of 3 years following the last operation. The technical log, however, must be retained for at least 7 years. You should be prepared to furnish copies of these logs upon request. Additionally, if you sell your drone, the purchaser may request access to these records. Operational log Retention Period: 3 years Applicable to: small and medium RPAs Key Information to include:

- Location and altitude of flight

- RPA type, model, and identification

- Dates and times of operation

- Nature and purpose of the operation

- Assessment of whether the drone is airworthy for the subsequent day's flight. Technical log Retention Period: 7 years Applicable to: medium RPAs Key Information to include:

- RPA type, model, and identification

- Total flight time of the RPA

- Component in-service durations

- Scheduled maintenance timings

- Details of maintenance carried out and certification of any conducted work. Remote pilot log Retention Period: 3 years Applicable to: medium RPAs Key Information to include:

- Accumulated flight time operating an excluded RPA

- Details identifying each operation, including RPA type, model, and identification

- Dates, locations, and durations of each flight.

Drone Regulations in the United Kingdom

In 2024, the Civil Aviation Authority of the United Kingdom (CAA), serving as the nation's governing body for aviation affairs, has introduced a comprehensive framework of drone regulations aimed at fostering the safe, conscientious, and legal operation of drones throughout the United Kingdom [49]. These regulations encompass a wide range of drone activities, spanning from recreational to commercial purposes.

In 2024, the prevailing drone regulations in the UK are grounded in the fundamental principle that Unmanned Aircraft Systems (UAS) operating within the country must adhere to safety and operational standards equivalent to those of manned aircraft performing similar operations in the same airspace, as delineated in CAP 722 – Unmanned Aircraft System Operations in UK Airspace – Guidance [50].

While this principle appears straightforward, most drones lack the inherent safety features of manned aircraft and are typically operated by individuals with less extensive training. Consequently, as the popularity of drones continues to soar, the UK Civil Aviation Authority (CAA) faces the challenging task of devising a regulatory framework that balances the imperative of safeguarding public safety and security with the imperative of nurturing an industry poised for substantial growth and requiring the capacity to expand operations significantly [50].

UAS operations in the UK are subject to regulation under two distinct frameworks: the Air Navigation Order 2016 (as amended within the framework of the Civil Aviation Act 1982) and the regulations stemming from UK Regulation (EU) 2018/1139, commonly referred to as the Basic Regulation.

These regulatory frameworks are accompanied by guidance provided by the CAA in the form of CAP722 (Unmanned Aircraft System Operations in UK Airspace – Guidance). Nonetheless, comprehending this guidance can prove challenging for many. Hence, on this platform, we aim to elucidate as clearly as possible the requirements for safely and lawfully operating drones in the UK in 2024 [50].

As of the latest data, the UK's drone registry is experiencing substantial growth, boasting over 513,860 active drones within UK airspace. In response to this surge, the CAA is continuously adapting and refining regulations to align with this expanding drone landscape.

Outlined below are the key provisions of the United Kingdom's 2024 Drone Laws [49]:

1. Minimum Age Requirement: Drone operators must be at least 12 years old to independently operate drones.

2. Altitude Limit: Drones are prohibited from flying above 400 feet (120 meters).

3. Line of Sight: Operators must maintain visual contact with their drones at all times during flight.

4. Restricted Airspace: Permission must be obtained before flying in restricted airspace.

5. Airport Proximity: Drones should not be flown within a 5-kilometer radius of airports.

6. Distance from People: A minimum distance of 50 meters must be maintained between drones and uninvolved individuals.

7. Weight-Based Restrictions: Drones weighing below 250 grams are allowed to fly closer to and over people. Drones weighing 250 grams or more must maintain a distance of at least 150 meters from parks, industrial areas, residential zones, and other built-up locations.

8. Camera-Equipped Drones: Operators of drones equipped with cameras must register for an Operator ID with the CAA.

9. Insurance Mandate: Commercial drone operators are required to have insurance

coverage.

10. Day and Night Compliance: Compliance with regulations is obligatory for both daytime and nighttime operations.

These regulations, effective as of 2024, apply to all drone operators in the United Kingdom. Adhering to these laws is imperative to ensure the safe and responsible use of drones within the country.

Additionally, when operating drones or model aircraft in the UK, it's essential to be aware of legal identification (ID) and registration requirements. These requirements are contingent upon factors such as drone weight and the presence of a camera and are applicable to all drones, irrespective of size.

Flyer ID:

- Necessary for drones weighing over 250 grams or equipped with a camera.

- Issued by the UK Civil Aviation Authority (CAA) after passing a 40-question theory test.

- Registration can be completed online through the CAA's website.

- Valid for 5 years and free of charge.

Operator ID:

- Mandatory for operators of camera-equipped drones engaged in commercial activities.

- Issued by the UK Civil Aviation Authority (CAA) after passing a theory test.

- Registration entails providing an email address and payment information.

- Valid for 1 year, with a fee of £10.

For individuals under 18 years old, the registration of an operator ID must be facilitated by a parent or guardian.

Figure 28: Drone Filming in Karst Closed Basin. Nick Chipchase, CC BY-SA 2.0, via Wikimedia Commons.

To ensure legal compliance, drones and model aircraft must be labelled with the operator ID. This unique identifier serves to distinguish the responsible party and facilitates accountability. When labelling drones, follow these guidelines [49]:

1. Clearly write the Operator ID in block letters, at least 3mm tall.

2. Securely attach the label to the aircraft's main body, ensuring visibility from the outside or easy accessibility within a compartment.

3. Protect the label from damage to maintain legibility throughout the drone's lifespan.

4. Repeat the labelling process for each drone or model aircraft under your supervision, utilizing the same Operator ID.

It's crucial to utilize the operator ID, not the flyer ID, when labelling drones and model aircraft. The operator ID specifically identifies the responsible party, while the flyer ID pertains to the pilot.

Under the Air Traffic Management and Unmanned Aircraft Act 2021, UK police have been granted authority to regulate drone usage. These powers include:

- Taking action if a drone is believed to be used in connection with an offense.

- Landing, inspecting, and seizing drones with a secured warrant.

- Mandating drone operators to land their drones.

- Conducting searches to locate drones or drone equipment.

- Confiscating and retaining drones or drone equipment.

If concerns arise regarding drone usage in your vicinity, contacting local law enforcement enables them to investigate and take necessary action to ensure compliance with UK drone laws.

Failure to comply with UK drone laws and regulations may result in consequences such as fines, confiscation of equipment, criminal charges, and liability for damages or injuries caused by drones. It's imperative to adhere to these laws to safeguard public safety and airspace integrity, flying drones responsibly, and following authorities' directives.

In 2024, UK drone pilots must adhere to specific categories of drone operations, categorized as follows [49]:

1. Open Category: Encompasses low-risk flights without the need for special CAA approval.

2. Specific Category: Pertains to higher-risk flights necessitating operational authorization from the CAA.

3. Certified Category: Involves even higher-risk flights, typically with larger aircraft, subject to stringent regulation and authorization akin to manned flights.

These categories, established by the Civil Aviation Authority (CAA), serve to classify drone operations based on risk factors such as proximity to individuals and drone weight. Most drone pilots operate within the Open Category, which advocates responsible drone usage and permits operation in the A1 and A3 subcategories with a Flyer ID.

By implementing these categories, the UK regulatory framework aims to ensure that drone pilots adhere to appropriate safety measures and risk assessments tailored to the nature of their flights, thereby promoting safe and responsible drone operations across the country.

Operating drones within the Open Category in the United Kingdom entails adhering to specific guidelines tailored for low-risk drone flights. This category does not necessitate special approval from the Civil Aviation Authority (CAA) and is commonly utilized by most drone pilots in the UK, emphasizing responsible drone operation.

The Open Category is subdivided into three distinct subcategories, which are delineated based on drone weight and proximity to individuals:

1. A1 – "Fly over people": Intended for very lightweight drones posing minimal risk, permitting flight directly over individuals.

2. A2 – "Fly close to people": Involves lightweight drones capable of flying near people, presenting slightly higher risk than A1 drones.

3. A3 – "Fly far from people": Designed for heavier drones, mandating a safe distance from individuals to mitigate potential hazards.

Most UK drone pilots can operate within the A1 and A3 subcategories without additional training, provided they possess an Operator ID and have passed the drone code test. This framework ensures adherence to responsible drone usage guidelines while mitigating risks associated with drone flights across various environments.

To operate drones within the Open Category, specific operational restrictions and requirements are delineated based on drone weight and subcategory:

- Drones weighing under 250 grams fall under the A1 subcategory, allowing flight over uninvolved individuals with no flight over assemblies of people. Operator registration is required, and remote pilot competence is essential.

- Drones weighing under 900 grams can operate in the A1 subcategory, with no flight over uninvolved people. Operator registration is mandatory, and completion of online training for A1/A3 subcategories is required.

- Drones weighing under 4kg can operate in the A2 subcategory, necessitating no flight over uninvolved people and maintaining a horizontal distance of 30 meters from individuals. Operator registration and an A2 Certificate of Competency (A2 CofC) are required.

- Drones weighing under 25kg operate in the A3 subcategory, prohibiting flight near people and mandating flight outside urban areas. Operator registration and an A2 CofC are necessary.

Drone operations fall under the Open Category if they meet specific requirements, including adherence to class specifications outlined in Delegated Regulation (EU) 2019/945, maintaining safe distances from individuals, and complying with visual line of sight (VLOS) regulations [49].

As an average drone pilot operating within the Open Category, adherence to key points is essential:

1. Prioritize Safety: Employ reasonable, proportionate, and common-sense measures to manage flight risks, ensuring the safety of individuals and property.

2. Registration and Flyer ID: Register as an operator and obtain a Flyer ID in most cases, ensuring compliance with regulatory requirements.

3. Distance from People: Maintain safe distances from individuals during flight, prioritizing safety and injury prevention.

4. Safety Rules Adherence: Follow safety protocols, including maintaining visual line of sight, respecting altitude limits, and observing flight restriction zones.

5. Local Restrictions and Permissions: Familiarize yourself with local restrictions and obtain necessary permissions before flying, recognizing that airspace and land permissions are separate entities.

Operating drones within the Specific Category entails engaging in higher-risk flights that do not align with the low-risk criteria of the Open Category. Pilots operating in this category must secure operational authorization from the Civil Aviation Authority (CAA).

The Specific Category is typically utilized for flights with more intricate or specialized demands, such as industrial inspections, agricultural monitoring, or aerial photography in congested areas. To apply for operational authorization, operators must conduct a comprehensive risk assessment and develop an operational safety case to demonstrate their ability to safely execute the planned drone operation.

Upon submission of the application, including the risk assessment and mitigating measures, the CAA evaluates the operational risks and issues an Operational Authorization if it deems the risks adequately mitigated. This authorization may pertain to a single operation or multiple operations specified by time or location. Alternatively, the CAA may approve a Light UAS Certificate (LUC) in accordance with Part C of the Annex.

Operators holding an LUC with appropriate privileges or conducting operations within model aircraft clubs and associations with proper authorizations are exempt from the requirement of obtaining Operational Authorizations.

The Certified Category is designated for even higher-risk flights, often involving larger drones or aircraft. The regulatory and authorization requirements for this category mirror those for manned flights. Pilots must obtain the necessary certifications, permits, and approvals to operate drones within the Certified Category. Activities within this category may include package delivery, drone taxi services, or flights in highly controlled airspace.

Drone operations fall under the Certified Category if the drone is certified according to Article 40 of Delegated Regulation (EU) 2019/945 and meets specific conditions, such as flying over assemblies of people, transporting people, or carrying dangerous goods. Additionally, operations may be classified as Certified Category if the CAA determines, based on the risk assessment, that the risks cannot be adequately mitigated without certification of the drone and the operator, and, where applicable, the licensing of the remote pilot.

Drone pilots in the United Kingdom in 2024 must comprehend and adhere to the requirements of the Open, Specific, and Certified categories to ensure the safe and lawful operation of drones.

As of January 1, 2024, the United Kingdom will enforce new regulations governing drones, requiring all new drones to meet specific standards and be categorized into one of four classifications: C0, C1, C2, or C3. These classifications are determined based on the weight and capabilities of the drone, dictating its permissible usage and operational boundaries [49].

The drone classes and their associated subcategories are outlined as follows:

- Class C0: Eligible for operation in all subcategories.

- Class C1: Eligible for operation in all subcategories.

- Class C2: Permissible for operation only in subcategories A2 (with an A2 Certificate of Competence [CofC]) or A3.

- Class C3: Permissible for operation exclusively in subcategory A3.

- Class C4: Permissible for operation exclusively in subcategory A3.

Outlined below are the five drone classes along with their corresponding regulations:

Drone Class: C0
- Description: C0 drones comprise very small unmanned aircraft, including toys, weighing less than 250 grams. They boast a maximum speed of 42.5 mph and are mandated to remain within 400 feet of the control device.

Drone Class: C1
- Description: C1 drones must weigh less than 900 grams and possess a maximum speed of 42.5 mph. They are engineered to minimize injury in the event of collision with a person. Additionally, these drones adhere to noise and height limitations and must meet specific requirements for remote identification and situational awareness.

Drone Class: C2
- Description: C2 drones must weigh less than 4 kilograms and prioritize injury minimization upon potential collision with a person. They are equipped with a low-speed mode, capping their maximum speed at 6.7 mph when activated by the operator. Furthermore, C2 drones comply with noise and height restrictions and must satisfy prerequisites for remote identification and situational awareness. Additional requirements apply if these drones are utilized while tethered to the ground.

Drone Class: C3
- Description: C3 drones are unmanned aircraft featuring automatic control modes and weighing less than 25 kilograms. They are subject to height restrictions and must fulfill specified criteria for remote identification and situational awareness. Supplementary requirements come into play if these drones are deployed while tethered to the ground.

Drone Class: C4
- Description: C4 drones are unmanned aircraft devoid of any automation beyond basic flight stabilization, weighing less than 25 kilograms. They adhere to height restrictions and must meet designated criteria for remote identification and situational awareness. Additional prerequisites apply if these drones are utilized while tethered to the ground.

UK Drone Licensing Options Ensuring drone pilots possess the requisite certifications is paramount to guaranteeing safe and legal drone operations. Various drone license types cater to diverse operational needs and requirements, offering pilots the necessary qualifications to navigate the skies responsibly. Among these licenses are [49]:

1. A2 Certificate of Competency (A2 CofC) Drone License:

    - Description: This qualification enables drone pilots to legally operate certain drones in challenging locations and closer to uninvolved individuals.

    - Validity: 5 years

    - Applicable Operations: A2 subcategory of the Open category, suitable for both commercial and recreational drone pilots.

    - Renewal Process: Completion of a training course and passing a qualification exam.

2. General Visual Line of Sight Certificate (GVC) Drone License:

    - Description: The GVC serves as a remote pilot competency qualification, authorizing pilots to safely fly drones weighing up to 25 kg in built-up areas.

    - Validity: 5 years

    - Applicable Operations: Most Visual Line of Sight (VLOS) operations within the Specific category.

    - Renewal Process: Completion of a refresher course with a training provider every 5 years.

3. Permission for Commercial Operations (PfCO) Drone License [No Longer Valid]:

    - Description: Previously required for commercial drone operations in the UK, the PfCO has been replaced by the GVC since January 2021.

    - Validity: N/A

    - Applicable Operations: N/A

- Renewal Process: N/A

Drone License Details: A2 Certificate of Competency (A2 CofC) Drone License: The A2 Certificate of Competency (A2 CofC) qualifies drone pilots to operate certain drones in challenging environments and closer to uninvolved individuals. Obtaining this certification entails completing a training course and passing a qualification exam. While there is no formal practical requirement, pilots must self-declare their drone flying experience to demonstrate competency. The A2 CofC is valid for five years and requires renewal to maintain legal standing.

General Visual Line of Sight Certificate (GVC) Drone License: The GVC enables pilots to operate drones up to 25 kg in built-up areas, covering most VLOS operations. Valid for five years, the GVC necessitates a refresher course every five years to ensure continuous competency. Pilots must complete the refresher course with a training provider to renew their GVC license. Course fees vary depending on the training provider, with additional application fees payable to the CAA.

Operating Drones Within Visual Line of Sight (VLOS): In the United Kingdom, drone regulations stipulate that drones must be operated within Visual Line of Sight (VLOS) when flying within the Open category or under operational authorization for the Specific category. VLOS operations, outlined by UK Regulation (EU) 2019/947, involve the remote pilot maintaining continuous unaided visual contact with the drone to control its flight path and avoid collisions with other aircraft, people, or obstacles.

Ensuring VLOS operations allows the remote pilot to monitor the drone's position, orientation, and the surrounding airspace effectively. While corrective lenses are permissible, the use of binoculars, telescopes, or other image-enhancing devices is prohibited. The maximum VLOS distance varies for each operation, influenced by factors such as the drone's size, onboard lighting, weather conditions, the remote pilot's eyesight, and terrain and obstacles obstructing the view. It is the remote pilot's responsibility to determine the maximum safe distance while maintaining unaided visual contact with the drone.

Beyond Visual Line of Sight (BVLOS): Drone Operations Beyond Visual Line of Sight (BVLOS) operations involve drone flights where the remote pilot cannot maintain direct, unaided visual contact with the drone during flight [49]. This allows drones to cover larger distances and undertake tasks that would be challenging within the confines of VLOS operations, such as aerial mapping, infrastructure inspection, and delivery services. However, BVLOS operations necessitate stringent safety measures to protect airspace users, as well as people and property on the ground.

The Civil Aviation Authority (CAA) is developing drone laws pertaining to BVLOS operations to enable authorized operators to conduct BVLOS flights in a scalable and sustainable manner while ensuring safety. This initiative comprises four primary areas of focus, known as "the four-pillars":

1. Pilot Competency: Collaborating with industry partners to establish a standardized mechanism for demonstrating pilot competence beyond the current General Visual Line of Sight Certificate (GVC).

2. Flightworthiness: Establishing a formal mechanism for assessing the robustness of aircraft when applying for operational authorization, including developing requirements for certain unmanned aircraft systems (UAS) assessed by Flightworthiness Recognized Assessment Entities.

3. Risk Assessment: Implementing a suitable mechanism to assess and mitigate risk for authorizing complex UAS operations, adopting an amended version of the JARUS 2.5 Specific Operations Risk Assessment (SORA) to account for exemptions to the UK Standardized European Rules of the Air.

4. Airspace: Exploring the integration of BVLOS operations into the UK's airspace through atypical air environment utilization to address mid-air collision risk initially. Long-term strategies involve supporting the adoption of detect and avoid technologies and electronic conspicuity within a regulatory framework.

Specific Operating Risk Assessment (SORA): The Specific Operating Risk Assessment (SORA) methodologically evaluates and addresses risks associated with Unmanned Aircraft System (UAS) operations. It empowers drone operators to discern operational constraints, aircraft technical requisites, personnel training objectives, and formulate suitable operational protocols. Although introduced in 2023, SORA's development is ongoing in the UK as of 2024.

Current Guidance and Future Implementation of SORA in the UK: While awaiting full implementation of the UK SORA, drone operators applying for the Specific category should adhere to the methodology and templates outlined in the CAP 722A publication. Upon introduction, the UK SORA may deviate from the European Aviation Safety Agency (EASA) SORA to accommodate domestic requisites.

Regulatory Status and Timeline for UK SORA: Considered an Acceptable Means of Compliance (AMC) to Article 11 of Regulation (EU) No 2019/947, the UK SORA will be retained and amended under the European Union (Withdrawal) Act 2018. It does not necessitate regulatory alterations for implementation, being a set of recommendations and guidelines rather than a regulation. Expected for consultation in Q1 2024, the UK SORA aims for implementation in Q3/4 2024. The comprehensive implementation plan encompasses various facets, including its impact on Recognized Assessment Entities (RAEs) and the design of training courses for drone operators.

Operational Authorizations and Operating Safety Cases: Valid Operational Authorizations (OAs) will persist post-SORA implementation and remain valid within the specified duration. However, Operating Safety Cases (OSCs) will require adjustments to accommodate SORA, with a transition period provided for drone operators to make necessary updates.

SORA Methodology and Comparison to CAP 722A: Compared to the primarily qualitative approach of CAP 722A, the SORA methodology adopts a more quantitative stance. Developed internationally with consensus from multiple National Aviation Authorities (NAAs) and industry specialists, SORA establishes an acceptable safety threshold for proposed Specific category operations.

Guidance for UK Drone Operators in the Interim Period: Pending the release of the UK SORA, applicants should adhere to the CAP 722A guidance when conducting Specific category risk assessments and planning applications. It is advised against blending SORA elements with the CAP 722A methodology, as it may prolong assessment duration and necessitate additional compliance evaluations with Article 11 of UK Regulation (EU) 2019/947.

The Specific Operating Risk Assessment (SORA) marks a significant stride for UK drone pilots, ushering in a more quantifiable approach to risk appraisal and mitigation. While its full rollout is underway, drone operators are recommended to adhere to CAP 722A guidance until further updates are issued.

Authorized Areas for Drone Operations 2024

This section delves into the regulations governing the permissible locations for drone flights. It encompasses legal altitude restrictions, required distances from individuals, and areas where drone operations are prohibited. Additionally, it addresses constraints on flying in proximity to airports and spaceports. Familiarizing oneself with these regulations is crucial to ensure safe and responsible drone operation.

Adherence to 400ft Maximum Altitude

Maintaining a limited altitude is vital to mitigate the risk of collision with other aircraft. In the UK, the legal altitude limit for drone operations is set at 120m (400ft). This means drones should not ascend beyond 120m (400ft) to minimize the chance of encountering other airborne vehicles, including air ambulances, police helicopters, and military aircraft, which may fly at lower altitudes for various operational reasons like emergency response or surveillance.

Adaptation in Mountainous Terrain

When operating drones over hilly or mountainous terrain, adjustments to flight paths may be necessary to ensure compliance with the legal altitude limit. For instance, flying over a mountain may require reducing altitude to remain within the 120m (400ft) height constraint, considering the elevated terrain compared to the surrounding landscape.

Maintaining a Safe Distance from Individuals

Drone pilots must uphold a safe distance from individuals to prevent potential accidents or injuries. The standard minimum distance from people is set at 50 meters (164 feet), encompassing individuals on the ground and those within structures or vehicles. This regulation creates a designated "no fly zone" within a 50-metre (164-foot) radius around individuals, extending vertically to the legal altitude limit, typically around 120 metres (400 feet). Therefore, flying directly over people, even at higher altitudes, is prohibited.

Exception for Involved Participants and Lightweight Drones

While maintaining a safe distance from individuals is crucial, exceptions apply to individuals actively participating in drone-related activities and lightweight drones under 250g. In such cases, closer proximity to participants is permissible, deviating from the standard 50-meter (164-foot) rule. Additionally, drones under 250g are allowed to fly closer to individuals and even over them, provided the activity remains within safe parameters.

Official UK Drone Distancing Regulations

In addition to the general 50-metre (164-foot) rule, specific circumstances may necessitate increasing the distance from individuals to ensure flight safety. Factors such as altitude, weather conditions, and flight speed influence the required distance. Areas with high population density, including shopping centres, sports events, religious gatherings, and concerts, warrant increased caution and adherence to safety protocols to minimize risks associated with crowded environments.

Figure 29: Flying a drone on Newbiggin Point. Russel Wills, CC BY-SA 2.0, via Wikimedia Commons.

UK Drone Regulations for International Operators 2024

International drone pilots intending to operate drones within the UK must comply with the country's established regulations governing drone and model aircraft flights. These regulations are applicable to all drone pilots, irrespective of their nationality, with the overarching goal of ensuring safe and responsible drone operations within UK airspace [49].

In most instances, foreign drone pilots are required to obtain both a UK flyer ID and operator ID prior to commencing drone flights within the UK. The flyer ID serves as a unique identifier for the pilot and must be visibly displayed on the drone, whereas the operator ID identifies the individual or entity accountable for the drone's operation.

Moreover, if the nature of the flight necessitates a valid UK permission, foreign drone pilots must obtain one accordingly. The requirement for a UK permission hinges on various factors including the drone's size and weight, the purpose of the flight, and the intended flight location.

Foreign drone pilots who have undergone requisite online training, passed a drone pilot examination, and acquired a remote pilot competency certificate in any EASA Member State are permitted to travel with their drones to the UK. Nevertheless, the process for obtaining a valid UK permission is contingent upon the specific type of flight being conducted, with each application evaluated on its individual merits.

Given the potential complexity and time-consuming nature of the permission acquisition process, it is advisable for foreign drone pilots to seek guidance from either a UK-based drone operator or the Civil Aviation Authority (CAA) prior to submitting an application. While the CAA typically grants permissions to foreign operators seeking to undertake work in the UK, compliance with fundamental safety prerequisites akin to those required of UK-based operators is imperative.

However, the CAA reserves the right to impose additional requirements or limitations based on the nature of the intended flight. It is essential for foreign operators to recognize that approvals and qualifications obtained from other countries do not automatically hold validity within the UK. Hence, adherence to UK drone laws and regulations is paramount prior to engaging in drone flights within UK airspace.

Failure to comply with these regulations may result in severe penalties or legal ramifications, including fines or imprisonment.

UK Drone Laws For Residential, Recreational, Commercial and Industrial Sites

UK drone regulations impose a minimum distance requirement of 150 meters from specific types of locations, encompassing residential, recreational, commercial, and industrial sites. This stipulation aims to safeguard individuals and property on the ground during drone operations. However, it's essential to recognize that this distance serves as a baseline, and adjustments may be necessary to ensure safe drone or model aircraft operation.

For instance, smaller drones weighing less than 250 grams are permitted to fly within residential, recreational, commercial, and industrial sites. Nevertheless, maintaining safety remains paramount, prompting the need to extend the distance beyond the prescribed 150 meters if deemed necessary for safe operation.

Residential areas encompass various settings, including individual dwellings, gardens, parks, clusters of residential buildings, housing developments, villages, urban centers, and educational institutions such as schools. Similarly, recreational sites span tourist destinations, sports venues, beaches, parks, theme parks, and other public recreational areas.

Commercial locations encompass diverse environments such as shopping complexes, storage facilities, business parks, and major transportation routes like motorways. On the other hand, industrial sites encompass factories, ports, railway stations, and governmental facilities such as police stations and correctional facilities.

By adhering to these regulations and exercising caution, drone operators can contribute to the safe and responsible integration of drones into various environments, mitigating potential risks to individuals and property while ensuring compliance with legal requirements.

Airport Restricted Zones and Other No-Fly Drone Laws 2024

Flight restriction zones (FRZs) denote specific areas surrounding airports, airfields, and spaceports where flying drones or model aircraft is deemed unsafe. These zones serve to mitigate the risk of collisions with aircraft or spacecraft. To operate a drone within or in proximity to these zones, obtaining prior permission from the respective airport, airfield, or spaceport authority is imperative.

Even in the absence of designated FRZs, exercising caution around airports, airfields, and spaceports is paramount to prevent endangering aircraft safety. As a general rule, maintaining a distance of at least 5 kilometres from an airport is advisable unless explicit permission to fly closer has been granted.

Various resources are available to assist in identifying flight restriction zones and other airspace limitations. The UK Civil Aviation Authority (CAA) offers an online map delineating these restrictions, while certain drone applications may also furnish relevant information regarding these zones.

However, it's crucial to acknowledge that not all small airfields may be cataloged in these resources. Hence, vigilance is essential, and any indicators of nearby airfields, such as light aircraft or associated infrastructure, should prompt caution.

In essence, refraining from flying within or in close proximity to airports, airfields, and spaceports unless authorized is imperative. Furthermore, maintaining awareness of potential hazards to aircraft safety is crucial for responsible drone operation.

Obtain the Necessary Permissions for Your Flight

When preparing for a drone flight within the UK, acquiring the requisite permissions is not only vital for compliance with legal regulations but also crucial for ensuring the safety of the flight and preventing any potential disturbances or harm to the environment and individuals.

Securing permission from landowners is the initial step before launching or landing a drone on private property. For properties owned by local councils or governmental bodies, seeking additional permissions may be necessary to avoid any legal infringements.

Local authority permissions play a pivotal role in the planning phase of a drone flight. Each jurisdiction may impose specific requirements and regulations for drone operations within their area, necessitating thorough verification to ensure adherence to local ordinances and regulations.

Informing local law enforcement agencies of the intended drone flight is another essential step towards ensuring public safety and minimizing disruptions. Proactively notifying authorities about the flight details, including the location, date, and time, facilitates coordinated efforts to manage any potential risks or disturbances.

Obtaining permission from the Civil Aviation Authority (CAA) is indispensable for compliance with regulations governing drone flights in the UK. While the CAA delineates guidelines for general drone operations through categories like the Open category and Operational Authorisation, specific flight plans may warrant additional permissions, such as an Operational Safety Case (OSC).

Notifying Network Rail of intended drone flights near railways is crucial to mitigate safety risks, as flights within 50 meters of railway tracks are prohibited. Collaboration with Network Rail and other authorized entities ensures adherence to safety protocols and regulatory requirements.

Seeking permission from local Air Traffic Control (ATC) is imperative when planning drone flights in proximity to airports. Unauthorized flights within airport-controlled airspace pose significant safety risks and legal liabilities, necessitating prior approval from ATC to ensure compliance with airspace regulations.

Understanding and adhering to Flight Restriction Zones (FRZs) around Nuclear Facilities is paramount to prevent legal repercussions and safeguard public safety. Acquiring permission from authorized personnel at these facilities is a prerequisite for legally conducting drone flights in these areas.

Before initiating drone flights near sites like prisons, military bases, or sports stadiums, verifying the presence of restriction zones and obtaining necessary permissions are essential steps. Adhering to site-specific regulations helps prevent legal violations and ensures public safety.

Requesting permission from the National Trust for drone filming activities in their properties requires adherence to competency and insurance standards. Commercial filming endeavours must align with the Trust's guidelines and receive prior approval from the filming office to proceed lawfully.

Obtaining the requisite permissions for drone flights entails meticulous planning, collaboration with relevant authorities, and strict adherence to legal regulations to ensure safety, compliance, and the protection of public interests.

Other Considerations

Privacy considerations are paramount when operating drones or model aircraft, necessitating a conscientious approach to respect the privacy rights of others and ensure compliance with relevant laws and regulations. It's imperative to refrain from infringing on individuals' privacy while engaging in drone activities and to remain mindful of legal constraints.

Adherence to certain protocols is essential when capturing photos or videos with drones, particularly to avoid encroaching on private spaces such as homes or gardens. Employing cameras or listening devices on drones for intrusive purposes may contravene data protection laws and could lead to legal repercussions under the General Data Protection Regulation (GDPR).

Visibility and accountability are integral aspects of responsible drone operation, emphasizing the importance of notifying individuals before recording or photographing them. While practicality may pose challenges in every scenario, making reasonable efforts to inform others of drone activities fosters transparency and demonstrates respect for their privacy rights.

Ethical considerations should guide decisions regarding the dissemination of drone-captured media, prioritizing fairness and harm avoidance. Careful assessment of potential implications and recipients of shared content is crucial, with a focus on securing and responsibly managing drone imagery to safeguard individuals' privacy.

In addition to standard flight regulations, unique scenarios and flying activities require special attention from drone operators to ensure compliance and safety. Flying over tall structures, emergency incidents, and engaging in First Person View (FPV) flying necessitate adherence to specific guidelines and regulations outlined by the Civil Aviation Authority (CAA).

Follow-me mode, a feature enabling drones to autonomously track and follow subjects, is permissible within defined parameters set by the CAA. While offering flexibility for recreational and small commercial flights, adherence to maximum distance limitations is essential to maintain visual contact and ensure safe operations.

Understanding and abiding by privacy laws and flight regulations are fundamental responsibilities for drone operators, underpinning safe and ethical drone usage while fostering respect for privacy rights and legal obligations.

Drone Regulations in Europe

Drone regulations in Europe are primarily governed by the European Union Aviation Safety Agency (EASA), which establishes rules and standards for the safe operation of unmanned aircraft systems (UAS) across the European Union (EU) member states. These regulations aim to ensure the safety of airspace users, including both manned and unmanned aircraft, as well as people and property on the ground.

As of 2024, the main regulatory framework for drone operations in Europe is Regulation (EU) 2019/947, commonly known as the EU Drone Regulation. This regulation categorizes drones into three operational categories based on their level of risk: Open, Specific, and Certified. Each category has its own set of requirements and operational limitations.

1. Open Category: This category covers low-risk drone operations. It includes drones flown for recreational purposes as well as some commercial and educational activities. Operating within the Open category requires compliance with specific operational limitations, such as maximum altitude and distance from people.

2. Specific Category: The Specific category encompasses medium-risk drone operations that do not fall within the Open category. It includes more complex drone operations, such as flights near crowds or over urban areas. Operators in this category must obtain an operational authorization from the national aviation authority and conduct a risk assessment for each flight.

3. Certified Category: The Certified category is reserved for high-risk drone oper-

ations, such as beyond visual line of sight (BVLOS) flights or operations over densely populated areas. Drones in this category must meet rigorous certification standards, similar to those for manned aircraft.

In addition to the EU Drone Regulation, individual EU member states may have their own national regulations and requirements for drone operations. These regulations may include additional restrictions or permissions for certain types of flights, such as flights near sensitive areas or infrastructure.

The goal of drone regulations in Europe is to strike a balance between promoting innovation and economic growth in the drone industry while ensuring safety, security, and privacy for all stakeholders.

The backdrop of EU drone regulations underscores a continual adaptation to the rapid advancements in drone technology. Originally crafted to manage the burgeoning use of drones across diverse sectors, these regulations aim to tackle challenges pertaining to safety, privacy, and efficient airspace management. The 2024 revisions signify a substantial evolution in this regulatory landscape, seeking to further standardize drone operations across the EU while addressing complexities and inconsistencies that have emerged over time. These changes reflect not only the EU's dedication to technological progress but also its commitment to public safety and privacy concerns [51].

Commencing January 1, 2024, pivotal changes in the EU's drone regulations herald a paradigm shift. A key facet of this transformation is the introduction of drone classes based on risk assessment. This novel classification system aims to streamline operations and bolster safety throughout EU nations, ushering in a more structured and comprehensible framework for drone utilization. These revisions represent more than just minor adjustments; they constitute a significant overhaul of the existing framework, aimed at aligning drone regulations with current and future technologies and applications.

Manufacturers will encounter heightened requirements for marketing drones within the EU starting in 2024. Each drone must bear a specific class designation, akin to the CE mark found in electronics, affirming compliance with EU standards. This change is poised to significantly impact manufacturers, setting a higher benchmark for quality and safety. It signifies a shift towards enhanced accountability and reliability in the drone industry, ensuring consumers have access to drones meeting stringent safety standards. This shift is likely to reshape the industry landscape, phasing out subpar products and fostering a market focused on quality and adherence to regulations.

The new regulations introduce a nuanced classification system for all existing and new drones, with profound implications for drone usage within the EU:

Drones Under 250 grams fall under the Open A1 category, offering maximum operational freedom. While no drone license is required, valid insurance and registration with the national aviation authority are necessary. This category primarily benefits hobbyists and professionals using smaller, less risky drones. Drones Over 250 grams are categorized under the more restrictive Open A3 category [51]. Pilots of these drones must hold a license for operation and adhere to operational limits, such as maintaining a distance of at least 150 meters from residential, industrial, and recreational areas. This category significantly impacts professional drone operators utilizing larger drones for commercial purposes [51].

A detailed examination of drone classes provides insight into the evolving landscape of drone technology, enabling tailored regulation to ensure safer skies. These classifications simplify the regulatory framework while aligning it with the capabilities and risks associated with different drone types, catering to hobbyists, professionals, and commercial users alike. From lightweight drones used for leisure activities to robust models deployed for commercial endeavours, understanding these classes is essential for all drone operators.

In the realm of EU drone regulations, the categorization into different classes delineates distinct operational parameters and regulatory requirements tailored to various drone types and applications. Here's a breakdown of the classes:

- Class C0: Regulatory Requirements: Subject to minimal regulations. License Needs: No flying license is mandated. Mandatory Registration and Insurance: Operators must ensure drone registration and insurance. Operational Category: Eligible for Open A1 category operations. Proximity to People: Permitted to fly in close proximity to people. Ideal Users: Suited for hobbyists and light commercial use. Drone Examples: Typically encompasses very small drones, commonly utilized for leisure activities. Advantages: Provides the highest level of operational freedom within urban and populated areas.

- Class C1: Weight Limit: Encompasses drones weighing up to 900 grams. License Requirements: Basic flying license is required. Operational Category: Also categorized under Open A1 category operations. Flexibility: Offers greater operational flexibility compared to Class C0. Target Activities: Suitable for a wider range of activities, including commercial operations. Usage Examples: May involve small commercial drones utilized for photography, videography, and inspections. Regulatory Compliance: Pilots must adhere to specific airspace restrictions and privacy regulations.

- Class C2: Weight Bracket: Includes drones exceeding 900 grams. Initial Restrictions: Initially placed in the Open A3 category with operational limitations. Advantages with A2 License: Acquisition of an A2 flying license enables operations closer to urban areas and people. Targeted Towards: Geared towards professional and commercial use. Potential Uses: Ideal for advanced commercial applications such as aerial surveying, agricultural monitoring, and more. Operational Flexibility: The A2 license significantly broadens the operational scope for these drones. Regulatory Compliance: Mandates strict adherence to safety and operational guidelines.

The Open Category serves as the primary framework for leisure drone activities and low-risk commercial ventures across European nations. Within this category, there exist three distinct sub-categories, namely A1, A2, and A3, each tailored to specific operational parameters [52]:

- A1: Permits flying over individuals but not over gatherings of people.

- A2: Allows flying in close proximity to individuals.

- A3: Requires flying at a considerable distance from individuals.

Each subcategory entails its own set of criteria and prerequisites. Therefore, it is crucial for operators within the Open Category to ascertain the subcategory that aligns with their activities to determine the applicable regulations and requisite training for remote pilots.

For those who comply with the stipulated requirements of the subcategories (A1, A2, and A3), no operational authorization is necessitated prior to commencing a flight. However, if a drone operation falls outside the purview of the Open Category, recourse to the 'Specific Category' or 'Certified Category' is mandated.

Certain conditions must be fulfilled to circumvent the need for authorization:

- Drone operators must be duly registered, adhering to specific procedures based on residency.

- Adequate insurance coverage for all operated drones is mandatory, with varying limits across different countries.

- Drone pilots must possess proof of competency, contingent upon the subcategory of the drone operation.

- Adherence to visual line of sight (VLOS) requirements, ensuring constant visibility of the drone.

- Limiting drone altitude to a maximum of 120 meters above ground level.

- Prohibition of carrying hazardous materials or releasing any objects during flight.

Commencing January 1, 2024, operations falling within the open category necessitate the utilization of a drone equipped with a class identification label denoted as C0, C1, C2, C3, or C4. Alternatively, operations may also employ privately constructed drones or those lacking a class identification label, provided they were introduced to the market prior to December 31, 2023. The markings are shown as Figure 30.

Figure 30: Class identification labels.

Starting January 1, 2024, operations within the open category will adhere to the guidelines outlined below. It's important to note that "privately built" refers to drones constructed for personal use, distinct from those assembled from market-available kits.

If you've purchased a drone lacking a class identification label before January 1, 2024, you can still operate it within subcategory A1 if it weighs under 250g or in subcategory A3 if it weighs under 25kg.

Drone Categories and Operational Subcategories

The open category is subdivided into three subcategories: A1, A2, and A3. Here's a breakdown of each:

Privately Built and Drones Bought before 1/1/24 (Under 250g)

- **A1**: Allows flight over people but not assemblies, and may also fly in subcategory A3. Flight over uninvolved people is permitted, with overflight minimized when possible. No operator registration is required unless a camera or sensor is onboard, and the drone is not classified as a toy. No training is necessary, and there's no minimum age requirement.

- **C0 (Under 250g)**: Falls under A1 operations, allowing flight over people but not assemblies. Maintaining flight altitude below 120m above ground level is mandated. No operator registration is necessary unless a camera or sensor is onboard and the drone isn't a toy. Minimum age for operation is 16 years, though some states may lower it to 12 for their jurisdiction.

C1 (Under 900g)

- **A1**: Similar to C0, allowing flight over people but not assemblies. Operator registration is required, and pilots need proof of completion for online training. Minimum age for operation varies by state, with some potentially lowering it to 12.

C2 (Under 4 kg)

- **A2**: Allows flight close to people but mandates a horizontal distance of 30m from uninvolved individuals, extendable to 5m in low-speed mode. Operator registration is necessary, along with proof of completion for online training and a remote pilot certificate of competency for A2 operations.

C3 and C4 (Under 25 kg)

- **A3**: Requires flying far from people, maintaining a horizontal distance of 150m from uninvolved individuals and urban areas. Operator registration is required, along with proof of completion for online training. Minimum age for operation varies by state, with some potentially lowering it to 12.

Privately Built and Drones Bought before 1/1/24 (Under 25 kg)

- **A3**: Similar to C3 and C4, mandating flight far from people and urban areas. Operator registration, proof of completion for online training, and compliance with age requirements are necessary.

From January 1, 2024, drones in the specific category and those with class marks operating in the open category must have an active and up-to-date remote identification system.

DRONE OPERATIONS

DRONE REGULATIONS IN INDIA

Drone regulations in India are governed by the Directorate General of Civil Aviation (DGCA), the regulatory body responsible for civil aviation in the country. The regulations were first introduced in 2018 and have since undergone several revisions to accommodate the evolving drone industry while addressing safety and security concerns. India's Directorate General of Civil Aviation announced the country's first Civil Aviation Requirements (CAR) for drones on August 27, 2018 to go into effect December 1, 2018 [53].

Drone regulations in India include:

1. Drone Categories: The regulations classify drones into five categories based on their weight: Nano (up to 250 grams), Micro (251 grams to 2 kilograms), Small (2 kilograms to 25 kilograms), Medium (25 kilograms to 150 kilograms), and Large (above 150 kilograms).

2. Registration and Operator Permits: All drone operators in India are required to register their drones and obtain an Operator Permit (OP) and a Unique Identification Number (UIN) from the DGCA. Different categories of drones require different levels of permits, with heavier drones requiring more stringent permits.

3. Remote Pilot License (RPL): Pilots operating drones in the 'Small' and above categories are required to obtain a Remote Pilot License (RPL) from the DGCA. To qualify for an RPL, pilots must undergo training from DGCA-approved drone training organizations and pass written and practical exams.

4. No-Permission No-Take-off (NPNT): The NPNT system is a mandatory compliance requirement for all drones operating in India. It ensures that drones can only take off after receiving clearance from the Digital Sky platform, which verifies the drone's compliance with airspace restrictions and safety norms.

5. Geo-Fencing and Restrictions: Drones in India are required to have geo-fencing capabilities to prevent them from entering restricted airspace, such as airports, military installations, and other sensitive areas. Additionally, drones are prohibited from flying over certain designated areas, including eco-sensitive zones and strategic locations.

6. Flight Permissions: Operators must obtain specific flight permissions from the Digital Sky platform for each drone operation, specifying details such as flight path, altitude, and duration. Commercial drone operators are also required to obtain additional clearances from local authorities for certain types of operations.

7. Operational Restrictions: Drones are prohibited from flying beyond visual line of sight (BVLOS) and must be operated during daylight hours only. They are also subject to altitude restrictions, with different limits depending on the category of the drone.

8. Payload Restrictions: Drones in India are not permitted to carry hazardous materials or payloads that pose a risk to public safety or security.

9. Insurance Requirements: Drone operators are required to have third-party liability insurance coverage for their drones, as specified by the DGCA.

Overall, India's drone regulations aim to strike a balance between promoting innovation and ensuring safety and security in the airspace. While the regulations have introduced some complexities for drone operators, they are essential for fostering the growth of the drone industry while addressing regulatory concerns.

Hobbyist Drone Laws for Residents of India

In India, individuals have the opportunity to engage in drone flying for recreational purposes, commonly referred to as hobbyists. While the operation of drones is generally permissible for non-commercial use, certain regulations must be adhered to. Specifically, individuals operating drones weighing up to 2 kg for recreational purposes are exempt from requiring an India Remote Pilot Certificate, provided the activity remains non-commercial [54]. However, registration of hobbyist drones is mandatory for those intending to fly drones for recreation or non-commercial purposes. Although hobbyists are not required to obtain a Drone Remote ID, it is essential to ensure proper drone insurance coverage for recreational drone flights, with the exception of Nano UAVs.

Commercial Drone Laws for Residents of India

For individuals in India looking to utilize drones for commercial purposes, specific regulations apply. Commercial drone operations necessitate the possession of a Commercial India Drone Pilot license and the registration of commercial drones. While commercial drone operators are not mandated to acquire a Drone Remote ID, securing appropriate drone insurance coverage is a prerequisite for conducting commercial drone operations in India.

Commercial Applications of Drones in India

The utilization of drones for various commercial applications has gained significant traction in India. These applications encompass a wide array of industries and activities, including aerial photography and videography, agricultural and crop monitoring, package delivery and logistics, infrastructure inspection and maintenance, environmental conservation and wildlife monitoring, security and surveillance, as well as surveying and mapping.

Drone Laws for Visitors to India

Visitors to India are subject to specific regulations regarding drone operations. Foreign visitors are not permitted to operate drones within the country, and the possession of a Drone Pilot License by foreigners is not applicable in India. Furthermore, requirements such as Drone Remote ID and registration, as well as drone insurance, do not apply to tourists and visitors engaging in drone activities in India.

Drone Laws for Government Drone Operators in India

Government entities involved in drone operations within India must adhere to distinct regulations. While government drone flights with a valid Drone Pilot License are permissible, neither Drone Remote ID nor drone insurance is obligatory for government drone operations. However, the registration of government drones remains mandatory to ensure compliance with regulatory standards.

Recent Laws for Drone Operations in India

The Government of India has taken significant steps to enhance and streamline drone operations across the country. Notably, the Ministry of Civil Aviation introduced the

New Drone (Amendment) Rules 2023, which came into effect on September 27, 2023. Among the amendments was the clarification that identity and address proof issued by the government, such as Voter ID, Driving License, or Ration Card, could be accepted for Remote Pilot Certificate applications in the absence of a passport. This amendment aimed to address previous barriers faced by individuals in rural areas, particularly those engaged in agricultural activities, by removing the requirement for a passport as a prerequisite for Remote Pilot Certification. To qualify for Remote Pilot Certification, individuals must meet certain eligibility criteria, including being between the ages of 18 and 65, possessing at least a Class X qualification from a recognized board, and completing Remote Pilot Training as specified by the DGCA from an authorized Remote Pilot Training institute [54].

General Rules for Flying a Drone in India

To ensure compliance with drone regulations in India, it's essential to be familiar with the key rules governing drone operations. Here are the most crucial guidelines to keep in mind [53]:

Firstly, all drones, except those classified as Nano category, must undergo registration and be issued a Unique Identification Number (UIN). For commercial drone activities, except for those in the Nano category flown below 50 feet and the Micro category flown below 200 feet, a permit is mandatory.

Furthermore, drone pilots are obligated to maintain a direct visual line of sight while operating drones. Vertical flight is restricted to a maximum altitude of 400 feet, and drones cannot be flown in designated "No Fly Zones," including areas near airports, international borders, and various strategic locations such as Vijay Chowk in Delhi and military installations.

Obtaining permission to fly in controlled airspace necessitates the submission of a flight plan and securing a unique Air Defense Clearance (ADC)/Flight Information Center (FIC) number.

Figure 31: MedCOPTER drone during the BVLOS operations conducted in Karnataka, India. Nambi2015, CC BY-SA 4.0, via Wikimedia Commons.

Drone Categories in India

Drone classification in India is categorized based on weight, with registration requirements varying accordingly:

- Nano: Drones weighing less than or equal to 250 grams (.55 pounds)

- Micro: Drones ranging from 250 grams (.55 pounds) to 2kg (4.4 pounds)

- Small: Drones weighing from 2kg (4.4 pounds) to 25kg (55 pounds)

- Medium: Drones with weights between 25kg (55 pounds) to 150kg (330 pounds)

- Large: Drones exceeding 150kg (33 pounds)

Required Drone Equipment in India

Apart from registration, certain mandatory features are stipulated for drones operating in India, excluding those in the Nano category. These features include GPS, Return-to-home (RTH) capability, anti-collision lights, identification plates, a flight controller with flight data logging, as well as RF ID and SIM/No Permission No Take-off (NPNT) functionality.

India's No Permission, No Take-off Policy

Under the "No Permission, No Take-off" (NPNT) policy, drone pilots are required to obtain permission for each flight via a mobile app linked to the Digital Sky Platform.

Without receiving clearance through this platform, drone operators are unable to initiate take-off. All drone operators must register their drones and seek permission for every flight through India's Digital Sky Platform, with further details available on the DGCA website.

Zone Classifications for Drone Operations

In accordance with the Drone Rules 2021, Indian airspace is divided into three distinct zones: Red Zone, Yellow Zone, and Green Zone. Here's a detailed overview of each zone:

Red Zone: The Red Zone pertains to the airspace above land areas or territorial waters of India, which includes specified installations or notified port limits beyond territorial waters. Only operations conducted by the Central Government are permitted within this zone. Stringent restrictions are imposed on drone activities, with specific dimensions delineated.

Yellow Zone: The Yellow Zone encompasses airspace above land areas or territorial waters of India. Drone operations within this zone are subject to restrictions and necessitate permission from the relevant air traffic control authority. This zone includes airspace above 400 feet or 120 meters in designated green zones and airspace above 200 feet or 60 meters within a lateral distance of 8 to 12 kilometres from the perimeter of an operational airport.

Green Zone: The Green Zone covers airspace above land areas or territorial waters of India, extending up to a vertical distance of 400 feet or 120 meters. It encompasses areas not classified as Red or Yellow Zones on the drone airspace map. Additionally, the Green Zone includes airspace up to a vertical distance of 200 feet or 60 meters above the area located between a lateral distance of 8 to 12 kilometres from the perimeter of an operational airport.

Drone Airspace Map and Key Features:

The Central Government, led by Prime Minister Shri Narendra Modi, unveiled an interactive drone airspace map on the DGCA's digital sky platform on September 24, 2021. Key features of this map include:

- Interactive Interface: Users can visually identify yellow and red zones across India through the drone airspace map.

- Green Zone: Drones weighing up to 500 kg can operate freely in green zones without seeking prior permission.

- Yellow Zone: Operations within this zone require permission from relevant air traffic control authorities, with specific height restrictions near airports.

- Reduction of Yellow Zone: The yellow zone radius has been reduced from 45 km to 12 km from the airport perimeter.

- Red Zone: Drone operations in the red zone are strictly prohibited without permission from the Central Government.

- Modification of Airspace Map: Authorized entities have the capability to modify the airspace map as necessary.

- Regular Checking: Drone operators are advised to regularly check the airspace map for any updates or changes in zone boundaries.

- Accessibility: The drone airspace map is easily accessible on the digital sky platform without the need for login credentials.

Registration of Unmanned Aircraft Systems:

Drone operators are mandated to register their unmanned aircraft systems on the digital sky platform and obtain a unique identification number (UIN), unless exempted under the Drone Rules, 2021. The DGCA maintains a comprehensive registration record of all UIN-issued unmanned aircraft systems.

As per the Civil Aviation Ministry, an interactive airspace map will be accessible on its website, illustrating three distinct zones [55]:

Yellow denotes controlled airspace. Green signifies areas where no permission is required. Red indicates areas where flying is prohibited. Drone operators can utilize these delineations to ascertain where they are permitted or prohibited from flying their unmanned aircraft systems.

The yellow zone, previously spanning a 45-kilometer radius around airport perimeters, has now been reduced to a 12-kilometer radius. This adjustment implies that drone operators no longer need authorization to fly outside a 12-kilometer radius around airport perimeters.

The green zone encompasses airspace up to 400 feet and includes areas not designated as red or yellow zones. Additionally, it extends up to 200 feet above the region located between 8 to 12 kilometres from the perimeter of an operational airport.

In India, certain areas are designated as no-fly zones (Red Zone), where drone operations are strictly prohibited. These areas include:

- Within 5 kilometres of the perimeters of international airports in Mumbai,

Delhi, Chennai, Kolkata, Bengaluru, and Hyderabad.

- Within a 3-kilometer radius of boundaries of any civil, private, or defense airports.

- Within 25 kilometres of the international border (AGPL), encompassing Line of Control (LoC), Line of Actual Control (LAC), and Actual Ground Position Line.

- Within 3 kilometres of military installations or facilities without clearance.

- Within a 5-kilometer radius of Delhi's Vijay Chowk.

- Within 2 kilometres of the perimeter of strategic locations or vital installations notified by the Ministry of Home Affairs unless clearance is obtained.

- Within 3 kilometres of the State Secretariat Complex in State Capitals. For ground stations situated on a fixed platform on land, placement beyond 500 meters into the water from the coast is permissible.

- Flying from a moving vehicle, ship, or any other improvised floating platform is prohibited. Over eco-sensitive zones around National Parks and Wildlife Sanctuaries without prior approval from the Ministry of Environment, Forests and Climate Change.

- Within Prohibited, Restricted, and Danger zones, whether permanent or temporary.

To ensure safe and responsible drone flying, it's essential to adhere to the following guidelines:

Do's:

Obtain a Unique Identification Number (UIN) from the DGCA and seek pre-flight permission from the Digital Sky Platform. Ensure compliance with safety conditions and be cautious of mobile device interference and signal blockage. Limit flights to daytime hours and monitor weather conditions, staying informed about changes in climatic situations. Follow all guidelines and regulations for flying drones, conducting thorough research before investing in a drone. Understand operational and regulatory aspects before each flight and respect airspace restrictions and No Drone Zones. Choose flight locations away from airports and heliports, respecting people's privacy and maintaining a log of flights. Notify authorities in case of incidents or accidents.

Don'ts:

Do not exceed altitude limits specified for different drone categories or fly drones near airports, heliports, and crowded areas without permission. Do not operate drones over government facilities, military bases, or no-drone zones, and refrain from flying over private property without permission. Avoid operating in regulated airspace near airports without proper approval and do not use drones for carrying or dropping hazardous material. Never operate drones under the influence of drugs or alcohol, and refrain from flying drones from moving vehicles, ships, or planes.

Drone Regulations in 2022

Exemptions from Prior Approval - With the exception of the nano and micro categories, which are limited to non-commercial use, all drone operations require prior approval from the Digital Sky online platform for individual flights or a series of flights.

Drone operators are required to ensure that the aircraft remains within the designated area for which permission was granted, and to maintain an online log of each flight.

According to the 2022 regulations, no permit is necessary for flying and operating tiny drones falling under the nano and micro categories.

Furthermore, the government is establishing drone corridors to facilitate cargo delivery operations.

Perform Operational Inspections on Remote Operated Systems

Performing operational inspections on remote-operated systems involves a systematic approach to ensure safety, compliance, and efficiency. This includes:

- Suitable maps, charts, and weather briefings are selected for the intended remote operation. An operations plan is prepared, and geofencing is set if required. This involves carefully choosing maps and charts that provide accurate and relevant information about the operational area. Weather briefings help in understanding the current and forecasted weather conditions that may impact the operation. Geofencing, if necessary, involves setting virtual boundaries to restrict the drone's flight path.

- Pre-operational information, including Notice to Airmen (NOTAM) or industry equivalents, is accessed, analysed, and applied to the operational plan. This step ensures that any relevant information regarding airspace restrictions, temporary flight restrictions, or other operational considerations is taken into account.

- Hazards are clearly indicated on charts, and risk controls are implemented. Identifying potential hazards such as obstacles, terrain features, or airspace restrictions is crucial for safe operation. Risk controls, such as adjusting the flight path or altitude, are implemented to mitigate identified hazards.

- Effects of wind velocity, adverse environmental conditions, and contingency actions are planned for. Understanding how wind and environmental conditions may affect drone operations is essential for safe and effective flight. Contingency plans are developed to address unexpected situations or emergencies.

- The lost link profile and routing are prepared and validated. This involves planning for communication loss between the remote pilot and the drone and establishing procedures for re-establishing communication or safely returning the drone to the ground in case of a lost link.

- Awareness of current and forecast weather conditions is maintained throughout the operation. Continuous monitoring of weather conditions helps in making informed decisions and adapting the operational plan as needed to ensure safety.

- Information about the remote-operated system is obtained, read, and used to guide work as required. Understanding the capabilities and limitations of the remote-operated system is essential for safe and effective operation.

- Pre- and post-operational planning and documentation are completed. This involves preparing all necessary paperwork, including flight plans, checklists, and any required permits or authorizations, before and after the operation.

- The remote system's operating weight and configuration are confirmed to ensure compliance with regulatory requirements and operational limitations.

- Pre- and post-operation technical release and remote system operation administration documentation are completed to document the operational process and ensure accountability.

- System serviceability is determined by approved technical inspection to ensure that the remote-operated system is in good working condition and safe for operation.

- Certification of inspection for technical release is completed to certify that the remote-operated system has been inspected and approved for operation.

- Equipment and documentation are identified and accessible in accordance with regulatory requirements to ensure that all necessary equipment and paperwork are readily available during the operation.

- Internal and external checks are completed in accordance with approved system checklists to verify that the remote-operated system is functioning properly and free from defects or damage.

- Deployment administration tasks and communications are conducted to coordinate the operation with relevant stakeholders and ensure that all necessary protocols are followed.

- The remote-operated system is secured in accordance with manufacturer specifications and organizational procedures to prevent unauthorized access or tampering.

- Pre-operating inspection of the remote-operated system and ancillary equipment is performed in accordance with original equipment manufacturer (OEM) documentation and operations manual to ensure that all components are functioning correctly and meet operational requirements.

- Appropriate actions are undertaken to rectify discrepancies, and they are recorded to document any issues or problems encountered during the pre-operating inspection and ensure that they are addressed promptly.

- Pre-operating inspection is recorded in accordance with the operations manual to maintain a record of the inspection process and demonstrate compliance with regulatory requirements.

Several civil aviation regulations govern pilot actions before flight, such as, in an Australian context, including CAR 78 for Navigation logs, CAR 92 for Use of aerodromes, CAR 233 for the Responsibility of the pilot in command before flight, CAR 234 for Fuel requirements, CAR 235 for Take-off and landing of aircraft, CAR 235A for Minimum runway width, CAR 239 for Planning of flight by the pilot in command, CAR 244 for Safety precautions before take-off, and CAR 282 for Offences in relation to licenses, certificates, and authorities.

Before flight, it is prudent to conduct a thorough check of flight planning, navigation equipment, and aircraft equipment to ensure compliance with all requirements. Have you:

1. Established the safest route and minimum safe altitude, avoiding hazardous terrain, restricted areas, and designated remote areas?

2. Double-checked all magnetic bearings and distances on the flight plan?

3. Verified the suitability of refuelling stops, destination airfield, and alternate landing areas?

4. Checked details in ERSA and contacted owner/operators for airfield information and potential hazards?

5. Reviewed weather forecasts, NOTAMs, and daylight duration for en-route, destination, and alternate airfields?

6. Checked weather radars and lightning tracker sites for weather patterns?

7. Ensured proper functioning of essential instruments and avionics?

8. Confirmed functionality and loaded required frequencies for the VHF transceiver?

9. Provided backup batteries for handheld equipment?

10. Secured tie-down gear properly?

11. Ensured all necessary documents and checklists are current and available?

12. Checked fuel and oil levels and inspected for contamination?

13. Confirmed sufficient fuel/battery load with a safety margin?

14. Verified aircraft weight and balance within specified limits?

15. Calculated density altitude and take-off distance required, considering runway dimensions and conditions?

16. Calculated density altitude for destination and alternate airfields, ensuring safety margins for landing, take-off, and climb-out performance?

All pilots and operators must adhere to relevant rules and regulations and maintain their equipment in airworthy condition at all times.

Area and Environment

When selecting a site for UAV operations, it's crucial to assess potential hazards and environmental factors. This includes checking for wires or cables, the presence of animals, nearby people or bystanders, and property in the vicinity. Ensuring the site is away from nonessential participants and maintaining adequate buffer zones between aircraft and personnel is essential. Additionally, minimizing departures and landings over populated areas is important for safety. Consideration of local topography is necessary to maintain a visible line of sight towards the UAV and ensure the telemetry connection is not obstructed. Investigate potential alternative landing sites in case the take-off site is obstructed. Psychological considerations such as fatigue, time pressure, or external pressure from clients should also be taken into account.

Weather considerations, including temperature, visibility, and precipitation, play a significant role in flight safety. Wind speed, both at ground level and at altitude, should be carefully assessed, especially considering rotor effects on the lee side of large objects. Before flight, notify any bystanders or nearby property owners of your intentions and seek permission if necessary. Discuss the flight plan with your co-pilot or spotter to ensure mutual understanding and coordination. If flying in controlled airspace, notify the airspace authority and adhere to relevant NOTAMs. Ensure you have the means to maintain communication if required.

First Aid Kit stocked, readily accessible and visible to anyone in the area is essential for immediate response to emergencies.

Equipment / UAV / Drone

Before each flight, conduct a thorough walk-around inspection of the UAV and its equipment. Check for any cracks in joints and structural members, loose or damaged screws, ties, fasteners, straps, wiring, and connections. Inspect prop mounts and screws, applying slight counter pressure on arms to check for loosened components. For FPV, inspect and clean the camera lens, ensuring it is secured and connections are firmly attached. Verify that camera settings are correct for still images, video, and framerate.

Ensure that the battery or batteries are fully charged, properly seated, and securely fastened. Verify the functionality of fail-safe equipment such as Return to Home (RTH), recovery chute, and firmware airport proximity detection. Check that props are smooth and free of damage or defects, including blade, surface, and hub. Tighten and secure prop adapters, and ensure that voltage alarm and arming/idle timeout are properly configured.

Confirm that the correct model is selected in the transmitter (if applicable), and perform a range test to ensure proper communication. Balance the weight before each flight, adjusting the battery position for optimal balance. Regularly check the nose and tail loading, moving the battery back and forth to find the sweet spot for the best balance.

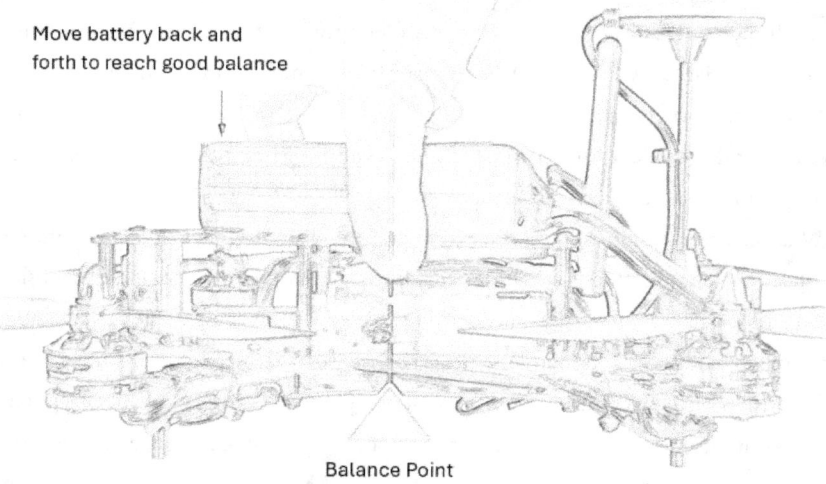

Figure 32: Balancing the drone with battery fitted.

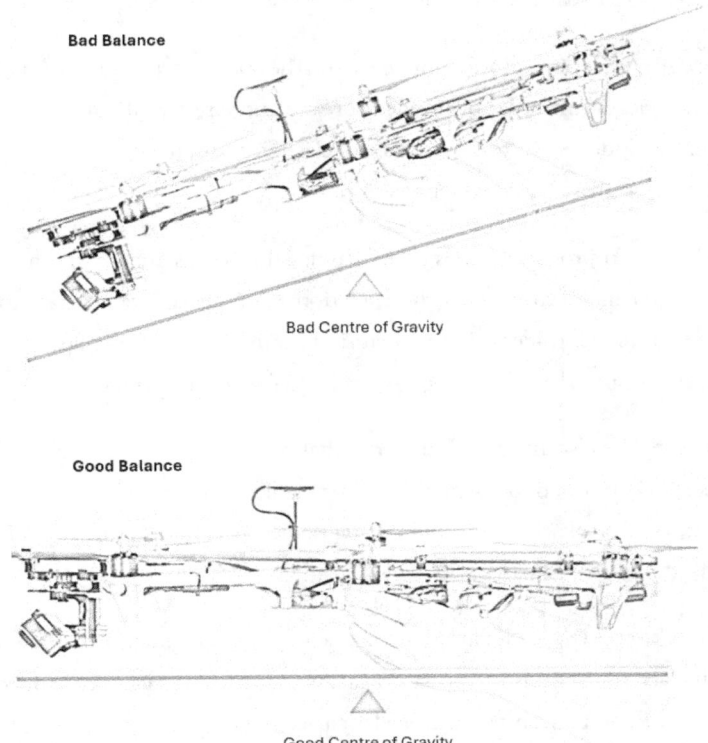

Figure 33: Drone should be balanced around the point of the centre of gravity.

Mission Plan

For every mission, thorough planning is essential to ensure all actions and contingencies are considered. Contingency planning should encompass safe routes in the event of system failure, degraded performance, or lost communication link, if such failsafes exist. It's crucial to share mission plans and flight plans with other operators in the vicinity to promote coordination and safety.

To select suitable maps, charts, and weather briefings for a drone operation, follow these steps:

1. Assess Operational Requirements: Determine the specific requirements of the drone operation, including the intended flight path, altitude, and duration. Consider factors such as the purpose of the flight (e.g., aerial surveying, photog-

raphy, or surveillance) and any regulatory restrictions or airspace considerations.

2. Identify Relevant Information: Based on the operational requirements, identify the types of information needed for safe and effective flight planning. This may include terrain features, airspace classifications, navigation aids, obstacles, restricted areas, and weather conditions.

3. Choose Appropriate Maps and Charts: Select maps and charts that provide comprehensive coverage of the operational area and relevant details for drone navigation. Consider using aeronautical charts, topographic maps, satellite imagery, or specialized mapping tools tailored for drone operations.

4. Ensure Detailed Information: Verify that the selected maps and charts contain detailed information essential for flight planning and navigation. Look for features such as elevation contours, water bodies, landmarks, roads, buildings, and geographic coordinates.

5. Check for Airspace Restrictions: Review the maps and charts to identify any airspace restrictions or special-use areas that may impact the planned drone flight. Pay attention to controlled airspace, military training areas, prohibited zones, and temporary flight restrictions (TFRs) issued by aviation authorities.

6. Assess Potential Hazards: Evaluate the maps and charts for potential hazards or obstacles that could pose risks to the drone operation. This may include natural features like mountains, cliffs, or dense vegetation, as well as man-made structures such as power lines, towers, and buildings.

7. Conduct Weather Briefings: Gather current and forecasted weather information relevant to the operational area. Consult official weather sources, such as meteorological agencies, aviation weather services, or online weather platforms, to obtain data on temperature, wind speed and direction, visibility, precipitation, and atmospheric conditions.

8. Analyse Weather Impact: Analyse the weather briefings to assess how meteorological conditions may affect the drone operation. Consider factors such as wind gusts, turbulence, icing conditions, cloud cover, and visibility restrictions. Determine whether the weather conditions meet the safety requirements for the

planned flight.

9. Document Findings: Document the findings from the map, chart, and weather briefing assessments to inform the operational plan and ensure all relevant information is considered during flight planning and execution. This documentation may include annotated maps, weather reports, and notes on airspace restrictions and hazards.

For drone operations, various types of charts and maps can be utilized to ensure safe and effective flight planning and navigation. Here's a breakdown of the types of charts and maps commonly used:

1. Aeronautical Charts: These charts, provided by aviation authorities like the Federal Aviation Administration (FAA) or Civil Aviation Authority (CAA), offer detailed information on airspace structure, navigation aids, airways, and restricted areas. They are essential for understanding airspace regulations and planning drone routes to avoid restricted or controlled airspace.

2. Topographic Maps: Topographic maps, typically issued by government agencies such as the United States Geological Survey (USGS) or national mapping organizations, depict terrain features such as elevation contours, rivers, forests, and landmarks. These maps are valuable for assessing terrain suitability, identifying obstacles, and planning flight paths over varied landscapes.

3. Satellite Imagery: Satellite imagery obtained from online mapping platforms like Google Earth or Bing Maps provides high-resolution visual representations of the Earth's surface. Drone operators can use satellite imagery to visualize the operational area, identify landmarks, assess terrain conditions, and plan flight routes with precision.

4. Digital Elevation Models (DEMs): DEMs are digital representations of terrain elevation data, often derived from radar or LiDAR technology. They provide accurate elevation information, allowing drone operators to analyse terrain features, calculate slope gradients, and assess elevation changes for safe flight planning.

5. Vector Maps: Vector maps consist of geometrically defined features such as points, lines, and polygons, stored as digital vector data. They offer flexibili-

ty in displaying various map layers, including roads, buildings, land use, and administrative boundaries. Vector maps are suitable for importing into drone flight planning software and integrating with navigation systems for real-time guidance.

6. Specialized Mapping Tools: Some mapping tools and software platforms are specifically designed for drone operations, offering features tailored to the needs of UAV pilots. These tools may include 3D terrain visualization, obstacle detection, route optimization, and geofencing capabilities to define no-fly zones and safety boundaries.

By considering the operational requirements, available resources, coverage, detail, scale, resolution, accuracy, currency, format compatibility, and specialized features of these charts and maps, drone operators can make informed decisions to ensure safe and successful flight planning and execution. Testing and verifying the chosen maps and charts before the operation is crucial to confirm their reliability and suitability for the mission at hand.

The term "aeronautical chart" encompasses various maps utilized for air navigation, provided they contain essential information such as topographic features, hazards, navigation routes, airspace delineations, and airport details. In the United States, there are nine commonly used types of aeronautical charts, primarily geared towards instrument flying, including en-route low altitude charts, en-route high altitude charts, instrument approach procedures, instrument departure procedures, and standard terminal arrival procedures. However, our focus here will be on charts pertinent to visual flight rules (VFR) operations.

Irrespective of location, pilots are likely to encounter sectional aeronautical charts, colloquially known as sectionals. These charts, scaled at one to 500,000, serve as aids for visual navigation in slow or medium-speed aircraft. Sectionals prioritize visual checkpoints and topographic details, featuring vital information such as obstacle and terrain elevations, radio frequencies for navigation, communication, and weather, airport particulars, controlled airspace designations, and restricted areas. Pilots predominantly utilize sectionals for cross-country flights [56].

In contrast to sectionals, VFR terminal area charts are available only for specific regions, utilizing a scale of one to 250,000. Pilots should utilize terminal charts for navigation when accessible, as they offer enhanced insights into busy areas within and around

Class B airspace. These charts contain similar information to sectionals but provide additional details, particularly concerning airspace, airports, obstructions, terrain, and visual checkpoints [56].

World aeronautical charts (WACs) employ a scale of one to 1 million and are primarily suited for long-distance navigation by pilots of high-speed aircraft [56]. Each WAC covers a sizable geographical area, albeit with less detail compared to terminal and sectional charts. Nonetheless, WACs include essential features such as cities, towns, major roads, railroads, prominent landmarks, frequencies, airways, and restricted areas.

Lastly, airport taxi charts, though primarily utilized by VFR pilots, are available for many major airports. These charts assist pilots in navigating within airport premises, facilitating the smooth flow of air traffic. Identified by the official airport name, such as Dulles International Airport, taxi charts aid pilots in efficiently manoeuvring on the ground [56].

Mastering the ability to interpret sectional charts stands as a fundamental skill for any drone pilot. By honing this proficiency, a drone operator gains insights into airspace hazards, topographical features, airport data, and controlled airspace. Particularly for individuals seeking to obtain a Part 107 remote pilot certificate (USA), competence in reading and comprehending sectional charts constitutes a substantial portion of the knowledge test required for certification.

Before delving into sectional charts, it's essential to grasp the basics of map reading, particularly the concept of latitude and longitude coordinates. These coordinates serve as the foundational framework for pinpointing any location on the globe. Latitude and longitude coordinates delineate positions along an imaginary grid pattern. To distinguish between the two, it's crucial to understand the role of key reference points—the equator and the prime meridian.

The prime meridian, denoted as the "zero longitude," traverses from the North to South poles, passing through Greenwich, England. Conversely, the equator serves as the "zero latitude," lying perpendicular to the prime meridian and equidistant from the North and South poles. Latitude lines run parallel to the equator, while longitude lines extend from pole to pole.

Latitude and longitude coordinates can be expressed in two primary formats. The traditional method involves degrees, minutes (where 1 degree equals 60 minutes), and seconds (where 1 minute equals 60 seconds). However, modern GPS systems typically utilize decimal notation. Familiarity with both formats is advantageous for map reading proficiency.

In sectional charts, the entire map is divided into quadrants to facilitate precise delineation of smaller areas. Each quadrant, defined by boundaries within 30 minutes of latitude and longitude, serves as a convenient reference point for pilots navigating sectional charts. Understanding quadrant identifiers aids pilots in indicating specific yet expansive areas within the charts.

Across sectional charts, airports stand out as significant landmarks. These pivotal locations come in various types, each offering distinctive features that are denoted on sectional charts. Differentiating factors include the presence of a control tower, the runway surface type, and fuel availability. Understanding these distinctions is essential for drone pilots, as it guides them on which radio frequencies to monitor for pertinent air traffic updates concerning specific airports.

Figure 34: FAA Sectional Chart showing Capital Region International Airport (FAA: LAN), formerly Capital City Airport, in Lansing, Clinton County, Michigan. United States FAA, Public domain, via Wikimedia Commons.

Primarily, airports are categorized based on the presence or absence of control towers, represented by distinct symbols on sectional charts. Airports with control towers are marked with blue symbols, while those without control towers are denoted by magenta symbols [57].

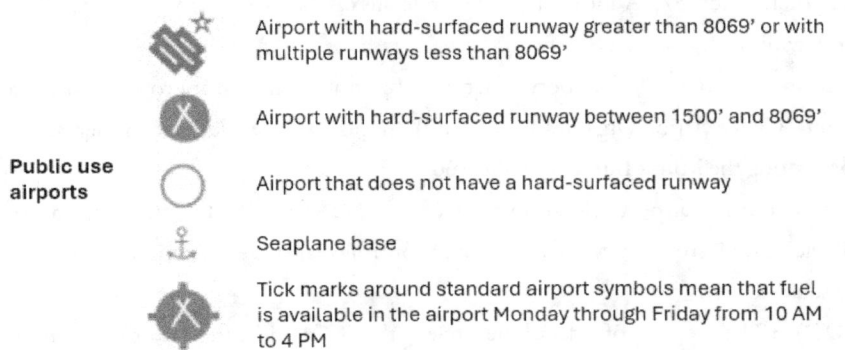

Figure 35: For public-use airports, this list of symbols can be used as reference.

On the other hand, distinguishing military airports is straightforward, as they are designated by abbreviations like AAF (Army Air Field), NAS (Naval Air Station), and NAV (Naval Air Facility), among others.

Regarding additional details about a particular airport, attention should be paid to the alphanumeric sequence associated with each airport symbol. This will be outlined using an example, shown as Figure 36.

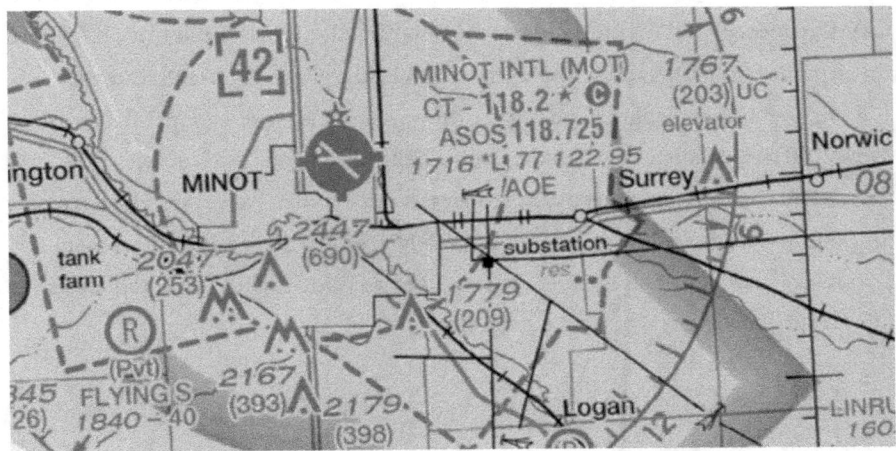

Figure 36: Sectional chart around Minot International Airport. FAA-CT-8080-2G, Figure 21, United States FAA, Public domain.

Based on the information provided, we can deduce that the airport denoted by the symbol possesses a control tower, a hard-surfaced runway shorter than 8069 feet, and offers fuel service [57]. Additional pertinent details can be gleaned from the text adjacent to the symbol.

Airport Identifier: Each airport is identified by an abbreviation approved by the International Civil Aviation Organization (ICAO). In this case, the 3-letter identifier is MOT, representing the Minot International Airport.

Elevation: The airport's elevation is specified as 1716 feet MSL (above mean sea level). This elevation factor influences the extent of controlled airspace surrounding the airport, as discussed later.

CTAF: The presence of a dark blue circle with a 'C' signifies the use of the Common Traffic Advisory Frequency (CTAF) at the airport. Pilots passing through are expected to self-announce their location and intentions. This suggests that although the airport has a control tower, it operates on a part-time basis. The designated frequency for drone pilots to monitor for self-announcements is 118.2 MHz.

ASOS Frequency: The symbol indicates that the airport's Automated Surface Observing System (ASOS) frequency is 118.725. ASOS automatically provides essential weather information such as barometric pressure, wind speed and direction, visibility, and precipitation.

UNICOM Frequency: Given the intermittent operation of the control tower, UNICOM frequency 122.95 is utilized when the tower is active. It's advisable to monitor both the airport's UNICOM and CTAF channels while scanning for communications.

Longest Runway Length: The longest runway at Minot International Airport measures 7700 feet, denoted by '77' in the symbol, representing hundreds of feet.

In addition to highlighting points of interest, sectional charts serve as crucial references for pilots to navigate around obstacles and safely manoeuvre over dynamic terrain. Key features indicating terrain include contour lines or shaded relief maps, serving as the foundational map layers for the sectional chart.

Terrain (contour lines)		Contour lines connect points of equal elevation. The graduations between the lines may vary based on the resolution of the map, but intervals of 50 to 250 feet are common.
Terrain (shaded relief)	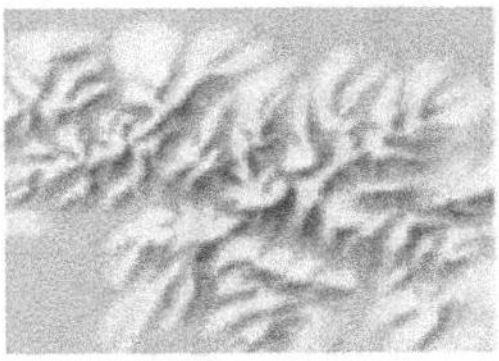	Shaded relief maps are a way of visually representing the terrain of the map by allowing the viewer to see the terrain features as if there is a light source from the northwest.

Figure 37: Terrain Indications.

In addition to visual terrain cues, sectional charts include symbols and data enabling pilots to adapt their flight paths and altitudes. Among these, the Maximum Elevation Figure (MEF) is paramount, featured in each quadrant of the sectional chart. The MEF signifies the highest point of elevation within the quadrant, encompassing both natural and man-made features [57].

Furthermore, sectional charts incorporate numerous symbols denoting different types of obstacles.

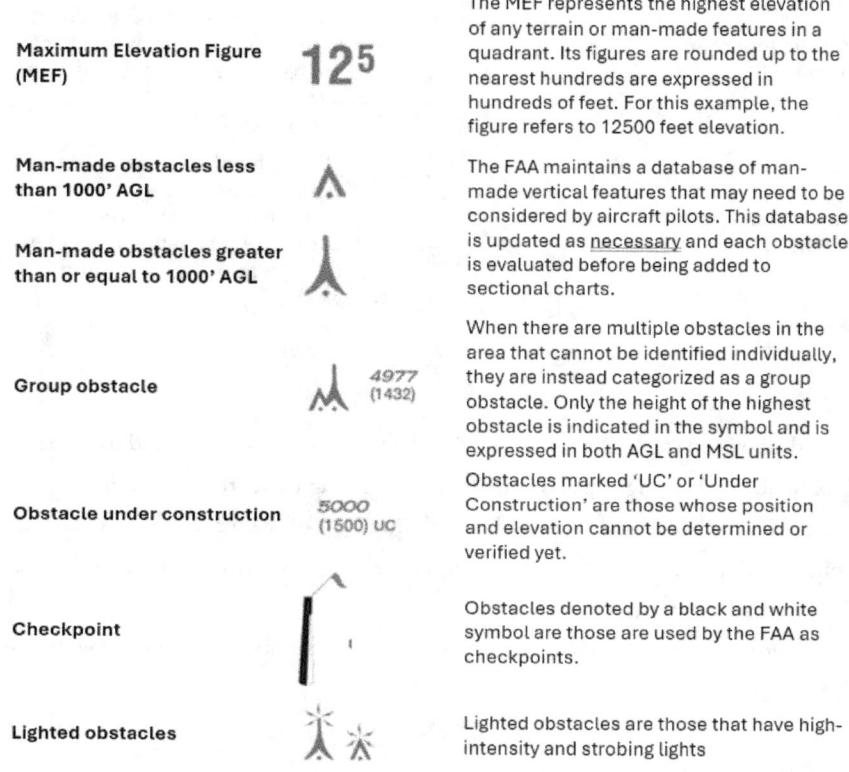

Figure 38: *Map symbols used to indicate obstacles.*

Controlled airspace, often encircling airports, is regulated by air traffic control (ATC) services, necessitating airspace authorization for drone flights due to the volume of air traffic. Conversely, uncontrolled airspace, also known as Class G airspace, lacks ATC regulation, permitting drone operations under visual flight rules (VFR).

Special use airspace entails restricted areas, denoted by distinctive symbols on sectional charts, which impose flight limitations unrelated to routine air traffic. These limitations can range from military exercises to public events.

In a US context, controlled Airspace Types: Class A: Ranging from 18,000 to 60,000 feet, primarily utilized by commercial airlines for long-haul flights, thus less relevant for drone operations. Class B: Designated around major airports, featuring extensive airspace coverage and requiring airspace authorization for drone flights. Its configuration often resembles an "upside-down cake" shape. Class C: Similar to Class B airspace but associated with smaller airports, represented by solid magenta lines on sectional charts, and requiring airspace authorization for drone flights. Class D: Assigned to smaller airports, characterized by a smaller extent and always starting at the surface, necessitating airspace authorization for drone flights. Class E: Encompassing areas not covered by previous categories, constituting a majority of national airspace, with most drone operations permitted without airspace authorization, barring certain airport proximities [57].

Understanding these airspace classifications aids drone pilots in navigating through regulatory requirements and safely conducting flights within designated airspace.

Uncontrolled Airspace: Class G, or uncontrolled airspace, stands as the least restrictive category among airspace types. Not subject to any ATC facility's jurisdiction, Class G airspace allows drone operation without requiring specific authorization. Despite this freedom, adherence to FAA flight regulations remains imperative within Class G airspace. Pilots should maintain flight altitudes below 400 feet AGL and ensure visual line-of-sight. Although uncontrolled, Class G airspace may still witness manned aircraft activity, necessitating drone pilots to yield right of way [57].

Special Use Airspace: Special use airspace encompasses a diverse array of flight restrictions, often associated with national security or event-related crowd protection. Varied types of special use airspace may cater to drone pilot safety during military operations or artillery testing. Identifying these airspace classifications typically relies on distinct codes and symbols.

Prohibited Areas: Designated by labels such as P-XXX, Prohibited Areas feature solid blue lines with hash marks on sectional charts. Strictly off-limits for drone flight, Prohibited Areas prioritize national security concerns, mandating avoidance irrespective of airspace authorization status.

Restricted Areas: Labelled R-XXX, Restricted Areas are demarcated by solid blue lines with hash marks. While not entirely off-limits, drone operation within Restricted Areas requires explicit authorization from the relevant controlling agency. Approval is contingent upon factors such as military testing activities, necessitating compliance with agency directives.

Warning Areas: Indicated by labels like W-XXX, Warning Areas are enclosed by solid blue lines with hash marks. Although drone pilots may operate within Warning Areas without prior authorization, exercising caution is paramount due to potential air traffic hazards.

Alert Areas: Identified by A-XXX labels, Alert Areas feature solid magenta lines with hash marks. Typically characterized by heightened air traffic volume, Alert Areas necessitate vigilant drone operation despite the absence of a controlling agency. While not explicitly prohibited, cautionary flight practices are advised.

Military Operation Areas (MOA): MOAs, marked by solid magenta lines with hash marks, denote military training or operational zones. Drone flight within MOAs is strongly discouraged due to potential hazards posed by military activities. Guidance from controlling agencies may provide clarity on drone flight permissions within MOAs.

Military Training Routes (MTR): Depicted by arrow symbols on sectional charts, MTRs bear labels such as VR (visual rules) or IR (instrument rules) followed by a numerical identifier. Given the high-speed nature of military flight training within MTRs, drone pilots are urged to steer clear of these routes to avoid potential conflicts [57].

Public Awareness

Maintaining a courteous and polite demeanour is important as a drone operator. Remember that you are an ambassador for the industry, and your actions will influence other pilots and the public perception of drones. Professionalism should be maintained at all times to uphold industry standards and foster positive relationships.

Pre-flight / Run-up

Before take-off, a comprehensive pre-flight check is necessary to ensure the safety and functionality of the UAV. Verify that all transmitter, on-board aircraft, and camera batteries are fully charged, confirming voltage levels. Check for any frequency conflicts between video and transmitter/receiver systems. Inspect all control surfaces for signs of damage or loose hinges, and ensure the overall condition of the UAV is sound.

Examine the motor/engine and mounting attached to the airframe, as well as the propellers, mounting hardware, and rotor blades for chips and deformation. Check the landing gear for damage and proper function. Test all electrical connections to ensure they are secure and operational. Verify that the photo/video equipment mounting system is secure and functioning properly.

Check the location of GPS equipment controlling the autopilot and verify IMU movements in the ground control software. Ensure that the UAV is in stabilization mode and that control surfaces move towards the correct positions. Position the UAV in a level location safe for take-off.

Power up the FPV ground station and video receiver/goggles, if applicable. If using a video recorder, turn on the camera system and ensure that camera settings are correct. Clear the SD camera memory and insert it into the camera.

Begin the pre-flight checklist by confirming that all transmitter controls move freely in all directions, with trims in the neutral position and switches in the correct position. Set the transmitter throttle to zero and turn on the radio transmitter.

Connect and power on the battery to the airframe, ensuring that LED indicators and audible tones are correct. Start the timer if applicable. Confirm that FPV video is displayed on the monitor or goggles.

Before take-off, scan the area for nearby cars, people, or animals. Announce "CLEAR!" to alert others of imminent flight. Arm the flight controller and increase throttle slightly, listening for any abnormalities. Conduct a short 20-30 second hover at 3-5 feet to check for vibrations or loose items. Finally, confirm that voltage levels are correct before proceeding with the flight.

Personal Fitness for Flight

Before taking to the skies, it's essential to conduct a personal assessment to ensure you are fit to fly. A mnemonic checklist, known as the I'M SAAFE checklist, has been devised for this purpose. Answering 'yes' to any of these questions may indicate that your alertness, perception, judgment, general performance, or situational awareness capabilities are compromised, potentially leading to forgetfulness or impaired decision-making.

- Illness: Do you have any symptoms of illness, disorder, or known conditions that could pose an in-flight hazard?

- Medication and Other Drugs: Have you been using prescription, over-the-counter, or recreational drugs, or have you mixed medications that could affect your ability to operate safely?

- Stress and Distraction: Are you under psychological pressure from work or personal circumstances? Are you preoccupied with financial, health, family, emotional, or relationship issues? Are you feeling anxious about undertaking the flight?

- Age: If you are in your later years, have you considered whether your ability to handle emergencies or unfamiliar situations may have declined to the point where it's advisable to fly accompanied by another qualified pilot?

- Alcohol: Have you consumed alcohol within the past 8 hours? Even if it's been 8-16 hours since consumption, blood alcohol levels can still be significant. It's important to ensure that your average alcohol consumption falls within the 'very low risk' category to maintain safety standards.

- Fatigue: Are you feeling tired, inadequately rested, or experiencing a lack of sleep? Fatigue can impair cognitive function and reaction times, posing a risk during flight operations.

- Eating and Drinking: Have you consumed enough food and fluids to maintain adequate nourishment and hydration levels? Dehydration and inadequate nutrition can impact cognitive and physical performance, affecting your ability to fly safely.

Set Up Operations Plan and Geofencing

To set up operations plan and geofencing for drone operations, follow these steps:

1. Define Objectives: Clearly outline the objectives of the drone operation, including the purpose of the flight, desired outcomes, and any specific tasks to be accomplished.

2. Identify Flight Paths: Determine the optimal flight paths for achieving the objectives while considering factors such as airspace restrictions, terrain features, and potential hazards. Plan routes that minimize risks and maximize efficiency.

3. Assess Safety Measures: Evaluate safety measures to mitigate risks and ensure safe operation of the drone. This may include establishing emergency procedures, implementing altitude limits, and identifying areas to avoid.

4. Develop Operations Plan: Create a detailed operations plan that encompasses all aspects of the drone operation, including pre-flight preparations, in-flight procedures, and post-flight protocols. Specify roles and responsibilities for each team member involved in the operation.

5. Implement Geofencing Technology: If necessary, utilize geofencing technology to define virtual boundaries for the drone's operation. Geofencing helps ensure that the drone remains within designated areas and prevents it from entering restricted airspace or other prohibited zones.

6. Configure Geofencing Parameters: Set up geofencing parameters based on the specific requirements of the operation, taking into account factors such as altitude limits, geographic boundaries, and no-fly zones. Adjust settings as needed to align with safety protocols and regulatory requirements.

7. Test Geofencing System: Conduct thorough testing of the geofencing system to verify its functionality and effectiveness in maintaining compliance with operational boundaries. Identify any potential issues or limitations and make adjustments as necessary.

8. Communicate Plan to Stakeholders: Communicate the operations plan and geofencing parameters to all relevant stakeholders, including drone operators, ground crew members, and any authorities or organizations involved in the operation. Ensure everyone understands their roles and responsibilities and complies with safety protocols.

9. Monitor and Adapt: Continuously monitor the drone operation and geofencing system throughout the flight to ensure adherence to the established plan and parameters. Be prepared to adapt the plan in real-time based on changing conditions or unforeseen circumstances.

10. Evaluate Performance: After the operation, conduct a comprehensive evaluation of the performance of both the drone and the geofencing system. Identify any areas for improvement and incorporate lessons learned into future operations plans.

Access and Analyse Pre-Operational Information

To access and analyse pre-operational information for drone operations, follow these steps:

1. Identify Information Sources: Determine the sources of pre-operational information available to you, such as Notice to Airmen (NOTAM) systems, aviation authorities, weather services, and industry-specific alerts or publications.

2. Access NOTAM System: Log in to the NOTAM system or access relevant aviation authority websites to retrieve the latest notices and updates related to airspace restrictions, temporary flight restrictions (TFRs), airport closures, and other pertinent information.

3. Review NOTAMs: Thoroughly review all NOTAMs applicable to the planned operation, paying close attention to any notices that may impact the intended flight area, altitude restrictions, or airspace usage. Note the effective times and areas affected by each NOTAM.

4. Check Industry Alerts: Stay informed about any industry-specific alerts or publications that provide additional insights into airspace conditions, regulatory changes, or other relevant factors that could influence the drone operation.

5. Analyse Information: Analyse the pre-operational information gathered from NOTAMs and other sources to assess its impact on the planned operation. Evaluate the severity and duration of any airspace restrictions or TFRs and consider how they may affect the flight path, altitude requirements, or scheduling.

6. Incorporate into Operational Plan: Integrate the findings of your analysis into the operational plan, adjusting flight paths, altitudes, or schedules as necessary to comply with airspace regulations and ensure safe operation. Clearly communicate any changes or updates to the team members involved in the operation.

7. Monitor for Updates: Continuously monitor NOTAMs and other relevant information sources leading up to the scheduled flight time to stay informed about any new developments or changes that may arise. Be prepared to adapt the operational plan accordingly based on updated information.

8. Document Findings: Maintain a record of the pre-operational information accessed and analysed, including any NOTAMs reviewed and decisions made based on their content. Documenting this information ensures accountability and provides a reference for future operations.

9. Coordinate with Authorities: If necessary, coordinate with relevant aviation authorities or air traffic control agencies to clarify any uncertainties or seek additional guidance regarding airspace restrictions or regulatory requirements impacting the planned operation.

10. Verify Compliance: Before initiating the drone operation, verify that the operational plan aligns with all relevant pre-operational information, including NOTAMs and airspace restrictions. Ensure that the drone flight will be conducted in accordance with regulatory requirements and safety protocols.

Identify Hazards and Implement Risk Controls

To identify hazards and implement risk controls for drone operations, follow these steps:

1. Review Charts and Maps: Begin by thoroughly examining charts and maps of the planned flight area, including sectional charts, topographic maps, and any other relevant mapping resources. Pay close attention to terrain features, obstacles, airspace designations, and environmental conditions that could pose risks to the operation.

2. Identify Potential Hazards: Use the information provided by the charts and maps to identify potential hazards along the planned flight path. This may include natural obstacles such as mountains, trees, or bodies of water, as well as man-made structures like buildings, power lines, or communication towers. Additionally, note any airspace restrictions, such as controlled airspace, restricted areas, or temporary flight restrictions (TFRs).

3. Document Identified Risks: Clearly document all identified hazards and risks associated with the planned flight, noting their location, nature, and potential impact on the operation. Organize this information in a systematic manner to ensure comprehensive coverage of all relevant risks.

4. Assess Risk Severity: Evaluate the severity of each identified hazard based on its potential to cause harm or disruption to the drone operation. Consider factors such as altitude, proximity to the flight path, and the likelihood of encountering the hazard during the operation.

5. Develop Risk Controls: Once hazards have been identified and assessed, develop risk controls to mitigate the identified risks and ensure the safety of the operation. This may involve implementing measures such as adjusting the flight path to avoid obstacles, establishing buffer zones around airspace restrictions, or modifying operational procedures to account for environmental conditions.

6. Prioritize Risk Controls: Prioritize risk controls based on the severity and likelihood of encountering each hazard, focusing on mitigating the most significant risks first. Allocate resources and attention accordingly to address high-priority risks effectively.

7. Communicate Risk Controls: Clearly communicate the identified hazards and corresponding risk controls to all team members involved in the drone operation. Ensure that everyone understands their roles and responsibilities in implementing the risk controls and maintaining situational awareness during the operation.

8. Continuously Monitor Hazards: Throughout the drone operation, maintain vigilance and continuously monitor for any new hazards or changes in conditions that may affect the safety of the flight. Remain flexible and prepared to adjust risk controls as needed to respond to evolving circumstances.

9. Document Risk Management Process: Keep detailed records of the hazard identification process, risk assessments, and implemented risk controls for the drone operation. Document any deviations from the planned risk controls and the rationale behind these decisions to facilitate post-flight review and learning.

10. Review and Learn: After the completion of the drone operation, conduct a thorough review of the risk management process to identify lessons learned and areas for improvement. Use this feedback to refine risk management practices for future operations and enhance overall safety performance.

Plan for Wind Velocity and Adverse Environmental Conditions

To plan for wind velocity and adverse environmental conditions in drone operations, follow these steps:

1. Weather Analysis: Begin by accessing up-to-date weather forecasts and reports for the planned flight area. Pay close attention to wind speed and direction, as well as other relevant weather conditions such as precipitation, visibility, and temperature. Use reputable sources such as official meteorological services or aviation weather websites to gather accurate and reliable information.

2. Assess Wind Conditions: Evaluate the impact of wind velocity on drone operations by considering factors such as the drone's maximum wind speed tolerance, its ability to maintain stability in windy conditions, and the effects of wind on flight performance and battery life. Determine the prevailing wind direction and identify any areas of turbulent or gusty winds that may pose challenges during the flight.

3. Plan Flight Route: Based on the analysis of wind conditions, adjust the planned flight route and trajectory to optimize performance and minimize risks. Consider flying into the wind during outbound legs of the mission to conserve battery power and ensure safe return to the launch point. Identify suitable waypoints or landmarks that can provide shelter from strong winds or serve as reference points for navigation.

4. Account for Environmental Factors: In addition to wind velocity, consider other adverse environmental conditions that may affect drone operations, such as rain, snow, fog, or extreme temperatures. Assess the drone's ability to withstand these conditions and make adjustments to the operational plan as necessary to mitigate risks and ensure safe operation.

5. Monitor Weather Changes: Continuously monitor weather conditions leading up to and during the drone operation to identify any changes or developments that may impact flight safety. Be prepared to adapt the operational plan in real-time based on evolving weather patterns and forecasts. Maintain communication with relevant stakeholders, such as airspace authorities or clients, to

coordinate adjustments to the flight plan as needed.

6. Implement Safety Measures: Incorporate safety measures into the operational plan to address potential risks associated with adverse weather conditions. This may include setting operational limits for wind speed, establishing emergency procedures for adverse weather events, and ensuring that all equipment and personnel are adequately prepared to handle challenging environmental conditions.

7. Pilot Training and Skill Development: Ensure that drone pilots are adequately trained and proficient in flying in varying weather conditions. Provide opportunities for pilots to practice flying in windy or adverse weather conditions under controlled circumstances to build confidence and proficiency. Emphasize the importance of situational awareness and decision-making skills in managing weather-related risks during flight operations.

8. Contingency Planning: Develop contingency plans for adverse weather scenarios, including options for alternative flight routes, emergency landing sites, and procedures for safely aborting or returning the drone in case of unexpected weather changes or equipment malfunctions. Communicate these contingency plans to all team members involved in the operation and ensure that everyone understands their roles and responsibilities.

In the realm of aviation, in the US for example weather services are a collaborative effort involving entities such as the National Weather Service (NWS), Federal Aviation Administration (FAA), Department of Defense (DOD), various aviation organizations, and individuals [45].

The demand for global weather information has prompted involvement from international weather agencies as well. While weather predictions are not infallible, meteorologists utilize meticulous scientific analysis and computer modelling to increasingly forecast weather patterns, trends, and characteristics with greater precision. This wealth of knowledge is disseminated to pilots and aviation professionals through an intricate network of weather services, government bodies, and independent observers, furnishing them with current weather reports and forecasts for informed decision-making regarding flight safety.

Surface aviation weather observations aggregate current weather data from individual ground stations across the United States. This network comprises both government-operated and privately contracted facilities that continuously provide updated weather information. Automated weather systems, including Automated Weather Observing Systems (AWOS), Automated Surface Observing Systems (ASOS), and other mechanized setups, significantly contribute to data collection from ground stations.

These surface observations furnish localized weather conditions and pertinent details specific to each airport. Information conveyed encompasses report type, station identifier, timestamp, modifiers as necessary, wind speed, visibility, runway visual range (RVR), weather phenomena, sky condition, temperature/dew point, altimeter readings, and relevant remarks. Data for surface observations may originate from human observers, automated stations, or automated setups supplemented by manual oversight. Irrespective of the data source, surface observations offer valuable insights into individual airports nationwide, covering a limited geographical area and proving advantageous to remote pilots.

Aviation weather services in Australia are provided by several agencies, each playing a crucial role in ensuring the safety and efficiency of air travel. Here's an overview of the key components of aviation weather services in Australia:

1. Bureau of Meteorology (BoM): The Bureau of Meteorology is the primary agency responsible for providing weather forecasts, warnings, and observations across Australia. It offers a wide range of aviation-specific products and services tailored to the needs of pilots, airlines, and other aviation stakeholders. These include terminal aerodrome forecasts (TAFs), aviation routine weather reports (METARs), area forecasts, and significant weather charts. The BoM also issues severe weather warnings and advisories for thunderstorms, turbulence, icing, and other hazardous conditions that may affect aviation operations.

2. Airservices Australia: Airservices Australia is a government-owned corporation responsible for managing air traffic control, navigation, and aviation rescue and firefighting services in Australia. It collaborates with the Bureau of Meteorology to provide aviation-specific weather information to pilots and air traffic controllers. Airservices Australia operates a network of weather observation stations, such as Automatic Weather Stations (AWS) and Automatic Terminal Information Service (ATIS) units, to collect real-time weather data at airports and aerodromes across the country. This data is used to generate METARs,

TAFs, and other aviation weather products.

3. Civil Aviation Safety Authority (CASA): The Civil Aviation Safety Authority is Australia's national aviation authority, responsible for regulating civil aviation safety and overseeing the certification and licensing of pilots, aircraft, and air operators. CASA works closely with the Bureau of Meteorology and other agencies to ensure that pilots receive accurate and timely weather information to make informed decisions about flight planning and operations. CASA publishes advisory circulars and guidance material on weather-related topics, including the effects of weather on aircraft performance, fuel planning, and flight operations.

4. Aviation Meteorological Services: In addition to the Bureau of Meteorology and Airservices Australia, several private meteorological service providers offer specialized aviation weather forecasting and consulting services to airlines, general aviation operators, and airports. These companies employ meteorologists with expertise in aviation meteorology to provide tailored weather briefings, route optimization services, and risk assessments for flight planning and dispatch operations. They may also develop customized weather products and tools to meet the specific needs of their clients.

Aviation weather services in Europe are provided through a collaborative effort involving various national meteorological agencies, aviation authorities, and international organizations. This includes:

1. European Organisation for the Safety of Air Navigation (EUROCONTROL): EUROCONTROL is a pan-European organization that coordinates air traffic management (ATM) and aviation safety across the continent. It operates the European Aviation Safety Agency (EASA) and collaborates with national meteorological services and aviation authorities to ensure the provision of timely and accurate weather information to support safe and efficient air travel. EUROCONTROL provides a range of aviation weather products and services, including weather forecasts, warnings, and observations, to assist pilots, air traffic controllers, and airlines in making informed decisions about flight planning and operations.

2. National Meteorological Services: Each European country has its own national

meteorological service responsible for providing weather forecasts, observations, and warnings within its territory. These services collect and analyse weather data from a network of observation stations, satellites, and radar systems to generate aviation-specific weather products such as METARs (aviation routine weather reports), TAFs (terminal aerodrome forecasts), SIGMETs (significant meteorological information), and AIRMETs (airman's meteorological information). These products are disseminated to pilots, air traffic controllers, and aviation stakeholders through various channels, including the internet, radio, and dedicated aviation weather briefing services.

3. European Aviation Safety Agency (EASA): EASA is the European Union's regulatory agency responsible for aviation safety and standardization. It works closely with national aviation authorities and meteorological services to develop regulations, standards, and guidance material related to aviation weather services. EASA ensures that aviation weather information meets international standards and is consistent across European airspace, thereby enhancing safety and interoperability in the region.

4. Volcanic Ash Advisory Centres (VAACs): Europe is home to several Volcanic Ash Advisory Centres responsible for monitoring and forecasting volcanic ash hazards in the atmosphere. These centres, operated by national meteorological agencies and international organizations such as the Met Office in the UK and Météo-France in France, provide timely information on volcanic ash plumes and ash dispersion forecasts to support aviation safety and decision-making. Pilots and airlines use VAAC advisories to avoid areas affected by volcanic ash, which can pose significant risks to aircraft engines and flight operations.

Aviation weather services in India are provided by several key organizations and agencies to ensure the safety and efficiency of air travel throughout the country. Here's an overview of how aviation weather services are managed in India:

1. India Meteorological Department (IMD): The India Meteorological Department is the primary agency responsible for weather forecasting, monitoring, and issuing weather advisories across the country. It operates a network of observatories, weather stations, and meteorological centres to collect and analyse weather data from various sources, including satellites, radars, and weather balloons. IMD provides a wide range of aviation-specific weather products

and services, including aerodrome forecasts (TAFs), aviation routine weather reports (METARs), significant weather charts, and forecasts for en-route and terminal areas. These products are disseminated to pilots, air traffic controllers, and aviation stakeholders through dedicated channels such as the Aeronautical Meteorological Services (AMS) and the IMD website.

2. Airports Authority of India (AAI): The Airports Authority of India manages and operates most of the airports in the country, including major international airports, domestic airports, and civil enclaves. AAI collaborates with IMD to ensure the provision of accurate and timely weather information to support safe and efficient air traffic management at airports. AAI's Air Traffic Management (ATM) division utilizes aviation weather forecasts and observations to make decisions regarding flight planning, runway operations, and air traffic control services.

3. Regional Meteorological Centres (RMCs): India is divided into several regions, each served by a Regional Meteorological Center responsible for providing weather forecasts, warnings, and advisories tailored to the specific needs of the region. These RMCs supplement the services provided by IMD by issuing local weather forecasts, severe weather warnings, and specialized products for aviation, agriculture, and other sectors. RMCs work closely with IMD and AAI to coordinate aviation weather services and ensure seamless integration with air traffic management operations.

4. Automated Weather Observing Systems (AWOS): Many airports in India are equipped with Automated Weather Observing Systems, which automatically collect and disseminate real-time weather data, including temperature, humidity, wind speed, and visibility. AWOS installations enhance the accuracy and reliability of aviation weather observations, enabling pilots and air traffic controllers to make informed decisions about flight operations and safety.

5. Indian Meteorological Satellite Program (INSAT): India operates a fleet of meteorological satellites as part of the Indian Meteorological Satellite Program (INSAT), which provides continuous coverage of weather systems and atmospheric conditions over the Indian subcontinent and surrounding regions. INSAT satellites contribute to the monitoring of weather patterns, tropical

cyclones, and other meteorological phenomena, enhancing the capability to forecast weather and issue timely warnings for aviation and other sectors.

Accessing aviation weather services involves obtaining weather information relevant to flight planning, decision-making, and in-flight operations. To access aviation weather services:

1. **Official Websites and Apps**: Aviation weather information is available through official websites and mobile applications provided by meteorological agencies, aviation authorities, and other relevant organizations. These platforms offer a wide range of weather products, including forecasts, observations, charts, and advisories tailored for aviation purposes. Examples of such websites and apps include:

   - National Meteorological Services: Many countries have national meteorological services that offer aviation-specific weather information on their websites or through dedicated apps. These services may include the National Weather Service (NWS) in the United States, the India Meteorological Department (IMD), the UK Met Office, and others.

   - Aviation Authorities: Aviation regulatory authorities such as the Federal Aviation Administration (FAA) in the United States, the European Union Aviation Safety Agency (EASA), and the Civil Aviation Authority (CAA) in various countries provide aviation weather information on their websites and mobile apps.

   - Third-Party Providers: Some third-party providers offer aviation weather services through their websites and apps. These platforms may offer additional features or customized weather products for pilots and aviation professionals.

2. **Aviation Weather Briefings**: Pilots can obtain comprehensive weather briefings from certified flight service stations (FSS) or automated flight service stations (AFSS) before flight. These briefings include current weather conditions, forecasts, NOTAMs (Notices to Airmen), SIGMETs (Significant Meteorological Information), and other pertinent information relevant to the planned route of flight. Briefings can be obtained via phone, radio, or online platforms such as

DUATS (Direct User Access Terminal System) in the United States.

3. **Aviation Weather Products**: Meteorological agencies and aviation authorities produce a variety of weather products specifically designed for aviation purposes. These products include:

   - METARs (Aviation Routine Weather Reports): Observations of current weather conditions at airports and aerodromes.

   - TAFs (Terminal Aerodrome Forecasts): Forecasts of weather conditions at specific airports for the next 24 to 30 hours.

   - SIGMETs (Significant Meteorological Information): Advisories for significant weather phenomena affecting aviation safety.

   - Graphical Weather Charts: Maps and charts depicting weather features such as fronts, pressure systems, and turbulence.

   - Radar and Satellite Imagery: Real-time images of precipitation, cloud cover, and other meteorological phenomena captured by radar and satellite sensors.

4. **Automated Weather Stations**: Many airports and aerodromes are equipped with Automated Weather Observing Systems (AWOS) or Automated Surface Observing Systems (ASOS) that provide continuous updates of weather conditions. Pilots can access these observations through radio frequencies or online platforms.

5. **Subscription Services**: Some aviation weather providers offer subscription-based services that provide enhanced weather information, advanced forecasting models, and customized weather alerts tailored to specific flight operations or geographical areas.

By utilizing these channels, pilots and aviation professionals can access the latest weather information to make informed decisions and ensure the safety of flight operations.

Aviation weather reports aim to provide precise portrayals of present weather conditions. These reports are regularly updated and come in various types, such as METARs and PIREPs. To access a weather report in the United States, visit http://www.aviation weather.gov/ and in Australia at http://www.bom.gov.au/aviation/observations/metar-speci/.

The Aviation Routine Weather Report, abbreviated as METAR, serves as a detailed observation of the current surface weather conditions, presented in a standardized international format. These reports are typically issued at regular intervals unless significant weather changes prompt the issuance of a special METAR (SPECI) report. For instance, a METAR report for Gregg County Airport might look like this [45]:

METAR KGGG 161753Z AUTO 14021G26KT 3/4SM +TSRA BR BKN008 OVC012CB 18/17 A2970 RMK PRESFR.

Let's delve into the components of a typical METAR report:

1. Type of Report: METAR reports are categorized into routine reports, transmitted at regular intervals, and special reports (SPECI) for immediate updates on rapidly changing weather conditions or critical information.

2. Station Identifier: This four-letter code, established by the International Civil Aviation Organization (ICAO), uniquely identifies the reporting station. For example, Gregg County Airport in Longview, Texas, is identified as "KGGG."

3. Date and Time of Report: Depicted in a six-digit group, where the first two digits represent the date and the last four indicate the time in coordinated universal time (UTC). The appended "Z" denotes Zulu time (UTC).

4. Modifier: Indicates if the report is automated (AUTO) or corrected (COR). The presence of "AO1" or "AO2" in the remarks section indicates the type of precipitation sensors employed.

5. Wind: Reported with direction, speed, and gusts. Variable winds are denoted as "VRB," and gusting winds are indicated with a "G" followed by the peak gust recorded.

6. Visibility: Prevailing visibility is reported in statute miles (SM), often accompanied by runway visual range (RVR) for pilot reference.

7. Weather: Describes weather phenomena, including intensity, proximity, and descriptors. It may include precipitation types, obscurations, and other atmospheric conditions.

8. Sky Condition: Reports cloud coverage, height, and type. Cloud heights are provided in hundreds of feet above ground level (AGL).

9. Temperature and Dew Point: Given in degrees Celsius, with temperatures below zero indicated by the letter "M" for minus.

10. Altimeter Setting: Barometric pressure reading in inches of mercury ("Hg"), typically preceded by the letter "A."

11. Zulu Time: Indicates the time in coordinated universal time (UTC), commonly used in aviation.

12. Remarks: Contains additional information, such as wind data, visibility variations, and notable weather phenomena. Remarks often begin with "RMK" and may include equipment maintenance notices.

In the provided example, the METAR report for Gregg County Airport depicts various weather parameters, including wind speed, visibility, precipitation, cloud cover, temperature, and barometric pressure.

Let's consider a sample METAR report for Sydney Airport (KSYD) in Australia:

METAR KSYD 221200Z AUTO 18010KT 10SM SCT030 BKN050 25/18 Q1015 NOSIG

Explanation:

- METAR: This indicates that it is a routine weather report.

- KSYD: Station identifier for Sydney Airport.

- 221200Z: Date and time of the report, where "22" represents the day of the month, "1200Z" indicates the time in UTC.

- AUTO: Indicates that the report comes from an automated source.

- 18010KT: Wind from the south (180 degrees) at 10 knots.

- 10SM: Visibility is 10 statute miles.

- SCT030 BKN050: Sky condition with scattered clouds at 3000 feet and broken clouds at 5000 feet.

- 25/18: Temperature is 25 degrees Celsius, and dew point is 18 degrees Celsius.

- Q1015: Altimeter setting is 1015 hectopascals.

- NOSIG: No significant change is expected in weather conditions in the near future.

And further, a sample METAR report for Indira Gandhi International Airport (VIDP) in New Delhi, India:

METAR VIDP 221500Z 07008KT 5000 HZ SCT020 BKN080 33/24 Q1008 NOSIG

Explanation:

- METAR: This indicates that it is a routine weather report.

- VIDP: Station identifier for Indira Gandhi International Airport.

- 221500Z: Date and time of the report, where "22" represents the day of the month, "1500Z" indicates the time in UTC.

- 07008KT: Wind from the east-northeast (070 degrees) at 8 knots.

- 5000: Visibility is 5000 meters.

- HZ: Haze is present.

- SCT020 BKN080: Sky condition with scattered clouds at 2000 feet and broken clouds at 8000 feet.

- 33/24: Temperature is 33 degrees Celsius, and dew point is 24 degrees Celsius.

- Q1008: Altimeter setting is 1008 hectopascals.

- NOSIG: No significant change is expected in weather conditions in the near future.

METAR reports for airports in India can be accessed through various sources, including:

1. India Meteorological Department (IMD) website: The IMD provides meteorological services in India and offers access to METAR reports for airports across

the country on their website.

2. Aviation Weather Services: Aviation weather services in India may also provide access to METAR reports through their platforms or websites. These services cater specifically to the aviation industry and offer comprehensive weather information for pilots and other aviation professionals.

3. Mobile Applications: There are several mobile applications available for smartphones that provide access to real-time weather information, including METAR reports. These apps often allow users to search for specific airports and view METAR reports along with other weather data.

4. Aviation Authorities: The Directorate General of Civil Aviation (DGCA) or other relevant aviation authorities in India may also provide access to METAR reports through their official websites or portals dedicated to aviation-related information and services.

5. Third-Party Websites: There are various third-party websites that aggregate weather data from different sources, including METAR reports. These websites may offer user-friendly interfaces for accessing METAR reports for airports in India and around the world.

And finally, a METAR report for Warsaw Chopin Airport (EPWA) in Warsaw, Poland:
METAR EPWA 221800Z 28010KT 7000 SCT025 BKN050 10/06 Q1012 NOSIG
Explanation:

- METAR: This indicates that it is a routine weather report.

- EPWA: Station identifier for Warsaw Chopin Airport.

- 221800Z: Date and time of the report, where "22" represents the day of the month, "1800Z" indicates the time in UTC.

- 28010KT: Wind from the west (280 degrees) at 10 knots.

- 7000: Visibility is 7000 meters.

- SCT025 BKN050: Sky condition with scattered clouds at 2500 feet and broken clouds at 5000 feet.

- 10/06: Temperature is 10 degrees Celsius, and dew point is 6 degrees Celsius.

- Q1012: Altimeter setting is 1012 hectopascals.

- NOSIG: No significant change is expected in weather conditions in the near future.

METAR reports for airports in Europe can be accessed through several channels, including:

1. National Meteorological Services: Each European country typically has its own national meteorological service responsible for providing weather information, including METAR reports. These services often have websites where METAR reports can be accessed for airports within their respective countries.

2. Eurocontrol: Eurocontrol, the European Organisation for the Safety of Air Navigation, provides centralized air traffic management services across Europe. They may offer access to METAR reports through their website or dedicated aviation weather portals.

3. Aviation Weather Services: Various aviation weather services cater specifically to the aviation industry and offer comprehensive weather information, including METAR reports, for airports in Europe. These services may provide access through their websites, mobile applications, or other platforms.

4. Airport Websites: Some airports in Europe publish METAR reports on their official websites for the convenience of pilots and passengers. These reports are typically available on the airport's weather or operational information page.

5. Mobile Applications: There are numerous mobile applications available for smartphones that provide access to real-time weather information, including METAR reports, for airports in Europe. These apps often offer user-friendly interfaces and customizable features for pilots and aviation enthusiasts.

6. Aviation Authorities: National aviation authorities in European countries may also provide access to METAR reports through their official websites or portals dedicated to aviation-related information and services.

Weather forecasts for aviation purposes often rely on observed weather condition reports to provide accurate predictions for the same area. Various forecast products are generated specifically for preflight planning [45]. These include Terminal Aerodrome Forecast (TAF), Aviation Area Forecast (FA), Inflight Weather Advisories (SIGMET, AIRMET), and Winds and Temperatures Aloft Forecast (FB).

A TAF is a forecast issued for a five-statute-mile radius around an airport, typically for larger airports. Each TAF is valid for a 24 or 30-hour period and is updated four times daily at 0000Z, 0600Z, 1200Z, and 1800Z. The TAF utilizes descriptors and abbreviations similar to those used in METAR reports. This information is crucial for flight planning. The TAF includes:

1. Type of report: TAF or TAF AMD (amended).

2. ICAO station identifier: The same as used in METAR reports.

3. Date and time of origin: Given in a six-number code indicating the date and time in UTC.

4. Valid period dates and times: Indicate the forecast period's start and end times in UTC.

5. Forecast wind: Direction and speed in a five-digit group.

6. Forecast visibility: Given in statute miles.

7. Forecast significant weather: Weather phenomena coded similarly to METAR reports.

8. Forecast sky condition: Similar to METAR reports but only includes CB clouds.

9. Forecast change group: Describes any significant weather changes expected during the forecast period, indicated by FM (rapid change) or TEMPO (temporary).

10. PROB30: Percentage describing the probability of thunderstorms and precipitation within the forecast period, not applicable for the first 6 hours.

Example TAF [45]: TAF VABB 111130Z 1112/1212 TEMPO 1112/1114 5SM BR FM1500 16015G25KT P6SM SCT040 BKN250 FM120000 14012KT P6SM BKN080

OVC150 PROB30 1200/1204 3SM TSRA BKN030CB FM120400 1408KT P6SM SCT040 OVC080 TEMPO 1204/1208 3SM TSRA OVC030CB

Explanation: Routine TAF for Mumbai, India, issued on the 11th day of the month at 1130Z, valid for 24 hours from 1200Z on the 11th to 1200Z on the 12th. Wind from 150° at 12 knots, visibility greater than 6 SM, scattered clouds at 4,000 feet, broken clouds at 25,000 feet. Temporary mist between 1200Z and 1400Z. From 1500Z, wind from 160° at 15 knots, gusting to 25 knots, visibility greater than 6 SM, scattered clouds at 4,000 feet, broken clouds at 25,000 feet. Probability of thunderstorms with moderate rain showers from 1200Z to 0400Z with broken clouds at 3,000 feet and cumulonimbus clouds. Wind from 140° at 8 knots from 0400Z, visibility greater than 6 miles, scattered clouds at 4,000 feet, overcast at 8,000 feet. Temporary thunderstorms with moderate rain showers between 0400Z and 0800Z with overcast clouds at 3,000 feet and cumulonimbus clouds. End of report.

Here's a sample TAF and explanation for a European city:

Sample TAF: TAF EHAM 220505Z 2206/2312 18008KT 9999 BKN025 TEMPO 2206/2209 4000 -DZ BR BKN008 BECMG 2209/2212 9999 SCT030 BECMG 2216/2219 6000 BKN012 TEMPO 2303/2307 4000 -RA BR BKN008 BECMG 2308/2311 9999 SCT018

Explanation: This TAF is for Amsterdam Airport Schiphol (EHAM) issued on the 22nd day of the month at 0505Z, valid from 0600Z on the 22nd to 1200Z on the 23rd.

- Wind: From 180 degrees at 8 knots.

- Visibility: 10 kilometres or more (9999).

- Clouds: Broken clouds at 2,500 feet above ground level (BKN025).

- Temporary Conditions (TEMPO): Between 0600Z and 0900Z, temporary conditions are expected with visibility reduced to 4 kilometres, light drizzle (-DZ), mist (BR), and broken clouds at 800 feet (BKN008).

- Becoming (BECMG): Between 0900Z and 1200Z, conditions are expected to improve with visibility returning to 10 kilometres or more and scattered clouds at 3,000 feet (SCT030).

- Becoming (BECMG): Between 1600Z and 1900Z, conditions are expected to deteriorate with visibility reduced to 6 kilometres and broken clouds at 1,200 feet (BKN012).

- Temporary Conditions (TEMPO): Between 0300Z and 0700Z on the 23rd, temporary conditions are expected with visibility reduced to 4 kilometres, light rain (-RA), mist (BR), and broken clouds at 800 feet (BKN008).

- Becoming (BECMG): Between 0800Z and 1100Z on the 23rd, conditions are expected to improve again with visibility returning to 10 kilometres or more and scattered clouds at 1,800 feet (SCT018).

This forecast provides crucial information for pilots planning flights into or out of Amsterdam Airport Schiphol, allowing them to anticipate changes in weather conditions over the forecast period.

Convective Significant Meteorological Information (WST) alerts are disseminated to warn pilots of severe weather conditions associated with thunderstorms. These alerts are issued when surface winds exceed 50 knots, hail with a diameter of at least ¾ inch is observed at the surface, or tornadoes are present. Additionally, they are issued to notify pilots of embedded thunderstorms, lines of thunderstorms, or thunderstorms with heavy or intense precipitation affecting a significant portion (40% or more) of a region covering 3,000 square miles or larger. Remote pilots will benefit from these weather advisories when planning their flights.

As an example of a SIGMET:

SIGMET LSJH VALID 051830/052230 LSJH- SIGMET 01 VALID 051830/052230 LSJH LJLX- LJLX SIGMET 01 VALID 051830/052230 OVRBLD CONVECTV ACT INVOF STNRY FNT AFFECTING AREA=

Explanation: This SIGMET, issued for LSJH (a hypothetical European city), is valid from 1830 UTC on the 5th to 2230 UTC on the 5th. It indicates significant meteorological information about convective activity. The convective activity is associated with an overdeveloped convection in the vicinity of a stationary frontal boundary, affecting the specified area. Pilots in this region should exercise caution as severe weather conditions such as thunderstorms may be present, impacting flight safety and navigation.

Unmanned Aerial Vehicle (UAV) pilots can access SIGMETs through various channels to stay informed about significant meteorological information that may impact their flights. Here's how they can access SIGMETs:

1. Aviation Weather Websites: Many aviation weather websites provide access to SIGMETs along with other pertinent weather information. Pilots can visit these

websites to view SIGMETs relevant to their operating area. Websites such as the Aviation Weather Center (AWC) in the United States or the European Aviation Safety Agency (EASA) website for Europe typically offer SIGMET information.

2. Weather Apps: There are several weather apps designed specifically for pilots, which include SIGMET data among other weather-related information. These apps often provide real-time updates and notifications about SIGMETs affecting the pilot's designated operating area.

3. Official Aviation Authorities: UAV pilots can also obtain SIGMETs directly from official aviation authorities or agencies responsible for meteorological services. These authorities often publish SIGMETs on their websites or distribute them through email subscriptions or other communication channels.

4. Aviation Weather Briefings: Prior to flight operations, UAV pilots can request aviation weather briefings from certified weather briefing sources. These briefings include SIGMETs along with other relevant weather information tailored to the pilot's intended route and operational area.

5. NOTAMs: Notices to Airmen (NOTAMs) sometimes include information about SIGMETs affecting specific regions. UAV pilots should check NOTAMs for any SIGMET-related notices applicable to their flight area.

By utilizing these resources, UAV pilots can access SIGMETs and stay informed about significant meteorological phenomena that may impact their operations, allowing them to make informed decisions and ensure flight safety.

Maintaining awareness of current and forecast weather conditions is crucial for safe drone operations. To do so effectively, it's important to access reliable weather sources. Utilize reputable sources such as official meteorological agencies, aviation weather services, and weather forecasting websites or apps. These sources provide up-to-date and accurate information relevant to drone operations.

Before initiating the flight, it's essential to monitor current weather conditions at the drone's location and along its planned flight path. Pay attention to factors such as wind speed and direction, visibility, temperature, humidity, and precipitation. This step ensures that you have a clear understanding of the immediate weather environment.

In addition to monitoring current conditions, stay informed of forecasted weather for the duration of the planned flight. Review both short-term and long-term predictions, looking for anticipated changes in weather patterns such as thunderstorms, high winds, fog, or other adverse conditions.

Aviation-specific weather reports like METARs (Aviation Routine Weather Reports) and TAFs (Terminal Aerodrome Forecasts) provide detailed information tailored to aviation needs. Access these reports for essential data on wind, visibility, cloud cover, and other parameters relevant to drone flight.

Keep an eye on weather alerts, warnings, and advisories issued by meteorological authorities. These notifications highlight significant weather events or hazards that could impact drone operations, such as severe storms, strong winds, or airspace restrictions.

Integrate weather assessment into your pre-flight checklist. Assess how current and forecasted weather conditions may affect the drone's performance, flight stability, and safety. Consider factors like wind velocity, gusts, temperature extremes, and precipitation.

Remain flexible and be prepared to adjust your operational plan based on evolving weather conditions. If conditions deteriorate or become unsafe for drone flight, postpone or cancel the mission until conditions improve. Safety should always take precedence over meeting operational objectives.

Maintain continuous awareness of weather conditions throughout the flight. Monitor weather updates and changes in real-time, especially for longer-duration flights. Utilize onboard weather monitoring tools if available to track conditions during flight.

Lastly, develop contingency plans for unexpected weather events or emergencies. Identify alternative flight routes, landing sites, or emergency procedures to mitigate risks associated with adverse weather conditions. By consistently monitoring weather conditions and adjusting operational plans accordingly, drone operators can enhance safety and mitigate the impact of adverse weather on their flights.

Prepare Lost Link Profile and Routing

A drone lost link refers to the loss of communication between the drone and its operator or ground control station. This loss of connection can occur due to various reasons, including technical issues, signal interference, or environmental factors. When a drone experiences a lost link, it may no longer receive commands from the operator, making it difficult or impossible to control remotely.

In some cases, drones are equipped with failsafe mechanisms that are activated when a lost link is detected. These mechanisms may include features such as automatic return-to-home functions, where the drone autonomously navigates back to its take-off point, or predefined safety protocols to minimize the risk of accidents.

The term "lost link" underscores the critical importance of maintaining communication between the operator and the drone during flight operations. Losing this link can pose significant challenges and risks, particularly in scenarios where the drone is flying over populated areas or sensitive locations. Therefore, drone operators must have contingency plans and procedures in place to mitigate the impact of a lost link and ensure the safe operation of their drones.

Preparing a lost link profile and routing plan is essential for maintaining safety and control in the event of a communication link loss between the drone operator and the drone. Here's how to do it:

1. Define Lost Link Profile: Start by outlining a comprehensive lost link profile that specifies the actions to be taken in the event of a communication failure. This profile should include step-by-step procedures for various scenarios, such as total loss of communication or intermittent signal loss.

2. Emergency Procedures: Define emergency procedures for regaining control or safely recovering the drone in case of a lost link. This may involve activating failsafe modes, initiating return-to-home functions, or manually piloting the drone back to a safe location if possible.

3. Contingency Routing Options: Establish alternative routing options that the drone can follow autonomously in the event of a lost link. These routes should prioritize safety and compliance with airspace regulations. Identify specific waypoints or flight paths that the drone can follow to minimize risks to people, property, and other aircraft.

4. Validate Procedures: Test and validate the lost link procedures and routing options in a controlled environment to ensure they function as intended. Conduct simulated flights with simulated communication failures to verify the effectiveness of the contingency plans.

5. Safety Protocols and Compliance: Ensure that the developed procedures and routing options align with safety protocols and regulatory requirements set

forth by aviation authorities. Consider factors such as airspace restrictions, altitude limits, and collision avoidance measures to mitigate potential risks.

6. Operator Training: Provide comprehensive training to drone operators on how to execute the lost link procedures and contingency routing options effectively. Emphasize the importance of remaining calm and following established protocols during emergency situations.

7. Documentation and Review: Document the lost link profile and routing plan, including any updates or revisions made during testing or operational experience. Periodically review and update the procedures based on feedback, changes in regulations, or technological advancements.

8. Emergency Communication: Establish protocols for communication with relevant authorities, such as air traffic control or local emergency services, in the event of a lost link incident that poses a safety risk to airspace or ground operations.

By developing a thorough lost link profile and routing plan, drone operators can effectively manage communication failures and ensure the safe operation of drones in various scenarios. Regular training, testing, and adherence to safety protocols are essential for maintaining readiness and responsiveness during emergency situations.

Impacts of Weather on Drone Flights

Let's now consider the factors influencing aircraft performance, encompassing aircraft weight, atmospheric conditions, runway environment, and the fundamental physical laws governing aircraft forces. Among these factors, atmospheric characteristics, particularly pressure and temperature, wield significant influence.

Density Altitude

Density Altitude emerges as a critical concept in understanding aerodynamic performance within the nonstandard atmosphere. It represents the altitude in the standard atmosphere corresponding to a specific air density value. Aircraft performance directly correlates with air density: as air density increases (lower density altitude), performance improves, while a decrease in air density (higher density altitude) diminishes performance [45]. This altitude directly impacts aircraft operations and is shaped by altitude, temperature, and humidity variations.

Density altitude is a fundamental concept in aviation that plays a crucial role in understanding aerodynamic performance, especially in nonstandard atmospheric conditions. It refers to the hypothetical altitude in the standard atmosphere where the air density matches a specific value at the actual altitude. In simpler terms, density altitude indicates the altitude at which the air density is equivalent to the air density at the current location, but in a standard atmosphere.

Aircraft performance is significantly influenced by air density. Generally, as air density increases, aircraft performance improves, and as air density decreases, aircraft performance diminishes. Therefore, density altitude serves as a key indicator of how atmospheric conditions affect aircraft operations.

Several factors contribute to the determination of density altitude:

1. Altitude: The actual altitude above sea level affects air density. As altitude increases, air density decreases, leading to a higher density altitude. Conversely, lower altitudes result in higher air density and lower density altitudes.

2. Temperature: Temperature variations impact air density. Higher temperatures cause air molecules to spread out, reducing air density, while lower temperatures increase air density. Consequently, higher temperatures result in higher density altitudes, and lower temperatures lead to lower density altitudes.

3. Humidity: Although humidity's effect on air density is relatively minor compared to altitude and temperature, it still plays a role. Moist air is less dense than dry air because water vapor molecules displace air molecules. Therefore, higher humidity levels contribute to lower air density and higher density altitudes, while lower humidity levels increase air density and lower density altitudes.

Understanding density altitude is essential for pilots because it directly affects aircraft performance. Higher density altitudes decrease engine power output, reduce aircraft lift, and increase take-off and landing distances. Pilots must account for density altitude when planning flights, especially in mountainous regions or during hot weather, to ensure safe and efficient aircraft operations. By considering density altitude along with other factors like temperature, pressure, and humidity, pilots can make informed decisions to optimize flight performance and safety.

Density altitude impacts drones in a similar manner to manned aircraft, albeit with some nuances. Density altitude affects drones as follows:

1. Flight Performance: Just like manned aircraft, drones experience changes in flight performance based on density altitude. Higher density altitudes, typically associated with higher elevations, warmer temperatures, and lower atmospheric pressure, result in decreased air density. This reduction in air density affects the drone's aerodynamic performance, including its lift capability, manoeuvrability, and stability. Drones may struggle to generate sufficient lift to maintain altitude or perform manoeuvres effectively in high-density altitude conditions.

2. Battery Performance: Density altitude can also affect the performance of drone batteries. In environments with high density altitude, where the air is less dense and temperatures may be elevated, drone batteries may experience increased stress and reduced efficiency. High temperatures can cause batteries to degrade more quickly and reduce their overall capacity, leading to shorter flight times and diminished performance.

3. Motor and Propulsion System: The motor and propulsion system of a drone are impacted by density altitude changes. In high-density altitude conditions, where the air is less dense, drone motors may need to work harder to generate the necessary thrust for flight. This increased workload can lead to higher motor temperatures, increased power consumption, and potential overheating issues. Conversely, in low-density altitude conditions, where the air is denser, motors may operate more efficiently, but drones may still face challenges related to temperature regulation and battery performance.

4. Flight Stability: Density altitude variations can affect the stability of drone flight. In high-density altitude environments, where air density is reduced, drones may experience decreased stability due to changes in aerodynamic forces and wind conditions. This reduction in stability can make it more challenging to control the drone accurately, especially during manoeuvres or in gusty wind conditions. Pilots must account for these stability issues when flying drones in high-density altitude environments to ensure safe and precise operation.

Overall, density altitude impacts drones by influencing their flight performance, battery efficiency, motor operation, and flight stability. Pilots need to consider density altitude variations when planning drone flights, especially in mountainous regions, high-temperature environments, or areas with significant atmospheric pressure changes, to optimize drone performance and ensure safe and effective operations.

Pressure plays a pivotal role in air density dynamics. As air, being a gas, is compressed, it occupies a smaller volume, thus increasing density. Conversely, reduced pressure expands the air, lowering its density. Density remains directly proportional to pressure, with doubling pressure resulting in doubled density, holding true at constant temperature [45].

Pressure is a fundamental factor influencing the density of air, which in turn affects various aspects of aviation and atmospheric dynamics. Understanding the relationship between pressure and air density is crucial for pilots, meteorologists, and aviation enthusiasts alike.

Air, being a gas, is highly compressible. When air is subjected to pressure, it responds by compressing or expanding to occupy the available space. This behaviour is governed by the ideal gas law, which states that the pressure of a gas is directly proportional to its temperature and density, provided that the volume remains constant.

When air is compressed, such as in a high-pressure system or by external forces like the descending motion associated with subsidence, it becomes denser. In other words, a greater mass of air is packed into a smaller volume, leading to an increase in air density. This phenomenon is particularly evident near the Earth's surface, where atmospheric pressure is highest.

Conversely, reduced pressure, as observed in low-pressure systems or at higher altitudes, causes the air to expand. With less pressure exerted on the air molecules, they spread out over a larger volume, resulting in decreased air density. This decrease in density is a significant factor contributing to the challenges of high-altitude flight, where aircraft encounter thinner air and reduced lift.

The relationship between pressure and air density is directly proportional, meaning that changes in pressure lead to corresponding changes in air density. If the pressure is doubled, the density of the air also doubles, assuming constant temperature and volume. Similarly, a decrease in pressure results in a proportional decrease in air density.

However, it's important to note that the relationship between pressure and density holds true only under constant temperature conditions, as outlined by the ideal gas law. Changes in temperature can alter the density of air independently of pressure variations. Therefore, when considering the impact of pressure on air density, it's essential to account for temperature changes as well.

Pressure plays a pivotal role in governing air density dynamics. Understanding how changes in pressure affect air density is essential for predicting atmospheric behaviour, analysing weather patterns, and optimizing aircraft performance in different flight conditions.

The impact of pressure on drones is significant and multifaceted, influencing various aspects of their performance and operation. Here's how pressure dynamics affect drones:

1. Flight Performance: Pressure variations directly impact air density, affecting the aerodynamic performance of drones. In high-pressure conditions, where air density increases, drones may experience enhanced lift and stability due to

denser air providing more lift. Conversely, in low-pressure conditions, such as at higher altitudes, reduced air density can lead to decreased lift and performance challenges for drones.

2. Altitude Capability: Drones rely on lift generated by their rotors to stay airborne. As pressure decreases with altitude, air density also decreases, making it more challenging for drones to generate lift. This limits the altitude capability of drones, as they may struggle to maintain flight stability and control in thin air at higher elevations.

3. Battery Performance: Pressure variations can indirectly affect drone battery performance. In high-pressure conditions, where air density is higher, drones may experience increased aerodynamic drag, requiring more power to maintain flight. This can lead to faster battery depletion and reduced flight endurance. Conversely, in low-pressure conditions, drones may encounter less drag and conserve battery power more efficiently.

4. Weather Adaptability: Understanding pressure patterns is essential for drone pilots to anticipate weather changes and adapt their flight plans accordingly. High-pressure systems typically bring stable weather conditions with clear skies and light winds, providing optimal flying conditions for drones. In contrast, low-pressure systems often signify inclement weather, such as storms, strong winds, and turbulence, posing risks to drone operation.

5. Flight Planning: Pilots must consider pressure variations when planning drone missions, especially when operating at different altitudes or in diverse geographic regions. Knowledge of pressure gradients and atmospheric pressure trends helps pilots assess the feasibility and safety of their intended flight routes, ensuring optimal performance and minimizing risks associated with pressure-induced challenges.

Pressure is a fundamental atmospheric parameter that significantly influences drone performance, altitude capability, battery usage, weather adaptability, and flight planning. By understanding the relationship between pressure and air density, drone operators can make informed decisions to optimize flight operations and ensure safe and efficient drone missions across various environmental conditions.

Temperature serves as another determinant of air density. A rise in temperature decreases density, while a decrease conversely increases it. This inverse relationship holds true under constant pressure. Despite conflicting effects, the decrease in pressure with altitude typically outweighs the temperature's impact, leading to a decrease in density with increasing altitude.

Temperature exerts a significant influence on air density, playing a crucial role in atmospheric dynamics and aviation operations. Here's a detailed explanation of how temperature affects air density:

1. Temperature and Molecular Motion: Temperature is a measure of the average kinetic energy of molecules in a substance. When the temperature of air rises, the molecules within it gain energy and move more vigorously, increasing their speed and kinetic energy. Conversely, a decrease in temperature results in reduced molecular motion and lower kinetic energy.

2. Effect on Density: The density of a gas is determined by the mass of its molecules and the space they occupy. In warmer air, where molecules are moving faster and colliding more frequently, the air becomes less dense because the molecules are more spread out. This is analogous to increasing the volume while keeping the mass constant, resulting in decreased density.

3. Inverse Relationship: There exists an inverse relationship between temperature and air density under constant pressure conditions. As temperature rises, air density decreases, and conversely, as temperature drops, air density increases. This relationship holds true as long as the pressure remains constant.

4. Impact on Aviation: In aviation, changes in air density due to temperature variations have significant implications for aircraft performance, especially during take-off, landing, and climbing to altitude. Warmer air, with its lower density, provides less lift and aerodynamic performance, requiring longer runways for take-off and reduced climb rates. Conversely, cooler air offers better aerodynamic conditions, enhancing aircraft performance.

5. Altitude Variation: Despite the influence of temperature on air density, its impact is often overshadowed by changes in pressure with altitude. As altitude increases, atmospheric pressure decreases exponentially, causing a corresponding decrease in air density. While temperature may fluctuate with altitude, the

decrease in pressure typically outweighs its effects on density, resulting in a net decrease in air density at higher altitudes.

6. Weather Considerations: Temperature variations play a crucial role in shaping weather patterns and atmospheric stability. Warm air masses tend to rise, leading to the formation of convective clouds and thunderstorms, while cold air masses sink, promoting stable atmospheric conditions. Understanding temperature gradients and their impact on air density is essential for weather forecasting and aviation safety.

Temperature serves as a key determinant of air density, influencing aircraft performance, atmospheric stability, and weather patterns. Its inverse relationship with density, coupled with changes in pressure, contributes to the dynamic nature of the Earth's atmosphere and its effects on aviation operations.

Temperature's impact on air density significantly affects drone operations across various aspects.

Firstly, temperature directly influences lift generation by affecting air density. In warmer air, characterized by lower density due to heightened molecular motion, drones encounter reduced lift capacity. This can impede their ability to ascend, carry payloads, and manoeuvre effectively.

Secondly, battery performance is affected by temperature fluctuations. High temperatures can accelerate battery discharge rates and diminish overall battery efficiency. Conversely, cooler temperatures can enhance battery performance by maintaining optimal operating conditions.

Thirdly, temperature variations impact a drone's flight endurance. Warmer temperatures may cause the drone's motors and electronic components to operate at elevated temperatures, potentially leading to overheating and reduced flight times. Conversely, cooler temperatures can prolong flight endurance by maintaining lower operating temperatures.

Additionally, changes in air density due to temperature fluctuations can influence a drone's stability and control during flight. Warmer air may lead to increased turbulence and air disturbances, resulting in reduced stability and potentially affecting flight precision and navigation accuracy.

Temperature variations also merit consideration in altitude scenarios. While temperature primarily affects air density near the Earth's surface, it can also influence drone operations at higher elevations. As drones ascend to colder altitudes, air density may increase slightly, impacting parameters like lift capacity and flight stability.

Furthermore, temperature fluctuations are indicative of changing weather patterns, including convective currents, wind shear, and turbulence. Drones operating in warmer conditions may encounter thermals and updrafts, altering flight trajectories and stability. Conversely, colder temperatures may yield stable atmospheric conditions, offering smoother flight experiences.

Drone operators must integrate temperature considerations into flight planning processes. Understanding how temperature influences air density and drone performance enables operators to anticipate challenges and adjust flight parameters for safe and efficient operations.

Temperature significantly influences drone performance, battery efficiency, flight endurance, stability, and operational considerations. By accounting for temperature variations and their effects on air density, drone operators can optimize flight operations and ensure safe and effective mission outcomes.

Humidity, or moisture content, further modulates air density. Moist air, containing water vapor lighter than air, exhibits decreased density compared to dry air. Consequently, increased water content elevates humidity, reducing air density, thereby influencing aircraft performance. Relative humidity, denoting the water vapor amount relative to air's capacity, varies with temperature, with warmer air holding more vapor [45].

Humidity, or moisture content, is an essential factor in determining air density and consequently affects aircraft performance. Firstly, moisture in the air reduces its density. Unlike dry air, which consists solely of nitrogen, oxygen, and other gases, moist air contains water vapor, which is lighter than the other components of the atmosphere. As a result, the overall mass of air in a given volume is reduced when water vapor is present, leading to decreased air density.

Secondly, the level of humidity in the atmosphere directly affects air density. Higher humidity levels indicate a greater concentration of water vapor in the air, further reducing its density. Conversely, lower humidity levels result in denser air, as there is less water vapor present to displace the heavier gases.

Relative humidity is a key metric used to measure the moisture content of the air. It represents the ratio of the amount of water vapor present in the air to the maximum amount of water vapor the air can hold at a given temperature and pressure. Warmer air has a higher capacity to hold moisture, leading to higher relative humidity levels compared to cooler air.

Temperature plays a crucial role in determining relative humidity. As air temperature increases, its ability to hold moisture also increases, leading to higher relative humidity levels. Conversely, cooler air has a lower capacity to hold moisture, resulting in lower relative humidity levels.

The impact of humidity on air density is particularly significant for aircraft performance. Reduced air density due to higher humidity levels can adversely affect aircraft lift, aerodynamic performance, and engine efficiency. Denser air provides better lift and propulsion for aircraft, while less dense air can lead to reduced performance and increased fuel consumption.

Humidity influences air density by introducing water vapor into the atmosphere, which decreases overall air density. Relative humidity levels vary with temperature, with warmer air holding more moisture. Understanding the relationship between humidity and air density is crucial for pilots, meteorologists, and aircraft engineers in assessing aircraft performance and optimizing flight operations.

While humidity alone may not be a primary factor in density altitude calculations, it still contributes to overall performance considerations. Thus, understanding these atmospheric dynamics aids in assessing aircraft performance and ensuring safe operations amidst varying environmental conditions.

Performance and Weight

Performance refers to an aircraft's capacity to fulfill specific tasks essential for its intended purposes. It encompasses various factors crucial for flight operations, including take-off and landing distances, climb rate, maximum altitude, payload capacity, range, speed, manoeuvrability, stability, and fuel efficiency [45].

Factors such as weight, altitude, and configuration changes significantly influence climb performance. Climb performance relies on the aircraft's ability to generate either excess thrust or excess power, both of which are affected by these variables.

Weight plays a particularly significant role in aircraft performance. An increase in weight necessitates a higher angle of attack (AOA) to maintain a given altitude and speed. This leads to an increase in induced drag on the wings and parasite drag on the aircraft, requiring additional thrust to overcome. Consequently, less reserve thrust is available for climbing. Aircraft designers prioritize minimizing weight to mitigate its adverse impact on performance parameters.

When an aircraft's weight increases, it directly affects its aerodynamic characteristics and operational capabilities.

One of the primary effects of increased weight is the need for a higher angle of attack (AOA) to maintain a constant altitude and speed during flight. The angle of attack refers to the angle between the chord line of the wing and the direction of the oncoming airflow. By increasing the angle of attack, the lift generated by the wings compensates for the added weight, allowing the aircraft to remain aloft.

However, a higher angle of attack also results in increased induced drag on the wings. Induced drag is the drag force generated as a byproduct of lift production. As the aircraft's weight increases, the wings must work harder to generate the necessary lift, leading to higher induced drag. Additionally, the overall drag experienced by the aircraft, including parasite drag from other components such as the fuselage and empennage, also increases with weight.

To overcome the increased drag and maintain performance, the aircraft's engines must produce additional thrust. This additional thrust requirement reduces the amount of reserve thrust available for climbing. In other words, a heavier aircraft has less surplus thrust available to accelerate and climb compared to a lighter aircraft.

Aircraft designers recognize the critical importance of weight management in optimizing performance parameters. They strive to minimize the aircraft's weight through various design strategies, such as using lightweight materials, optimizing structural components, and employing efficient propulsion systems. By reducing weight, designers can enhance the aircraft's climb performance, manoeuvrability, fuel efficiency, and overall operational flexibility.

Changes in weight also have a dual effect on climb performance. As altitude increases, the power required for climbing rises while the power available decreases. Consequently, an aircraft's climb performance diminishes with altitude due to these combined effects on power dynamics. This dual effect stems from the interplay between the power required for climbing and the power available to the aircraft's engines.

As altitude increases, several factors come into play that affect the power dynamics of the aircraft. Firstly, the air density decreases with altitude, resulting in reduced engine performance. The engines receive less oxygen-rich air, which diminishes their power output. This reduction in available power affects the aircraft's ability to climb efficiently.

Simultaneously, the power required for climbing increases with altitude. As the aircraft ascends, it encounters lower air density and reduced lift generation from the wings. To maintain a steady climb rate, the engines must compensate by producing more thrust, requiring additional power.

This combined effect of decreasing power available and increasing power required results in a diminishing climb performance as altitude increases. Essentially, the aircraft's engines struggle to generate sufficient thrust to overcome the aerodynamic forces acting against the climb.

The altitude at which this diminishing climb performance becomes noticeable depends on various factors, including the aircraft's weight, engine efficiency, aerodynamic design, and atmospheric conditions. However, in general, as altitude rises, the climb rate of the aircraft progressively decreases due to the decreasing power margin available to sustain the climb.

Understanding these power dynamics is crucial for pilots and aircraft operators, especially during high-altitude operations or when planning climbs to elevated regions. By considering the effects of weight on climb performance and the challenges posed by increasing altitude, pilots can make informed decisions to optimize their flight profiles and ensure safe and efficient operations.

Atmospheric Pressure

To establish a consistent benchmark for atmospheric conditions, the International Standard Atmosphere (ISA) has been devised. These standard conditions serve as the foundation for most aircraft performance data. Standard sea level pressure is defined as 29.92 inches of mercury ("Hg) and a standard temperature of 59 degrees Fahrenheit (15 degrees Celsius). Atmospheric pressure is also measured in millibars (mb), with 1 inch of mercury equal to approximately 34 millibars. Standard sea level pressure is standardized at 1,013.2 millibars. Typical pressure readings in millibars range from 950.0 to 1,040.0 millibars. Surface charts, high and low-pressure systems, and hurricane data are reported using millibars [45].

Since weather stations are distributed worldwide, all local barometric pressure readings are converted to sea level pressure to ensure standardized records and reports. To achieve this, each station adjusts its barometric pressure by adding approximately 1 inch of mercury for every 1,000 feet of elevation. For instance, a station situated 5,000 feet above sea level, recording a pressure reading of 24.92 inches of mercury, reports a sea level pressure reading of 29.92 inches of mercury [45].

By monitoring barometric pressure trends across a broad area, meteorologists can more accurately forecast the movement of pressure systems and the associated weather patterns. For example, observing a pattern of increasing pressure at a particular weather station generally signals the approach of fair weather conditions. Conversely, a decrease or rapid decline in pressure typically indicates the onset of inclement weather and, potentially, severe storms.

Effects of Wind

Wind can have several effects on drones, influencing their performance, stability, and overall flight characteristics:

1. Flight Stability: Wind can cause drones to experience turbulence, which may lead to instability during flight. Gusts of wind can disrupt the drone's balance and control, making it challenging for the pilot to maintain stable flight.

2. Drift: Strong winds can cause drones to drift off course, especially when flying in open areas or at higher altitudes. This can result in the drone deviating from its intended flight path and potentially posing a risk to nearby obstacles or structures.

3. Battery Consumption: Flying against strong headwinds requires the drone to exert more power, leading to increased energy consumption and reduced battery life. Conversely, tailwinds can enhance battery efficiency by reducing the drone's power requirements.

4. Speed Variations: Wind speed can affect the drone's ground speed and airspeed. Headwinds will reduce the drone's ground speed, while tailwinds will increase it. Pilots need to account for these variations when planning flights to ensure

accurate timing and adherence to schedules.

5. Altitude Changes: Wind shear, which is a sudden change in wind speed or direction with altitude, can impact the drone's altitude control. This phenomenon may cause the drone to ascend or descend unintentionally, requiring corrective action from the pilot to maintain desired flight levels.

6. Flight Endurance: Flying in windy conditions can reduce the drone's flight endurance, as it expends more energy to counteract the effects of wind resistance. Pilots may need to shorten flight durations or adjust flight paths to conserve battery power and ensure safe return-to-home capabilities.

7. Risk of Loss of Control: In extreme wind conditions, drones may become vulnerable to loss of control or even wind-induced crashes. High winds can overpower the drone's motors and stabilization systems, making it difficult for the pilot to maintain control, especially for smaller or lightweight drone models.

Wind is a critical environmental factor that drone pilots must consider when planning and executing flights. By understanding the effects of wind on drone performance and employing appropriate flight strategies, pilots can enhance safety, efficiency, and mission success.

The presence of obstructions on the ground poses a significant hazard to pilots, impacting wind flow patterns and creating unseen dangers. Ground features such as terrain variations and large structures disrupt the natural flow of wind, resulting in unpredictable wind gusts characterized by sudden changes in speed and direction. These obstructions encompass a wide range of structures, from man-made facilities like hangars to natural formations such as mountains, bluffs, and canyons [45].

The degree of turbulence caused by ground obstructions depends on the size of the obstacle and the prevailing wind velocity. This turbulence can significantly affect the performance of any aircraft and pose a serious safety risk to pilots and passengers alike.

This phenomenon is particularly pronounced when flying in mountainous regions. While the wind ascends smoothly on the windward side of a mountain, aided by upward currents that assist aircraft in crossing the mountain peak, the leeward side presents a different scenario. As the air descends on the leeward side, it follows the contours of the terrain, resulting in increasingly turbulent airflow. This turbulent airflow poses a risk of pushing aircraft into the mountain's side, particularly in strong wind conditions where the downward pressure and turbulence are more pronounced [45].

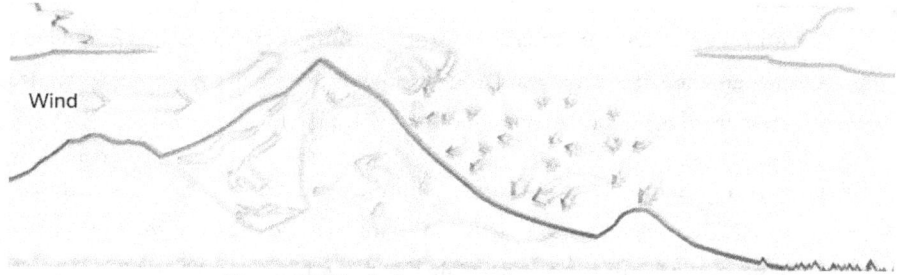

Figure 39: Turbulence in mountainous regions.

Wind shear refers to a sudden and significant alteration in wind speed and/or direction occurring over a very limited area. This phenomenon can subject an aircraft to abrupt vertical drafts, causing sudden changes in altitude, as well as rapid shifts in the aircraft's horizontal movement. Although wind shear can manifest at various altitudes, low-level wind shear poses particular risks due to the aircraft's close proximity to the ground. Factors contributing to low-level wind shear often include the passage of frontal systems, thunderstorms, temperature inversions, and the presence of strong upper-level winds exceeding 25 knots [45].

The impact of wind shear on aircraft can be perilous. It can swiftly alter the aircraft's performance and disrupt its normal flight characteristics. For instance, a sudden shift from tailwind to headwind can result in increased airspeed and performance, while the opposite transition can lead to decreased airspeed and performance. Pilots must remain vigilant and prepared to respond promptly to these fluctuations to maintain control of the aircraft.

Among the most severe forms of low-level wind shear is the microburst, typically associated with convective precipitation descending rapidly from cloud base into dry air. Microbursts may be indicated by intense surface rainfall coupled with virga at cloud base, although sometimes only a ring of blowing dust serves as a visible clue. These phenomena typically exhibit a horizontal diameter of 1–2 miles and a depth of approximately 1,000 feet. Microbursts have a relatively short lifespan of 5–15 minutes but can generate downdrafts reaching speeds of up to 6,000 feet per minute (fpm) and cause headwind losses ranging from 30 to 90 knots, significantly impairing aircraft performance [45]. Additionally, microbursts can produce severe turbulence and hazardous shifts in wind direction. During an inadvertent encounter with a microburst, a small unmanned aircraft (UA) may initially experience a performance-enhancing headwind, followed by performance-diminishing downdrafts, and then a sudden increase in tailwind velocity. Such conditions increase the risk of terrain impact or dangerously low flight altitudes, especially during approach manoeuvres.

It is essential to recognize that wind shear can affect flights across all altitudes. While wind shear may sometimes be detected and reported, it often remains unnoticed, posing a concealed threat to aviation safety. Pilots must maintain constant awareness of the potential for wind shear, particularly when operating in proximity to thunderstorms and frontal systems.

When preparing for a flight over mountainous regions, it's essential to gather comprehensive preflight data regarding cloud formations, wind patterns, wind velocities, and atmospheric stability. Utilizing satellite imagery can aid in identifying mountain waves. However, complete information may not always be readily available, necessitating vigilance for visual cues in the sky.

Wind speeds exceeding 25 knots at mountain peak levels indicate potential turbulence, while wind velocities surpassing 40 knots across mountain barriers warrant heightened caution. The presence of layered clouds typically indicates stable air conditions. Conversely, the appearance of standing lenticular or rotor clouds suggests the presence of a mountain wave, with anticipated turbulence extending several miles downwind of the mountains and relatively smoother flight conditions on the windward side [45].

The occurrence of convective clouds on the windward side of mountains signifies unstable air, indicating the likelihood of turbulence in close proximity to and surrounding the mountainous terrain.

Atmospheric Stability

The stability of the atmosphere hinges on its resistance to vertical motion. A stable atmosphere impedes vertical movement, causing small disturbances to dissipate. Conversely, an unstable atmosphere fosters the amplification of minor vertical air movements, leading to turbulent airflow and convective phenomena. Instability can result in pronounced turbulence, the development of expansive vertical clouds, and the occurrence of severe weather events.

The stability of the air and consequent weather patterns are determined by the interplay of moisture and temperature. Cool, dry air exhibits high stability, inhibiting vertical motion and promoting favourable, generally clear weather conditions. Conversely, the atmosphere is most unstable when warm and moist, as commonly observed in tropical regions during summer. In such environments, daily occurrences of thunderstorms arise due to the heightened instability of the surrounding air mass.

Inversion

As air ascends and expands within the atmosphere, its temperature typically decreases. However, an atmospheric anomaly, known as a temperature inversion, can disrupt this conventional behaviour. A temperature inversion occurs when the temperature of the air increases with altitude, leading to the formation of inversion layers. These layers consist of shallow, smooth, and stable air masses near the Earth's surface. The temperature within these layers rises with altitude until reaching the inversion's upper limit. The air at the top of the inversion layer acts as a barrier, trapping weather elements and pollutants beneath it. In the presence of high relative humidity, inversion layers may foster the formation of clouds, fog, haze, or smoke, consequently reducing visibility within the layer.

Surface-based temperature inversions commonly occur during clear, cool nights when the air in close proximity to the ground cools as a result of declining surface temperatures. This cooling process causes the air within a few hundred feet of the surface to become cooler than the air above it. Frontal inversions occur when warmer air displaces cooler air, either by spreading over a layer of cooler air or by forcing cooler air beneath a layer of warmer air.

Temperature/Dew Point

The connection between dew point and temperature defines the concept of relative humidity. Dew point, expressed in degrees, represents the temperature at which the air reaches its maximum moisture-holding capacity. When the air's temperature drops to the dew point, it becomes fully saturated, leading to the condensation of moisture in various forms such as fog, dew, frost, clouds, rain, or snow [45].

Methods of Reaching Saturation Point: When the temperature and dew point are in close proximity, air often reaches its saturation point, potentially resulting in the formation of fog, low clouds, or precipitation. Several methods can lead to air reaching its saturation point. Firstly, warm air cooling over a colder surface can cause the air temperature to decrease, reaching the saturation point. Secondly, the mixing of cold and warm air masses can also lead to saturation. Thirdly, nighttime cooling of air through contact with cooler ground surfaces can induce saturation. Lastly, air ascending or being forced upward in the atmosphere can reach its saturation point through expansion and cooling [45].

Dew and Frost Formation: During cool, clear, and calm nights, the temperature of the ground and nearby objects can cause the surrounding air temperature to fall below the dew point. This results in the condensation of moisture from the air onto surfaces such as the ground, buildings, vehicles, and aircraft. This condensed moisture, known as dew, is often visible on grass and other objects in the morning. In freezing temperatures, the condensed moisture forms frost instead of dew. While dew poses no significant threat to small unmanned aircraft (UA), frost presents a notable flight safety hazard. Frost disrupts the airflow over the wings, reducing lift production, and increases drag, adversely affecting take-off performance. Therefore, it's imperative to thoroughly remove any frost from a small UA before initiating a flight to ensure safe operations.

Clouds

Among pilots, the cumulonimbus cloud stands out as one of the most perilous cloud types. It manifests either individually or in clusters and is referred to as either an air mass thunderstorm, resulting from heating of the air near the Earth's surface, or an orographic thunderstorm, induced by upslope air motion in mountainous areas. Cumulonimbus clouds arranged in a continuous line form non-frontal bands of thunderstorms or squall lines.

Figure 40: Cumulonimbus cloud at the Baltic Sea near island of Öland, Sweden. Arnold Paul, CC BY-SA 2.5, via Wikimedia Commons.

Due to the upward movement of air currents, cumulonimbus clouds are highly turbulent, presenting a considerable hazard to flight safety. Entering a thunderstorm can subject a small unmanned aircraft (UA) to updrafts and downdrafts exceeding 3,000 feet per minute (fpm). Moreover, thunderstorms can generate large hailstones, dangerous lightning, tornadoes, and substantial amounts of precipitation, all posing potential risks to aircraft.

Figure 41: Cumulonimbus cloud with Pileus in the Northern Territory. Bidgee, CC BY 3.0, via Wikimedia Commons.

Standing Lenticular Altocumulus Clouds: Standing lenticular altocumulus clouds form atop wave crests generated by obstructions in the wind flow. These clouds exhibit minimal movement, earning them the designation "standing." Nevertheless, the wind blowing through them can be quite forceful. They are distinguished by their smooth, well-defined edges. The presence of these clouds signals the presence of intense turbulence, warranting avoidance.

Figure 42: Standing Jellyfish Lenticular Could over the Wasatch Mountains, Utah. The Weather Nutz, CC BY-SA 4.0, via Wikimedia Commons.

Stability

The stability of an air mass dictates its prevailing weather characteristics. When one air mass overlays another, conditions undergo vertical changes.

In meteorology, distinguishing between stable and unstable air masses is essential for understanding prevailing weather conditions. Here's a breakdown of the characteristics associated with each:

Unstable Air: Unstable air masses typically give rise to cumuliform clouds, characterized by their towering, cauliflower-like appearance. These clouds often indicate convective activity and the potential for thunderstorms. Showery precipitation is a common feature of unstable air masses. The precipitation tends to occur in scattered, localized bursts, resulting in irregular patterns of rainfall or showers. Due to convective currents and rapid vertical motion, unstable air can cause rough air conditions, leading to turbulence. This turbulence can be particularly intense in regions experiencing convective activity, such as thunderstorms. Despite the turbulent conditions, unstable air often results in good visibility, except in areas affected by blowing obstructions like dust or sand, which can reduce visibility.

Cumuliform clouds are a type of cloud formation characterized by their distinct, puffy appearance with sharp, well-defined edges. These clouds often resemble heaps, mounds, or towers, hence the term "cumulus," which is Latin for "heap" or "pile." Cumuliform clouds typically develop vertically, with their bases forming at lower altitudes and their tops extending into higher regions of the atmosphere.

There are several types of cumuliform clouds, including:

1. Cumulus Congestus: These clouds are characterized by their towering structure and significant vertical development. Cumulus congestus clouds are often associated with unstable atmospheric conditions and can develop into cumulonimbus clouds, which are capable of producing thunderstorms.

2. Cumulus Humilis: Also known as fair-weather cumulus, cumulus humilis clouds are small, fluffy clouds with flat bases and rounded tops. They typically form on sunny days when atmospheric instability is relatively low. Cumulus humilis clouds are generally benign and do not produce precipitation.

3. Cumulus Fractus: Cumulus fractus clouds are small, fragmented clouds that appear torn or shredded. These clouds often form as larger cumulus clouds dissipate, and their appearance is indicative of changing weather conditions, such as the onset of a storm or a shift in wind patterns.

4. Cumulus Castellanus: These clouds have a castle-like appearance, with vertical towers protruding from their tops. Cumulus castellanus clouds are often associated with increasing atmospheric instability and may indicate the potential for thunderstorm development later in the day.

Cumuliform clouds typically form as a result of convective processes, where warm air near the Earth's surface rises and cools, leading to the condensation of water vapor into visible cloud droplets. They are most commonly observed during the daytime when surface heating is at its peak but can also form in association with other weather phenomena such as frontal boundaries or mountainous terrain.

Figure 43: Cumulus congestus clouds over Long Island, New York, viewed from Fire Island. Jsayre64, CC BY-SA 3.0, via Wikimedia Commons.

Figure 44: Cumulus humilis clouds showing the typical flatness of the humilis kind. Kr-val, Public domain, via Wikimedia Commons.

Stable Air: In contrast, stable air masses tend to produce stratiform clouds and fog. These clouds are typically layered or sheet-like in appearance, forming a blanket of clouds that can extend over large areas. Precipitation in stable air masses is more continuous and widespread compared to the showery nature seen in unstable air. This precipitation tends to be more uniform and persistent over time. Stable air masses are associated with smoother air conditions, characterized by reduced turbulence compared to unstable air masses. Flight through stable air tends to be more stable and predictable. While stable air masses generally result in fair to poor visibility, particularly in haze and smoke, the conditions are more consistent and less prone to sudden changes compared to unstable air masses.

Stratiform clouds are a type of cloud formation characterized by their horizontal, layered appearance. Unlike cumuliform clouds, which are puffy and vertically developed, stratiform clouds typically extend over large areas and have relatively uniform bases and tops. These clouds often cover the sky in a continuous layer, obscuring the sun and producing diffuse, muted lighting conditions.

There are several types of stratiform clouds, including:

1. Altostratus: Altostratus clouds are mid-level clouds that form at altitudes ranging from 6,500 to 20,000 feet (2,000 to 6,100 meters) above the Earth's surface. They appear as gray or bluish-gray sheets covering the sky and often precede or accompany warm fronts. Altostratus clouds may produce light precipitation, such as drizzle or light rain.

2. Nimbostratus: Nimbostratus clouds are thick, dark clouds that extend over large areas of the sky. They are typically associated with steady, moderate to heavy precipitation, such as rain or snow. Nimbostratus clouds often form at lower altitudes than altostratus clouds and are commonly observed during frontal passages.

3. Stratus: Stratus clouds are low-level clouds that form at altitudes below 6,500 feet (2,000 meters). They appear as gray, uniform layers covering the sky and are often associated with overcast conditions and light precipitation, such as drizzle or mist. Stratus clouds may form as a result of stable atmospheric conditions or the lifting of moist air over cooler surfaces.

4. Cirrostratus: Cirrostratus clouds are high-level clouds composed of ice crystals and often appear as thin, wispy sheets covering the sky. They are typically found at altitudes above 20,000 feet (6,100 meters) and can produce halo phenomena, such as solar and lunar halos, when light is refracted by the ice crystals. Cirrostratus clouds may precede the approach of warm fronts and indicate the potential

for precipitation.

Stratiform clouds form through processes such as lifting of air masses along frontal boundaries, convergence of air masses, or the cooling of air near the Earth's surface. They are commonly associated with stable atmospheric conditions and may persist for long periods, leading to prolonged periods of overcast skies and subdued weather conditions.

Figure 45: Altostratus undulatus cloud. Liridon, CC BY-SA 4.0, via Wikimedia Commons.

Understanding the characteristics of both stable and unstable air masses is crucial for meteorologists, pilots, and weather forecasters in predicting and preparing for various weather phenomena and their impacts.

Fronts

Fronts occur when air masses originating from distinct regions with different characteristics meet and interact. These encounters create a boundary known as a frontal zone or front, where significant changes in temperature, humidity, and wind direction can occur abruptly and over relatively short distances. These variations in atmospheric conditions along the front are often accompanied by dynamic weather phenomena [45].

Fronts can have several impacts on drone flying, influencing various aspects of flight operations:

1. Weather Conditions: Fronts are associated with changes in weather patterns, including shifts in temperature, humidity, and wind speed. Drones are sensitive to weather conditions, and sudden changes brought by fronts can affect their performance and stability during flight. For example, a cold front may bring strong winds and cooler temperatures, while a warm front can result in increased

humidity and precipitation, both of which can pose challenges for drone operation.

2. Wind Patterns: Frontal zones often exhibit significant changes in wind direction and speed. Drones rely on stable wind conditions for safe and efficient flight. However, the presence of fronts can lead to erratic and gusty winds, which may affect the drone's ability to maintain stability and control. Pilots need to be vigilant and adjust their flight plans accordingly to navigate safely through areas affected by fronts.

3. Visibility: Frontal zones can also impact visibility due to changes in atmospheric moisture and the formation of clouds or fog. Reduced visibility can pose risks for drone pilots, especially when flying beyond visual line of sight (BVLOS). Poor visibility conditions may necessitate the use of advanced navigation systems or alternative flight routes to maintain situational awareness and avoid obstacles.

4. Precipitation: Fronts often bring changes in precipitation patterns, including rain, snow, or sleet. Precipitation can affect drone performance and compromise electronic components if they are not adequately protected. Additionally, wet weather conditions may reduce visibility and increase the risk of accidents, making it essential for drone operators to exercise caution and consider postponing flights during adverse weather associated with fronts.

5. Thunderstorms: Certain types of fronts, such as cold fronts, are frequently associated with the formation of thunderstorms. Thunderstorms pose significant hazards to drone operations due to lightning, strong winds, turbulence, and hail. Flying drones near thunderstorms is extremely risky and should be avoided to prevent damage to the aircraft and ensure the safety of people and property on the ground.

Fronts can impact drone flying by altering weather conditions, wind patterns, visibility, precipitation, and the risk of encountering thunderstorms. Pilots must closely monitor weather forecasts and exercise caution when operating drones in areas affected by frontal activity to mitigate risks and ensure safe flight operations.

Structural Icing

Structural icing during flight requires two specific conditions [45]:

1. The aircraft must encounter visible water, like rain or cloud droplets.

2. The temperature at the location where the moisture contacts the aircraft must be at or below 0°C.

Aerodynamic cooling has the potential to decrease the temperature of an airfoil to 0°C, even if the surrounding ambient temperature is slightly warmer.

Two primary conditions must be met for structural icing to occur:

1. Presence of Visible Water: For icing to occur, the aircraft must encounter visible water in the form of rain or cloud droplets. These water droplets come into contact with the aircraft's surfaces, such as the wings, fuselage, and tail.

2. Temperature at or Below Freezing: The temperature at the point where the moisture contacts the aircraft must be at or below the freezing point of water, which is 0°C (32°F). When the temperature is at or below freezing, the water droplets can freeze upon impact with the aircraft's surfaces, leading to ice accumulation.

A phenomenon known as aerodynamic cooling further exacerbates the risk of structural icing. Even if the surrounding ambient temperature is slightly warmer than freezing, the rapid airflow over the aircraft's surfaces can cause a decrease in temperature, effectively cooling the airfoil to 0°C or below. This means that even in conditions where the air temperature might be slightly above freezing, the airflow dynamics around the aircraft can create localized areas where icing is possible.

In essence, structural icing occurs when airborne moisture encounters surfaces of an aircraft at freezing temperatures, leading to the formation of ice. The combination of visible water and sub-freezing temperatures poses a significant risk to aircraft performance and safety, making it crucial for pilots to be vigilant and take appropriate precautions when flying in conditions conducive to icing.

Structural icing presents significant obstacles for drone operations, particularly in environments prone to ice formation.

Flight Safety Concerns: Icing on drone surfaces, such as wings and propellers, can disrupt aerodynamics and compromise flight stability. Ice accumulation alters the shape of the drone's components, leading to increased drag and reduced lift. This can affect the drone's ability to maintain altitude and manoeuvre safely, potentially resulting in loss of control and accidents.

Reduced Performance: Ice buildup adds weight to the drone, affecting its overall performance. Increased weight due to ice accumulation requires more power to maintain flight, leading to higher energy consumption and reduced battery life. Additionally, the altered aerodynamic properties of the drone may result in decreased speed and agility, affecting its operational capabilities.

Flight Endurance: Structural icing can significantly impact the flight endurance of drones. Ice accumulation increases the drone's energy requirements, causing faster battery depletion and reducing the duration of flight missions. Drones operating in icy conditions may need to return to base for battery replacement or recharge more frequently, limiting their operational range and efficiency.

Risk of Damage: Ice formation on drone components, such as propellers and sensors, can pose a risk of damage. Ice buildup may interfere with the rotation of propellers, leading to imbalance and potential motor failure. Additionally, ice accumulation on sensors, cameras, and other critical equipment can impair functionality and compromise data collection and transmission capabilities.

Preventative Measures: To mitigate the risks associated with structural icing, drone operators must exercise caution and implement preventive measures. This includes monitoring weather conditions and avoiding flight in areas where icing is likely to occur. When flying in cold and moist environments, operators should regularly inspect the drone for ice buildup and take necessary actions to remove accumulated ice, such as landing and manually removing the ice or employing de-icing equipment if available.

Structural icing poses significant challenges for drone operations, affecting flight safety, performance, endurance, and equipment integrity. Drone operators must remain vigilant and proactive in managing the risks associated with icing to ensure safe and successful mission outcomes.

Thunderstorms

Throughout its life cycle, a thunderstorm cell progresses through three distinct stages: the cumulus, the mature, and the dissipating stages. Detecting the transition from one stage to another is challenging, as it occurs subtly and without abrupt changes. Moreover, a thunderstorm may consist of multiple cells in various stages of the life cycle simultaneously.

The Cumulus Stage Every thunderstorm begins as a cumulus cloud, although not all cumulus clouds evolve into thunderstorms. The defining feature of the cumulus stage is the presence of an updraft, illustrated in figure 3-4. The strength of the updraft varies and extends from the surface to the cloud top. During this stage, the cloud's growth rate can exceed 3,000 feet per minute, making it unsafe to operate small unmanned aircraft (UA) in areas with rapidly building cumulus clouds. Initially, water droplets within the cloud are small but grow as the cloud develops. The updraft carries liquid water above the freezing level, creating an icing hazard. As raindrops become heavier, they fall, dragging cold air downward and creating a cold downdraft alongside the updraft, signalling the transition to the mature stage [45].

The Mature Stage The onset of precipitation from the cloud base indicates the development of a downdraft, marking the entry into the mature stage. The cold rain within the downdraft prevents compressional heating, keeping the downdraft cooler than the surrounding air. Consequently, its downward speed accelerates, possibly exceeding 2,500 feet per minute. The downward rushing air spreads outward at the surface, generating strong, gusty surface winds, a sudden temperature drop, and a rapid increase in pressure. This surface wind surge, known as a "plow wind," is characterized by its "first gust" at the leading edge. Concurrently, updrafts reach maximum speeds, possibly exceeding 6,000 feet per minute. The proximity of updrafts and downdrafts creates strong vertical shear and a highly turbulent environment. All thunderstorm hazards peak during the mature stage [45].

The Dissipating Stage The dissipating stage is characterized by downdrafts dominating the thunderstorm cell, leading to the rapid demise of the storm. Once rain ceases and downdrafts diminish, the dissipating stage concludes. When all cells within the thunderstorm complete this stage, only benign cloud remnants remain.

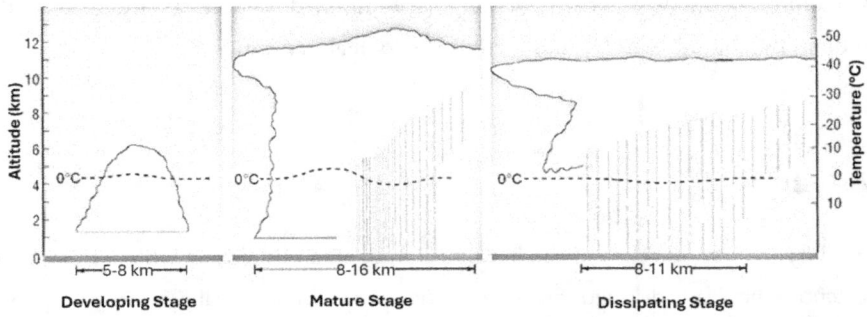
Figure 46: Life cycle of a thunderstorm.

Ceiling

In aviation, the term "ceiling" refers to the altitude of the lowest layer of clouds in the sky. It serves as a crucial parameter for pilots and air traffic controllers in assessing weather conditions and determining flight safety. The ceiling is determined based on observations of cloud cover and visibility.

Cloud cover is classified into different categories based on the extent of the sky covered by clouds. When five-eighths to seven-eighths of the sky is obscured by clouds, the cloud cover is termed as "broken" [45]. This means that there are significant breaks or openings in the cloud cover, allowing some sunlight to penetrate through. On the other hand, when the entire sky is covered by clouds with no breaks or openings, the cloud cover is described as "overcast." In this case, the sky appears uniformly gray or white, with no visibility of the sun or sky.

Additionally, the concept of ceiling extends beyond just cloud cover to include visibility into phenomena such as fog or haze. In situations where visibility is reduced due to fog or haze, the height at which objects or terrain become obscured from view is also considered as part of the ceiling.

Real-time ceiling data is essential for flight planning and navigation. This information is typically provided by aviation routine weather reports (METAR) and various types of automated weather stations located at airports and other key locations. Pilots rely on this data to assess the feasibility of flying under current weather conditions, especially when considering factors such as cloud cover, visibility, and potential hazards like fog or haze.

By monitoring ceiling reports, pilots can make informed decisions regarding take-off, landing, and route selection to ensure the safety of flight operations [45].

Visibility

Visibility in aviation refers to the maximum horizontal distance at which prominent objects can be clearly distinguished with the naked eye. It is a crucial parameter for pilots as it directly affects flight safety and navigation. Visibility information helps pilots assess the visibility conditions they can expect during a flight, enabling them to plan and execute their operations accordingly.

Visibility is closely related to factors such as cloud cover, fog, and haze, as these phenomena can significantly reduce visibility by obscuring objects in the surrounding environment. Pilots rely on accurate visibility reports to make informed decisions about take-off, landing, and navigation, especially when flying in conditions with reduced visibility.

Current visibility data is reported in aviation weather reports such as METAR (Aviation Routine Weather Report) and is also provided by automated weather systems installed at airports and other relevant locations. This information is crucial for pilots to understand the visibility conditions at their departure, destination, and along their route of flight.

During preflight weather briefings, pilots receive visibility forecasts from meteorologists, which help them anticipate visibility conditions they may encounter during their flight. By staying informed about visibility reports and forecasts, pilots can effectively plan their flights, adjust their routes if necessary, and ensure the safety of their operations, even in challenging visibility conditions.

Aircraft Loading

Before any flight, the remote pilot-in-command (PIC) must ensure that the aircraft is properly loaded by assessing its weight and balance status. Adherence to the weight and balance limitations set by the manufacturer or builder is paramount for flight safety. The remote PIC should anticipate the potential repercussions of operating an aircraft beyond its weight limitations in case of an emergency [45].

Although a maximum gross take-off weight is specified, it doesn't guarantee safe take-off under all conditions. Factors like high elevations, temperatures, and humidity can necessitate weight reduction before attempting flight. Additionally, runway conditions, wind, and obstacles must be considered, potentially requiring further weight reduction [45].

Changes in weight during flight, primarily due to fuel burn, directly impact aircraft performance and balance. In small unmanned aircraft (UA) operations, weight fluctuations may occur with expendable items. Adverse balance conditions can affect flight characteristics similar to excess weight, necessitating adherence to manufacturer-established centre of gravity (CG) limits. As load items shift or are expended, the CG location may change, requiring the remote PIC to anticipate and mitigate resulting effects. If the CG exceeds allowable limits, weight relocation or reduction is necessary before flight [45].

Weight

Gravity is the fundamental force that pulls all objects towards the centre of the Earth. Within the context of aircraft dynamics, the Center of Gravity (CG) is a pivotal concept. It can be visualized as a single point where the entirety of the aircraft's weight is concentrated. If an aircraft were suspended at its exact CG, it would maintain balance regardless of its orientation in space. The CG plays a crucial role in the stability of small Unmanned Aircraft (UA).

The permissible position of the CG is determined during the aircraft's design phase and is specific to each aircraft model. Designers also establish the range within which the centre of pressure (CP), the point where aerodynamic forces (such as lift) are concentrated, can move. It's important to grasp that while the weight of the aircraft acts at the CG, the aerodynamic forces generated by the wings act at the CP [45].

When the CG is located forward of the CP, there's a natural tendency for the aircraft to pitch its nose downward. Conversely, if the CP is situated ahead of the CG, it induces a nose-up pitching moment. To ensure flight stability, designers set the aft limit of the CG forward of the CP for a given flight speed, maintaining equilibrium.

Understanding the relationship between weight and lift is fundamental in aviation. Lift, generated by the wings, acts upward and perpendicular to both the relative wind and the aircraft's lateral axis. Its primary function is to counteract the force of gravity, which acts downward due to the aircraft's weight. In stable, level flight, when lift equals weight, the aircraft remains in equilibrium without any vertical acceleration. If lift decreases below weight, the aircraft's vertical speed decreases, while if lift exceeds weight, the vertical speed increases. This delicate balance between weight and lift governs the aircraft's ability to maintain altitude and control its vertical motion.

Stability

Stability is an essential aspect of aircraft design, referring to the aircraft's inherent ability to correct deviations from its intended flight path and return to or maintain its original trajectory. It's a characteristic primarily determined during the aircraft's design phase [45].

Stability influences two critical areas:
1. Manoeuvrability: This refers to how easily an aircraft can be maneuvered and its capacity to withstand the stresses imposed by manoeuvres. Various factors contribute to manoeuvrability, including the aircraft's weight, its inertia, the

size and placement of flight controls, its structural strength, and the powerplant. Manoeuvrability, like stability, is primarily influenced by the aircraft's design.

2. Controllability: This aspect concerns the aircraft's responsiveness to the pilot's control inputs, particularly regarding changes in flight path and attitude. Controllability measures how effectively the aircraft responds to the pilot's commands during manoeuvres, irrespective of its stability characteristics.

In essence, stability ensures the aircraft naturally tends to return to its intended flight path after disturbances, while manoeuvrability and controllability determine how effectively the pilot can manoeuvre the aircraft and exert control over its movements. These qualities are crucial for safe and efficient flight operations.

Load Factors

In aerodynamics, the maximum load factor, at a given bank angle, represents the ratio between the lift generated by the aircraft and its weight. This relationship follows a trigonometric pattern. Load factor is quantified in Gs, which stands for "acceleration of gravity." It denotes the force experienced by an object when it undergoes acceleration, equivalent to the force exerted by gravity on a stationary object. Any force applied to an aircraft to alter its straight-line flight path induces stress on its structure, with the magnitude of this force termed as the load factor.

While a formal education in aerodynamics isn't mandatory for obtaining a remote pilot certificate, it's crucial for pilots to possess a solid comprehension of the forces acting upon an aircraft, how to utilize these forces advantageously, and the operational constraints of the specific aircraft they operate.

For instance, a load factor of 3 indicates that the total stress on an aircraft's structure is three times its weight. Since load factors are expressed in terms of Gs, a load factor of 3 may be referred to as "3 Gs," and similarly, a load factor of 4 as "4 Gs."

Given that aircraft structural designs are engineered to withstand only a certain level of overload, understanding load factors has become indispensable for all pilots. Load factors carry significance for two main reasons:

1. Pilots can inadvertently subject aircraft structures to dangerous levels of stress, leading to potential structural failure.

2. Increased load factors result in higher stalling speeds, making stalls achievable even at seemingly safe flight speeds. This underscores the importance of pilots being aware of and managing load factors to maintain flight safety.

During a coordinated turn at a constant altitude, the load factor experienced by an aircraft is the result of two primary forces: centrifugal force and weight. Centrifugal force is the outward force experienced by an object in motion along a curved path, in this case, the aircraft's path during a turn. Weight, on the other hand, is the force acting downwards due to gravity.

The rate of turn (ROT) during a coordinated turn varies with the aircraft's airspeed. Generally, at higher speeds, the rate of turn is slower. This slower rate of turn compensates for the added centrifugal force generated during the turn, ensuring that the load factor remains constant.

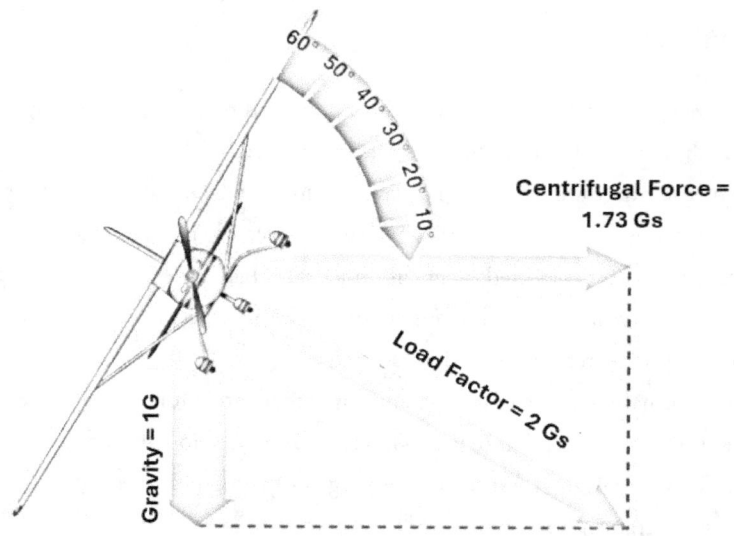

Figure 47: During turns, two forces contribute to the load factor experienced by an aircraft: centrifugal force and weight. Centrifugal force pushes outward, generated by the aircraft's curved path, while weight acts downward due to gravity. These forces combined determine the load factor, impacting the aircraft's stability and structural integrity during manoeuvres.

The Graph shown as Figure 48 indicates that as the bank angle of the aircraft increases, the load factor increases rapidly. Beyond a bank angle of approximately 45° to 50°, the increase in load factor becomes significant. For example, in a coordinated level turn with a bank angle of 60°, the load factor is 2 Gs. In an 80° bank, the load factor increases to 5.76 Gs. It's crucial to note that the wing must generate lift equal to these load factors to maintain altitude.

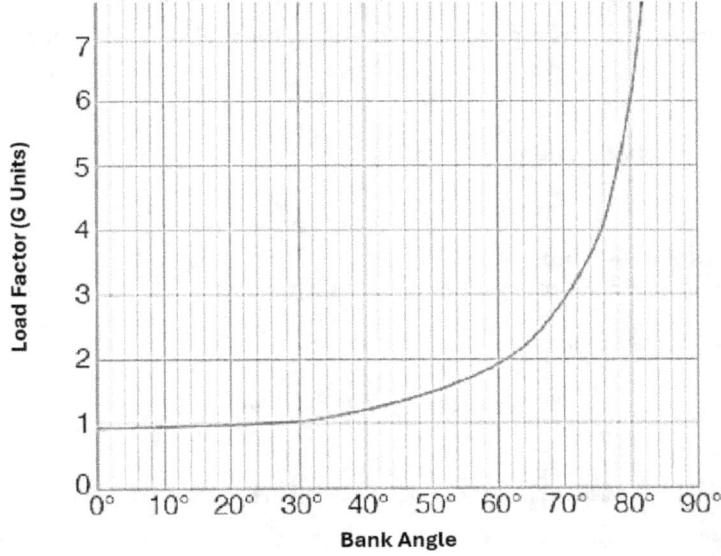

Figure 48: Angle of bank changes load factor in level flight.

The graph depicting the load factor rises rapidly as it approaches a bank angle of 90°. However, it never quite reaches 90° because a constant altitude turn at a 90° bank is not physically possible due to aerodynamic limitations.

While an aircraft can be banked to 90° in a coordinated turn if altitude is not a concern, holding altitude in such a turn is not mathematically possible. An aircraft capable of maintaining a 90° banked, slipping turn can also perform straight knife-edged flight. However, it's important to note that beyond a bank angle of slightly more than 80°, the load factor exceeds the limit of 6 Gs, which is the limit load factor for most acrobatic aircraft. Exceeding this limit can lead to structural damage or failure. Therefore, pilots must be aware of these load factors and the associated limitations to ensure safe flight operations.

Any aircraft, within its structural limitations, can experience a stall at any airspeed. When the angle of attack (AOA) becomes sufficiently high, the smooth airflow over the airfoil breaks up and separates, leading to a sudden change in flight characteristics and a loss of lift, resulting in a stall.

The occurrence of a stall in an aircraft is a critical aerodynamic phenomenon that can happen at any airspeed, provided certain conditions are met. Even within its structural limitations, any aircraft is susceptible to stalling. This vulnerability arises from the fundamental aerodynamic principle related to the angle of attack (AOA) of the aircraft's wings.

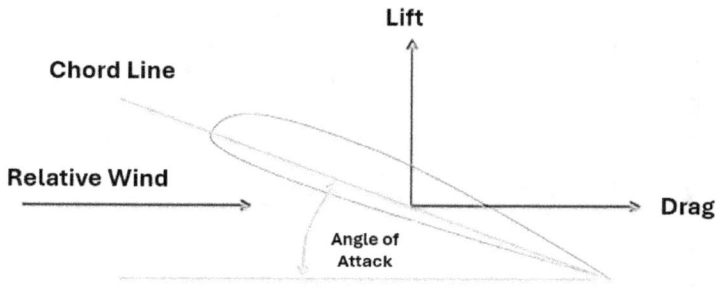

Figure 49: Angle of attack.

The angle of attack refers to the angle between the chord line of the wing (an imaginary line running from the leading edge to the trailing edge of the wing) and the relative airflow. As the angle of attack increases, the airflow over the wing's surface changes. At low angles of attack, the airflow remains attached and smooth over the wing's surface, generating lift. However, when the angle of attack becomes sufficiently high, the smooth airflow over the airfoil can break up and separate, leading to turbulent airflow and a loss of lift.

This critical angle of attack at which the airflow separation occurs varies depending on the airfoil's design and other factors. Once the airflow separation occurs, the wing can no longer generate sufficient lift to support the aircraft's weight. As a result, the aircraft experiences a sudden change in flight characteristics, often characterized by a nose-down pitch, a loss of altitude, and reduced control effectiveness. This abrupt reduction in lift is what is commonly referred to as a stall.

Stalls can occur during various phases of flight, including take-off, landing, and manoeuvres. They are particularly hazardous during critical phases such as low-altitude operations or when close to the ground. Recovery from a stall typically involves reducing the angle of attack by lowering the nose of the aircraft, applying full power if necessary, and regaining controlled flight.

In summary, a stall occurs when the angle of attack becomes sufficiently high to disrupt the smooth airflow over the wing, leading to a sudden loss of lift and a change in flight characteristics. Understanding the factors that contribute to stall conditions and how to recognize and recover from them is essential for pilots to ensure safe and effective flight operations.

Research has shown that an aircraft's stalling speed increases proportionally to the square root of the load factor [45]. For example, an aircraft with a normal stalling speed of 50 knots can stall at 100 knots with a load factor of 4 Gs. If the aircraft could withstand a load factor of nine, it could stall at a speed of 150 knots. Pilots should be cautious of inadvertently stalling the aircraft by increasing the load factor, such as during steep turns or spirals [45].

In steep turns exceeding a bank angle of 72°, the load factor reaches 3, significantly raising the stalling speed. For an aircraft with a normal stalling speed of 45 knots, maintaining an airspeed above 75 knots is necessary to prevent stalling during such manoeuvres [45]. Similar effects occur during rapid ascents or manoeuvres generating load factors exceeding 1 G. These sudden loss of control incidents, particularly during steep turns or abrupt elevator inputs near the ground, have led to numerous accidents.

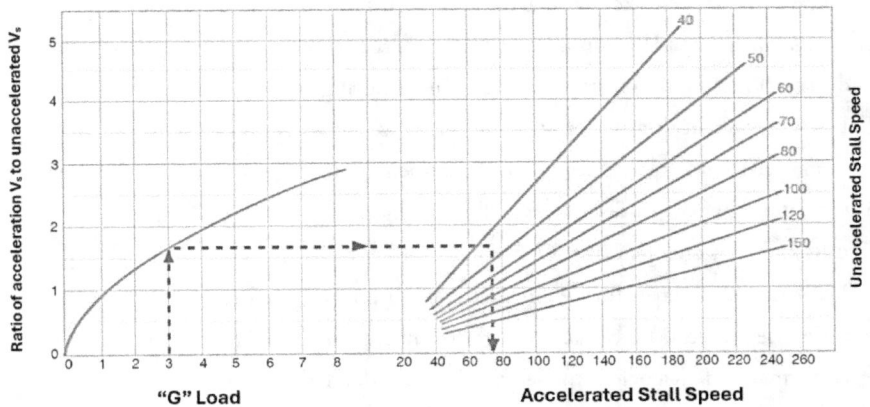

Figure 50: Changes in load factor directly affect the stall speed of an aircraft. As the load factor increases, the stall speed of the aircraft also increases. Conversely, when the load factor decreases, the stall speed decreases accordingly. Pilots must be aware of this relationship, as it impacts the safety margins during flight manoeuvres and influences the aircraft's handling characteristics.

As stalling an aircraft at higher airspeeds squares the load factor, it imposes tremendous stress on the aircraft structure, highlighting the importance of avoiding stalls at elevated speeds.

Weight and Balance

Adhering to the weight and balance limits of an aircraft is paramount for ensuring flight safety. Exceeding the maximum weight limitation compromises the aircraft's structural integrity and hampers its performance. Operating with the centre of gravity (CG) beyond approved limits can result in control difficulties. Therefore, pilots must regularly reassess the aircraft's weight and balance data.

Weight, the force exerted by gravity on a body, is a crucial aspect of aircraft design and operation. It is countered solely by the force of lift, which sustains the aircraft in flight. Loading an aircraft beyond the manufacturer's recommended weight must be avoided to ensure that lift generated is sufficient to counteract weight, preventing flight incapability.

The effects of excessive weight on aircraft performance are numerous and significant. Manufacturers strive to keep aircraft as light as possible without compromising strength or safety. Pilots should be mindful of the adverse consequences of overloading, which can lead to poor flight characteristics and difficulties during take-off and landing.

Excessive weight diminishes flight performance across various parameters, including take-off speed, climb rate, cruising speed, manoeuvrability, and stalling speed. Pilots must have a comprehensive understanding of how weight impacts the performance of the specific aircraft they are operating. Operating an overweight aircraft reduces safety margins and exacerbates hazards during emergency situations. Therefore, pilots must carefully consider the implications of excess weight to ensure safe and efficient flight operations.

Performance deficiencies experienced by an overloaded aircraft:

1. Higher take-off speed: Excess weight increases the required airspeed for achieving lift-off during take-off. This is because the additional weight adds to the aircraft's inertia, necessitating a higher velocity to overcome gravitational forces and generate sufficient lift for take-off.

2. Longer take-off run: With higher take-off speed requirements, an overloaded aircraft typically needs a longer distance to accelerate to the necessary speed for lift-off. This prolonged acceleration distance results from the increased momen-

tum that must be overcome due to the added weight.

3. Reduced rate and angle of climb: Once airborne, an overloaded aircraft experiences a diminished rate of climb, meaning it ascends at a slower vertical speed compared to its normal performance. Additionally, the angle of climb, which represents the steepness of the ascent trajectory, is also reduced. These reductions stem from the decreased excess power available to overcome gravitational forces and propel the aircraft upward.

4. Lower maximum altitude: Excess weight limits the altitude to which an aircraft can climb. The aircraft's engines may lack the necessary thrust to maintain climb rates at higher altitudes due to the increased aerodynamic drag and gravitational forces acting on the heavier aircraft.

5. Shorter range: Excessive weight decreases the aircraft's fuel efficiency, leading to a reduction in the distance it can travel on a given amount of fuel. This diminished range results from the increased fuel consumption required to lift and sustain the heavier aircraft in flight.

6. Reduced cruising speed: An overloaded aircraft typically operates at a slower cruising speed compared to its optimal performance. This reduction in speed results from the increased drag caused by the heavier aircraft, which requires more power to maintain forward momentum.

7. Reduced manoeuvrability: Excess weight impairs the aircraft's ability to manoeuvre effectively. The increased mass makes it more challenging for the aircraft to respond promptly and accurately to control inputs, resulting in decreased agility and responsiveness in flight.

8. Higher stalling speed: An overloaded aircraft has a higher stalling speed, meaning it requires a greater airspeed to maintain lift and prevent a stall. This higher stalling speed is a consequence of the increased wing loading resulting from the additional weight, which necessitates greater lift production to counteract gravitational forces.

9. Higher approach and landing speed: During the approach and landing phases, an overloaded aircraft requires a higher airspeed to maintain lift and control.

This increased approach and landing speed is necessary to compensate for the additional weight and ensure a safe touchdown within the available runway distance.

10. Longer landing roll: Upon touchdown, an overloaded aircraft requires a longer distance to come to a complete stop due to the increased kinetic energy resulting from its higher landing speed. This prolonged landing roll poses challenges in terms of runway length requirements and braking capabilities, particularly in constrained landing areas.

Overall, the cumulative effects of excessive weight significantly degrade an aircraft's flight performance, compromising its safety, efficiency, and operational capabilities. Pilots must carefully manage aircraft weight within specified limits to mitigate these performance deficiencies and ensure safe flight operations.

REMOTE PILOT AIRCRAFT AND THEIR COMPONENTS

The terms "Unmanned Aerial Vehicle" (UAV), "Unmanned Aircraft System" (UAS), "Remotely Piloted Aircraft System" (RPAS), and "Drone" generally refer to the same concept: an aircraft or aircraft system operated remotely without a pilot on board.

Typically, the operator controls such aircraft from the ground, but they may also operate from a vehicle, boat, or another manned aircraft.

Initially, "UAV" was adopted by CASA in July 2002 and remains widely used in certification, licensing, and guidance materials. This term was prevalent during the establishment of the Australian Certified UAV Operators.

"UAS" is now the internationally recognized term, endorsed by ICAO and CASA, serving as the overarching classification terminology.

"RPAS," defined by ICAO, denotes a type of UAS directly controlled by a pilot at all flight stages despite remote operation. CASA has recently transitioned to using "RPAS" as its primary terminology.

CASA's reference materials use "UAVs," "UAS," and "RPAS" interchangeably depending on the context of discussion. Historical background discussions involving ACUO, for instance, may utilize all three terms due to the association's origins.

Historically, "Drone" referred to UAS used as targets in military air defence training. Despite its original usage, popular culture, especially the media, now employs "drone" as a generic term for unmanned or remotely piloted aircraft, particularly those with military capabilities.

Recreational remotely piloted aircraft are categorized by CASA as "Model Aircraft" and are operated for sport and recreation under the oversight of the Model Aeronautical Association of Australia (MAAA) and Civil Aviation Safety Regulations (CASR) 1998 - Part 101.G.

ACUO observes ongoing technological advancements in the UAS sector, leading to continual revisions of terminologies and definitions. This evolution is typical in emerging industries, reminiscent of the terminological shifts seen in early 20th-century commercial aviation and motor transport. Nevertheless, ICAO's efforts to standardize terminology and definitions are expected to establish consensus in the near future, with "UAS" and "RPAS" already holding legal status in numerous jurisdictions.

Drone Components

While drone models may vary, certain components remain consistent and essential for their operation. When discussing quadcopter drones, the most prevalent type for drone pilots, we can delineate fundamental parts applicable to most RPAS.

Drone Components:

1. Frame or Chassis:

    - The frame or chassis serves as the drone's body, holding all components together in a configuration conducive to optimal aerodynamic performance. It determines the drone's size and structure.

2. Arms:

    - These support the motors and attach to the frame. Longer arms enhance stability, while shorter ones improve manoeuvrability. In some cases, arms are integral to the frame, not counted as separate parts.

3. Motors:

    - Vital for drone propulsion, motors are located at arm ends and generate lift. They work in conjunction with propellers to lift the drone.

4. Drone Propellers:

- Propellers, connected to motors, provide lift by rotating. Each motor typically has one or two propellers, comprising the powertrain.

5. Battery:
    - Powers motors and other electrical components. Li-po batteries are common, offering high performance and flight autonomy.

6. Flight Controller Board:
    - Acts as the drone's "brain," receiving and processing information from various sources to control flight movements.

7. Sensors:
    - Essential for performance, sensors include speed, height, altitude, and position sensors, providing crucial data for flight control.

8. Camera:
    - Integral for aerial photography or filming, cameras are commonly found on drones, with structures supporting camera installation.

9. Gimbal:
    - Stabilizes the camera during flight, preventing motor vibrations from affecting image quality.

10. Variable Speed Drives or Speed Controllers (ESC):
    - Enhance flight experience by allowing speed and direction adjustments.

11. Drone Control Station:
    - Comprises elements such as radio transmitter, receiver, data management components, and remote control, facilitating precise drone control.

12. Landing Gear:
    - Ensures drone integrity upon ground contact, maintaining distance be-

tween the drone body and the ground, especially crucial for drones carrying payloads.

Add-ons:
- Other drone parts, not standard but included depending on the intended activity. These may include cargo drones or drones for light shows, incorporating additional components for specific tasks.

Understanding these components is crucial for safe drone operation and effective flight control.

The frame of the drone serves as its structural backbone, connecting all components and parts. It facilitates the arrangement of various constituents and typically comes in two shapes: "X" or "+" designs, optimized for aerodynamics. The weight and size of the frame significantly influence the performance of flying drones.

Motor: Responsible for propelling the drone by spinning the propellers, the motor is a crucial component. In a Quadcopter, four motors power each propeller individually. It's important to note that higher RPM per volt of the motor results in faster propeller rotation.

ESC (Electronic Speed Control): Also known as ESC, this wired framework links the motor to the battery and regulates propeller spinning. ESC adjusts propeller speed and motion to enable various manoeuvres during flight. Another component involved in propeller speed control is the Flight Control Board (FCB), managing gyroscope and acceleration, ultimately governing the drone's operation.

Propellers: Functioning like wings, propellers direct the flight path of the drone. They rotate to lift the drone and provide roll, yaw, and pitch adjustments during flight.

Battery and Charger: The drone's power source is its battery, essential for its operation. Drones rely on batteries of varying capacities, influencing flight duration. Typically, drone batteries are rechargeable for extended use.

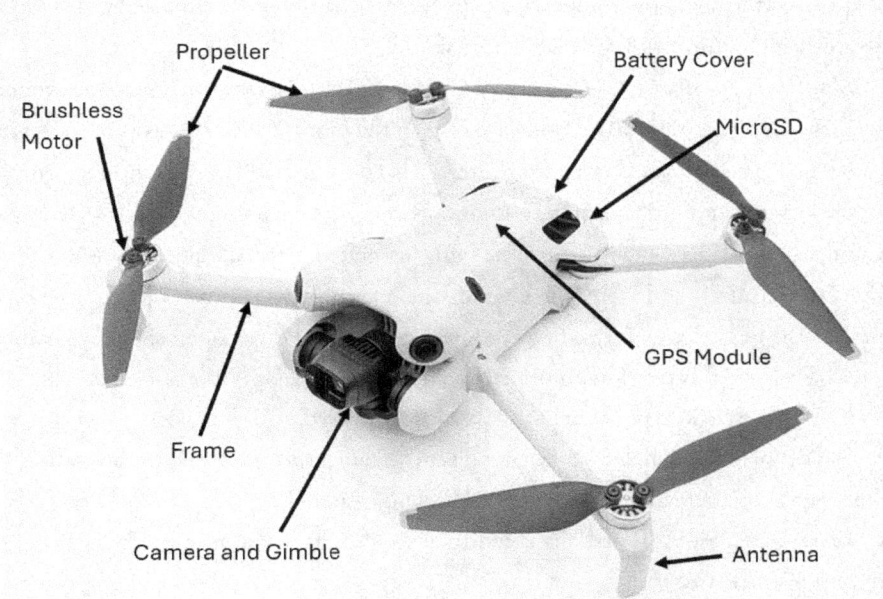

Figure 51: Parts of a Drone (DJI Mini 4 Pro). Back image: Jacek Halicki, CC BY-SA 4.0, via Wikimedia Commons.

In a quadcopter design, a torque-free architecture is achieved through a central frame (hub) housing all electronic components, with four arms (booms) extending outward to provide stable mounting positions for the rotors. Each rotor comprises a propeller driven by a motor controlled by an ESC (electronic speed controller), typically located in a ventilated area near the main hub. Following Newton's third law of physics, whereby every action force has an equal and opposite reaction, the clockwise and counterclockwise rotation of the quadcopter's rotors creates a torque-free system. This contrasts with conventional helicopters, where a single rotor forces the fuselage to rotate, necessitating a complex tail rotor system. With four rotors distributing the workload, quadcopter rotors do not need to spin as fast, resulting in less twitchy controls.

In a quadcopter, motors #1 and #3 rotate counterclockwise, while motors #2 and #4 rotate clockwise. Adjusting rotor speeds on each side enables pitch (forward or backward tilt) and roll (right or left bank) manoeuvres for lateral movement, while synchronized motor speeds provide throttle control for altitude adjustments. Yaw control (right or left turning) is achieved by varying the torque between clockwise and counterclockwise propellers, rather than using a tail rotor. For instance, speeding up the clockwise rotors and/or slowing down the counterclockwise rotors increases torque in the counterclockwise direction, turning the quadcopter leftward.

Maintaining a balanced Center of Gravity (CG) is essential for quadcopter operations, with the CG typically situated midway between the four rotors. Any payload, such as a camera or gimbal, located away from the CG is compensated by adjusting the battery position in the opposite direction. Without proper CG, one or more rotors may struggle to maintain balance. Flight controllers with integrated gyros should be positioned at the CG. To adjust and verify the CG, lift the quadcopter from two opposing points next to the flight controller using your index fingers. The quadcopter should resemble a well-levelled seesaw, indicating proper balance. If not, the operator can adjust the CG by moving the payload or battery until balance is achieved.

Quadcopter aerodynamics differ significantly from airplanes, with extensive surfaces creating substantial wind resistance. This becomes especially critical during windy conditions and descent. Advanced flight controllers and electronic firmware offer algorithms to address these issues.

Structural integrity is crucial for quadcopters, particularly larger systems. Rigidity is vital for larger quadcopters to maintain stability. Strong, lightweight materials such as carbon fibre or aluminium are preferred for booms, brackets, and propellers, ensuring uncompromised design. Cheaper quadcopters may utilize mass-produced plastic components, resulting in excessive flex and weight.

Remote Control

A remote control serves as a radio transmitter responsible for various functions, including signal reception and transmission. It oversees the flight, direction, and speed of the drone, facilitating instructions to be sent to the aircraft.

Right Stick: This stick governs the pitch and roll movements of the drone, dictating its left, right, backward, and forward motions during flight.

Left Stick: Associated with throttle and yaw control, the left stick manages flips and rolls of the drone. It controls the anticlockwise and clockwise rotations of the aircraft, as well as regulates flight altitude.

Trim Button: Present on all remote control units, the trim button is used to correct any imbalance in controls. Pressing the trim button adjusts control settings to restore balance.

Antenna: The antenna of a remote control functions as a receiver for transmissions. It receives signals sent from the controller and acts accordingly to control the drone.

Figure 52: Using a drone controller. Photo by David Montanari, via Pexels.

Working Principle of Drone and Flow Pattern

Fluid dynamics is a crucial aspect of aircraft and drone design and development, governing the aerodynamic principles underlying their operation. Lift, essential for counteracting gravity and raising the vehicle, relies on generating a sufficient upward force. This force is complemented by thrust, which propels the vehicle forward. Understanding these forces involves applying the kinematic laws of fluid flows [58].

When air interacts with an aerofoil or propeller, it incurs pressure, viscous, and drag forces, with the force exerted being directly proportional to the air velocity at the inlet.

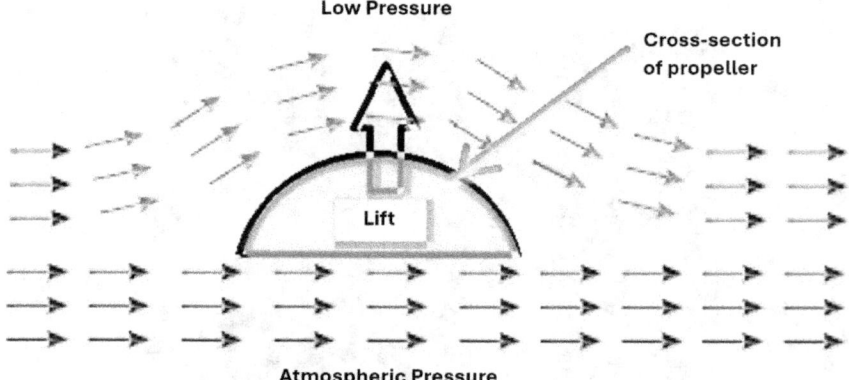

Figure 53: *Lift based on Bernoulli's principle.*

The flow pattern around the cross-section of the aerofoil or propeller demonstrates high fluid pressure beneath and low pressure above the propeller, resulting in an upward force known as lift. This lift force is responsible for elevating the weight of an aircraft or drone, with its magnitude influenced by the angle of inclination of the aerofoil or propeller [58].

Bernoulli's principle, based on the conservation of energy in fluid flow, elucidates how the sum of all energy forms within a fluid remains constant along the streamline. As air flows over an aerofoil or wing, its velocity increases at the upper portion, leading to decreased air pressure. Conversely, at the lower side of the blade, air velocity decreases, causing an increase in pressure. This pressure discrepancy across the aerofoil results in an upward lift force, crucial for flight [58].

Multirotor drones are equipped with various numbers of propellers. While having more propellers enhances stability and load-carrying capacity, it also demands increased battery power to drive additional motors for higher power output. Among these, the quadcopter stands out as a widely favoured option.

- Bicopter (2 propellers)
- Triplecopter (3 propellers)
- Quadcopter (4 propellers)
- Hexacopter (6 propellers)

- Octacopter (8 propellers)

Working Principle of Quadcopter [58]:
- A quadcopter features four propellers positioned at the corners of its frame.

- Each propeller's speed and rotation direction are independently controlled to ensure balance and manoeuvrability of the drone.

- In a conventional quadrotor design, all four rotors are uniformly spaced from each other.

- To maintain system equilibrium, one set of rotors rotates clockwise while the other set rotates counterclockwise.

- To ascend (hover), all rotors must operate at high speeds. Adjusting the rotor speeds enables the drone to move forward, backward, and sideways.

Quadcopter Dynamics:

A quadcopter's movements are classified into four types based on the relationship between its four propellers: 1) throttle, 2) pitch, 3) roll, and 4) yaw [58].

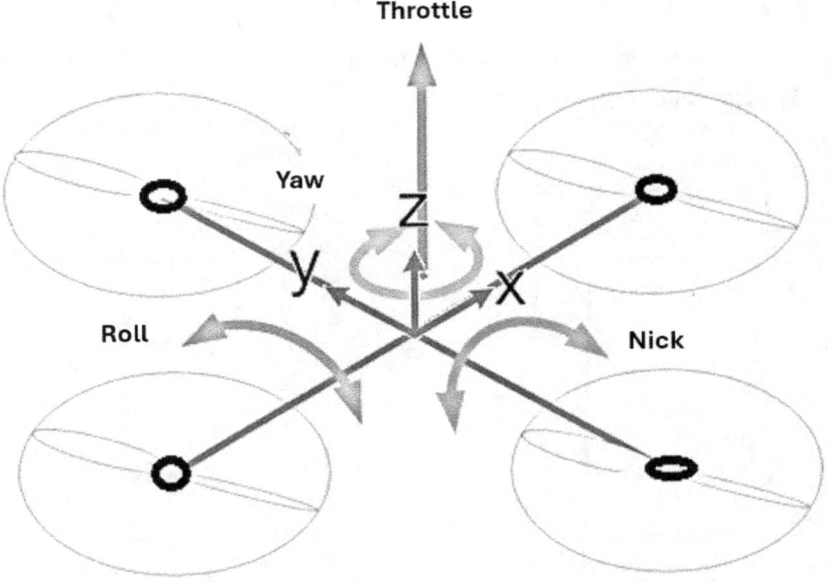

Figure 54: Quadcopter movements.

Throttle/Hover: Throttle refers to the vertical movement of the drone.
- If all four propellers operate at normal speed, the drone will descend.

- If all four propellers operate at a higher speed, the drone will ascend, resulting in hovering.

Pitch: Pitching motion involves the drone's movement along a lateral axis, either forward or backward.
- If the two rear propellers operate at high speed, the drone moves forward.

- If the two front propellers operate at high speed, the drone moves backward.

Roll: Rolling motion pertains to the drone's movement about the longitudinal axis.
- If the two right propellers operate at high speed, the drone moves left.

- If the two left propellers operate at high speed, the drone moves right.

Yaw: Yawing motion involves the rotation of the drone's head around the vertical axis, either left or right.
- If two propellers of the right diagonal operate at high speed, the drone rotates counterclockwise.

- If two propellers of the left diagonal operate at high speed, the drone rotates clockwise.

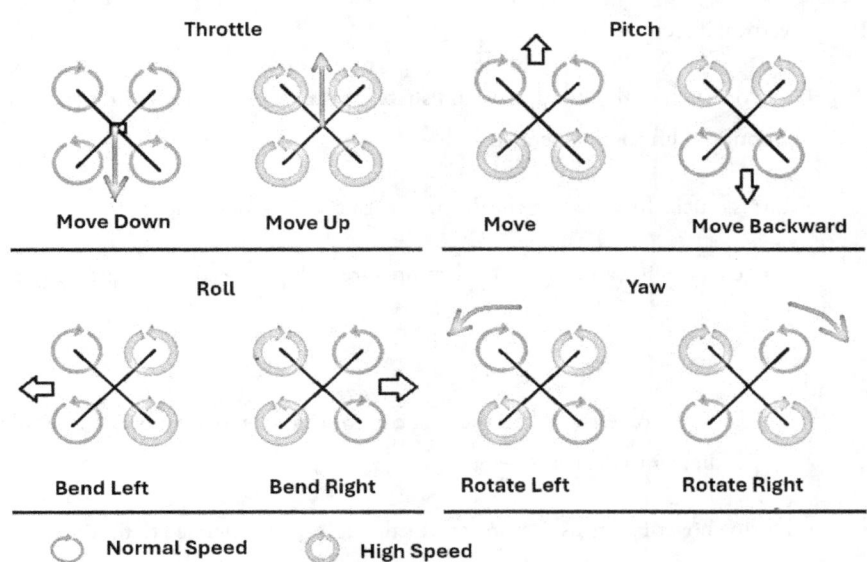

Figure 55: Quadcopter Controls.

Forces and Moments Acting on a Drone

When a drone is in flight, it experiences several forces that dictate its movement. These forces interact to determine the drone's overall behaviour. The primary forces acting on a drone are:

Weight:

- Weight is the force exerted on the drone due to its mass and gravity.

- It always acts downward toward the centre of the Earth.

- The greater the weight of the drone, the more power is required to lift and manoeuvre it.

- The weight of the drone can be calculated by multiplying its mass by the acceleration due to gravity.

Lift:

- Lift is the upward force generated on the drone, counteracting its weight.

- This force is produced by pressure differences across the drone's body in the vertical direction.

- Factors such as the speed, size, and shape of the propeller blades influence the amount of lift force generated.

- Lift is crucial for elevating the drone against the force of gravity.

- To generate lift, all four propellers operate at high speeds to create upward thrust.

Thrust:
- Thrust is the force exerted on the drone in the direction of its motion, typically perpendicular to the rotor plane.

- During hovering, thrust is purely vertical, but it can be inclined to tilt the drone forward or backward for directional movement.

- Thrust is essential for propelling the drone in the desired direction at a consistent speed.

- To achieve the desired motion, two propellers are often given higher speeds to produce greater thrust.

Drag:
- Drag is the force acting on the drone in the opposite direction of its motion, caused by air resistance.

- Factors contributing to drag include pressure differences and the viscosity of the air.

- To minimize drag, drones are designed with aerodynamic shapes that reduce air resistance and streamline airflow over the body.

Controlling a Multirotor Drone

Some general steps for operating a drone include:

1. Familiarize yourself with the manual: Begin by carefully reading the drone's manual. Each drone model is unique and comes with its own set of instructions and guidelines.

2. Register your drone: Depending on your location, you may need to register your drone with the relevant authorities before flying it.

3. Charge the drone battery: Ensure that the drone's battery is fully charged before attempting to fly it to avoid unexpected interruptions.

4. Choose an appropriate location: Select a location that is spacious, free from obstacles such as trees, buildings, or power lines, and complies with local regulations for drone operation.

5. Check the weather conditions: Avoid flying your drone in adverse weather conditions such as high winds or rain. Check the weather forecast before proceeding with your flight.

6. Power on the drone and remote control: Turn on both the drone and the remote control, ensuring they are properly synced and functioning.

7. Calibrate the drone: Follow the instructions provided in the manual to calibrate the drone before take-off, ensuring optimal performance and stability.

8. Take off: Gradually push the throttle stick upward to initiate take-off, maintaining smooth and controlled ascent.

9. Navigate the drone: Utilize the remote control to manoeuvre the drone through the air, maintaining a safe distance from people, buildings, and other structures.

10. Prepare for landing: When ready to conclude the flight, gently lower the drone back to the ground using the throttle stick, ensuring a controlled and stable descent.

11. Power down the drone: After safely landing the drone, power off both the drone and the remote control to conserve battery life and ensure safety.

Operating a Quadcopter:

- Pre-flight Preparation: Learning to fly a quadcopter is facilitated by a structured step-by-step approach. Before taking flight, ensure you are thoroughly familiar with the following procedures:

  - Quadcopter Familiarization: Begin by acquainting yourself with your quadcopter and carefully reviewing all instructional materials provided.

  - Transmitter Setup: Familiarize yourself with the remote control (RC) transmitter and ensure that batteries are properly inserted.

  - Control Understanding: Understand the functionality of each control:

  - The left stick controls throttle (altitude adjustment) and yaw (rotation).

  - The right stick controls pitch (forward/backward movement) and roll (side-to-side movement).

- Preflight Setup: Follow manufacturer-recommended preflight setup and adjustments:

  - Battery Charging: Charge the quadcopter's battery using the supplied charger according to the manufacturer's instructions.

  - Pre-flight Checks: Prepare the quadcopter for flight as per the provided instructions.

  - Select Flight Area: Ensure you have a spacious, uncluttered area indoors or outdoors, free from wind or drafts. Ensure the flight area is devoid of people, animals, or fragile objects.

- Initial Setup:

  - Positioning: Place the quadcopter in the centre of your open space, facing directly away from you.

  - Transmitter Activation: Lower the throttle (left stick) on the RC transmitter and switch it on. Always activate the transmitter before connecting the quadcopter's battery.

- Battery Connection: Connect the quadcopter's battery after activating the transmitter. When finished flying, disconnect the battery first before turning off the transmitter.

- Safe Distance: Step back three or four paces from the quadcopter and maintain facing towards it.

- Initial Flight:

  - Lift-off Practice: Gradually increase the throttle stick until the motors start spinning, then reduce it until they stop. Repeat to familiarize yourself with throttle control.

  - Hovering: Gradually increase throttle to lift the quadcopter slightly off the ground. Practice maintaining a stationary hover. Use trim buttons to adjust for any directional movement or rotation.

- Controlled Hovering:

  - Altitude Control: Use throttle control to maintain altitude. Make slight adjustments to the right stick to hold horizontal position.

  - Directional Stability: Utilize the left stick (yaw) to prevent rotation. Adjust trim buttons as needed for stability.

- Basic Manoeuvres:

  - Forward and Backward Movement: Practice moving the quadcopter forward and backward using the right stick (pitch).

  - Side-to-Side Movement: Experiment with side-to-side movement using the right stick (roll).

- Rotation Mastery:

  - Mental Reorientation: Understand the mental reorientation required for rotating the quadcopter.

  - Transmitter Control: Develop subconscious control over the RC transmitter.

- Advanced Rotations:

  - Gradual Rotation: Practice rotating the quadcopter gradually using the yaw stick.

  - Angle Adjustments: Experiment with rotating the quadcopter at different angles, gradually increasing to 180 degrees.

  - Pitch and Roll: Integrate pitch and roll movements while maintaining control over yaw.

  - Advanced Manoeuvres: Master more complex manoeuvres, such as flying in circles and figure eights, while maintaining orientation.

Operating a drone can be an enjoyable and fulfilling experience, but mastering the process requires patience, practice, and attention to detail. Here's a comprehensive guide to help you navigate the steps of operating a drone effectively:

- **Familiarization and Pre-flight Setup:**

  - Begin by acquainting yourself with your quadcopter and carefully reviewing all provided instructions.

  - Ensure your remote control transmitter is properly set up and equipped with batteries.

- **Preflight Preparation:**

  - Charge the drone's battery according to the manufacturer's instructions.

  - Ready your drone for flight, following the recommended procedures.

  - Select a suitable flying location, indoors or outdoors, ensuring it's spacious, obstacle-free, and shielded from wind and drafts.

  - Verify that the flight area is clear of individuals, animals, and fragile objects.

- **Initial Setup and Take-off:**

DRONE OPERATIONS

- Position the drone in the centre of your designated flying area, facing away from you.
- Confirm that the throttle (left stick) on the remote control transmitter is set to its lowest position before powering it on.
- Always turn on the transmitter first, followed by connecting the drone's battery.
- After completing the flight session, disconnect the drone's battery first before powering off the transmitter.
- Step back a few paces from the drone, maintaining a clear view of it.

- **Basic Flight Manoeuvres:**
  - Begin by gradually increasing throttle input until the drone's motors initiate and then reduce it to halt them, familiarizing yourself with throttle control.
  - Practice lifting the drone off the ground incrementally, ensuring it remains relatively stationary and non-rotating.
  - Adjust trim settings as necessary to achieve a stable hover without manual input.

- **Hovering and Altitude Control:**
  - Aim to achieve a controlled hover approximately one foot above the ground, utilizing throttle input to maintain altitude.
  - Employ subtle movements of the right stick to maintain horizontal position and counteract any yaw, roll, or pitch deviations.

- **Forward and Sideways Movement:**
  - Gradually introduce forward and backward movement using the pitch (right) stick, mastering directional control while keeping the drone oriented away from you.
  - Transition to lateral movement using the roll (right) stick, adjusting yaw (left

stick) input as needed to maintain orientation.

- **Rotation and Orientation Control:**

  - Develop proficiency in rotating the drone using the yaw (left) stick, maintaining orientation and adjusting control inputs accordingly.

  - Practice hovering at various angles and gradually increase rotation angles to 180 degrees, adjusting control responses as needed.

- **Advanced Manoeuvres and Coordination:**

  - Combine yaw, pitch, and roll stick movements to execute complex flight patterns such as circles and figure eights.

  - Refine your control and coordination skills through consistent practice, gradually increasing the complexity of manoeuvres and flight environments.

By following these step-by-step instructions and dedicating time to practice, you'll gradually enhance your proficiency and confidence in operating a drone effectively and safely.

Controls: Below is an illustration of the control mechanisms for piloting a quadcopter and an explanation of each control's function.

- Roll: Tilts the quadcopter left or right by adjusting the rotor speeds on one side while decreasing them on the other.

- Pitch: Tilts the quadcopter forward or backward in a similar manner to roll.

- Yaw: Rotates the quadcopter by accelerating all rotors spinning in one direction and decelerating those spinning in the opposite direction.

- Throttle: Manages the vertical axis by regulating the overall rotor speed. These controls are also referred to by other names; for instance, roll is known as aileron, pitch as elevator, and yaw as rudder.

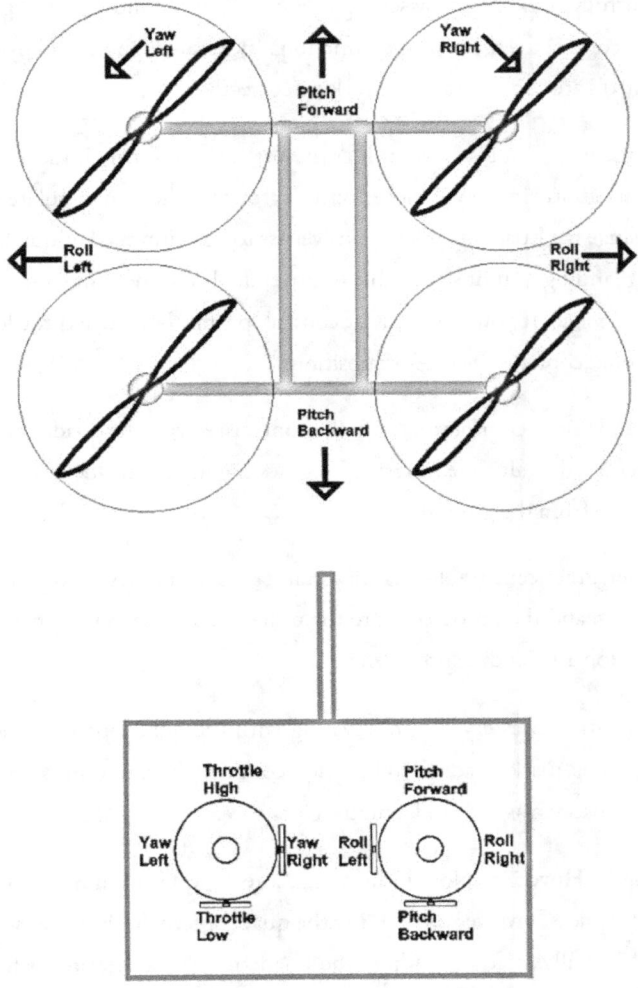

Figure 56: Quadcopter controls.

Stabilization: Quadcopters typically offer three primary stabilization modes:
1. Rate Mode, also referred to as manual, hard, or Acro.

2. Attitude Mode (distinct from Altitude Mode), also termed self-level or Auto-level.

3. GPS-hold Mode, also known as Loiter.

Quadcopter Hovering:

1. Control Check: Begin by setting the throttle at around 10% and gradually test each control to ensure proper functionality before flight. Avoid flying unless all controls are confirmed to be working correctly.

2. Quadcopter Familiarization: Increase the throttle slowly until the quadcopter hovers approximately 2 inches off the ground. Then, manipulate the controls to gauge the quadcopter's responsiveness to your inputs. For quadcopters with long landing gear, it's advisable to hover at about one foot to prevent ground interference. If you sense loss of control, promptly reduce throttle and return the quadcopter to its take-off position.

3. Ascend: Once comfortable with the controls, elevate the quadcopter to around 3 feet. Higher altitude hovering becomes slightly easier due to reduced air turbulence from the ground.

4. Target Practice: Establish landing targets and practice flying to each target, landing, and then proceeding to the next one. This exercise enhances hovering precision and landing proficiency.

5. Orientation Mastery: Begin hovering with the quadcopter positioned at the 10 o'clock mark, gradually becoming confident before transitioning to other positions such as 2, 9, and 3 on the clock face.

6. Nose-In Hovering: Nose-in hovering, a technique common among RC helicopter pilots, involves positioning the quadcopter with its nose facing towards you. Initially, manually adjust the quadcopter's orientation before take-off. Note that controls may feel reversed initially, requiring adjustment similar to balancing a stick. Mastering nose-in hovering aids in orientation practice, including hovering at the 7 and 5 o'clock positions.

7. Nose-In Landing Practice: Set up landing targets and attempt to land the quadcopter with its nose facing inward. This manoeuvre is challenging and requires patience to master.

Aerodynamics for Flight and Directional Maintenance for Fixed Wing Aircraft

While a basic understanding of aerodynamics and aircraft stability is not strictly necessary for flying, it proves beneficial, especially for those involved in aircraft design or modification. Nonetheless, mastering the theory can be more challenging than the act of flying itself. Personal preference dictates the extent to which one delves into the theoretical aspects.

The subsequent guide serves as a fundamental introduction to aerodynamics and aircraft stability. While it is not a prerequisite for flying, it aids in the construction of various models. At the very least, familiarity with the terminology used in aircraft design is advisable.

An aircraft requires four primary types of structures to achieve flight:

1. Lifting structures: These components generate lift to counteract gravity.

2. Stability structures: These elements maintain the craft's heading stability and controllability.

3. Control structures: These mechanisms facilitate control of the aircraft's movement.

4. Utility structures: These elements provide structural integrity, elevate the aircraft off the ground, and accommodate payload and propulsion systems.

Lifting Structures: The wing serves as the lifting structure, responsible for generating lift by directing airflow while in motion. It must strike a balance between generating lift and minimizing drag, the force that impedes the craft's forward motion. The performance of a wing is often quantified by its lift-to-drag ratio (LD), which determines its gliding capabilities and power efficiency.

Wings operate on both simple and intricate principles. While they intuitively push air downward as they move forward, they also create lift by "sucking" air above the wing. Understanding the complexities of wing operation involves concepts such as the Bernoulli effect and conservation of momentum. However, for practical purposes, it is essential to focus on relevant factors and not get bogged down in theoretical debates.

Key Points about Wings:
- The size of the wing is a crucial factor, with smaller crafts like insects experienc-

ing airflow differently than larger aircraft.

- The Reynolds number, which describes the object's scale in relation to fluid viscosity and density, influences wing performance.

- The wing's cross-section, known as the airfoil, plays a significant role in its efficiency, with extensive research aimed at improving aerodynamic performance.

- While small models may use simplistic wing designs, larger and faster aircraft require more sophisticated airfoil designs for optimal performance.

Lift and Drag: Drag, generated by friction and induced air movement, poses a challenge for wings, necessitating forward speed for effective operation. Lift is directly proportional to speed and the angle of attack (AOA), with an optimal AOA typically ranging from 2 to 3 degrees. However, exceeding a critical AOA leads to a stall, wherein the wing's performance deteriorates rapidly.

A stall event occurs when the wing's AOA surpasses a critical threshold, resulting in a significant increase in drag and loss of lift. This phenomenon, akin to a deep stall, can cause a drastic change in flight characteristics, leading to a loss of control. While some aircraft designs mitigate the risk of deep stalls through stability mechanisms, maintaining awareness of AOA limits is essential for safe flight.

The objective is not complete elimination but rather minimization of rotation. Achieving this goal involves three primary approaches:

1. Opt for long and slender wings to reduce the area of the wingtips.

2. Design elliptical wings to concentrate lift towards the center and minimize pressure differences at the tips. Alternatively, employ wing twisting, known as "washout," to progressively reduce lift towards the tips, thus preventing stalling during turns.

3. Incorporate winglets or vertical structures to disrupt the formation of vortices at the wingtips.

While winglets can effectively reduce tip vortices within a limited speed and angle of attack range, designing them to avoid compromising performance across various conditions can be challenging. Often, extending the wingspan proves more efficient unless constrained by factors such as airport gate limitations for large airliners.

Although elliptical wings offer enhanced efficiency, their construction complexity and associated costs are higher. Conversely, high aspect ratio wings, characterized by a greater wingspan compared to width, are more efficient but require stronger control mechanisms, leading to additional weight and cost penalties.

High aspect ratio wings necessitate a thinner profile to maintain relative thickness and camber, resulting in structural weakness unless compensated by stronger materials or thicker airfoils, which increase drag or weight. Thus, advanced materials and design techniques play a crucial role in optimizing aircraft performance.

Key Factors in Wing Design:

1. Wing Loading: The weight-to-wing-size ratio determines the lift required for flight. Lower wing loading facilitates slower flight and reduced power consumption.

2. Aspect Ratio: The ratio of wing width to length from an overhead perspective influences wing efficiency. High aspect ratio wings minimize wingtip vortices but require stronger construction.

3. Thickness: Thicker wings offer structural strength but induce more drag at higher speeds and lower angles of attack.

4. Camber: Wing curvature affects stall behaviour and drag at different angles of attack. High camber wings are suited for slow flight and short runways.

5. Sweep: Wing rotation back from a straight line influences stability and speed performance. Swept wings enhance stability at high speeds but compromise lift-to-drag ratio.

Wing Design Considerations:
- There is no universal wing design, as trade-offs must be balanced based on specific flight speeds and performance requirements.

- Achieving thinness requires reinforcement, increasing weight and wing loading.

- High aspect ratio wings demand additional strength and stiffness, adding weight and cost.

- High camber facilitates slow flight but limits speed and may pose challenges in windy conditions.

Wing Modification Devices: Various structures such as flaps and leading-edge extensions adjust wing characteristics to suit different flight phases. However, these modifications incur weight, cost, and reliability considerations.

Torque Counteraction: Efficient lift generation requires maintaining the wing at the optimal angle of attack, typically inducing a nose-down torque force. Stability structures are essential to counteract this torque and ensure efficient and stable flight.

Stability Structures

The importance of stability in aircraft design cannot be overstated, as it directly impacts the safety and control of flight. A popular saying among aviators underscores this significance: "A nose heavy plane may fly poorly but a tail heavy plane may fly well...once." Tail heavy aircraft, while capable of flight, are prone to sudden and uncontrollable manoeuvres, especially during stalls or when affected by air currents. Given that take-offs and landings occur at low speeds and close to the ground, there is minimal room for recovery in such situations. Pilots may possess considerable skill, but they cannot control the unpredictable movements of the air. Consequently, tail heavy aircraft have a short lifespan in aviation.

Stability is crucial for an aircraft to maintain control and manoeuvrability. In essence, stability refers to the ability of an aircraft to resist amplification of small positional changes. Without stability, even minor disturbances such as gusts of wind or slight control inputs can lead to escalating movements beyond the pilot's ability to compensate. While excessive stability can make an aircraft challenging to control, especially in the case of model aircraft, it is indispensable for safe human-operated flight.

Dynamic vs. Static Stability: Aircraft stability encompasses both dynamic and static aspects, each serving distinct functions. Unlike a bicycle, which is statically unstable when stationary but gains stability when in motion, aircraft require dynamic stability to maintain control during flight. Similarly, tricycles exhibit static stability but face limitations in dynamic stability, particularly during high-speed turns. Understanding this distinction is crucial, as static stability can sometimes hinder dynamic performance, as evidenced by the differences between bicycles and tricycles.

Center of Gravity: The balance point of an aircraft, known as the Center of Gravity (COG) or Center of Mass, plays a critical role in its stability. Like balancing a boat or bike, ensuring that the COG is properly aligned is essential for stable flight. While certain designs may position the COG below the wings to enhance static stability, this approach often compromises dynamic stability. Conversely, placing the COG above the lifting structure is uncommon, except for hovering craft, due to the destabilizing effects of higher COG positions. The interaction between static and dynamic stability further complicates aircraft design, highlighting the intricate nature of stability considerations.

Wing Modifications for Stability: Some aircraft designs incorporate stability structures directly into the wing, exemplified by all-wing "plank" designs and swept flying wings like hang-gliders. For swept wings, reducing the Angle of Attack (AOA) at the tips (known as "washout") or employing reflexed airfoils can enhance stability. However, these modifications often come at the cost of decreased lift or increased drag, underscoring the trade-offs inherent in stability enhancements. Even modern aircraft designs that utilize advanced technology to actively control flight face performance penalties, emphasizing the challenges of emulating natural flight mechanisms observed in birds.

The Three Axes of Stability: Aircraft stability encompasses three primary axes: roll, pitch, and yaw. Roll stability, achieved through dihedral wing configurations, relies on side-slip to correct deviations from horizontal flight. Yaw stability, facilitated by vertical stabilizers or swept wings, counters side-slip to maintain alignment with the relative wind. However, these stability axes must be carefully coordinated to ensure effective control during manoeuvres. For instance, dihedral alone cannot induce turns; instead, banking manoeuvres require coordinated roll and yaw inputs to initiate and maintain the desired trajectory.

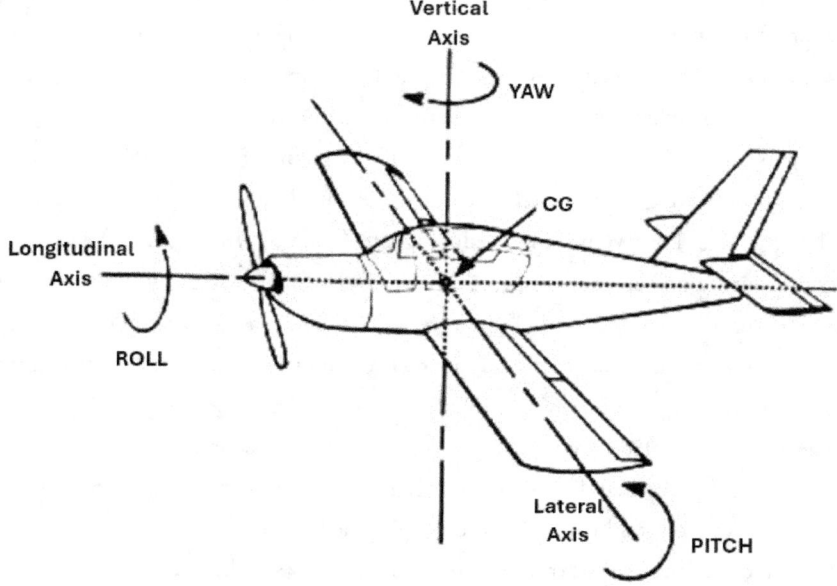

Figure 57: Axes of the aircraft.

Pitch Stability: Pitch stability, vital for maintaining proper orientation along the longitudinal axis, hinges on the placement of the COG relative to the lifting structure. Achieving the appropriate COG position ensures that the aircraft naturally tends to return to its optimal Angle of Attack (AOA) following disturbances. The horizontal stabilizer, positioned behind the main wing, counteracts the torque generated by changes in AOA, stabilizing the aircraft in pitch. Notably, the design of the horizontal stabilizer, including its camber and orientation, influences its effectiveness in pitch control.

In conclusion, stability structures are integral to the safe and efficient operation of aircraft. By understanding the principles of stability and employing appropriate design modifications, aircraft engineers can achieve a delicate balance between stability, control, and performance, ensuring optimal flight characteristics across a range of operating conditions.

Control Structures

In aviation, control structures are essential for manoeuvring aircraft along all three axes: roll, pitch, and yaw. While some aircraft, such as hang gliders, appear to lack traditional control structures, they rely on weight shift to adjust the craft's trim. Hang gliders enable pilots to manipulate pitch, roll, and yaw by shifting their weight, leveraging the pilot's heavier mass compared to the glider's components. Moreover, hang gliders utilize a centre keel that moves laterally, altering the wing's twist similar to a boom vang on a sailboat, amplifying the effect of weight shift.

Despite their apparent simplicity, even these designs can become surprisingly intricate. Control structures are typically integrated into stability structures, forming a cohesive system to ensure manoeuvrability and stability during flight. The elevator, located on the horizontal stabilizer, governs pitch control, while ailerons, typically mounted on each wing, regulate roll. The rudder, part of the vertical stabilizer, controls yaw.

Certain aircraft designs may feature only a rudder for yaw control, relying on yaw-roll coupling for turning. These designs necessitate dihedral for stability. Conversely, other designs may lack a rudder, employing roll-yaw coupling for turning, which requires either a vertical stabilizer or swept wings to convert side-slip into yaw. However, all aircraft designs incorporate some form of elevator control.

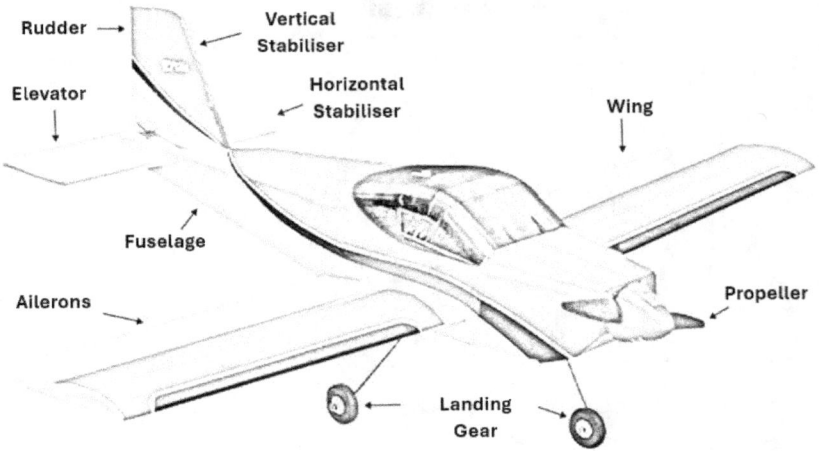

Figure 58: Aircraft control structures.

In flying wing designs, elevators often serve dual roles as ailerons, a configuration known as elevons. By employing control mixing, elevons enable pitch and roll adjustments: upward movement of both elevons causes the craft to pitch up, while differential movement induces roll. Yaw control is typically minimal during standard flight, with yaw-roll coupling compensating for turning forces. Trainer aircraft, designed with simplified 2-axis control systems, rely on built-in roll-yaw coupling to facilitate coordination during basic flight manoeuvres. However, more advanced manoeuvres necessitate control over all three axes.

Excessive control surface movement can introduce drag and destabilize the aircraft, leading to "snap" behaviour characterized by sudden and exaggerated responses to control inputs. While deliberately designed in some indoor or radical foam aircraft, such behaviour poses challenges that pilots must master for precise control.

In model aircraft, connecting control surfaces to servos presents a significant challenge. Typically, servos are mounted at a distance from the controls due to space or weight distribution constraints, connected via push-rods and levers known as "horns." To optimize control accuracy, appropriate leverage is employed, utilizing shorter levers at the servo and longer levers at the control surface to maximize servo arm movement. This meticulous setup ensures precise control over the aircraft's movements.

LAUNCH, CONTROL AND RECOVER A REMOTELY PILOTED AIRCRAFT

Preflight Procedures

Before taking your drone to the skies, it's crucial to adhere to a comprehensive preflight checklist and maintain detailed flight logs. Here's what you should include:

- **Preflight Checklist and Flight Log Information**:
    - Record the date and time of the flight.
    - Note the location and ensure a safe take-off and landing area.
    - Identify the operator and any team members involved.
    - Verify all wiring and hardware connections for security.
    - Document aircraft details, radio and channel information, and flight modes/settings.
    - Log details about propellers and batteries used, including labelling and tracking each battery's usage.
    - Check GPS status, noting the number of satellites locked in.
    - Monitor weather conditions, including sun direction, wind direction, and

speed. Ensure the aircraft is suited to handle the prevailing conditions.

- Define the purpose, subject, mission, and contact person for the flight.
- Assess potential dangers and devise a plan to mitigate each risk.
- Record the elevation and speed reached during the flight.
- Confirm payload security, preferably starting with no additional payload.
- Set camera settings and ensure sufficient memory card space.
- Document the flight length and any irregularities observed during the experience.

- **Flight Zone Safety Measures**:
  - Maintain a minimum distance of 30 feet between the UAV and any individuals or objects.
  - Utilize safety cones or large tarps to mark the perimeter of the safe zone.
  - Consider creating a physical boundary using rope, poles, paint, or field-lining powder to deter spectators from entering the flight zone.
  - If a spotter is present, instruct them to communicate with nearby individuals, direct spectators to stay away from the flight zone, and maintain awareness of the UAV's position.
  - Avoid flying near large stadiums with crowds in the stands.

- **Obstacle Awareness**:
  - Be vigilant for cables, power lines, loose cables, outstretched tree branches, light poles, and architectural features in the flight area.
  - Maintain a safe distance from potential obstacles to minimize risk.

- **Aircraft Inspection**:
  - Conduct a comprehensive systems check before each flight, even if the drone

performed flawlessly in previous sessions.

- Test motors and settings without propellers and perform a prop-directional test after attaching them.

- Document any repairs or alterations made to the drone on the spot.

- **Battery Procedures**:

  - Review battery procedures, including handling, storage, and disposal.

  - Monitor battery age and integrity to ensure safe operation.

  - Familiarize yourself with local drop-off centres for used LiPo batteries.

  - Keep a fire extinguisher nearby as a precaution.

- **Flight and Maintenance Logs**:

  - Maintain a detailed flight log documenting each flight, including relevant details from the preflight checklist.

  - Keep a separate maintenance log for UAV builds, recording repairs, improvements, and testing results.

  - Document the decision-making process throughout the drone build, including component selection and comparisons.

- **Resources**:

  - Utilize online forums and resources to seek advice and information on UAV safety and technology.

  - Don't hesitate to ask for help if uncertain about any aspect of drone design, build, or flight.

Remote Pilot Aircraft Launch

The initial phase of drone operation is known as take-off, a critical step that demands mastery. To commence take-off, the pilot engages the throttle to activate the propellers. Begin by positioning your drone on a level surface within an open space. Gradually increase the throttle to elevate the drone by a few inches initially. It's essential for the pilot to develop familiarity and comfort with the throttle's sensitivity to excel in take-off manoeuvres. If the drone begins to drift, it's recommended to refrain from using the right stick for adjustment and instead halt the process to restart it anew.

Before you can take off with your drone, there are a few final steps you need to take. These steps are generally applicable to launching, although each task may vary slightly depending on the drone model. Therefore, refer to your user manual if you're unsure. When preparing to launch your drone, your focus should be solely on the task at hand. Any distractions should be set aside to prevent injury. Follow these general steps:

1. Place your drone on the ground in a safe take-off and landing area. If your drone has an auto-return mode, it will return to this location automatically. Keep in mind that most auto-return modes do not avoid collisions, so choose an open area. Ensure the drone is pointed away from you and that your take-off and landing pad is at least 10 feet in front of you. Using your own launch pad ensures a clean and level surface for take-off and landing.

2. If your camera is integrated, ensure the lens cap is removed and set the camera to the desired flight mode. For add-on cameras like GoPro, power on the camera, remove the cap, and set it to the desired mode.

3. Verify the transmitter is off and throttle is set to zero before connecting the drone battery. Although the chance of the drone starting up upon battery connection is slim, proceed with caution.

4. Connect and power on the drone battery.

5. Calibrate the drone. High-end sensors in the drone need calibration before each flight to ensure proper control. Calibrate away from electromagnetic sources such as speakers and power lines.

6. Initiate GPS lock, similar to establishing a home location. Update home position if you change take-off and landing locations to prevent the drone from returning to an old location.

7. Arm the drone to indicate readiness for flight. Do not handle the drone while armed, especially in assisted flying modes, as it may attempt to correct and level out.

8. Slowly increase throttle to spin up the motors and take off. Hover about 10-20 feet above the ground to verify control and stability before proceeding.

Take-off and Landing

When a UAV operates at an aerodrome typically used by manned aircraft, it should adhere to standard procedures for take-off and landing and follow ATC instructions unless otherwise permitted.

For UAVs manually controlled during take-off by the launch controller, standard VFR procedures, local airfield pattern regulations, and VFR weather minimums for the airspace class apply. After take-off, the launch controller should adjust the UAV's position as needed to maintain visual contact. During take-off and transition from direct to autonomous control, the UAV supervising controller must monitor the UAV system to ensure compliance with navigational and flight path clearances and to verify system status. Collision avoidance is the responsibility of the supervising controller during this phase, but the launch controller may adjust the UAV's position per ATC instructions under IFR procedures.

For UAVs manually controlled during landing by the launch controller, the same VFR procedures, local airfield pattern regulations, and VFR weather minimums apply. The UAV should follow ATC instructions, with traffic separation provided by ATC, until reaching a predetermined recovery point. Upon visual sighting of the UAV by the supervising controller, they assume responsibility for traffic separation and collision avoidance. The supervising controller should monitor the recovery process to manual control to ensure compliance with navigational and flight path clearances. For UAVs equipped with automatic take-off and landing systems, the supervising controller should monitor UAV system status and compliance with ATC clearances, making flight path corrections as needed and directed by ATC.

Figure 59: Unmanned Aerial System UAS (Drone) Launches To Survey Fire. Mike McMillan - DNR, Public domain, via Wikimedia Commons.

Emergency Procedures

The UAV flight plan should encompass details and protocols concerning pre-planned emergency flight scenarios in the event of a loss of positive data link control over the UAV. Depending on system capabilities, these scenarios might entail:

(a) Autonomous transit of the UAV to a predetermined recovery zone followed by autonomous recovery.

(b) Autonomous transit of the UAV to a predetermined recovery zone followed by activation of a flight termination system (FTS).

Abort Procedures: The supervising UAV controller should formulate specific abort and flight termination procedures, which must be briefed to ATC as necessary. At a minimum, the briefing should cover information regarding pre-programmed loss-of-link flight profiles (including termination actions if control link restoration fails), flight termination capabilities, and UAV performance under termination conditions.

Continuous and automatic checks of the data link should be conducted, and real-time warnings should be promptly displayed to the UAV crew in case of failure. In the event of a complete loss of data link, excluding intermittent signal loss or programmed outage periods, the UAV controller should automatically and manually squawk SSR 7700 code and execute emergency recovery procedures. The parameters determining acceptable intermittent signal loss and total loss will be established by the manufacturer. A UAV operating under autonomous pre-programmed flight profiles due to a complete loss of control data link will be treated by ATC as an emergency aircraft.

If communication failure occurs between the supervising UAV controller and ATC, the UAV should squawk SSR code 7600 (mode 3A) and endeavour to establish alternative communications. Until communication with ATC is restored, the UAV will adhere to the last acknowledged instruction or be directed to orbit in its current position. Should communication with ATC remain unestablished, the UAV sortie should be terminated.

Interfacing with Air Traffic Services

In Australia, UAVs operating within radar-controlled airspace must be equipped with an SSR transponder capable of functioning in modes 3A and C. The supervising UAV controller should possess the ability to adjust the SSR code and squawk identification as needed.

Flight Deviations: Requests for flight deviations must adhere to established procedures and be directed to the appropriate ATS authorities.

Communications: The supervising UAV controller is responsible for initiating and maintaining two-way communications with the relevant ATC authorities throughout the entire flight.

Position Reporting: In controlled airspace, UAVs must be continuously monitored for adherence to the approved flight plan by the supervising UAV controller. All position and other required reports should be made to the appropriate ATC unit. Automatic Dependent Surveillance (ADS) systems may be utilized for this purpose.

Tracking: ATC will monitor the UAV's flight path continuously in areas with radar coverage. Outside radar coverage, additional equipment may be required by CASA to facilitate tracking of the UAV and maintain separation from other aircraft. ADS or similar equipment may be suitable for this purpose.

UAV Identification: Each UAV flight should have a means of indicating to ATC that it is unmanned. Therefore, all UAV call signs should include the term "UNMANNED."

Pre-Flight Checks

Area & Environment

- Hazards / Site Selection

  - Check for wires / cables

  - Animals

  - People / bystanders

  - Property in the vicinity

  - Site is away from nonessential participants

  - Ability to maintain adequate buffer zones between aircraft and personnel;

  - Minimize departures and landings over populated areas

  - Take into account local topography, ensuring a visible line of sight towards the UAV at all times. Ensure the telemetry connection is not obstructed.

  - Investigate potential alternative landing sites in case take-off site is obstructed.

- Psychological consideration (are you well rested, rushed, "get there-itis", are you being pressured by client)

- Weather considerations

  - Temperature

  - Visibility

  - Precipitation

- Wind Speed
  - Upper winds / at altitude
  - Rotor (lee side of large objects)
- Notify any bystanders or nearby property owners of your intentions (permission)
- Discuss flight plan with your co-pilot or spotter
- If flying in controlled airspace, have you notified airspace authority
  - NOTAMs
  - Can you reach authorities
  - Do you need to maintain communication?
- First Aid Kit stocked, readily accessible and visible to anyone in the area.

Equipment / UAV / Drone

- Walk-around
- Crack in joints and structural members
- Loose or damaged screws, ties, fasteners, straps
- Loose or damaged wiring
- Loose or damaged connections (solder, plugs, etc.)
- Inspect prop mounts and screws and apply slight counter pressure on arms to check for loosened components
- FPV , inspect / clean FPV (Camera) Lens and insure it is secured and connects are firmly attached
- Camera settings are correct (still images, video, framerate)

- Battery / Batteries are fully charged, properly seated and Secured
- Fail-safe equipment functioning
  - RTH (return to home)
  - Recovery chute
  - Firmware Airport Proximity Detection Functioning
- Props are smooth and free of damage / defect (check blade, surface and hub)
- Prop adapters are tight / secure
- Ensure voltage alarm is connected
- Ensure arming / idle timeout is properly configured
- Correct model is selected in transmitter (if applicable)
- Check RC transmitter shows the right range and centring for all sticks
- Perform range test

Mission Plan

- All actions and contingencies for the mission planned.
- Contingency planning should include safe routes in the event of a system failure, degraded performance, or lost communication link, if such a failsafe exists.
- Mission plans and flight plans should be shared with other operators in the vicinity.

Public Awareness

- Be courteous and polite

- You are an ambassador and your actions will affect other pilots and the industry in general

- Be professional / appear professional

Pre-flight / Run-up

- Verifying all transmitter, on-board aircraft and camera batteries are fully charged; (confirm voltages)

- Ensure no frequency conflicts with both video and transmitter / receiver

- Checking all control surfaces for signs of damage, loose hinges, and overall condition; Looking over the wing/rotors to ensure they are in good structural condition and properly secured;

- Check motor/engine and mounting attached to the airframe;

- Study propellers / mounting hardware (tight) / rotor blades for chips and deformation;

- Check the landing gear for damage and function

- Test electrical connections, plugged in and secure

- Ensure photo / video equipment mounting system is secure and operational.

- Check location of GPS equipment controlling the autopilot.

- Check the IMU movements in the ground control software.

- UAV in stabilization mode, ensure control surfaces move towards the correct positions

- UAV / Drone is in a level location safe for take-off

- FPV / Power up ground station

- FPV / Power up Video receiver / goggles

- If using Video recorder turn on camera system
- Camera settings are correct (still images, video, framerate)
- SD camera memory clear and inserted into the camera
- Action / Start filming
- All transmitter controls move freely in all directions
- All transmitter trims in neutral position
- All transmitter switches in correct position(typically away)
- Transmitter throttle to zero
- Radio transmitter on
- Connect / power on battery to airframe
- Ensure led indicators and audible tones are correct
- Timer on (if applicable)
- FPV, confirm video is in monitor / goggles
- Scan for nearby cars / people / animals
- Say "CLEAR!"
- Arm flight controller
- Increase throttle slightly listening for any abnormalities
- Short 20-30 second hover at 3-5 feet (listen for vibrations / loose items)
- Confirm Voltage levels are correct

Preflight - Failsafe

Confirm that a pre-established failsafe mechanism (typically involving return to home and motor throttle reduction) has been programmed into the RC link (refer to manufacturer's guidelines), and conduct a ground test by deactivating the transmitter and observing the response on both the receiver and ground station. Once satisfied, re-activate the transmitter.

Example Specific Fail-Safe – 3DR IRIS+ / X8+

Fail-Safe Configurations

By default, the drone's fail-safe settings are optimized for manual flight in open areas with strong GPS signals. However, for areas with weak GPS signals or for specific missions, it's recommended to adjust the fail-safe settings for enhanced fault tolerance.

Flying in Areas with Low GPS Signal: Some areas may experience weak GPS signal due to physical obstructions or limited satellite availability. If you encounter a pre-arm check failure indicating a lack of GPS 3D lock on your ground station, it's likely that you're in an area with low GPS signal. To fly without GPS lock, modify the fail-safe configuration to deactivate the horizontal geofence. This removes the GPS lock requirement before take-off and disables GPS-dependent flight modes, allowing manual control (standard – altitude-hold mode) only.

To Disable the Range Fail-Safe (Horizontal Geofence): Connect the drone to Mission Planner and navigate to Config/Tuning > Standard Params. Locate the Fence Type parameter, which is typically set to Altitude and Circle by default. Switch it to Altitude to disable the range fail-safe, and then select Write Params to save the changes to the drone.

Flying with Low GPS Signal: Before take-off, the status LED blinks blue to indicate readiness for arming without GPS lock. The drone can only fly in standard mode (altitude hold) without GPS lock. Avoid activating Loiter, RTL, Follow Me, or Auto modes if GPS lock is not obtained prior to take-off.

Flight Mode GPS Requirements:

Mode	GPS Requirement
Standard (altitude hold mode)	No GPS lock required
Loiter	GPS lock required
Auto	GPS lock required before take-off
RTL	GPS lock required before take-off
Land	No GPS lock required
Follow Me	GPS lock required

Figure 60: GPS Settings for various flight modes.

Flying Missions with Extended Range: To fly missions exceeding the default range limit of 300 meters, disable the horizontal geofence as instructed earlier. This allows the drone to travel beyond 300 meters from the launch point during the mission without triggering a return-to-launch (RTL) action.

For mission flights, GPS lock is essential before take-off. In case of GPS signal loss during the mission, the drone will activate the default GPS fail-safe behaviour. In such instances, switch to manual control (standard – altitude hold mode). When flying missions with extended range, it's advisable to configure the GPS fail-safe behaviour to land when GPS signal is lost, increasing the likelihood of safe recovery over longer distances.

To Configure GPS Fail-Safe Behaviour: Connect the drone to Mission Planner and access Config/Tuning > Standard Params. Locate the GPS Failsafe Enable parameter, typically set to AltHold by default. Switch it to Land to instruct the drone to land at the current position in the event of GPS signal loss, and then select Write Params to save the changes to the drone.

Range Check: Conduct a transmitter range check following the manufacturer's instructions. Ensure the transmitter is returned to its normal flying state before launching.

Drone Specific Launch Preparation

Example - DJI Phantom 3 Professional [59]

'*Aircraft*' is used to refer to the DJI Phantom 3 Professional and is considered interchangeable with UAV, Drone, Quadcopter.

'*iPad*' is used to refer to the iOS or Android SmartPhone or Tablet used to run the DJI GO App software. Note: This document is written specifically for use with an Apple iOS device and does NOT take into account any functional differences for Operators using an Android device to run the DJI GO App.

'*RC Unit*' is used to refer to the DJI Radio Control unit.

Figure 61: DJI Phantom 3 4K +. Rektoz, CC BY-SA 4.0, via Wikimedia Commons.

Operational Area Checklist

- Check for potential interference sources such as large metal surfaces, ferromagnetic materials on person, or nearby UAV, as well as metal underground structures (rebar, pipes, conduit, etc.) in or around the calibration area.

- Record and confirm distances (use Laser Range Finder if possible):

    ○ Take-off/Landing distance to POI.

    ○ Perimeter (corner to corner lengths).

    ○ Center of POI to Max Radius for Orbit Mode.

    ○ Max heights of all vertical structures (buildings, hydro wires, trees, etc.; hydro poles & light posts are typically 20 – 25 meters).

    ○ Ensure a clear "As the crow flies" direct path from POI to Launch/Land position.

    ○ Note the minimum altitude for RTH (Return to Home) flight path based on potential obstructions (posts, trees, structures), typically at least 50 meters.

- Confirm the maximum height of structures to be orbited or flown over (Minimum Collision Height).

Aircraft and Controller Preflight Checklist

- Firmware – Ensure Aircraft, RC Unit, Smart Batteries, and iOS device control software and firmware are updated before arriving on-site. This may require a WiFi connection which might not be available on-site.

- Props – Secure by hand or with DJI wrench (Gray cap props on gray posts and clockwise to tighten, Black cap props on black posts and counterclockwise to tighten).

- Battery (Aircraft) – Fully charged and correctly installed (fully seated and locked in-place flush with hull).

  - Red LED solid lit and not flashing.

  - Four (4) Green LEDs solid lit and not flashing.

- Battery (RC Controller) – Fully charged.

  - First LED solid lit red when powered on.

  - Next four (4) LEDs solid lit white when powered on.

- Battery (iPad) – Fully charged to 97-100%.

- Lens cover, gimbal lock, and Aircraft gimbal clamp removed and stored.

- Camera lens filters in place and securely tightened (Pilot preference if not stock camera setup).

- SD card inserted into Aircraft camera slot (metal contacts down) and clicked into place flush with slot. Reformat prior to flight.

- iPad securely mounted and locked into RC Unit clamping bracket.

- Apple MFI Certified Lightning cable plugged into iPad with USB connector plugged into RC Unit.

- If using Sun Shroud, ensure the cable is properly routed through the access hole and plugged in without sharp bends or binding.

- Antennas – Erected vertically.

- Flight Mode Toggle Switch in 'P Mode' (Positioning Mode) for assisted flight control using GPS, Vision positioning, and Barometer positioning.

iOS Device Preflight Checklist
- Battery (iPad) – Fully charged to 97-100%.

    ○ WiFi – Disabled in Settings.

    ○ Bluetooth – Disabled in Settings.

    ○ All Background Apps closed.

    ○ Allow Multiple Apps Enabled in Settings.

    ○ Gestures Disabled in Settings.

- Screen Brightness – Set to bright and Auto-Brightness Disabled in Settings.

- DJI GO App – Ensure the latest Stable Build is used.

- DJI GO settings – Pre-selected before mounting on RC Unit if possible for convenience.

- Mode – Toggle from 'P' to 'F' on the RC Unit to access additional 'Assisted Intelligent Flying Modes'. For this checklist, fly manually in 'P Mode' for complete control.

- Aircraft status bar – Shows Connected/Ready when all units are powered up.

- Control settings – Confirm all settings based on Mission and Flight Requirements. Specific Settings and Configurations are detailed in a separate SFOCS (Specific Flight Operations Cheat Sheet) document.

Pre-Launch Setup

1. Insert the micro SD card into the Aircraft camera slot.

2. Verify that the battery status shows fully charged for all devices.

3. Check that the propellers are securely locked and properly aligned (black to black and gray to gray).

4. Ensure the iPad is securely mounted, clamped, and connected to the RC Unit via cable.

5. Confirm that the RC Unit antennas are correctly positioned upright.

6. Verify that the RC Unit flight mode is set to "P" position.

7. Position the Aircraft on a level surface, indicating the appropriate HOME position.

8. Ensure that the Aircraft nose is pointing away from the operator (Direction of Flight).

9. Start the Power Up Sequence:

    - RC Unit – Power ON:

        - Press the Power button once, twice, then a third time and hold for 2-3 seconds before releasing. All LEDs will illuminate, and the unit will emit a beep.

    - iPad – Power ON.

    - Aircraft – Power ON:

        - Press the battery button once, twice, then a third time and hold for 2-3 seconds before releasing.

        - Note: When powering on the Aircraft, ensure hands and forearms are below the propellers. Use a second hand below propeller level to hold the Landing Gear to keep the Aircraft stationary during the Power Up sequence.

DRONE OPERATIONS

- The Aircraft should emit a series of beeps.

- The camera and gimbal will complete a few full rotations, stopping 'in-position' and forward-facing when ready.

- The under arm lights will remain Red on front-facing arms and change colours on the rear-facing arms to indicate Aircraft Status. Refer to Pg 12 in the Phantom 3 Professional User Manual.

- Battery display – Four Green LEDs lit and not flashing, and one Red LED lit and not flashing.

- UAV battery status OK (fully charged, no errors).

- UAV status OK and ready.

- Controller LED green.

- Controller status OK (no errors).

10. Launch the DJI GO App.

11. DJI GO App – Launch the App, select the correct Aircraft, and go to Camera Mode. The App should establish a connection with the Aircraft within a few seconds.

12. Compass – Calibrate as per instructions in the manual.

13. GPS lock – Calibrate as per instructions in the manual.

14. Tap "Camera" option.

15. If it's a new launch area, tap "Calibrate" option and follow on-screen instructions.

16. Adjust camera settings as desired.

17. Ready for Take-off:

    ○ DJI GO App flight status OK to go (Safe to fly – GPS).

- Both control sticks to lower-inner position to start motors (CSC).
- Execute auto or manual take-off and move to hover position (~2m) for 30 seconds.
- Confirm and record GPS settings:
  - Take-off/Landing location (confirm with visual check on displayed map).
  - Check stability of UAV.

18. Left Stick Forward to ascend 2-3 meters then hover.

19. Left Stick Backwards to descend 2-3 meters then hover.

20. Left Stick Left to rotate left then hover.

21. Left Stick Right to rotate right then hover.

22. Right Stick Forward to pitch/fly forward 2-3 meters then hover.

23. Right Stick Backwards to pitch/fly backward 2-3 meters then hover.

24. Right Stick Left to pitch/fly left then hover.

25. Right Stick Right to pitch/fly right then hover.

26. Return back to the original Take-off/Landing location at about 2 meters then hover.

27. Check and re-configure any flight or camera settings and confirm Home position.

28. All checks OK – ready to go.

Autonomous Take-off and Landing for Fixed Wing UAVs

In the past, UAVs required remote piloting by an operator on the ground, but advancements in technology now offer various levels of autonomy. Once an operator sets specific parameters for the UAV (altitude, airspeed, coordinates, etc.), autonomously operated UAVs can navigate to their destination, allowing operators to monitor the aircraft rather than constantly controlling it. Such a platform necessitates custom autonomous take-off and landing (ATOL) controllers in conjunction with existing flight control systems (FCS). High automation levels, particularly ATOL-based systems, offer several advantages, including enhanced flight safety, simplified operations, reduced operating costs, and decreased operator workload.

One notable benefit of ATOL-based systems is the removal of human operators (and consequently any potential operator error) during critical take-off and landing phases. Human error alone contributes to about 60% of UAV accidents during operations, with take-off and landing incidents accounting for over 50% of accidents despite comprising only a fraction of the flight phase. Eliminating the need for manual aircraft control during take-off and landing with an ATOL-based system can significantly enhance safety during operations.

Training operators to perform UAV take-offs and landings represents a significant investment in both time and money. Eliminating the need for this training could be advantageous to any program. Additionally, operators are often restricted by conditions such as nighttime or heavy fog when landing aircraft. Having an automated system that relies on onboard sensors rather than sight for landing purposes provides a more robust UAV platform.

Moreover, operators can redirect their focus to other tasks and responsibilities, allowing them to monitor the aircraft instead of spending time manually controlling take-off and landing. In military operations, ATOL systems could reduce the need for launching and recovery crews for larger UAV platforms, enabling the military to allocate valuable operators to other areas. During long-endurance operations lasting over 20 hours, operator fatigue can affect decision-making, performance, and focus—critical factors for landing. Implementing an ATOL system eliminates operator-related risk factors and replaces human operators with a system that does not tire or fatigue.

The first recorded autonomous landing of a fixed-wing aircraft occurred on August 23, 1937, at Wright Field in Dayton, Ohio, using the Army's C-14B transport plane. This achievement was made possible by Captain Carl Crane, who developed the necessary instruments and radios on board the C-14B to interact with ground radio beacons around the airfield [60]. Since then, significant technological advancements have led to more complex, compact, and robust autopilot systems capable of autonomous landings and take-offs. While switching to an ATOL system offers numerous benefits, implementation can pose several challenges.

The primary challenge in developing an autonomous take-off and landing system is the localization problem, which involves ensuring that the UAV precisely knows its position (including elevation) relative to the runway during take-off or landing. Other challenges in designing an ATOL system include runway centreline tracking, precision approach, ground effects, crosswinds (crab and decrab angles), descent rate, and braking actions.

Conventional Aircraft Taxiing and Take-off Phases: Taxiing involves propelling the aircraft forward on the ground using throttle control to approach and align with the runway. Steering is achieved by manoeuvring the nose wheel and rudder.

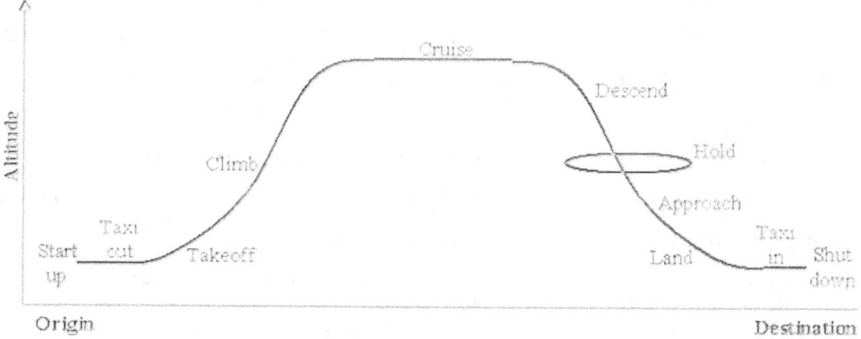

Figure 62: Aircraft Taxing, Take-off, Cruise, and Landing. Carnes (2014).

The take-off phase of flight marks the transition from taxiing to airborne flight. Typically, engines or motors are powered to full throttle to achieve the necessary take-off speed, which varies based on factors such as air density, aircraft weight, and configuration. Take-off speeds are influenced by the relative motion of the air; a headwind, for example, decreases the ground speed required for take-off by enhancing airflow over the wings, thereby generating more lift for the aircraft.

After take-off, the aircraft ascends to a designated altitude before proceeding to its cruising altitude safely. This ascent is accomplished by increasing the lift generated by the aircraft's wings until the lifting force exceeds the aircraft's weight.

Impact of Wind on Launch

The majority of aircraft incidents occur during take-off and landing phases, involving issues like obstacles during climb-out and runway overshoots during landing. In this section, we delve into the factors influencing aircraft performance during these critical phases, aiming to assist pilots in ensuring safe operations, as mandated by regulations [61].

The influence of wind on aircraft operations is a factor within our control to some extent. Selecting runways with the most favourable headwind component (where multiple runways exist) and utilizing tailwinds when flying towards our destination are strategies we can employ. Additionally, wind speed and direction may vary with altitude, providing further opportunities for optimization.

The final phase of flight, particularly landings, can be the most challenging for pilots. Significant time is dedicated to training in this area to attain near-perfection.

Headwinds and Tailwinds

Aircraft utilize wind flow over the wings to generate lift for flight. A minimum wind speed is necessary for take-off, often augmented by engine thrust.

Headwind

Taking off into the wind allows the wind to contribute to the required lift, resulting in an earlier liftoff and consequently a lower ground speed, leading to a shorter take-off run. This approach is not only safer but also reduces the runway distance required for aborted take-offs. Climbing into the wind facilitates a steeper ascent, ideal for clearing obstacles during climb-out [61].

Similarly, landing into the wind offers advantages such as reduced runway usage, lower ground speed at touchdown (reducing aircraft wear), and quicker runway availability for subsequent aircraft movements.

A general rule suggests that take-off and landing distances decrease by 1.5% for every knot of headwind up to 20 knots.

Tailwind

Taking off with a tailwind necessitates a longer runway distance to attain sufficient lift for flight, as the tailwind must be negated before any headwind effect is realized. Climbing angle is also diminished, increasing the risk of obstacle encounters. A five-knot tailwind can extend take-off distance by 25%, while a ten-knot tailwind can increase it by about 55%.

Similar effects are observed during landings, with higher ground speeds affecting approach dynamics. Landing with a tailwind raises the risk of inadvertently reducing airspeed due to visual perceptions, potentially leading to stalls. Vigilance and adherence to normal approach speeds are essential to mitigate this risk.

It's advisable to avoid tailwind operations during landing unless ample runway length and pilot experience are available to manage it safely.

Remember: Tailwinds do not alter indicated airspeed or stall speed; they influence ground speed only.

Turbulent and Gusting Winds

During take-off in gusting winds, it's prudent to keep the aircraft on the ground longer to provide a safety margin from stalling. During landing, adding half the gust factor to the final approach speed compensates for wind fluctuations. For instance, if tower reports winds of 240 degrees at 18 knots gusting to 28 knots, adding 5 knots to the airspeed is recommended [61].

Applying the same principle to take-off, adding half the gust factor to the normal liftoff speed ensures a safe margin from stalling. However, this may increase runway requirements, making it less ideal for shorter runways.

Considerations for Fixed Wing RPA Operations

Take-off and Landing Direction

Conventional wisdom dictates that aircraft should take off and land into the wind whenever possible. This approach reduces the required ground run for take-off, lowers ground speed upon landing, and facilitates steeper climb and descent angles. However, adhering to this advice may not always be feasible. Ultralight (UL) pilots, in particular, often operate from strips with obstacles at one end, necessitating a one-way take-off and landing. In such cases, flying against the wind may not be an option. General aviation (GA) pilots, on the other hand, typically operate from paved runways at "real airports," where taking off downwind is discouraged. Despite this, tailwind take-offs remain a topic with limited information available, indicating a lack of awareness regarding the associated risks. The following sections delve into the factors to consider when contemplating take-off or landing in unfavourable wind conditions, each variable playing a role to varying degrees [62].

Airspeed, Wind Speed, and Ground Speed

Airspeed represents the speed of airflow over the aircraft, while ground speed denotes the speed relative to the ground. In still air, both airspeed and ground speed align. However, when wind is present, discrepancies arise. For instance, flying into a headwind reduces ground speed, whereas flying with a tailwind increases it. This disparity affects take-off and landing distances significantly, highlighting the importance of wind awareness in flight planning [62].

Hovering

Understanding the interplay between airspeed, wind speed, and ground speed is crucial. In instances of strong winds, aircraft like the Challenger can effectively hover when positioned against the wind, showcasing the balance between these factors.

Aircraft Motion in Wind Once airborne, aircraft experience minimal ground friction, allowing them to drift with the wind's direction. This drift becomes evident during crosswind approaches, requiring pilots to adjust their heading to compensate for lateral movement. Similarly, landing in strong crosswinds necessitates crabbing to maintain alignment with the runway centreline [62].

Aircraft Performance in Wind

Despite drifting with the wind, aircraft performance parameters remain consistent, including climb rate and stall speed. However, variations in wind intensity, particularly gusts, may briefly impact performance. Ultimately, it is the aircraft's ground speed influenced by wind that significantly affects take-off and landing dynamics.

Surface Winds vs. Winds Aloft

Surface winds are typically weaker than winds aloft due to ground friction. Pilots should anticipate stronger winds at higher altitudes, with potential turbulence in the transition zone between slow-moving and fast-moving air masses. Maintaining focus on critical flight parameters, such as airspeed, helps mitigate the effects of turbulent conditions encountered in these shear layers.

Taking Off with a Tailwind versus a Headwind

Ultimately, a tailwind necessitates a longer runway for take-off, coupled with an increased distance required to clear obstacles at the runway's end. Consider a scenario where a plane needs a 200-foot ground run to achieve lift-off at 40 mph, climbing at a rate of 500 ft/min with an airspeed of 45 mph. Operating from a 1,000-ft runway, it becomes evident that clearing obstacles at the runway's end becomes significantly challenging with a tailwind, resulting in a notable decrease in altitude gained by the time the plane crosses the runway's end, especially evident with a 15 mph tailwind.

Additionally, as the plane ascends, it encounters stronger tailwinds aloft, causing a momentary drop in airspeed and subsequent decrease in climb rate due to the reliance of lift on airspeed. Simultaneously, turbulence may be experienced as the plane traverses the shear layer between slower and faster air masses.

This presents a challenging scenario for the pilot, characterized by a prolonged ground run, shallow climb angle, reduced climb rate, and potential turbulence. However, once the plane aligns with the wind, climb performance improves, albeit with a shallower angle due to increased ground speed, providing some relief to the pilot [62].

Considerations also extend to runway slope, where typically, taking off downhill and landing uphill is preferred for improved acceleration and deceleration. However, wind conditions may warrant reconsideration, with uphill take-off against a headwind potentially offering better performance than downhill take-off with a tailwind. Ultimately, the decision on take-off direction involves a judgment call based on factors such as slope degree and wind strength, highlighting the pilot's discretion in ensuring safe operations [62].

Tailwind Landings

Essentially, during a tailwind landing, you'll touch down at a significantly higher speed than usual, posing a risk of runway overrun and potential collision with obstacles or hazardous terrain beyond the runway's end [62].

When landing with a tailwind, the ground speed is the sum of the airspeed and wind speed. Consequently, the plane's touchdown speed will exceed the calm-air touchdown speed by the wind speed, necessitating a longer stopping distance. Additionally, the plane's descent angle will be shallower due to the increased ground speed.

To mitigate risks, if the approach is obstacle-free, the pilot may opt for a lower-than-usual approach to minimize potential energy from altitude, relying solely on increased speed energy to dissipate. A flatter approach allows for better reaction time to changes in wind speed as the plane descends through any shear layer present.

A critical consideration is maintaining vigilance on the airspeed indicator and promptly adding power if any hint of speed decrease arises. It's crucial not to judge speed based on ground objects, as they may appear to pass by faster than usual. Reacting to this perceived high ground speed by slowing down risks lowering airspeed, potentially leading to an unexpected stall or high sink rate.

When landing over an obstacle with a tailwind, it's advisable to cross the obstacle at the lowest altitude and airspeed feasible for safe operation. This minimizes excess speed at touchdown while ensuring safety. Turbulence above trees in windy conditions necessitates an extra margin between the trees and the aircraft's path. Additionally, the sudden disappearance of tailwinds as the plane approaches the runway may cause a rapid increase in airspeed, resulting in a longer float before touchdown.

These effects may vary depending on local conditions but warrant awareness and readiness to manage them effectively during flight [62].

Landing into a Headwind over an Obstacle

While headwinds are generally preferred over tailwinds, there's a potential pitfall when landing into a headwind, particularly over an obstacle like trees or woods surrounding the runway. Initially, the approach seems routine, but there's a notable steeper descent angle than usual due to the headwind. Adjusting power to maintain a shallower descent, the plane clears the trees and begins descent toward the runway. Here's the twist:

Because the runway is sheltered by surrounding trees, the headwind experienced above the trees suddenly disappears as the plane drops below their level. Consequently, the ground speed remains high, inherited from the headwind at higher altitude, while the airspeed drops upon descent into the calm air.

The outcome can vary from inconsequential to potentially concerning. If the approach had a buffer of extra airspeed, the sudden airspeed loss may have minimal impact. However, if the approach was near the minimum airspeed limit, the abrupt decrease could lead to a high sink rate. Without prompt correction through additional power, a hard and possibly damaging landing may ensue.

Additional Considerations Regarding Tailwind Take-offs

More often than not, when faced with the challenge of a tailwind take-off, various other factors compound the situation. Typically, it's not just one factor but a combination of elements that contribute to difficulties encountered by pilots. Here are several aspects to bear in mind [62]:

- Runway Slope: A downhill take-off is preferable as it shortens the take-off distance, while an uphill grade increases the distance required for take-off.

- Soft Field Conditions: Soft and spongy surfaces due to recent precipitation or melting snow significantly extend the take-off roll. Tall grass exacerbates this effect, making the situation even more challenging. For many aircraft, a nose-high attitude during take-off from soft fields is recommended to transition weight from the wheels to the wings swiftly. However, once airborne, promptly lowering the nose is crucial to return to a normal flight attitude.

- Wet Grass: Wet grass, whether from rain or dew, increases surface friction, resulting in a longer take-off run. Early lifting of the nose wheel can be advantageous, but extreme nose-high attitudes, like those used for soft field take-offs, may not provide substantial benefits unless the field is soft as well. Wet grass also diminishes braking effectiveness during high-speed landings due to reduced traction.

- Gusty Winds: Gusty or variable wind conditions make take-offs more challenging compared to steady winds. Pilots should anticipate a more dynamic experience during take-off in such conditions.

- Tire Pressure: Low tire pressure on hard surfaces leads to increased take-off distances due to tire flexing. While the impact is less noticeable on soft surfaces, the overall take-off run remains considerably longer compared to pavement. The trade-off involves tire footprint size, with higher pressure yielding a smaller footprint, potentially causing more sinking into soft surfaces.

- Tailwind with Crosswind Component: When faced with a tailwind accompanied by a crosswind, the aircraft tends to drift sideways upon liftoff. Pilots must promptly establish a crab angle to counter this drift, all while managing the shallow climb angle and high ground speed induced by the tailwind.

Pilots must remain vigilant regarding all factors influencing take-off. Focusing solely on the tailwind and potential obstacles at the runway's end may result in overlooking other critical variables, leading to unfavourable outcomes. Vigilance and thorough consideration of all factors are essential to ensure a safe take-off.

The Decision to Go or Not to Go

As the pilot, the responsibility falls on you to determine whether it's safe to attempt a take-off in challenging conditions. Consider the following points:

- Familiarity with Aircraft Performance: Understand your aircraft's capabilities. What's its typical take-off run? How steeply can it climb? What's the shortest stopping distance from take-off speed?

- Consideration of Weight: Heavy loading will extend take-off distance and slow climbing rate.

- Wind Assessment: Accurately assess wind speed. There's a significant difference between taking off in a 10 mph versus a 15 mph wind.

- Piloting Skills: Evaluate your own proficiency. Some pilots handle adverse conditions better than others. Have you flown recently? Have you faced similar conditions before?

- Avoiding Pressure: Don't succumb to pressure from other pilots, passengers, or spectators. Feeling obligated to proceed is a red flag.

- Comprehensive Evaluation: Take into account all variables such as wind, weight, runway conditions, tire pressure, etc.

- Trust Your Instincts: If you feel genuine nervousness or fear that impairs your concentration, it's best to halt. Discretion is key.

- Consider Landing: While assessing take-off feasibility, also contemplate the potential for landing. Planning for a safe return is essential.

- "When in Doubt, Get Out": If uncertainty persists, exiting the aircraft is a prudent choice. Tomorrow may offer better conditions, and preserving the aircraft's integrity is paramount.

Ultimately, prioritizing safety over pressure or discomfort is crucial. Trusting your judgment ensures a safer and more controlled flight experience.

Navigating Troublesome Situations

Every now and then, situations veer off course or catch us off guard. When faced with a tight spot, here are some scenarios along with tips to potentially salvage the situation:

- Deciding When to Abort a Take-off: A pilot's familiarity with their aircraft is paramount. Sensing any deviation from the norm, such as unusual sounds or sluggish acceleration, warrants caution. When contemplating an abort, it's advisable to act swiftly, ideally before considerable speed is attained. Assess the acceleration rate during the take-off run and visualize potential stopping points along the runway.

- Deciding When to Abort a Landing Attempt and Initiate a Go-Around: An optimal landing hinges on a well-executed approach. If the approach is flawed, the landing may follow suit. Early recognition of a subpar approach allows for a prompt go-around. When the runway permits, a go-around is feasible at any point, even post-touchdown. Once the decision is made, commit to it decisively. Identify the point of commitment and remain focused on the landing.

- Navigating a Departure with Limited Runway: In cases of surplus altitude and velocity during a departure, a well-executed slip manoeuvre might offer respite, provided the pilot is skilled enough. Ultralight aircraft's low inertia demands a smooth touchdown with controlled braking. If stopping before the runway's end seems improbable, maintain directional control and prepare for the terrain beyond.

- Navigating a Departure with Rapidly Approaching Obstacles: In a scenario where obstacles loom perilously close, maintaining a downward attitude to swiftly build airspeed is crucial. This expedites reaching the obstacle line, minimizing the wind's influence. After clearing obstacles, promptly correct the nose-down attitude to maintain airspeed. Prudent judgment dictates whether executing a zoom manoeuvre is viable. If the outlook appears dire, opting for an abort and controlled descent is the safer choice.

Fixed Wing Landing

The foundation of a successful landing lies in executing a proficient approach. Prior to initiating the final approach, the pilot conducts a thorough landing checklist, ensuring crucial tasks like confirming fuel flow, lowering the landing gear, and other aircraft specific functions are completed. Utilizing flaps during most landings allows for a reduced approach speed and a steeper descent angle, enhancing the pilot's visibility of the landing area. As the final approach commences, the aircraft's airspeed and rate of descent are stabilized, while aligning with the centreline of the runway.

A key skill acquired through practice is maintaining the correct attitude and descent rate during the approach. Over time, pilots develop an intuitive understanding, or "picture," of the aircraft's position relative to the runway, including the visibility of the nose cowling and the perspective of the runway. Adapting to land on runways of varying sizes requires mental adjustments to this visual picture. The numerical markers on the runway serve as important indicators; disappearance of the numbers beneath the aircraft's nose signals a long landing, whereas separation of the numbers from the nose indicates a short landing.

As the aircraft descends over the threshold of the runway, power is further reduced, possibly to idle. The pilot gradually decreases the rate of descent and airspeed by applying increased back pressure to the control wheel. Alignment with the runway centreline is primarily maintained using the rudder. Continuing back pressure on the control wheel as the aircraft enters ground effect slows its forward speed and descent rate. The objective is to keep the aircraft flying just inches above the runway's surface until it loses flying speed, allowing for a smooth touchdown on the main wheels.

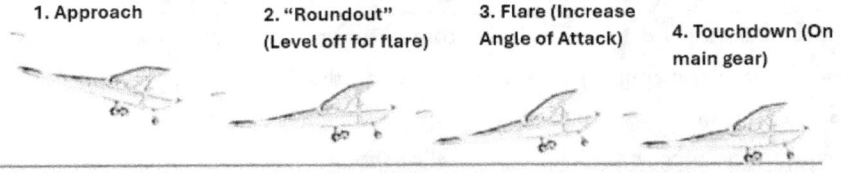

Figure 63: Landing sequence.

To prevent overstressing and damaging the nose gear upon touchdown, the pilot maintains a nose-high attitude by applying increasing back pressure on the control wheel until forward speed significantly decreases. The transition from flying to taxiing requires careful judgment and technique, as landing demands more skill than any other manoeuvre in flight. Crosswinds, wind shear, and variations in air density pose additional challenges during landing.

Considerations for landing include understanding the unique characteristics of each aircraft type, as detailed in its pilot operating handbook. Approaching at an optimal speed, typically 1.3 times the aircraft's stalling speed, is crucial, with adjustments made for varying aircraft weights. Wind conditions influence landing techniques, necessitating adjustments such as flying slightly faster in gusty conditions. Flaps play a significant role in the final approach, reducing stall speed and altering the aircraft's attitude for improved visibility.

The pilot's ability to handle adverse landing scenarios, such as bounces, wheelbarrowing, and balloons, is essential. Prompt decision-making, including the option to go around if any aspect of the landing feels unsatisfactory, is paramount for safety. Upon landing, ailerons should be turned into the wind to prevent gusts from tipping the aircraft.

Troubleshooting Launch Issues

Drone Flipping During Take-off: One of the most common dilemmas encountered by novice drone pilots who have assembled their own craft is the occurrence of flipping during take-off. While rectifying this issue can be straightforward, pinpointing the exact cause can prove challenging due to the various potential culprits.

Incorrect Motor Spin Direction: Flight controllers anticipate each motor to rotate either clockwise or counter-clockwise, contingent upon their placement. Refer to your flight controller manual or datasheet to ascertain the designated motor spin direction, ensuring alignment with the flight controller's configuration.

Improper Propeller Installation: Propellers should rotate to induce downward airflow, with the concave side of the blade facing downwards. Verify that your propellers are rotating in the correct direction and are not installed inverted.

Flight Controller Orientation: Certain flight controllers offer flexibility in mounting positions, allowing for sideways, angled, or upside-down placement. If your flight controller is positioned unconventionally, ensure its configuration reflects this adjustment.

Radio System Malfunction: Effective antenna placement is pivotal for optimal wireless connectivity. Factors such as power, antenna quality, and unobstructed line-of-sight significantly influence signal strength.

Radio Amplification: While amplifiers can enhance signal strength and extend operational range, they may cause receiver saturation at close proximity. Consequently, reliance on amplified signals heightens vulnerability to radio connection disruption due to minor obstructions.

Propeller Detachment Mid-flight: Though infrequent, propeller detachment poses a risk of substantial damage. Utilizing self-tightening propellers sourced from reputable suppliers can mitigate the likelihood of propeller dislodgement. Additionally, applying Loctite Threadlocker to prop securing bolts can prevent loosening during flight.

Shortened Battery Life: Optimal battery storage conditions entail room temperature, shaded environments with low humidity. Exposure to high temperatures and humidity can compromise internal battery chemistry, leading to diminished capacity and shortened flight durations.

Defective Manufacturer Batteries: Instances of defective batteries may necessitate replacement. Contact the manufacturer to explore options for battery replacement if you suspect a defect.

General Approach

Hovering and Landing: Hovering, the act of maintaining a stable position in mid-air, can pose a challenge for novice pilots but can be mastered with consistent practice. To begin, ensure the drone is at least 24 inches above the ground level. Utilize the throttle to elevate the drone and the right joystick to control its position. Practice hovering for at least 10-12 seconds to develop proficiency, adjusting the throttle gradually when preparing to land. Regular practice is key to honing hovering skills.

Take-off Procedure: Before initiating take-off, ensure all pre-flight checks have been completed. Power on the remote control without extending the RC antenna to prevent interference with the drone's GPS system. Position the drone on a level surface facing away from the pilot, then insert the LiPo battery pack. The drone will emit startup beeps, indicating readiness. Close the dome and refrain from manually moving the drone further to prevent engine activation on tilted surfaces. Power up the base station and start the downlink decoder software to receive communication and drone status updates. The drone will conduct a self-test and search for GPS signals, indicated by a rhythm of beeps. Wait until the drone signals readiness for take-off, then start the motors by adjusting the slider and joystick accordingly. Maintain a safe distance from the drone to prevent interference with the RC signal and ensure a stable take-off.

Manoeuvring: After mastering hovering and take-off, manoeuvring the drone involves flying it forward, backward, left, and right. Control the throttle to keep the drone airborne and use the right stick to manoeuvre. Begin by setting the drone to hover, then press the right stick to move it forward or backward. Use the same stick to shift the drone left or right. If the drone begins to rotate (yaw), adjust the left stick to maintain its direction. Regular practice and familiarity with stick movements are essential for precise manoeuvring.

Recovery

To avoid potential accidents, it's crucial to take certain precautions. Firstly, if you find yourself on the brink of a collision, swiftly reduce the throttle to zero to prevent damage to your quadcopter and avoid harming anyone nearby, including yourself. Additionally, always maintain a safe distance from the propellers to prevent accidental injury to your hands while they are in motion. When performing maintenance or adjustments on the drone, remember to remove the battery beforehand. This precaution prevents accidental activation of the propellers, reducing the risk of injury, especially to your fingers. For novice pilots flying indoors, consider securing the drone by tethering it down or enclosing it within a protective cage to minimize the risk of unintended collisions or damage.

UAV designers have explored a wider array of techniques for launching and recovering unmanned aircraft compared to their manned counterparts. This innovation stems not only from the freedom of not having to prioritize crew safety but also from design constraints such as deck space, transportability, and cost. For instance, the US Army's gun-launched Quick Look reconnaissance projectile/UAV experiences nearly 15,000 Gs of acceleration at launch, while the US Air Force's X-7 ramjet testbed was recovered javelin-like by burying its nose in the ground [63].

The selection of launch and recovery techniques for a particular UAV depends on its mission requirements, which typically revolve around three main considerations: operating environment, logistics, and cost. Environmental factors include the size and shape of the launch/recovery area, terrain features, mobility requirements, and the need for covert operations. Logistics considerations focus on transportability and expendables, while cost considerations involve design-to-cost trade-offs.

Launch and recovery techniques fall into three general categories: prepared surfaces, point methods, and airborne methods. Prepared surfaces, utilized by larger UAVs, do not require additional equipment but may pose challenges in handling crosswinds and securing the area. Point methods, such as zero-length launches or recoveries into nets, mitigate these concerns but may stress the UAV structure, leading to heavier airframes and reduced mission effectiveness. Airborne techniques offer solutions to environmental and logistical challenges but add complexity and expense to the UAV system [63].

Prepared surface methods include conventional take-offs, tow line launching, rotary launches, car rack launches, and catapult launches. Point launch methods involve catapults, zero-length launchers, artillery tube launches, mortar launches, and hand launching. Airborne launch methods include air drops, carrier launches, balloon or blimp tows, and parasail launches.

Recovery techniques encompass a variety of options, including conventional landings, arrested landings, net recoveries, parachute recoveries, parafoil recoveries, water landings, commanded stall landings, and vertical landings. Automated landing systems have also been developed to reduce aircraft losses and shorten pilot training, although they add weight, complexity, and cost to the system.

Looking ahead, UAVs may see advancements in launch and recovery methods, including operations from submarines and the deployment of swarms of micro air vehicles from manned or unmanned aircraft. Additionally, the development of unmanned spaceplanes could open new possibilities for aerial operations.

Deep stall refers to a flight condition wherein an aircraft tilts at exceptionally high angles beyond the stall angle, leading to a rapid loss of speed and altitude. This technique can be utilized for executing precise landings in constrained areas. Their compact size, lightweight, and specialized construction help prevent damage. Figure 1.2 illustrates the various phases of a vertical trajectory during a Deep Stall crash/landing manoeuvre.

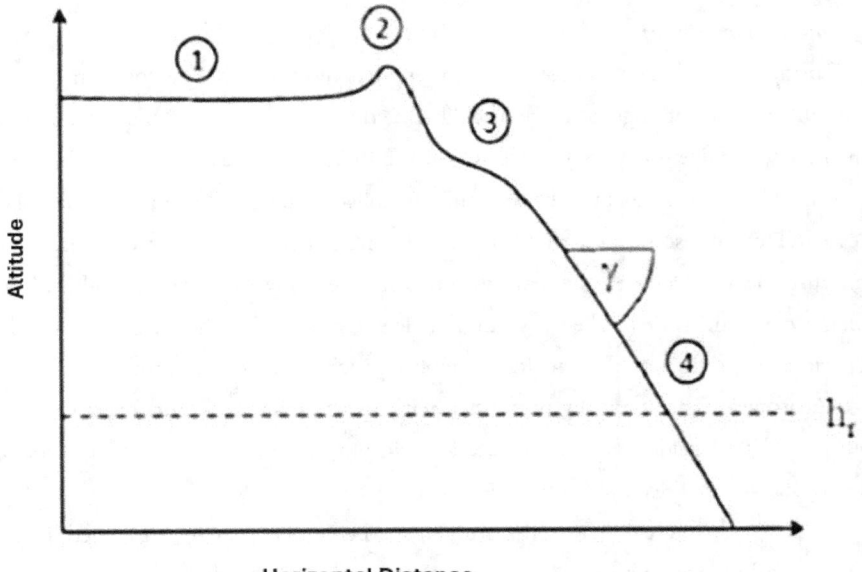

Figure 64: Phases of a deep stall crash landing.

Initially, at (1), the aircraft maintains steady level flight before initiating the deep stall crash/landing manoeuvre. Subsequently, at (2), the manoeuvre commences by shutting down the engine and tilting the UAV beyond the stall angle, thereby increasing Drag and reducing Lift forces, causing the UAV to descend and decelerate horizontally. The UAV briefly ascends due to its momentum before transitioning to the next phase. At (3), the UAV enters the descent phase to reach the target. The point marked as (4) indicates the minimum altitude where a recovery manoeuvre can be executed to prevent a complete crash in case of a missed approach. The angle γ is referred to as the flight path angle. However, flying at high degrees of tilt angle in deep stall conditions is often synonymous with a loss of control.

Furthermore, failing to control the descent of the aircraft increases the landing area. This occurs because as the wings enter deep stall flight, the airflow starts to separate from the wing's leading edge. This detached airflow is turbulent and unstable, making it challenging to model and control the UAV. Therefore, implementing a controlled Deep Stall crash-landing approach is essential for the UAV's functionality. Various approaches can achieve this task, with the most precise method involving predicting the aircraft's location beforehand. A highly accurate mathematical model can elucidate all the forces acting on the aircraft during flight.

Single Rotor Aircraft

During powered flight, helicopters utilize engine power to overcome rotor drag. However, in the event of engine failure or deliberate disengagement from the rotor system, an alternative force is required to sustain rotor RPM and enable controlled flight to the ground. This force is generated by adjusting the collective pitch, allowing for a controlled descent. During descent, the airflow provides the energy necessary to overcome blade drag and turn the rotor, a state known as autorotation. Essentially, the pilot trades altitude for energy, converting potential energy into kinetic energy stored in the turning rotor. This kinetic energy is then used to facilitate a smooth touchdown near the ground.

Autorotations are typically performed with forward airspeed, but for explanation purposes, let's consider vertical autorotation without forward airspeed. In this scenario, the rotor disk is divided into three regions:

1. The driven region, near the blade tips, experiences a drag force inclined slightly behind the rotating axis, slowing the rotation of the blade.

2. The driving region, spanning most of the blade radius, produces thrust inclined slightly forward of the axis of rotation, accelerating blade rotation.

3. The stall region, at the inboard section of the blade, operates above the stall angle of attack and causes drag, further slowing blade rotation.

The forces acting on each region vary due to differences in rotational relative wind speed along the blade length. Adjusting collective pitch, autorotative RPM, or rate of descent alters the size of each region, affecting blade rotation.

Entry into autorotation occurs after engine failure, indicated by rapid rotor RPM decay and an out-of-trim condition. The pilot must swiftly reduce collective pitch to prevent excessive RPM decay and establish a glide at the appropriate airspeed. Airflow changes as the helicopter descends, maintaining equilibrium and stabilizing rotor RPM and descent rate.

To prepare for touchdown, the pilot reduces airspeed and descent rate by adjusting the cyclic control to incline the rotor disk's total force rearward, increasing blade angle of attack and lifting force. This action slows forward speed and reduces descent rate, increasing RPM and kinetic energy for a smoother touchdown.

Successfully executing an autorotative landing requires precise control inputs to manage airspeed, descent rate, and rotor RPM, ultimately ensuring a safe touchdown.

Hazardous Attitudes, Aeronautical Decision-Making and Judgment

Throughout each flight, pilots are constantly faced with decisions concerning interactions between four key risk elements: the pilot in command, the airplane, the environment, and the operation. This decision-making process involves thoroughly evaluating each of these elements to gain an accurate perception of the flight situation. A pivotal decision for the pilot in command is the go/no-go determination, which hinges on assessing these risk elements to determine whether the flight should proceed or be aborted. Let's delve into each of these elements and their impact on decision-making in various scenarios.

Regarding the pilot, decisions must be made regarding competency, health condition, mental state, fatigue level, and other variables that may affect flight safety. For instance, if a pilot has had minimal sleep and is showing signs of illness, it may be wise to reconsider the feasibility of undertaking a long flight, as demonstrated by a pilot who declined a flight request due to fatigue and potential illness.

Assessing the airplane involves evaluating its performance, equipment functionality, and airworthiness. For example, a pilot's astute judgment led to delaying take-off after noticing oil leakage, resulting in the discovery of a loose oil cooler hose fitting during inspection by a mechanic.

The environment encompasses weather conditions, air traffic control, navigation aids, terrain features, and obstacles. Misjudgement of environmental factors can lead to errors, such as underestimating the impact of wake turbulence during landing, resulting in a hard landing due to the drifting wake turbulence from a preceding heavy jet.

Operation considerations involve evaluating the purpose of the flight operation and its associated risks. This includes questioning the necessity of the flight, the importance of adhering to the schedule, and weighing the risks involved. For instance, a pilot's decision to push the limits of fuel supply to maintain the schedule during a ferry flight resulted in a potentially hazardous situation that was not worth the risks involved.

To assess risk effectively, analysing accident reports and research data, such as those from the National Transportation Safety Board (NTSB), can provide valuable insights. Understanding accident patterns and statistics can help identify high-risk flight activities and inform decision-making to mitigate potential hazards. For example, recognizing that manoeuvring flight and certain phases like approaches carry a higher risk of fatal accidents can prompt pilots to adopt heightened vigilance and precautionary measures in these situations. Ultimately, informed decision-making based on thorough risk assessment is paramount to ensuring flight safety and reducing the likelihood of accidents.

Aeronautical Decision-Making

Aeronautical decision-making (ADM) entails the unique process of making decisions within the aviation environment. It involves a systematic approach wherein pilots consistently evaluate circumstances to determine the most appropriate course of action based on the latest available information. The significance of acquiring and comprehending effective ADM skills cannot be overstated. Despite advancements in pilot training methods, aircraft technology, and aviation services, accidents persist, with human error remaining a predominant factor. Studies suggest that approximately 80 percent of aviation accidents stem from human factors, with a significant portion occurring during take-off and landing [45]. ADM serves as a systematic framework for assessing risks and managing stress, with a focus on understanding how personal attitudes influence decision-making and how they can be adjusted to enhance safety.

Recognizing the pivotal role of good judgment in aviation safety, the airline industry pioneered training programs aimed at enhancing ADM and reducing accidents attributable to human factors. Crew resource management (CRM) training emerged to promote the effective utilization of available resources in decision-making processes, emphasizing collaboration among flight crew members. The FAA responded to research findings by incorporating decision-making training into pilot certification requirements, with ADM and risk management becoming mandatory topics for sUAS certification.

In 1987, the FAA released six manuals tailored to the decision-making needs of pilots at various skill levels, following extensive research and development efforts [45]. These materials aimed to mitigate decision-related accidents by providing comprehensive training resources. Independent studies confirmed the efficacy of ADM training, demonstrating that pilots who received such instruction made significantly fewer in-flight errors compared to those without ADM training. Moreover, operators implementing ADM training experienced a substantial reduction in accident rates, highlighting the tangible benefits of integrating ADM principles into pilot education and recurrent training programs.

Contrary to common belief, the skill of exercising good judgment can indeed be taught. Traditionally, it was thought that good judgment naturally developed with experience, as pilots accumulated accident-free flight hours. However, the process of decision-making has evolved with the introduction of Aeronautical Decision Making (ADM), which refines conventional decision-making to reduce the likelihood of human error and promote flight safety. ADM offers a structured approach to assessing the impact of changes during a flight on its safety outcome. It encompasses all facets of decision-making and outlines steps for effective decision-making:

1. Recognizing personal attitudes that pose risks to flight safety.

2. Learning techniques for modifying behaviour.

3. Identifying and managing stress.

4. Developing skills in risk assessment.

5. Utilizing all available resources.

6. Evaluating the efficacy of one's ADM skills.

Risk management, a crucial aspect of ADM, aims to proactively identify safety hazards and mitigate associated risks. By adhering to sound decision-making principles, pilots can reduce or eliminate inherent flight risks. Effective decision-making relies on both direct and indirect experiences, akin to the adoption of seat belt usage norms in automotive safety. As pilots navigate through the ADM process, it's imperative to uphold the four fundamental principles of risk management:

1. Avoid unnecessary risks.

2. Delegate risk decisions to those capable of implementing risk controls.

3. Accept risks only when the benefits outweigh the dangers.

4. Integrate risk management into all stages of flight planning and execution.

While lapses in judgment in daily life may not always result in tragedy, the stakes are considerably higher in aviation due to its unforgiving nature. ADM, by enhancing the management of the aeronautical environment, should be embraced and practiced by all pilots to ensure safe and responsible flight operations.

Crew Resource Management (CRM) and Single-Pilot Resource Management Although CRM traditionally targets pilots operating within crew environments, many of its principles are applicable to single-pilot operations. Several CRM concepts have been effectively adapted to single-pilot aircraft, leading to the emergence of Single-Pilot Resource Management (SRM). SRM encompasses the techniques employed by a single pilot to manage all available resources both before and during flight, ensuring a successful outcome. It integrates principles such as Aeronautical Decision Making (ADM), Risk Management (RM), Task Management (TM), Automation Management (AM), Controlled Flight Into Terrain (CFIT) awareness, and Situational Awareness (SA). SRM training assists pilots in maintaining situational awareness by effectively managing automation, aircraft control, and navigation tasks. This enables pilots to accurately evaluate and mitigate risks and make timely and informed decisions. Ultimately, SRM empowers pilots to gather, analyse, and utilize information effectively in their decision-making process.

Hazard and Risk

Two fundamental components of ADM involve hazard and risk. A hazard refers to a tangible or perceived condition, event, or circumstance encountered by a pilot. When confronted with a hazard, the pilot evaluates it based on various factors and assesses its potential impact, thereby determining its risk. Consequently, risk represents an evaluation of either a single or cumulative hazard that a pilot faces; however, different pilots may perceive hazards differently.

Hazardous Attitudes and Antidotes

Being fit to fly encompasses more than just a pilot's physical state and recent experiences; attitude also plays a crucial role in decision-making quality. Attitude, in this context, refers to a motivational predisposition to respond to people, situations, or events in a certain manner. Research has identified five hazardous attitudes—anti-authority, impulsivity, invulnerability, macho, and resignation—that can impede sound decision-making and proper exercise of authority. These hazardous attitudes contribute to poor pilot judgment but can be effectively mitigated by redirecting them towards corrective action. The key to neutralizing hazardous thoughts lies in recognizing them first. Once identified, pilots should acknowledge the hazardous nature of the thought and recall the corresponding antidote. Memorizing these antidotes for each hazardous attitude ensures they are readily available when needed.

Being fit to fly encompasses more than just a pilot's physical condition and recent experiences; attitude plays a crucial role in decision-making quality. Attitude, defined as a personal motivational predisposition to respond to persons, situations, or events, significantly influences a pilot's decision-making process. Studies have identified five hazardous attitudes—anti-authority, impulsivity, invulnerability, macho, and resignation—that can impede sound decision-making and proper exercise of authority.

The Five Hazardous Attitudes:

1. **Anti-Authority:** Pilots exhibiting this attitude resist authority and rules, often feeling resentful or considering regulations unnecessary. However, it is essential to acknowledge the importance of following rules and regulations, recognizing that they are usually in place for safety reasons.

2. **Impulsivity:** Pilots with this attitude act hastily without proper consideration or evaluation of alternatives. It's crucial to remember to pause and think before acting, ensuring a more deliberate and calculated approach to decision-making.

3. **Invulnerability:** Pilots who feel invulnerable believe accidents won't happen to them, leading to a false sense of security and increased risk-taking behaviour. Recognizing that accidents can happen to anyone is vital for maintaining a cautious and safety-conscious mindset.

4. **Macho:** Pilots demonstrating this attitude often seek to prove themselves by taking unnecessary risks, aiming to impress others with their abilities. However, risking safety for the sake of bravado is irresponsible and should be avoided.

5. **Resignation:** Pilots with this attitude feel helpless and passive, believing they have little control over outcomes. It's important to recognize that individuals can make a difference and take proactive steps to ensure safe outcomes.

The pilot must carefully examine decisions to ensure they are not influenced by hazardous attitudes. These attitudes can lead to poor decision-making and actions involving unnecessary risk. Therefore, pilots should be familiar with positive alternatives, or antidotes, to counteract hazardous attitudes. Recognizing hazardous attitudes during flight operations and applying the appropriate antidote when needed is essential for ensuring safety.

Stress Management: Effective stress management is crucial for maintaining performance and decision-making abilities during flight. While a certain level of stress can enhance alertness, prolonged or excessive stress can impair judgment and performance. Recognizing and managing stressors before they impact performance is essential for ensuring safe operations.

Use of Internal & External Resources: Pilots must be aware of both internal and external resources available during flight operations. Internal resources include instruments, procedures, and shared crew knowledge, while external resources encompass air traffic control (ATC) and flight dispatchers. Recognizing and accessing these resources, evaluating their relevance and impact on flight safety, and utilizing them effectively are essential aspects of ADM training.

Workload Management: Effective workload management involves planning, prioritizing, and sequencing tasks to avoid overload. Pilots should anticipate workload requirements and prepare accordingly, especially during high-demand situations. Prioritizing tasks, delegating when necessary, and maintaining focus on essential flight operations are key strategies for managing workload effectively. Recognizing signs of overload and implementing strategies to decrease workload, such as delegating tasks or enlisting ATC assistance, are essential for maintaining safe operations.

Risk assessment is a critical aspect of each flight for single pilots, who must navigate hazardous conditions while making numerous decisions. However, this process is far from straightforward. For instance, single pilots often act as their own quality control when making decisions, leading to potential biases and oversights. A fatigued pilot, for example, may downplay their exhaustion and prioritize mission goals over personal limitations. This tendency to overlook tangible hazards in favour of intangible factors, such as patient welfare in the case of helicopter EMS pilots, poses significant challenges for single pilots without the benefit of crew consultation. Consequently, single pilots face heightened vulnerability when grappling with these intangible factors.

Mitigating risk is a multifaceted endeavour. Single pilots can employ strategies like the IMSAFE checklist to evaluate their physical and mental readiness for flying. This checklist includes assessing factors such as illness, medication effects, stress levels, alcohol consumption, fatigue, and emotional state, all of which can significantly impact flying abilities and safety. Considering these factors proactively is essential for minimizing risk and ensuring safe flight operations.

Utilizing the PAVE checklist is an effective method for mitigating risk by systematically identifying potential hazards in preflight planning. The acronym stands for Pilot-in-command (PIC), Aircraft, enVironment, and External pressures, encompassing key areas of a pilot's decision-making process.

By employing the PAVE checklist, pilots can easily assess each category for risk factors before embarking on a flight. Once risks are identified, pilots must determine if they can be safely managed. If not, the prudent decision is to cancel the flight. For those choosing to proceed, developing strategies to mitigate risks is crucial. One such strategy is setting personal minimums tailored to the pilot's experience and proficiency level.

In the PAVE checklist:

- P stands for Pilot-in-Command, where the pilot evaluates their readiness for the flight based on experience, currency, physical, and emotional condition using the IMSAFE checklist.

- A represents Aircraft, prompting considerations about aircraft suitability, familiarity, and capacity to carry the planned load.

- V denotes enVironment, encompassing weather conditions, terrain evaluation, airspace checks, and awareness of any temporary flight restrictions (TFRs).

- E addresses External Pressures, which are external influences that may compel a pilot to complete a flight despite safety concerns. These pressures include the desire to demonstrate qualifications, impress others, or fulfill personal goals.

Effectively managing external pressures is crucial as they can override other risk factors. Personal standard operating procedures (SOPs) offer a method for mitigating external pressures by providing a structured approach to decision-making and offering a release from the pressures associated with flight operations.

The 3P model, consisting of Perceive-Process-Perform, offers a straightforward and systematic approach applicable to all flight phases. Pilots begin by "perceiving" the current circumstances of the flight, then "processing" by assessing their impact on safety, and finally "performing" by executing the best course of action. This cyclical process is repeated continuously throughout the flight, promoting vigilance and proactive safety measures.

In contrast, the DECIDE Model for ADM (Aeronautical Decision Making) presents a six-step deductive reasoning process for decision-making. While particularly beneficial for novice pilots, it may not fully capture the nuanced decision-making abilities of expert pilots due to differences in mental processing. Nevertheless, the DECIDE model enhances conventional decision-making for novices by increasing awareness, facilitating information gathering, and fostering motivation in selecting and executing actions, ultimately promoting safer outcomes. The steps of the DECIDE model include Detect (detecting changes), Estimate (estimating the need for counter-measures), Choose (choosing a safe outcome), Identify (identifying effective actions), Do (implementing chosen actions), and Evaluate (evaluating the effectiveness of actions and flight progress).

Human Factors

Why are human factors, such as fatigue, complacency, and stress, critical in aviation? These factors, among others, collectively known as human factors, directly contribute to or cause a significant portion of aviation accidents, accounting for over 70 percent of such incidents. While traditionally associated with flight operations, human factor incidents and accidents have increasingly become a concern in aviation maintenance and air traffic management. In response, the FAA has prioritized the study and research of human factors, collaborating with professionals across various aviation domains to integrate the latest insights into daily operations, aiming to enhance safety and efficiency [45].

Human factors science, or human factors technologies, encompasses a multidisciplinary approach drawing from psychology, engineering, industrial design, statistics, operations research, and anthropometry. It encompasses understanding human capabilities, applying this understanding to system design and deployment, and ensuring the successful application of human factor principles throughout aviation, including pilots, air traffic controllers, and maintenance personnel. Although often equated with Crew Resource Management (CRM) or Maintenance Resource Management (MRM), human factors extends beyond these domains in both its breadth of knowledge and application. It involves collecting research specific to various contexts, such as flight operations, maintenance, and stress levels, to inform the design of tools, machines, systems, tasks, jobs, and environments, with the aim of facilitating safe, comfortable, and effective human interaction. The aviation community as a whole benefits significantly from ongoing human factors research and development, as it enhances understanding of how individuals can perform their roles safely and efficiently while improving the tools and systems with which they interact.

Situational Awareness

Situational awareness encompasses the accurate perception and understanding of all factors and conditions within the five fundamental risk elements of aviation: flight, pilot, aircraft, environment, and type of operation [45]. This awareness is crucial for ensuring safety before, during, and after a flight. Maintaining situational awareness involves comprehending the relative significance of various flight-related factors and their potential impact on the flight trajectory. Rather than fixating on one perceived significant factor, a pilot needs to have an overview of the entire operation. Knowing the geographical location of the aircraft is important, but understanding the unfolding events is equally essential.

Several factors can impede the maintenance of situational awareness, including fatigue, stress, and work overload. These factors may cause a pilot to focus excessively on one particular aspect, thereby diminishing their overall awareness of the flight. Distractions, in particular, can divert the pilot's attention away from monitoring the aircraft, increasing the risk of accidents.

Effective workload management is essential for ensuring that essential operations are completed without overwhelming the pilot. This involves planning, prioritizing, and sequencing tasks to avoid excessive workloads. With experience, pilots learn to anticipate periods of high workload during times of lower activity. Additionally, staying informed about weather conditions through sources like ATIS, ASOS, or AWOS, and monitoring traffic conditions via tower frequency or CTAF can provide valuable situational context.

Recognizing signs of work overload is crucial for managing workload effectively. Symptoms may include increased effort with reduced productivity, inability to focus on multiple tasks, and incomplete decision-making due to information overload. When facing work overload, pilots should pause, assess, slow down, and prioritize tasks to mitigate the risk of errors. Understanding strategies to decrease workload is essential for maintaining situational awareness and ensuring safe flight operations.

Communications

Clear and effective communication between pilots and controllers is crucial for safe aerodrome operations. You can contribute to enhancing the controller's understanding by responding appropriately and adhering to standard phraseology.

Here are guidelines to ensure clear and accurate communications:

- Utilize standard phraseology when contacting ATC to facilitate clear and concise communication. Your initial transmission should include:

    - The entity you are addressing

    - Your call sign

    - Your current location

    - A brief description of your request or intention.

- Always state your position when initiating contact with any tower or ground controller, regardless of whether you've previously communicated your position to another controller.

- Focus solely on ATC instructions during communication and avoid engaging in non-essential tasks.

Ensure good radio technique by following these practices:

- Prepare your transmission beforehand, ensuring it is well thought out. Before transmitting, confirm you are on the correct frequency and won't interrupt ongoing communications.

- Keep communications concise and to the point, especially for unusual situations or lengthy communications.

- Acknowledge all clearances by reading back the required elements and concluding with your call sign.

- Read back any holding points or instructions related to runway activities, such as holding short, entering, landing, or crossing a runway.

- Monitor the assigned tower frequency for potential conflicts involving your runway when holding on a runway for take-off or on final approach.

- Clarify any misunderstandings or confusion regarding ATC instructions or clearances promptly.

In case you encounter an aircraft on the runway you've been cleared to land on:
- Assume the controller is aware of the situation and has issued appropriate instructions to the other aircraft. However, if you have doubts or feel uncomfortable with the spacing, query the clearance with the controller, referencing the other traffic, and be prepared to execute a go-around if necessary.

Here are examples (Australian) of taxi instructions to illustrate proper communication:

[Initial Call-up Example]

Pilot: "Essendon Ground, Alpha Bravo Charlie, GA Park, received Alpha, to Sydney, request taxi."

Controller: "Alpha Bravo Charlie, Essendon Ground, taxi to Holding Point Echo, Runway One Seven."

Pilot: "Holding Point Echo, Runway One Seven, Alpha Bravo Charlie."

[Another Example]

Pilot: "Bankstown Ground, Helo Forty Four, request air taxi from Heli Tours to the main pad."

Controller: "Helo Forty Four, Bankstown Ground, air taxi to the main pad, cross Runway Two Niner Left, Centre, and Right."

Pilot: "Cross Runway Two Niner Left, Centre, and Right, Helo Forty Four."

Initial call-up with specific request

Make clear any special requests on initial contact

EXAMPLE

Pilot: Melbourne Ground, Qantas Five Forty Two, Boeing 737, received Alpha, squawk four three two one, Bay Twenty, IFR, to Sydney request taxi and intersection departure from Juliet.

Controller: Qantas Five Forty Two, Melbourne Ground, taxi to Holding Point Juliet, Runway Three Four.

Pilot: Holding Point Juliet, Runway Three Four, Qantas Five Forty Two.

'Line up and wait'

Read back all 'line up' and 'line up and wait' instructions, including the runway designator when transmitted by ATC or when there is a possibility of confusion.

EXAMPLE

Controller: Virgin Two Thirty Two, line up and wait Runway Two Seven.

Pilot: Line up and wait, Runway Two Seven, Virgin Two Thirty Two.

Conditional clearance

A pilot receiving a conditional clearance must identify the aircraft or vehicle causing the conditional clearance before proceeding in accordance with the clearance.

EXAMPLE

Controller: Alpha Bravo Charlie, behind Cessna on short final line up behind.

Pilot: Behind the Cessna, lining up, Alpha Bravo Charlie.

Take-off clearance/landing clearance

Read back all take-off and landing clearances with a call sign, including the runway designator when transmitted by ATC or when there is a possibility of confusion.

EXAMPLE

Controller: Alpha Bravo Charlie, Runway Three Four, cleared for take-off.

Pilot: Runway Three Four, cleared for take-off, Alpha Bravo Charlie.

EXAMPLE

Controller: Qantas Two Twenty-Two, Runway Three Four, cleared to land.

Pilot: Cleared to land, Runway Three Four, Qantas Two Twenty-Two.

'Land and hold short' (LAHSO)

Land and hold short instructions require pilot readback.

EXAMPLE

Controller: Virgin Five Thirty Four a Cessna 441 landing on crossing runway, hold short Runway Two Seven, cleared to land Runway Three Four.

Pilot: Hold short Runway Two Seven, cleared to land Runway Three Four, Virgin Five Thirty Four.

EXAMPLE

Controller: Qantas Thirty Three, Boeing 737 landing on crossing runway will hold short – Runway Two Seven cleared for take-off.

Pilot: Runway Two Seven, cleared for take-off, Qantas Thirty-Three.

Initial contact after exiting runway

You are expected to exit the runway at the first available taxiway or as instructed by ATC.

You should contact ground control as soon as possible after exiting the runway.

EXAMPLE

Pilot: Cairns Ground, Alpha Bravo Charlie, Bay Two.

Controller: Alpha Bravo Charlie, Cairns Ground, taxi to Bay Two, cross Runway One Two.

Pilot: Cross Runway One Two, Alpha Bravo Charlie.

When instructed to taxi to a runway for departure, you must read back the holding point specified in the taxi clearance.

EXAMPLE

Controller: Alpha Bravo Charlie, taxi to Holding Point Tango Runway One Seven.

Pilot: Holding Point Tango, Runway One Seven, Alpha Bravo Charlie.

Radio Operations (USA Perspective)

Effective radio communications are vital for ensuring the safe operation of aircraft within the National Airspace System (NAS). Pilots rely on radio communications to exchange crucial information before, during, and after flights. This exchange of information facilitates the smooth flow of aircraft traffic, both in complex airspace areas and in less populated regions. Additionally, pilots use radio communications to report unexpected weather conditions and in-flight emergencies, enhancing overall safety.

While small unmanned aircraft (UA) pilots may not typically communicate over radio frequencies, it is still essential for them to grasp the fundamentals of aviation language.

Understanding common radio conversations aids UA pilots in maintaining situational awareness when operating within the NAS [45]. Although much of the guidance provided pertains to manned aircraft pilots, it is equally important for UA pilots to comprehend the unique communication protocols used within the NAS.

Understanding proper radio procedures is crucial for pilots to operate safely and efficiently within the airspace system. Familiarizing oneself with the Pilot/Controller Glossary found in the Aeronautical Information Manual (AIM) assists pilots in understanding standard radio terminology. Moreover, the AIM provides numerous examples of radio communications to further enhance understanding [45].

The International Civil Aviation Organization (ICAO) has adopted a phonetic alphabet for radio communications, which pilots should utilize when identifying their aircraft to air traffic control (ATC).

When operating at airports without operating control towers, pilots must remain vigilant and maintain awareness of other air traffic in the vicinity. This is especially important as some aircraft may not have communication capability, or pilots may not communicate their presence or intentions. To enhance safety, all radio-equipped aircraft should transmit and receive on a common frequency, and small UA pilots should monitor other aircraft identified for airport advisories.

Airports without operating control towers may have various communication facilities, including flight service stations (FSS), universal communications (UNICOM) stations, or no aeronautical stations at all. Pilots can communicate their intentions and obtain airport/traffic information by contacting an FSS, a UNICOM operator, or by making self-announce broadcasts.

Many airports now offer automated weather, radio check capability, and airport advisory information through automated UNICOM systems. These systems provide various features selectable by microphone clicks on the UNICOM frequency, with availability published in the Airport/Facility Directory and approach charts.

Effective communication at airports without operating control towers relies on selecting the correct common frequency, often referred to as the Common Traffic Advisory Frequency (CTAF). The CTAF serves as the designated frequency for conducting airport advisory practices when operating to or from airports without operating control towers. This frequency may be a UNICOM, MULTICOM, FSS, or tower frequency, as indicated in relevant aeronautical publications.

For airports without FSS or UNICOM facilities, a MULTICOM frequency of 122.9 is typically used for communication and broadcast procedures.

While it's not mandatory for a remote pilot-in-command to engage in radio communication with manned aircraft near non-towered airports, safety within the National Airspace System dictates that remote pilots should be well-versed in traffic patterns, radio protocols, and phraseology.

When planning to operate near a non-towered airport, the first step in radio procedures is identifying the appropriate frequencies. Most non-towered airports will have a UNICOM frequency, typically 122.8, although it's essential to verify this information through the Chart Supplements U.S. or sectional chart, as frequencies can vary [45]. In cases where a non-towered airport lacks a UNICOM or any listed frequency, the MULTICOM frequency of 122.9 is utilized. These frequencies are accessible on sectional charts or in the FAA's Chart Supplements publication.

For manned aircraft inbound to a non-towered airport, standard operating practice involves broadcasting "in the blind" when approximately 10 miles from the airport. This initial call should include the aircraft's position relative to north, south, east, or west from the airport. For instance: "Town and Country traffic, Cessna 123 Bravo Foxtrot is 10 miles south inbound for landing, Town and Country traffic."

During broadcasts at a non-towered airport, manned aircraft should mention the airport's name at both the beginning and end of the broadcast to confirm the destination for others on the frequency. Subsequent broadcasts include: "Town and Country traffic, Cessna 123 Bravo Foxtrot, is entering the pattern, mid-field left downwind for runway 18, Town and Country traffic."

As the aircraft enters the traffic pattern, it may follow a standard 45-degree entry to the downwind leg or opt for a straight-in approach, typically utilized for instrument approaches: "Town and Country traffic, Cessna 123 Bravo Foxtrot, is one mile north of the airport, GPS runway 18, full stop landing, Town and Country traffic."

During the landing phase, additional broadcasts should be made: "Town and Country traffic, Cessna 123 Bravo Foxtrot, left base, runway 18, Town and Country traffic." "Town and Country traffic, Cessna 123 Bravo Foxtrot, final, runway 18, Town and Country traffic."

Once clear of the runway, the following broadcast is necessary: "Town and Country traffic, Cessna 123 Bravo Foxtrot, is clear of runway 18, taxiing to park, Town and Country traffic."

Similar procedures apply when departing a non-towered airport: "Town and Country traffic, Cessna 123 Bravo Foxtrot, departing runway 18, Town and Country traffic."

While manned aircraft making radio broadcasts near non-towered airports is a recommended practice, it's not mandatory by regulation. Therefore, remote pilots must remain vigilant, scanning the area for other aircraft, and using radio communication to enhance situational awareness for added safety.

Understanding aircraft call signs is crucial for a remote pilot operating near any airport, whether it's towered or non-towered. While 14 CFR part 107 mandates remote pilots to obtain authorization for certain airport areas, it's advisable for them to have a radio to monitor relevant frequencies. However, it's imperative for remote pilots to refrain from transmitting over any active aviation frequency unless faced with an emergency.

Aviation communication involves unique procedures, unfamiliar to remote pilots without prior exposure to "aviation language." One such aspect is aircraft call signs. Every aircraft registered in the United States is assigned a unique registration number, commonly known as an "N" number. For instance, N123AB would be articulated using the phonetic alphabet as "November One-Two-Three-Alpha-Bravo." Typically, "November" is substituted with the aircraft manufacturer's name (make), or occasionally the aircraft type (model). Light general aviation (GA) aircraft usually use the manufacturer's name, such as "Cessna, One-Two-Three-Alpha-Bravo" for a Cessna 172. Conversely, heavier GA aircraft like turbo-props or turbo-jets use the aircraft's model, such as "Citation, One-Two-Three-Alpha-Bravo" for a Cessna Citation. Commercial airliners typically use their company name along with their flight number, for example, "Southwest-Seven-One-One" for Southwest Airlines flight 711. However, there are exceptions like British Airways, which uses "Speedbird" instead of its company name.

In summary, remote pilots are not required to communicate with other aircraft near airports unless in an emergency. However, for safety within the National Airspace System (NAS), it's essential for remote pilots to grasp aviation terminology and be aware of the various types of aircraft that may be operating in the vicinity of a small UA.

Drones Utilizing 4G Technology in the UK

As of January 20, 2023, the UK Spectrum Licensing Authority, also known as Ofcom, introduced a new UAS Radio Operators Licence, marking a significant advancement in enabling drones to operate beyond visual line of sight (BVLOS). This license provides authorization for a diverse range of equipment that operators may choose to employ or may be obliged to carry onboard as per the stipulations of the Civil Aviation Authority (CAA) [64]. Notably, this includes drones equipped with 4G LTE technology. The issuance of this license is indefinite, contingent upon the annual payment of a license fee.

For drones solely utilizing spectrum designated for Wi-Fi or model aircraft, there is no requirement to obtain a license, as they are already exempt under existing regulations. Therefore, there is no alteration for drones currently in operation.

The UAS Operator Radio Licence grants spectrum authorization for the utilization of various radio equipment on drones. This encompasses equipment for command and control, encompassing mobile and satellite terminals, as well as other safety systems [64]. This facilitates UAS operators to access a breadth of technologies that could enhance their capability to offer a wider array of services over extended distances.

Furthermore, the UAS Operator Radio Licence provides spectrum access authorization for drones employing alternative technologies that permit higher powers, thereby enabling an expanded operational range.

This license encompasses spectrum authorization for a variety of radio equipment, including:

- UAS 'command and control' functions, facilitating remote pilot control and navigation commands, as well as managing the launch, flight, and recovery of the drone.

- Payload data relaying, enabling the transmission of video and data back to the remote pilot.

- 'Electronic Conspicuity', allowing other users to track the UAS's location and flight path.

- 'Detect and Avoid' capabilities, enabling drones to autonomously evade obstacles, such as other drones, that pose a risk.

- Communications, navigation, and surveillance systems, enabling Air Traffic Controllers to monitor and manage flights as required by the CAA.

VHF Transmitter Licensing (Australia)

Licensing for VHF transmitters is managed by the Australian Communications and Media Authority (ACMA), which issues a class license permitting individuals to operate aircraft stations or aeronautical mobile stations, provided they adhere to the license conditions. The Recreational Aviation Administration Organizations (RAAO) provide VHF radio operator endorsements as a certification of compliance with the Authority's standards for operating VHF aircraft or aeronautical mobile stations. However, it's essential to note that RAAOs cannot issue endorsements for HF transceivers, and individuals intending to make airborne radio transmissions on aviation HF frequencies must hold a CASA flight radiotelephone operator license.

The ACMA issues a class license to license all operational radio transmitters, including VHF and HF aviation radiotelephony transceivers, transponders, or distress beacons carried in aircraft. This class license, known as the Radiocommunications (Aircraft and Aeronautical Mobile Stations) Class Licence 2006 (CL2006), replaces the previous Aircraft Station Class Licence 2001. CL2006 permits qualified operators to operate various aeronautical radiocommunications and radionavigation equipment installed on aircraft or used in most ground-based aeronautical mobile radiocommunications.

Aircraft stations can transmit only when onboard an aircraft, using the aircraft's station call sign for identification. Any breach of CL2006 conditions renders the operator unauthorized to operate under the class license and may lead to prosecution by the ACMA.

Aeronautical mobile stations, like aircraft stations, are authorized for communications related to safe flight conduct, emergencies, or specific occupational or industry-related matters. Operators must clearly identify the mobile station during transmissions.

Equipment used for aircraft stations must comply with specified standards, and only Civil Aviation Safety Authority (CASA) approved apparatus may be used for fixed installations. Hand-held VHF aviation band radiotelephones may be used by pilots of recreational aircraft in Class G airspace if they meet safety criteria outlined in regulatory documents.

Aircraft stations must have individual identification or call signs, typically derived from the aircraft's registration marking. Different call-sign formats are used for recreational and sport aircraft, each following specific patterns based on the type and registration number.

Aeronautical stations, including those operated by aero clubs, flying schools, or parachute clubs, are licensed by ACMA to operate in the aviation VHF band. Communication frequency symbols are denoted in kilohertz (kHz) for HF and megahertz (MHz) for VHF and UHF bands.

Regulations govern communication limitations, unauthorized communications, and the confidentiality of transmitted messages. It is mandatory for all transmissions to be conducted in English, using standard phraseology and phonetic alphabets, without profanity, deception, or improper use of call signs.

Operating frequencies for aircraft stations, approved by Airservices Australia, are chiefly within the aviation VHF communications band, with channel separations depending on airspace classification and frequency stability standards. A dedicated aviation VHF band exists for navigation facilities, known as the NAV band, while the full aviation VHF band serves both navigation and communication purposes.

Some specific aviation operational frequencies are:

- Aero club operations — 119.1 MHz

- Flying school operations — 119.1 MHz

- Fire spotting — 119.1 MHz

- Parachute club operations — 119.2 MHz

- Aviation sport — 120.85 MHz

- Emergency location — 121.5 MHz (plus 243.0 and 406.025 in the UHF band)

- Glider/sailplane operation — 122.5, 122.7, 122.9 MHz

- Fishing or agricultural operations or stock mustering — 122.8 MHz

- Pilot-to-pilot communications — 123.45 MHz

- Traffic information aircraft broadcasts — 126.35 MHz

- Aircraft industry testing — 129.1 MHz

- Crop dusting — 129.6 MHz

- Aerodrome operator, including refueller — 129.9 MHz

- Air show — 127.9 MHz

- Charter and other purposes not listed — 126.4, 128.9, 135.55 MHz

- Search and rescue only — 121.5, 123.1, 123.2 MHz (plus the 156.3, 156.8 MHz marine band frequencies)

At airfields situated within Class G airspace, there are designated areas known as common traffic advisory frequency (CTAF) areas. These areas encompass all reasonably active airfields and require pilots to adhere to specific monitoring and reporting procedures to ensure safe separation and facilitate movement priorities when necessary.

The VHF frequency designated for communication at each CTAF is specified in documents such as the En Route Supplement Australia (ERSA), as well as Visual Navigation Charts (VNC), Visual Terminal Charts (VTC), Planning Charts Australia (PCA), and En Route Charts (ERC-L). Additionally, some CTAF airfields may operate a private ground-based information service called 'Unicom', with its operating frequency aligning with the airfield's VHF frequency specified in ERSA.

For inter-pilot air-to-air communication while en route, a designated frequency of 123.45 MHz is utilized. This frequency serves as the regional air-to-air channel when aircraft are operating in remote areas beyond the range of VHF ground stations. Communications on this frequency are limited to the exchange of information pertinent to aircraft operations, and only authorized call signs may be used.

Regarding radio operator qualification, individuals operating aircraft stations must meet the requirements outlined in the Radiocommunications (Aircraft and Aeronautical Mobile Stations) Class Licence 2006 (CL2006). This entails being qualified in accordance with the Civil Aviation Regulations and relevant Civil Aviation Orders. The Chief Flying Instructor of an approved flight training facility has the authority to recommend the issuance of a radio operator's endorsement following an evaluation of the applicant's performance during flight operations and an oral or written examination. The examination covers the syllabus outlined in manuals provided by Recreational Aviation Administration Organizations (RAAOs), such as the RA-Aus Operations Manual section 3.08.

In Class G airspace, transmissions from aircraft stations primarily fall into three categories. Firstly, there are advisory broadcasts, which serve to inform other nearby stations of the pilot's whereabouts and intentions for traffic separation purposes. Acknowledgement of these broadcasts is not expected. Secondly, there are station-to-station calls, where a pilot requests specific information from Airservices Australia flight information service, another aircraft station, or an aerodrome ground station. Thirdly, responses to other aircraft or ground stations involve supplying specific information in response to a request or an advisory broadcast indicating a potential traffic conflict.

Most transmissions within Class G airspace occur when aircraft are near non-controlled airfields. These transmissions typically take the form of broadcasts, as mandated by CAR 166C, whenever necessary to prevent collisions or the risk thereof with other aircraft in the vicinity. While broadcasts to avoid collisions are mandatory, other transmissions are discretionary, but pilots should adhere to a standard broadcast structure to minimize frequency congestion.

To ensure effective communication, it's essential to use aviation English and keep transmissions concise. However, it's crucial to balance the need for communication with the goal of minimizing frequency congestion. Pilots must exercise judgment to determine when and what transmissions are necessary for safe and efficient traffic flow, considering the diverse backgrounds of pilots, including those from overseas.

In the vicinity of airfields within Class G airspace, common traffic advisory frequencies (CTAFs) play a vital role. Airservices Australia assigns discrete VHF frequencies to public-use non-controlled aerodromes with significant daily movements. Pilots operating near these airfields should monitor the designated CTAF frequency specified in ERSA, VNC, VTC, and ERC-L charts. If an airfield lacks a discrete CTAF, the default Multicom frequency of 126.7 MHz should be used. Larger broadcast areas have defined airspace volumes with allocated CTAFs, indicated on aeronautical charts.

Pilots should also be aware of regulatory requirements outlined in CARs 166, 166A, 166B, 166C, 166D, and 166E for operations at non-controlled aerodromes. Compliance with these regulations ensures safe and efficient communication practices. Additionally, the use of certified air/ground radio services (CA/GRS) and Unicom services can provide valuable assistance to pilots, offering essential information such as wind, weather, and traffic advisories within the CTAF. Access to AIP Book and ERSA resources online facilitates access to relevant information for effective communication and navigation.

Prescribed CTAF broadcast formats adhere to a structured sequence, ensuring clear and concise communication among aircraft stations within Class G airspace. These broadcasts typically consist of six key elements, presented in a consistent order:

1. **Location**: The general area or airfield name.

2. **Called station's ID**: Typically "TRAFFIC," addressing all nearby aircraft stations and possibly ground stations maintaining a listening watch on the CTAF.

3. **Calling station's ID**: The aircraft call-sign, including aircraft type and registration.

4. **Calling station's position**: Where the aircraft is located, often referenced to the airfield.

5. **Calling station's intentions**: The pilot's intended actions.

6. **Location repeated**: Reiterating the general area or airfield name for clarity.

For broadcast transmissions where a specific response is not expected, such as taxiing or entering a runway, the called station's ID is usually "TRAFFIC." However, if seeking a response, the called station's ID may be "ANY STATION" or "ANY TRAFFIC" preceded by the location name.

The format varies depending on the purpose of the transmission. For instance, a taxiing call notifies other aircraft of the intention to taxi to a runway, while an entering runway call alerts traffic in the circuit or clearing the runway of the intent to use the runway for take-off. Similarly, inbound, transit, and joining circuit calls provide relevant information to other pilots about the aircraft's position, intentions, and altitude.

Broadcast etiquette emphasizes the importance of clarity, brevity, and adherence to aviation English. Pilots are encouraged to compose their messages mentally before transmitting, speak distinctly and at a normal pace, and avoid superfluous words or non-aviation English phrasing. Additionally, pilots should listen out for ongoing transmissions to avoid broadcasting over others and operate the press-to-talk switch before speaking to ensure the full message is transmitted.

Overall, adherence to prescribed CTAF broadcast formats and broadcast etiquette enhances communication effectiveness and contributes to safe operations within Class G airspace.

During flight, there are instances where additional or discretionary radio calls can enhance safety and situational awareness among aircraft operating within Class G airspace. Although it's generally advised to minimize radio transmissions, certain traffic conditions or actions, such as a go-around or departure from the circuit, may warrant extra communication. These discretionary calls, while typically briefer than standard broadcasts, serve to keep all pilots informed and maintain safe separation.

Going Around Call Format: If a landing must be aborted, broadcasting a go-around call can alert other aircraft. The format typically includes the location, aircraft call-sign, and the action being taken, such as "GOING AROUND" followed by the runway number.

Departure Call Format: When departing from the circuit after activities like touch-and-goes, informing other aircraft about your departure intentions can be beneficial. This call typically includes the location, aircraft call-sign, and details of departure, such as "DEPARTING FOR [destination]."

Requesting Information: There are situations where requesting information from other aircraft is appropriate, such as inquiring about the active runway. Using the call "ANY STATION" followed by the location and the request, pilots can seek relevant details.

Communicating with Unicom or CA/GRS Stations: When inbound to an airfield with Unicom or CA/GRS service, pilots may request information regarding wind and traffic. Ground operators provide relevant details, and pilots acknowledge receipt of the information.

CTAF Response Calls: In response to broadcasts from other aircraft indicating possible traffic conflicts, maintaining situational awareness is crucial. Pilots must project the movements of other traffic and communicate intentions clearly to avoid conflicts. Additionally, recreational pilots are encouraged to yield priority to certain aircraft for safety and courtesy.

En Route Procedures: In Class G airspace, there are no mandatory reports for VFR aircraft operating en-route. However, maintaining a listening watch on the appropriate frequency and announcing potential conflicts with other aircraft is advised. The appropriate frequency depends on factors such as proximity to major airports or designated frequencies for specific areas.

In Class E airspace, similar procedures apply, with the addition of the necessity to use the appropriate ATC frequency to take advantage of Radar Information Service. Overall, discretionary radio calls serve to enhance safety and coordination among pilots operating within non-controlled airspace.

VHF Characteristics and Radio Operation

VHF (Very High Frequency) communication offers a straightforward, dependable, and high-fidelity means of communication. Its effectiveness, however, is constrained by its short-range nature, relying on a direct line-of-sight connection between the transmitting and receiving stations. While modern VHF aircraft communication systems are adaptable and user-friendly when properly installed, the presence of noise within the cockpit environment can pose challenges to both reception and transmission.

VHF Radio Wave Propagation

The transmission of electromagnetic waves occurs in straight lines but is subject to alterations due to various factors such as interaction with the Earth's surface and atmospheric phenomena like reflection, refraction, and diffraction. The ionospheric layers play a significant role in modifying the paths of radio waves. This process of conveying the signal between transmitter and receiver is known as propagation. As radio waves traverse through the atmosphere or other mediums, there is a loss of signal energy, known as attenuation, which amplifies with distance.

In the High Frequency (HF) band (ranging from 3 MHz to 30 MHz), radio wave propagation is notably influenced by reflection and refraction within the ionospheric layers, enabling long-distance transmission with minimal power and antenna size. Conversely, in the VHF band (30 MHz to 300 MHz), propagation primarily occurs along a direct path. Although VHF signals are less affected by atmospheric phenomena like reflection and refraction, they face significant attenuation due to the Earth's surface and can be obstructed, deflected, or reflected by terrain and structures, akin to VHF-band TV reception. Thus, clear reception of VHF transmissions necessitates an unobstructed line-of-sight (LOS) path between transmitter and receiver antennas, with sufficient RF output energy to counteract signal attenuation over the LOS distance.

Line-of-Sight (LOS) Distance

The LOS distance between a ground station and an aircraft, or between two aircraft, is governed by the curvature of the Earth's surface and influenced by the elevation/height of the stations and intervening terrain. A rule-of-thumb for estimating the maximum direct path distance (to the horizon) between an aircraft and a ground station is the square root of the aircraft's height, in feet, above the underlying terrain. Though technically 1.06 times the square root, this slight adjustment is typically disregarded for practical purposes.

Aircraft height (feet)	Maximum LOS distance (nm)
10	3.2
100	10
1000	32
5000	70
10 000	100

Figure 65: Theoretical LOS distance to horizon.

Estimating Square Roots

When mentally calculating square roots, simplification can expedite the process. By disregarding the two least significant digits of the height and estimating the square root of the remaining one or two digits, followed by multiplication by 10, estimation becomes more manageable. For instance, with a height of 3200 feet, ignoring the 00 leaves us with 32. The square root of 32 falls between 5 and 6, approximately 5.5, which, when multiplied by 10, gives us a line-of-sight (LOS) distance of 55 nautical miles (nm). Similarly, for a height of 700 feet, disregarding 00 and considering the square root of 7, estimated between 2 and 3, yields approximately 2.6, resulting in an LOS distance of 26 nm.

Air-to-Air Communications

In air-to-air communication, the LOS distance comprises two 'distance to horizon' calculations. For instance, with one aircraft at 5000 feet and the other at 10,000 feet, the combined maximum LOS distance would be 70 + 100 = 170 nm, with possible adjustments due to wave diffraction or intervening terrain affecting the actual distance.

Considerations for VHF Transceiver Operation

The LOS distance represents the theoretical maximum range for direct-path VHF transmission and reception. However, actual distances vary depending on factors such as transmitter/receiver system quality, antenna type and placement, receiver/headset quality, and other factors. Effective range typically ranges from 5 nm to the full LOS distance, with approximately 50 nm being likely for a well-implemented low-power installation.

Transceiver Components and Operation

Aircraft station apparatus includes an antenna system, radio transmitter/receiver unit (transceiver), speaker/earphones, microphone, interconnection cables, and matching devices. These components must be electrically compatible with each other and any cockpit intercommunication unit in a two-seat aircraft.

Transmission and Reception

Transmitters use amplitude modulation (AM) to impress voice information on a fixed RF carrier wave. Receivers demodulate selected signals, isolating voice information for amplification and conversion to sound waves.

Setting and Changing Frequencies

Frequencies are typically input via electronic keyboards or knobs, with options to set channel steps at 25 kHz or 50 kHz. Most transceivers allow setting of an active and standby frequency, with the ability to switch between them as needed. Some units offer dual-monitoring capability, enabling listening on multiple frequencies while transmitting on one.

Features and Considerations

Transceivers often include memory positions for storing frequencies, fast-scanning functions, access to emergency/distress frequencies, adjustable transmit power settings, and compatibility with aircraft antennas. Headsets serve dual roles of hearing protection and improved communication, with passive and active noise reduction options available.

Using Squelch Control

Squelch control filters out background noise while allowing strong signals to pass through. It should be adjusted only after establishing contact with the active frequency, as improper adjustment may filter out active transmissions. Automatic gain control may override squelch, permitting background noise monitoring when necessary.

C2 Link

A C2 link, or Command and Control link, is a communication link that facilitates the exchange of information between the pilot or operator and a remotely piloted aircraft (RPA), commonly known as a drone or unmanned aerial vehicle (UAV).

The C2 link serves as the primary means for the pilot or operator to command and control the RPA during its flight. It enables the transmission of instructions, commands, and operational data between the ground control station (GCS) or Remote Pilot Station (RPS) and the RPA itself. This communication is crucial for monitoring the aircraft's status, adjusting its flight parameters, and ensuring its safe operation throughout the mission.

The C2 link supports various functions, including:

1. Control: Allows the pilot to modify the behaviour of the RPA, such as adjusting

flight controls, propulsion systems, or landing gear.

2. Monitoring: Provides real-time feedback on the RPA's health, status, and operational parameters, such as speed, altitude, and system warnings.

3. Detect and Avoid Systems: Manages onboard systems designed to detect and avoid obstacles or other aircraft, enhancing safety and collision avoidance.

4. Handover and Flight Data Recording: Facilitates communication between the RPA and the pilot or operator, indicating the aircraft's operational state and recording flight data for analysis and review.

The C2 link can operate through various communication architectures, including direct radio communication (Radio Line of Sight - RLOS), satellite communication (Beyond Radio Line of Sight - BRLOS), or relay through the RPA itself. The choice of communication architecture depends on factors such as the operational range, terrain, and regulatory requirements.

The C2 link is an essential component of RPA operations, enabling effective command and control of the aircraft to ensure safe and successful mission execution.

Functions Supported by the C2 Link:

The Command and Control (C2) Link facilitates various critical functions for Remotely Piloted Aircraft (RPA) operations:

- **Control:** Allows the Pilot-in-Command (PIC) to modify RPA behaviour, including flight control, propulsion, and landing gear.

- **Detect and Avoid System Control:** Manages onboard systems like transponders, ADS-B, and radar for collision avoidance.

- **Support for Handover and Flight Data Recording:** Facilitates communication between RPA and Remote Pilot Station (RPS) for operational status indication and data recording.

- **Health and Status Monitoring:** Monitors RPA parameters such as speed, attitude, and system warnings.

- **Monitor Detect and Avoid System:** Observes target tracks and advisories for collision avoidance.

C2 Link Terminology:

- **Radio Line of Sight (RLOS):** Direct communication between RPA and ground radio, typically used for take-off and landing.

- **Beyond Radio Line of Sight (BRLOS):** Communication when distance exceeds the curvature of the earth, requiring satellite or ground radio networks.

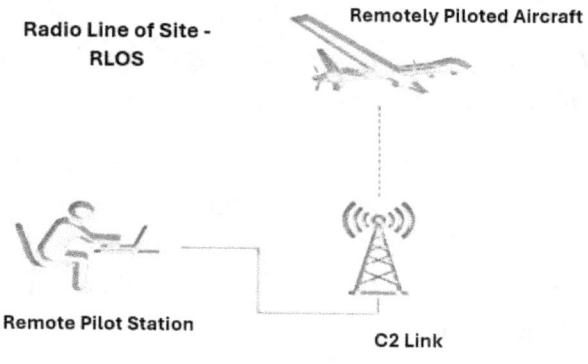

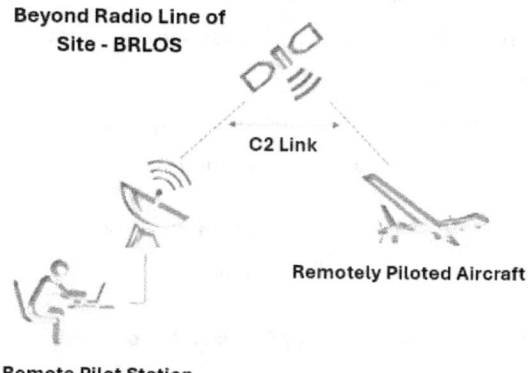

Figure 66: C2 Link Control Architectures.

C2 Link Communications Architectures:

- **Relay through the RPA:** RPA relays communications to ATC, resembling manned aircraft to ground stations.

- **Non-Relay through the RPA:** Direct VHF radio communication between

RPS and ATC, limited by range.

- **Ground to Ground Link:** Wired network connection for lower latency and higher reliability, especially suitable for international/oceanic operations.

C2 Link Characteristics:
- **Safety Critical Functions:** Ensures reliable connection between PIC and RPA, with adequate data rates, link budgets, and protection from interference.

- **Performance:** Supports various services such as voice/data transmission, navigation, surveillance, and collision avoidance.

- **Lost C2 Link Procedures:** Defines actions in case of C2 link failure, considering equipment failure, human error, and RF propagation conditions.

Lost C2 Link:
- **Causes:** Equipment failure, human error, interference, or RF propagation conditions like atmospheric/weather effects, terrain reflection, and airframe obstruction.

- **Effects:** Temporary link outages due to signal fades, with varying depths and durations depending on terrestrial or satellite links.

- **States:** Nominal State (C2 link available), Lost C2 Link State (C2 link unavailable, but flight plan executed), and Lost C2 Link Decision State (C2 link unavailable, decision pending).

Understanding these concepts ensures effective communication and control in RPA operations, enhancing safety and reliability.

The functions supported by the Command and Control (C2) Link have a significant impact on drone operators, as they directly influence the effectiveness, safety, and reliability of remotely piloted aircraft (RPA) operations. Let's explore the implications of each aspect:

1. Control: The ability for the Pilot-in-Command (PIC) to modify RPA behavior is crucial for executing flight plans, adjusting flight parameters, and responding to changing conditions. This allows operators to maintain control over the aircraft's flight path, propulsion systems, and landing gear, ensuring safe and

precise operation.

2. Detect and Avoid System Control: Managing onboard systems for collision avoidance is essential for ensuring the safety of both the drone and other airspace users. Effective control over transponders, ADS-B, and radar systems enables operators to detect and avoid potential obstacles or conflicts, reducing the risk of mid-air collisions.

3. Support for Handover and Flight Data Recording: Facilitating communication between the RPA and Remote Pilot Station (RPS) allows operators to monitor the aircraft's operational status and record essential flight data. This information is invaluable for analyzing performance, identifying issues, and improving future operations.

4. Health and Status Monitoring: Monitoring RPA parameters such as speed, attitude, and system warnings provides operators with real-time feedback on the aircraft's condition. This allows them to identify any anomalies or malfunctions promptly and take appropriate corrective action to maintain safety and operational efficiency.

5. Monitor Detect and Avoid System: Observing target tracks and advisories for collision avoidance enhances situational awareness and allows operators to make informed decisions to avoid potential conflicts.

In terms of C2 Link terminology, understanding concepts like Radio Line of Sight (RLOS) and Beyond Radio Line of Sight (BRLOS) is crucial for selecting the appropriate communication method based on operational requirements and regulatory constraints.

Similarly, familiarity with different communication architectures such as relay through the RPA, non-relay through the RPA, and ground-to-ground links enables operators to establish reliable and efficient communication channels with air traffic control (ATC) and other stakeholders.

Moreover, being aware of C2 Link characteristics, including safety-critical functions, performance requirements, and lost C2 link procedures, empowers operators to anticipate and address potential challenges effectively during RPA operations.

A comprehensive understanding of the functions, terminology, architectures, characteristics, and procedures related to the Command and Control Link is essential for drone operators to ensure safe, efficient, and compliant operations in diverse environments and scenarios.

Communications when in Difficulties

When facing difficulties such as low fuel, loss of navigation, failing light, or engine failure, recreational pilots must prioritize their actions to ensure safety. The following steps are essential:

1. **Assessment of Probable Outcomes:** Evaluate the potential consequences of available actions, considering factors such as terrain, visibility, and aircraft controllability.

2. **Fly the Aircraft:** Maintain control of the aircraft while addressing the emergency situation.

3. **Execute Pre-planned Emergency Drills:** Continue flying the aircraft while following predetermined emergency procedures.

4. **Select Landing Area:** Identify the best possible landing site considering factors like terrain, obstacles, and population density.

5. **Assess Landing Outcome:** Evaluate the likely outcome of the landing in terms of potential injuries and survival.

The decision to communicate distress depends on various factors:

- **Nature of Difficulty:** Control difficulties or challenging terrain may warrant immediate distress communication.

- **Aircraft Type and Situation:** Certain situations may pose a higher risk of injury, necessitating a distress broadcast.

- **Urgency of Assistance:** If time permits and there is uncertainty or urgency, pilots may request assistance without declaring an emergency.

Understanding distress communication protocols is crucial:

- **Distress Call Priority:** MAYDAY calls have absolute priority over other communications.

- **Urgency Call Priority:** PAN-PAN calls have priority except for distress calls.

- **Communication Channels:** Select VHF frequencies based on availability and response time.

- **Emergency Communication Format:** Follow standardized formats for MAYDAY and PAN-PAN calls to convey essential information clearly and efficiently.

Utilizing GPS and other communication means can aid in distress situations:

- **GPS Coordination:** Functional GPS devices provide accurate position information for efficient search and rescue operations.

- **Alternative Communication:** Consider using UHF CB radios or cellular mobile devices to communicate with ground stations or other aircraft.

Emergency procedures must prioritize safety:

- **Activation of Emergency Locator Transmitter (ELT):** Follow recommended procedures for activating ELT devices to signal distress.

- **Survival Preparedness:** Be familiar with survival procedures and resources outlined in aviation manuals and publications.

By adhering to established protocols and utilizing available resources, pilots can effectively communicate distress situations and receive timely assistance, enhancing the likelihood of a safe outcome in emergency scenarios.

Aircraft Radar Beacon Transponders Mode A/C Transponders

Transponders serve as specialized radio devices within the Air Traffic Control Radar Beacon System (ATCRBS). When triggered by a 1030 MHz interrogation pulse from an air traffic control secondary surveillance radar (SSR), transponders emit a high-energy 1090 MHz pulse, enhancing the radar's return signal. While primary surveillance radar (PSR) operates within 50 nautical miles of major airports, it does not interrogate airborne transponders. SSR, with a range of at least 100 nautical miles, provides bearing and distance information, with target height determined by the airborne transponder.

Mode A/C transponders, common in smaller civilian aircraft, transmit a 12-bit ATC-assigned identity/status code and altitude reading (in 100-foot units). These units, referred to as Mode A/C or Mode 3A/C transponders, utilize octal notation for the identity code, with each numeral ranging from 0 to 7. The standard non-discrete squawk code for VFR aircraft is '1200', with discrete codes assigned by ATC when needed.

Mode A/C transponders feature an 'identify' or 'special position identification' (SPI) function. When activated, this temporarily alters the aircraft's code, causing it to stand out on the controller's display. Pilots should only activate this function when instructed by ATC or when initially squawking an emergency code.

For emergency situations, pilots may use specific non-discrete transponder squawk codes:

- 7700 for emergency
- 7600 for VHF communications failure
- 7500 for unlawful interference (hijacking).

Mode S Transponders: Mode S transponders, found on passenger transport aircraft, utilize a permanent ICAO 24-bit Aircraft Address assigned by the National Airworthiness Authority. This address, provided in 6-digit hexadecimal notation, ensures unique identification. Mode S transponders can be selectively addressed by ground stations or other aircraft for data transfer. Additionally, they retain Mode A/C functionalities.

TCAS (Traffic Alert and Collision Avoidance Systems): TCAS II, installed on larger passenger aircraft, emits Mode C interrogation pulses and utilizes responses from Mode A/C transponders within a 14-nautical-mile range to assess collision risk. TCAS systems also use Mode S capabilities for data exchange between aircraft and ground stations.

Transponder Operating Regulations: All aircraft operating in Class A, C, and E airspace or above 10,000 feet must have an operating Mode A/C transponder. Transponders must be constantly operated when equipped, with exemptions in Class E airspace for aircraft with insufficient electrical capacity. Aircraft operating within 40 nautical miles of a Class D tower in Class E airspace must have a functioning transponder.

Transponder Emergency Procedure: In case of distress or navigational difficulties, pilots should select the emergency status code '7700', activate the 'IDENT' function, and contact the appropriate ATC service on the en-route area control frequency.

Monitoring 121.5 MHz

Monitoring 121.5 MHz en route offers numerous advantages, including:

- Immediate response to distress calls from other aircraft.

- Detection of ELT signals for rapid response to crashes.

- Contactability by ground stations for urgent messages.

- Compliance with ICAO requirements and recommendations.

- Usefulness in summoning assistance in emergencies.

- Requirement for intercepting aircraft to communicate before taking action.

Air Safety Australia encourages pilots to adopt the practice of monitoring 121.5 MHz, emphasizing its silent nature and critical role in aviation safety.

Radio Equipment Operation

Procedure for Troubleshooting Radio Equipment Issues

a. Troubleshooting Information: Refer to the specific handbook for the radio model in use for detailed troubleshooting instructions. The following serves as a general guide applicable to most types of equipment.

b. No Power to the Radio:

- Ensure the internal battery (if present) is securely housed.

- Check the condition of any external battery being used.

- Confirm that the radio or avionics master switch is turned ON.

- Verify the operation of the ON/OFF switch.

- Check for intact fuses or circuit breakers in the power circuit supplying the radio.

Note: Some checks may necessitate the use of a multimeter or similar equipment. Individuals unfamiliar with such equipment should seek guidance from someone with appropriate expertise.

c. No Acknowledgment of Transmissions:

- Confirm that the correct frequency is selected.

- Check the settings of the volume and squelch controls.

- Ensure the antenna connections are properly secured.

- Verify that the transmission indicator (if available) indicates carrier wave generation.

- Check for obstacles or the transmitter's position potentially interfering with transmission or reception.

- Try selecting another frequency, such as an ATC control frequency, where acknowledgment could be expected.

d. Other Problems:
  - Reception of all hash or squeals:

    - Ensure only one station transmits at a time to avoid conflicts.

    - If simultaneous transmission occurs, the result may include the transmission of "Two in together," despite being not recommended.

    - Note that a significantly more powerful transmitter may overpower transmissions from a weaker one.

  - Loud squeal during transmissions:

    - This issue often arises due to problems with antenna connections, location, or suitability, particularly with hand-held radios adapted for aircraft use.

    - Consider replacing the supplied whip antenna with an aftermarket antenna specifically designed for Airband VHF and repositioning it away from the handset and other metallic influences.

    - Antennas must be tuned to specific frequencies for efficient operation, which may require specialized equipment and knowledge.

  - Signal present but no voice heard:

    - Described as "Carrier wave only, no modulation."

- This issue is likely due to a faulty microphone, press-to-talk switch, or associated wiring.

Radiotelephony Phrasing — Aviation English

Ensuring Clear and Effective Aviation Radiotelephony Communication: The clarity and effectiveness of each aviation radiotelephony transmission hinge on the clear articulation of its intent, ensuring it is readily comprehensible and memorable to recipients. Prior to transmitting, assembling the requisite words, maintaining brevity, adhering to standard terminology and phrasing — known as aviation English — and consistently employing one's complete and accurate call sign are pivotal in conveying valuable operational information.

Radiotelephony Pronunciation: In radiotelephony (R/T) communications, a phonetic alphabet is utilized when individual letters need to be transmitted. Originating from the North Atlantic Treaty Organisation, this phonetic alphabet serves as an international standard for use by the armed forces of NATO nations.

Letters

Phonetic	Pronunciation	Phonetic	Pronunciation
A ALFA	AL fah	B BRAVO	BRAH voh
C CHARLIE	CHAR lee	D DELTA	DELL tah
E ECHO	ECK ho	F FOXTROT	FOKS trot
G GOLF	GOLF	H HOTEL	hoh TELL
I INDIA	IN dee A	J JULIETT	JEW lee ETT
K KILO	KEY loh	L LIMA	LEE mah
M MIKE	MIKE	N NOVEMBER	no VEM ber
O OSCAR	OSS cah	P PAPA	pah PAH
Q QUEBEC	keh BECK	R ROMEO	ROW me oh
S SIERRA	see AIR rah	T TANGO	TANG go
U UNIFORM	YOU nee form	V VICTOR	VIK tah
W WHISKY	WISS key	X X-RAY	ECKS ray
Y YANKEE	YANG key	Z ZULU	ZOO loo

Numbers

The R/T pronunciation of numbers should be the following phonetic form:

0 ZE–RO	5 FIFE
1 WUN	6 SIX
2 TOO	7 SEV en
3 TREE	8 AIT
4 FOW er	9 NIN er
Hundred HUN dred	
Thousand TOU SAND	
Decimal DAY SEE MAL	

Figure 67: Phonetic Alphabet used in Radiotelephony.

Expressing Numerical Values: When conveying altitude, cloud height, and visibility information containing whole hundreds and whole thousands, it's essential to articulate each digit individually, followed by the appropriate term "HUNDRED" or "THOUSAND" without including the suffix 'feet'. For instance:

- ALTITUDE:

  - (800 feet) – "EIGHT HUNDRED"

  - (1500 feet) – "ONE THOUSAND FIVE HUNDRED"

  - (4750 feet) – "FOUR SEVEN FIVE ZERO"

- (10 000 feet) – "ONE ZERO THOUSAND"

- **CLOUD HEIGHT:**

  - (2200 feet) – "TWO THOUSAND TWO HUNDRED"

  - (4300 feet) – "FOUR THOUSAND THREE HUNDRED"

- **VISIBILITY:**

  - (1500 feet) – "ONE THOUSAND FIVE HUNDRED"

  - (3000 feet) – "THREE THOUSAND"

For all other numerical values except VHF frequencies, each digit should be pronounced separately, such as:

- **HEADING:**

  - (150° M) – "ONE FIVE ZERO"

  - (080° M) – "ZERO EIGHT ZERO"

  - (305° M) – "THREE ZERO FIVE"

- **WIND DIRECTION:**

  - (020°) – "ZERO TWO ZERO DEGREES"

  - (100°) – "ONE ZERO ZERO DEGREES"

  - (210°) – "TWO ONE ZERO DEGREES"

- **WIND SPEED:**

  - (10 knots) – "ONE ZERO KNOTS"

  - (15 knots, gusting to 25) – "ONE FIVE KNOTS GUSTING TWO FIVE"

- **ALTIMETER SETTING – QNH:**

  - (995 hPa) – "NINE NINE FIVE"

- (1010 hPa) – "ONE ZERO ONE ZERO"

- (1027 hPa) – "ONE ZERO TWO SEVEN"

Regarding VHF frequencies, in Australia, the introduction of 25 kHz spacing is ongoing due to frequency congestion, but currently, only 50 kHz spacing operates in Class G airspace. The transmission method varies based on whether the frequency is a 50 kHz multiple or a 25 kHz multiple.

When expressing time in radiotelephony communications, the 24-hour clock system is utilized. Hours are denoted by the first two figures, and minutes by the last two figures. For instance:

- (0001 hrs) – "ZERO ZERO ZERO ONE"

- (1920 hrs) – "ONE NINE TWO ZERO"

Time checks are provided to the nearest minute, and Australian civil aviation employs Coordinated Universal Time [UTC]. The suffix 'Zulu' is appended when referencing UTC.

Standard Words and Phrases:

A set of standard words and phrases are employed in radiotelephony communications, each with specific meanings and usage, such as shown in Figure 68:

ACKNOWLEDGE	Let me know that you have received and understood this message.
AFFIRM	Yes.
APPROVED	Permission for proposed action granted.
BREAK	I hereby indicate the separation between portions of the message (to be used where there is no clear distinction between the text and other portions of the message).
CANCEL	Annul the previously transmitted clearance.
CHECK	Examine a system or procedure (no answer is normally expected).
CLEARED	Authorised to proceed under the conditions specified.
CONFIRM	Have I correctly received the following ... ? or Did you correctly receive this message ... ?
CONTACT	Establish radio contact with ...
CORRECT	That is correct.
CORRECTION	An error has been made in this transmission (or message indicated) the correct version is ...
DISREGARD	Consider that transmission as not sent.
HOW DO YOU READ	What is the readability (i.e. clarity and strength) of my transmission?
I SAY AGAIN	I repeat for clarity or emphasis.
MAINTAIN	Continue in accordance with the condition(s) specified or in its literal sense, e.g. "Maintain VFR".
MAYDAY	My aircraft and its occupants are threatened by grave and imminent danger and/or I require immediate assistance.
MONITOR	Listen out on (frequency).
NEGATIVE	"No" or "Permission is not granted" or "That is not correct".
OVER	My transmission is ended and I expect a response from you (not normally used in VHF communication).
OUT	My transmission is ended and I expect no response from you (not normally used in VHF communication).
PAN PAN	I have an urgent message to transmit concerning the safety of my aircraft or other vehicle or of some person on board or within sight but I do not require immediate assistance.
READ BACK	Repeat all, or the specified part, of this message back to me exactly as received.
REPORT	Pass me the following information.
REQUEST	I should like to know or I wish to obtain.
ROGER	I have received all of your last transmission (Under NO circumstances to be used in reply to a question requiring READ BACK or a direct answer in the affirmative or negative. Do not use the term 'COPY THAT' or double click the transmit button.)
SAY AGAIN	Repeat all or the following part of your last transmission
SPEAK SLOWER	Reduce your rate of speech.
STANDBY	Wait and I will call you.
VERIFY	Check and confirm with originator.
WILCO	I understand your message and will comply with it. (Do not use the term 'COPY THAT' or double click the transmit button.)

Figure 68: Standard words and phrases.

Clarity of Transmission: The readability scale is utilized in response to inquiries about transmission clarity or requests for a radio check. The scale ranges from "Unreadable" to "Perfectly Readable" to ensure effective communication.

Managing Human Factors in Remote Pilot Aircraft Systems Operations

Human factors encompass various aspects influencing how individuals perform their tasks. These factors include social and personal skills such as communication and decision-making, which complement technical expertise, thereby playing a crucial role in ensuring safe and efficient aviation operations.

The study of human factors involves applying scientific knowledge about the human body and mind to understand human capabilities and limitations better. By leveraging human factors knowledge, it becomes possible to minimize the likelihood of errors and develop more error-tolerant and resilient systems.

Human error stands as the most significant threat to aviation safety. While human factors are recognized as a primary contributing factor to incidents and accidents, they also offer substantial potential to enhance aviation safety.

In recent times, the proliferation of Remotely Piloted Aircraft Systems (RPAS) has raised concerns due to their increasing complexity and diverse operations, potentially leading to safety conflicts with conventionally piloted aviation systems in the near future.

For instance, a drone conducting surveillance over a crowded area or a sensitive facility could serve both defensive and potentially threatening purposes if mishandled.

Even a small-scale incident involving an RPAS can have serious consequences, as demonstrated by a past incident in Hungary where a model plane crashed during an air show, resulting in loss of life.

In aviation, safety traditionally relies on three factors: technical aspects (such as aircraft, systems, and maintenance), environmental factors (like weather conditions), and human factors, which our team considers paramount.

Regardless of advancements in technology, safety ultimately remains in human hands. Whether it's a recreational drone or a sophisticated combat RPAS, human control and decision-making are indispensable for ensuring safe operations.

However, RPAS operations present unique human factors challenges, including:

1. Reduced sensory cues: Pilots lack the rich sensory feedback available in conventional aircraft, making it harder to maintain awareness of the aircraft's state.

2. Design of the Remote Pilot Station (RPS): Some RPS designs may not meet ergonomic standards, posing challenges for pilot performance.

3. Handovers: Transferring control of an RPAS between pilots or control stations can introduce risks associated with coordination breakdowns.

4. Collision avoidance and separation assurance: Pilots must rely on alternative sources of information for situational awareness, particularly in the absence of a direct view.

5. Human factors implications of link performance: Latencies in radio signal transmission may affect pilot control and communication.

6. Flight termination considerations: Pilots may need to make critical decisions in emergencies, such as attempting an off-airport landing or terminating the flight safely.

Additionally, managing the command and control (C2) link, workload management, and maintenance considerations pose further challenges that require careful attention. Overall, addressing these human factors challenges is essential for ensuring the safe and effective integration of RPAS into the aviation system.

Working Non-traditional Hours Shift work has become increasingly common in our society, reflecting the evolving nature of work beyond the traditional Monday-to-Friday, 9-to-5 routine. A growing segment of the workforce now engages in various shift patterns and non-traditional schedules.

Shift work serves several purposes in the labour market, allowing employers to optimize production by utilizing the full 24 hours of each day. Moreover, it ensures the continuous provision of essential services, such as transportation and healthcare, to the community throughout the day and night.

For the purposes of this discussion, a 'shift worker' refers to individuals working rotating shifts, irregular shifts, evening shifts, afternoon shifts, morning shifts, or split shifts, commonly known as 'non-traditional work hours.'

Engaging in regular or permanent shift work involves more than just adhering to a work schedule; it becomes a lifestyle that significantly impacts sleep patterns, health management, family life, and social interactions. Research indicates that shift work affects both physical and mental health, as well as work performance.

The Body Clock (Circadian Rhythms): The human body operates on a circadian rhythm closely tied to the cycle of night and day, influencing patterns of sleepiness, wakefulness, hormone production, and body temperature. These rhythms, operating on a roughly 24-hour cycle, do not easily adjust to work schedules, especially those involving night shifts. Night schedules disrupt natural sleep/wake patterns and other biological rhythms, leading to fatigue, sleep disruption, and various health issues, such as gastrointestinal disorders.

Performance Impacts: Work performance is significantly influenced by fluctuations in alertness, with time of day or night playing a crucial role. Factors like task type, individual differences, and adaptation to routine changes also affect performance. Fatigue-related effects on performance include reduced attention, communication difficulties, mood changes, decreased concentration, increased omissions and carelessness, decreased vigilance, slowed comprehension and learning, encoding/decoding difficulties, faulty short-term memory, muddled thinking, slow perception, and uneven responsiveness, among others.

Individual Differences: Individual responses to shift work vary based on factors such as age, lifestyle habits, and chronotype (morning or evening preference). Coping with shift work becomes more challenging with age due to physiological changes, although past experiences and coping strategies may mitigate some effects. People can be categorized as morning or evening types (chronotypes), influencing their ability to adapt to different work hours. Morning types may struggle with night work but adapt better to early morning shifts, while evening types cope more easily with evening and night shifts. Additionally, individual differences may extend beyond simple chronotype categorizations.

Physiological Factors (Including Drugs and Alcohol) Affecting Pilot Performance

In USA, 14 CFR part 107 prohibits the operation of small unmanned aircraft (UA) if the remote pilot in command (remote PIC), the person manipulating the controls, or the Visual Observer (VO) is unable to perform their duties safely [45]. The remote PIC is tasked with ensuring that all crew members are not impaired during the operation. While it's well-known that drug and alcohol consumption can impair judgment, certain over-the-counter (OTC) medications and medical conditions may also impact the ability to safely operate a small UA. For instance, some antihistamines and decongestants can induce drowsiness.

Part 107 specifically forbids individuals from serving as a remote PIC, person manipulating the controls, VO, or any other crew member if they have recently consumed alcohol, are currently under its influence, have a blood alcohol concentration of .04 percent or higher, or are using drugs that affect their mental or physical capabilities. Certain medical conditions, such as epilepsy, may also pose risks to operations. It is the responsibility of the remote PIC to ensure that their medical condition is managed and that they can safely conduct a small UA operation.

Physiological and Medical Influences on Pilot Performance

Various physiological and medical factors can significantly impact a pilot's performance. It's crucial for pilots to understand and recognize these factors to ensure safe flight operations. Some of the key factors include:

Hyperventilation: Hyperventilation refers to excessive breathing, leading to a loss of carbon dioxide from the blood. While hyperventilation rarely causes complete incapacitation, it can induce alarming symptoms that may disrupt flight. Symptoms may include visual impairment, dizziness, tingling sensations, and muscle spasms. Breathing normally or into a paper bag can help restore proper carbon dioxide levels and alleviate symptoms.

Stress: Stress is the body's response to physical and psychological demands, triggering the release of hormones like adrenaline and increasing metabolism. Stressors can be physical, physiological, or psychological, and they can be acute (short-term) or chronic (long-term). While acute stress can trigger a "fight or flight" response, chronic stress can impair performance significantly. Pilots experiencing chronic stress should seek medical advice.

Fatigue: Fatigue is a common contributor to pilot error, affecting attention, coordination, and decision-making abilities. It can result from factors like sleep loss, physical exertion, stress, and cognitive work. Acute fatigue, typically short-term, can be managed with rest and sleep. However, chronic fatigue, lasting over a prolonged period, often requires medical intervention. Pilots experiencing acute fatigue should refrain from flying until adequately rested, while those experiencing chronic fatigue should consult a physician.

It's essential for pilots to be aware of these physiological and medical factors and take appropriate measures to mitigate their effects, ensuring safe and effective flight operations.

Dehydration: Dehydration occurs when the body loses a critical amount of water, often due to factors such as hot temperatures, wind, humidity, and the consumption of diuretic drinks like coffee, tea, alcohol, and caffeinated soft drinks. Common signs of dehydration include headache, fatigue, cramps, sleepiness, and dizziness. Fatigue is typically the first noticeable effect of dehydration, which can hinder both physical and mental performance, particularly during long periods of flying in hot weather or at high altitudes. To prevent dehydration, it's recommended to consume two to four quarts of water every 24 hours. However, individual physiological differences should be considered, and thirst should not be relied upon as the sole indicator of dehydration. Carrying a container to measure water intake, avoiding excessive caffeine and alcohol consumption, and staying ahead of thirst sensations are essential steps to prevent dehydration.

Heatstroke: Heatstroke occurs when the body is unable to regulate its temperature properly. Symptoms may include those of dehydration, and in severe cases, collapse may occur. To prevent heatstroke, it's crucial to carry and consume an ample supply of water at frequent intervals, even when not feeling thirsty. The body can typically absorb water at a rate of 1.2 to 1.5 quarts per hour, so individuals should aim to drink one quart per hour in severe heat stress conditions or one pint per hour in moderate stress conditions.

Medication Usage: The Federal Aviation Regulations (Title 14 CFR) do not explicitly address medication usage, but they prohibit individuals from acting as pilots if they have a medical condition or are taking medication that impairs their ability to meet the medical certification requirements. Additionally, regulations prohibit the use of any drug that affects a person's faculties contrary to safety. Many medications, including over-the-counter drugs, have the potential for adverse side effects, which can impact a pilot's judgment and performance. Pilots should assess their physical condition before every flight using the IMSAFE mnemonic (Illness, Medication, Stress, Alcohol, Fatigue, and Emotion). They should also wait at least 48 hours after taking a new medication before flying to ensure they do not experience adverse effects that could compromise flight safety. Other considerations include avoiding unnecessary medications, maintaining balanced meals, staying hydrated, getting adequate sleep, and staying physically fit.

Alcohol: Alcohol significantly compromises the body's functioning, as evidenced by research linking its consumption to a decline in performance. Pilots are tasked with making numerous decisions, many of which are time-sensitive, throughout a flight. The successful outcome of any flight relies on the ability to make correct decisions and respond appropriately to routine and abnormal situations. However, the influence of alcohol significantly diminishes the likelihood of completing a flight without incident. Even small amounts of alcohol can impair judgment, reduce sense of responsibility, impact coordination, narrow visual field, impair memory, decrease reasoning ability, and shorten attention span. Just one ounce of alcohol can slow muscular reflexes, impair eye movements during reading, and increase the frequency of errors. Vision and hearing impairments can occur after consuming even a single drink.

It's important to note that a pilot remains under the influence of alcohol while experiencing a hangover. Despite feeling as though they are functioning normally, both motor and mental responses are still impaired. Alcohol can remain in the body for over 16 hours after consumption, emphasizing the importance of pilots exercising caution and refraining from flying shortly after drinking.

Intoxication is determined by the concentration of alcohol in the bloodstream, typically measured as a percentage by weight. According to 14 CFR part 91, the blood alcohol level must be below 0.04 percent, and there must be a minimum of 8 hours between consuming alcohol and piloting an aircraft. If a pilot's blood alcohol level is 0.04 percent or higher after 8 hours, they cannot fly until it falls below that threshold. Even if the blood alcohol level is below 0.04 percent, a pilot still cannot fly within 8 hours of consuming alcohol. While the regulations provide clear guidelines, it is advisable to err on the side of caution and exercise even greater restraint than what is mandated.

Vision and Flight

Understanding vision and its mechanics enhances a pilot's ability to utilize sight effectively and address potential issues. Effective scanning techniques involve systematic movements from right to left or left to right. Starting from the farthest detectable point (top), pilots gradually shift their focus inward toward the aircraft's position (bottom). Each viewing point encompasses an area approximately 30° wide, with durations adjusted based on required detail but capped at 2 to 3 seconds per stop. Transitioning between viewing points should involve a 10° overlap with the previous field of view.

Fatigue

Fatigue, as defined by the US Federal Aviation Authority, refers to a condition characterized by heightened discomfort, reduced capacity for work, decreased efficiency, loss of energy or responsiveness, often accompanied by feelings of weariness and tiredness.

The development of fatigue can stem from various sources, with the critical concern being its adverse impact on an individual's task performance. For instance, prolonged periods of mental concentration, such as studying or report writing, can induce fatigue comparable to physical labour.

Numerous studies have shown that fatigue significantly hampers a person's ability to carry out tasks requiring sustained focus, intricate thinking, and manual dexterity. Fatigue can manifest rapidly after intense physical or mental exertion or gradually over days or weeks due to factors like insufficient sleep, caregiving responsibilities, travel, sleep disorders, or demanding work schedules.

Furthermore, the effects of fatigue can be exacerbated by inadequate hydration and nutrition, exposure to harsh environments, prolonged mental or physical exertion, or lack of familiarity or fitness for the tasks at hand.

Physiologically, fatigue is a natural response to prolonged stress, whether physical or mental. After 17 hours of wakefulness, cognitive function declines equivalent to a blood alcohol level of 0.05 percent, escalating to 0.1 percent after 24 hours. Fatigue impairs cognitive processing speed, memory, concentration, and increases susceptibility to distractions.

Various factors contribute to fatigue, including emotional strain, mental workload, physical exertion, insufficient food/fluid intake, adverse environmental conditions, monotony, and disrupted sleep patterns. Sleep, both in terms of quantity and quality, plays a pivotal role in combating fatigue and maintaining alertness and performance.

Factors such as non-traditional work shifts, especially night shifts, can disrupt sleep patterns and diminish the opportunity for adequate rest and recovery. Work-related factors like demanding schedules, task pressures, and inadequate sleep environments, as well as non-work-related issues such as disturbed or disrupted sleep, untreated sleep disorders, and lifestyle choices, contribute to fatigue.

In today's wired and globally connected society, social and recreational activities, along with work demands, often encroach upon sleep time, exacerbating fatigue levels.

Detecting our own levels of fatigue accurately can be challenging, often making it difficult to determine when it becomes unsafe to continue working or driving. However, there are observable signs and symptoms that serve as indicators.

These signs and symptoms of fatigue are typically categorized into physical, mental, and emotional aspects. The diagram presented in the subsequent section outlines key signs within each category. Additionally, depending on the nature of the task at hand, there may be specific indicators of fatigue tailored to that activity.

For instance, in the context of flight crew, indicators of fatigue may include:

- Reduced thoroughness in instrument scans

- Diminished coordination among crew members

- Increased instances of errors of omission

- Heightened sensitivity to noise

- Adoption of more passive flight control strategies

- Tolerance of elevated risk levels

- Misinterpretation of instructions or instrument readings

- Delayed corrections in response to system deviations

- Disregard of peripheral cues

- Lowered performance standards

- Increased lapses in prospective memory

- Impaired visual perception

- Occurrence of micro-sleeps

- Falling asleep while operating controls

Experiencing multiple symptoms from the outlined list suggests a significant decline in alertness. Although fatigue is not the sole cause of such symptoms, their co-occurrence often indicates fatigue-related impairment.

Consistent manifestation of fatigue-related symptoms warrants consideration of consulting a relevant medical specialist. This is especially crucial for individuals with a body mass index exceeding 30 and a 'large' neck size (43 cm or greater in men; 40 cm or greater in women), as these characteristics are associated with a notably higher risk of sleep disorders, particularly sleep apnea.

Times of heightened fatigue risk exist throughout the day, regardless of recovery sleep patterns. Understanding these periods is crucial when determining work hours, overtime, contingency planning, and emergency response strategies.

High-risk times for fatigue include:

- Working from midnight to dawn, especially between 2 a.m. and 5 a.m., coinciding with the body's circadian rhythms' low points associated with alertness and performance.

- Instances where regular breaks have not been taken.

- Shifts exceeding eight hours in duration, as depicted in Figure 2 showcasing the mean relative risk of error for various shift lengths.

- Commencing early shifts before 6 a.m., which often results in shortened sleep due to challenges in adjusting bedtime schedules or anxiety about waking up on time.

- Periods when employees are new to their job or workplace, as the learning curve and acclimatization process can disrupt sleep patterns.

Major causes of fatigue include:

1. Inadequate sleep, with adults requiring seven to eight hours nightly.

2. Sleep apnea, interrupting breathing during sleep.

3. Poor diet leading to blood sugar fluctuations and sluggishness.

4. Anemia, particularly common in women due to menstrual blood loss.

5. Depression, contributing to fatigue alongside emotional symptoms.

6. Hypothyroidism, slowing metabolism and causing sluggishness.

7. Excessive caffeine consumption leading to increased heart rate and fatigue.

8. Diabetes, hindering sugar metabolism and energy conversion.

9. Dehydration, leading to fatigue and reduced bodily function.

10. Heart disease, manifesting in fatigue during routine activities.

Addressing these factors through lifestyle changes, medical interventions, and appropriate hydration can help mitigate fatigue-related risks and improve overall well-being.

Sleep

Sleep is characterized as a state of partial or complete unconsciousness where voluntary functions are suspended, allowing the body to rest and rejuvenate itself. Despite its evident significance, the precise purpose of sleep remains incompletely understood. In a general sense, it is believed that during sleep, both the mind and body "recover" from daily stresses and "prepare" or "recharge" for the challenges of the following day. Insights into the function of sleep have primarily emerged from studies involving sleep deprivation in animals and humans.

The Need for Normal Sleep: Sleep requirements vary among individuals and evolve across different stages of life. Newborns typically sleep for 16 to 18 hours per day, while preschool children generally require 10 to 12 hours. School-aged children and teenagers typically benefit from at least 9 hours of sleep each night. For most adults, optimal functioning throughout the subsequent day is typically achieved with 7 to 8 hours of sleep nightly.

Both the quality and quantity of sleep are significantly influenced by the timing of sleep within the 24-hour day cycle. Humans have naturally adapted to sleeping during nighttime hours and being active during the day.

Understanding Sleep Cycles and Structure: Sleep is not uniform throughout the night; rather, it progresses through various stages characterized by distinct brain wave patterns.

These stages form a continuous cycle lasting approximately 90 to 120 minutes, comprising five distinct phases:

1. Stage 1: Initiation of sleep, occasionally accompanied by muscle twitches or starts.

2. Stage 2: Light sleep phase, during which individuals are easily roused.

3. Stages 3 and 4: Deep sleep stages, crucial for physical regeneration, wherein awakening is challenging.

4. Stage 5 (REM sleep): Rapid eye movement phase, characterized by dreaming and noticeable eye movements under closed eyelids. REM sleep plays a vital role in memory consolidation and mental well-being, and recent studies suggest its contribution to physical restoration.

In the early part of the night, individuals spend more time in stages 3 and 4 of each sleep cycle. However, as the night progresses, the relative duration of REM sleep increases. When sleep-deprived, the body prioritizes catching up on deep sleep (stages 3 and 4) and REM sleep. Consequently, sleep-deprived individuals often transition rapidly from light sleep to deep slumber upon falling asleep.

Recovering from Sleep Deprivation: Experiencing unwanted sleepiness and fatigue can pose both an inconvenience and a hazard, particularly in situations such as driving or piloting an aircraft, where it could lead to fatal consequences.

Numerous strategies have been identified to mitigate the likelihood or effects of fatigue, some of which are discussed later in this workbook, such as managing caffeine intake or paying attention to dietary choices.

More extreme measures include the use of stimulants like amphetamines. However, while pharmacological interventions may offer temporary relief, they do not address the underlying need for restorative sleep, which is essential for both physical and mental recovery.

The specific amount of sleep required for optimal performance varies for each individual but generally falls between 7 and 9 hours within a 24-hour period. Despite age-related changes that may affect sleep patterns, the necessity for sleep remains constant throughout life. Most individuals naturally gravitate towards a sleep schedule that aligns with a typical night-time routine, although variations exist, especially among older individuals who may tend to sleep earlier.

While uninterrupted sleep is ideal, fragmented sleep, consisting of multiple short sleep periods, is preferable to total sleep deprivation. Even a brief nap can significantly enhance alertness. However, it's crucial to recognize that napping cannot fully substitute for a full night of sleep and should not be relied upon as a sole remedy for sleep deficits.

The Impact of Aging on Sleep: As we age, it typically becomes increasingly challenging to both initiate and maintain sleep, a difficulty that is often more pronounced during daytime rest periods but can also affect nighttime sleep patterns. These changes in sleep behaviour are not solely limited to difficulty falling asleep and shortened sleep duration; other age-related physiological alterations further compound the challenges of adapting to non-traditional work hours.

Recent studies indicate that age-related changes in bladder function can significantly contribute to sleep disruptions, prompting more frequent awakenings for trips to the bathroom. Coupled with other physiological shifts associated with aging, these disruptions can result in a heightened frequency of awakenings throughout the sleep cycle. Consequently, increased daytime sleepiness may ensue as a consequence of these interrupted sleep patterns.

Sleepwalking: Sleepwalking, also known as somnambulism, involves engaging in complex behaviours, such as walking, while still asleep, typically occurring during the second or third hour of sleep. Activities during sleepwalking episodes may range from simply sitting up and appearing awake, despite being asleep, to walking around. The individual remains unaware of these actions and usually has no recollection of them upon awakening.

Sleepwalking can manifest in more elaborate behaviours, including rearranging furniture, using the bathroom, or dressing and undressing. In extreme cases, there have been reports of individuals driving vehicles while in a sleepwalking state.

During sleepwalking episodes, the sleepwalker's eyes may be fully or partially open, and they may navigate their surroundings, avoid obstacles, and even respond to simple commands, albeit unconsciously. Awakening a sleepwalker typically results in surprise as they find themselves out of bed. Episodes of sleepwalking are usually brief, lasting only seconds or minutes, although they can persist for longer periods, even up to 30 minutes or more. Sleepwalking occurs during the rapid eye movement (REM) stage of sleep.

The causes of sleepwalking remain poorly understood, and there has been limited focus on treatment options for adults.

Sleep Apnea: Sleep apnea is a sleep disorder characterized by breathing interruptions, which can impair wakefulness during daytime activities such as work or driving.

There are three primary types of sleep apnea: central sleep apnea, obstructive sleep apnea, and mixed sleep apnea. Central sleep apnea occurs when the brain fails to send signals to the muscles responsible for breathing, resulting in a lack of effort to breathe.

Obstructive sleep apnea occurs when the brain sends signals to the breathing muscles, but airflow is obstructed due to a blockage in the airway, preventing adequate breathing. This form of sleep apnea is the most prevalent in Western societies.

Mixed sleep apnea involves a combination of central and obstructive sleep apnea.

If you suspect or have been informed that you exhibit symptoms suggestive of sleep apnea, it is crucial to consult with a healthcare professional. Classic symptoms of sleep apnea include making choking sounds, experiencing pauses in breathing during sleep, and abruptly waking up with gasping for air.

Napping: Benefits of Napping: Short naps offer several advantages, providing many of the benefits associated with longer sleep in a condensed timeframe. These benefits encompass enhanced short-term memory, heightened performance, increased alertness, and improved reaction time. However, it's worth noting that the effects of naps typically don't endure as long as those of lengthier sleep sessions.

Defining a Nap: The definition of a nap varies across literature. In this context, a nap refers to any sleep lasting up to three hours, while a "short sleep" extends from three to five hours. Naps as brief as 10 to 15 minutes have been shown to yield measurable benefits. Generally, the longer the nap, the more pronounced its advantages in terms of recovery and performance enhancement. Naps shorter than 10 minutes are generally not considered beneficial.

Timing of Naps: Research on the timing of naps suggests conflicting perspectives. While some studies indicate that the timing of a nap influences its restorative effects, particularly in combating fatigue, others propose that the timing is less critical when fatigue is significant, with the primary focus being on obtaining any sleep. It's advisable to adopt a nap schedule that best aligns with individual preferences. However, it's important to recognize that napping may interfere with subsequent sleep later in the day or at night.

Challenges in Implementing Napping Policies: Despite the potential benefits of napping for mitigating the adverse effects of fatigue and ensuring alertness in safety-critical roles, organizational attitudes toward workplace napping can pose obstacles. Some organizations may not endorse napping in the workplace, irrespective of its efficacy.

Key Points in a Napping Policy:
- Naps serve as supplements to primary sleep when insufficient or extended operations are required.
- Preventative naps aimed at averting fatigue are generally more effective in maintaining performance than recovery naps taken when fatigue has already set in.
- Fatigue is a foreseeable hazard, and napping can effectively mitigate its effects.
- Napping policies should not be exploited to extend schedules beyond reasonable limits but should prioritize safety.
- Encourage napping as a planned strategy for fatigue prevention.
- Naps are most beneficial when taken before dangerous drowsiness occurs.
- They can help maintain performance when longer sleep is occasionally missed or when work periods are extended.
- Allow at least fifteen minutes after waking from a nap to fully regain alertness before resuming duties.
- Whenever possible, schedule naps during periods of natural drowsiness, such as the afternoon or early morning for night shift workers.
- A single nap of 45 minutes is generally sufficient to prevent fatigue, although exceptions may exist in aviation operations.
- Napping policies should also promote information on diet, fitness, and the use of alcohol and other drugs.
- Optimal napping conditions include a dark, quiet environment with comfortable temperature and good ventilation.

Food and Fatigue

As previously discussed in this guide, the ability to maintain wakefulness is primarily linked to adequate rest and recovery. Nevertheless, additional factors may contribute to feelings of weariness, sluggishness, and overall fatigue. One significant factor is the impact of low blood sugar levels, which many individuals underestimate or fail to recognize in relation to their alertness and safety.

Digestion and Appetite

Human biological rhythms dictate wakefulness during the day and sleep at night, influencing various bodily processes, including digestion. Digestive efficiency is naturally higher during daylight hours, with the secretion of digestive juices such as stomach acids and enzymes being most active during this time.

Food consumed at night is metabolized at a slower pace, often resulting in sensations of bloating, constipation, and potential discomfort like heartburn and indigestion. Individuals who eat outside typical meal times may experience gastrointestinal disturbances, exacerbated by the consumption of beverages like tea, coffee, or alcohol. Studies have shown that night workers are at a heightened risk of developing peptic ulcers compared to their daytime counterparts.

Moreover, individuals working non-traditional hours may notice shifts in their hunger patterns, experiencing unexpected bouts of hunger at unconventional times.

Maintaining Blood Sugar Levels with Diet

Given the disruptions to digestion and appetite caused by non-traditional work hours, stabilizing blood sugar levels becomes challenging. Stable blood sugar is crucial for minimizing fluctuations in energy levels, particularly common among shift workers.

Contrary to popular belief, recent research has debunked the notion that sugary snacks cause rapid spikes and drops in blood sugar levels. Instead, the glycemic index (GI) of foods determines how blood sugar levels respond to different food types.

High GI foods cause a swift rise and fall in blood sugar levels, making them suitable for replenishing energy quickly after physical exertion or exercise. Conversely, low GI foods facilitate a gradual change in blood sugar levels, helping to sustain stable energy levels over time. Incorporating low GI snacks throughout a shift can help prevent drastic fluctuations in energy.

The findings on GI foods also have significant implications for individuals with diabetes, as medical advice typically advises against high GI foods to regulate blood sugar levels. However, high GI foods may serve as occasional energy boosts for non-diabetic individuals, especially following physical activity. Nonetheless, low GI foods are generally more beneficial for maintaining consistent energy levels in daily life.

Here are examples of foods categorized based on their glycemic index (GI):

Low GI Foods:

1. Oatmeal

2. Sweet potatoes

3. Lentils

4. Apples

5. Oranges

6. Chickpeas

7. Greek yogurt

8. Whole grain bread

9. Quinoa

10. Nuts and seeds

Intermediate GI Foods:

1. Bananas

2. Brown rice

3. Couscous

4. Whole wheat pasta

5. Green peas

6. Pineapple

7. Raisins

8. Buckwheat

9. Popcorn

10. Muesli

High GI Foods:
1. White bread

2. White rice

3. Potatoes (mashed or baked)

4. Cornflakes

5. Sugary cereals

6. Watermelon

7. Instant oatmeal

8. Pretzels

9. White bagels

10. Dates

These examples provide a general idea of how different foods rank on the glycaemic index scale. However, it's essential to consider individual factors such as portion size, cooking methods, and overall dietary composition when assessing the impact of specific foods on blood sugar levels.

Alternative dietary strategies for shift workers have been suggested by research, one of which involves incorporating low-fat protein foods into your meals to help maintain alertness. This is attributed to a biochemical process involving the amino acid tyrosine, which leads to the elevation of stimulating chemicals in the body.

Low-fat, high-protein food options are readily available in modern supermarkets, often indicated through nutrition labelling. Additionally, high-protein foods contribute to overall health by providing essential nutrients for muscle strength and development. Opting for both low-fat and high-protein food choices is a prudent approach to maintaining a balanced diet.

Examples of low-fat protein sources include fish, poultry, and lean cuts of red meat. For those preferring vegetable-based proteins, options such as beans, lentils, and green vegetables like broccoli and peas are favourable choices.

Assess Your Current Dietary

Habits Chances are, some of the information presented in this section is new to you, offering fresh insights and strategies. Experiment with these approaches for a period and observe their impact on your well-being, particularly when you're feeling fatigued.

Maintaining a balanced diet is key. Generally, evidence suggests that a low-fat diet rich in low and intermediate GI foods, supplemented with quality protein, yields the most benefits. Remember to practice moderation in your eating habits.

Additionally, consider the fibre content of your diet, sourced from fresh fruits and vegetables, as well as the levels of essential minerals and salt.

The recommended daily salt intake is 3.8 grams (about half a teaspoon), adequate for replenishing the amount lost through daily perspiration and ensuring sufficient intake of other vital nutrients. Excessive salt consumption beyond this recommendation can contribute to high blood pressure, increasing the risk of stroke, heart disease, or kidney problems.

Hydration

As previously discussed, alertness is influenced not only by sleep but also by factors such as digestion and nutrition. Similarly, hydration plays a significant role in maintaining alertness and ensuring safety.

When the body experiences dehydration, it initiates mechanisms to conserve water, resulting in reduced activity and a tendency to relax and slow down. This state of relaxation increases the likelihood of drowsiness. Dehydration can also lead to symptoms like light-headedness and headaches.

Many individuals fail to consume adequate water, leading to suboptimal hydration levels. While severe dehydration can lead to medical issues, most dehydration-related effects are short-term and can be alleviated by increasing water intake.

Various factors contribute to dehydration, including:
- Engaging in physically demanding tasks.

- Working in hot environments.

- Consuming caffeinated beverages, as caffeine acts as a diuretic, promoting water loss.

- Drinking alcohol, which also has diuretic properties.

- Consuming soft drinks, which may not hydrate as effectively as plain water.

- Consuming salty foods, which necessitate additional water for processing.

Furthermore, limited access to water in certain workplaces, such as for professional drivers, can exacerbate dehydration risks.

To optimize alertness and vigilance, it's essential to monitor fluid intake closely. Some individuals may need to significantly increase their fluid intake to achieve optimal hydration levels. Interestingly, many people find that increasing water intake enhances alertness without significantly increasing urinary frequency; rather, their urine output increases with each instance.

Caffeine and Other Stimulants

Understanding the dynamics of caffeine usage can significantly enhance one's ability to leverage its effects effectively and manage potential drawbacks.

Caffeine Basics: Caffeine is a substance known for its addictive properties. Individuals may develop a dependence on caffeine if they feel unable to function without it and require daily consumption. It occurs naturally in various plants, such as coffee beans, tea leaves, and cocoa nuts, and is present in numerous food and beverage items, including chocolate and cola drinks.

Effects of Caffeine: Consuming caffeinated beverages is commonly associated with increased alertness. Caffeine operates by blocking adenosine reception, a neurotransmitter that promotes relaxation and drowsiness. Consequently, after consuming caffeine, individuals may experience heightened energy levels, muscle tension, excitement, and increased heart rate.

Timing and Duration of Effects: Caffeine typically takes 15 to 30 minutes to enter the bloodstream, with its peak physiological effects occurring about an hour later. The stimulant effects of caffeine can last for approximately five hours. Therefore, consuming caffeinated beverages too close to bedtime may hinder sleep onset.

Advantages and Disadvantages of Caffeine: While caffeine is widely used and legally available, it is essential to recognize both its benefits and drawbacks. The immediate sense of alertness experienced after caffeine intake may be partially attributable to psychological factors, such as anticipation and social interactions. Additionally, individuals who regularly consume caffeine may experience withdrawal symptoms when attempting to reduce or eliminate their intake.

Strategic Use of Caffeine: To maximize the effectiveness of caffeine and mitigate potential negative effects, strategic consumption is crucial. Some key strategies include avoiding caffeine when not tired to prevent tolerance buildup, refraining from excessive consumption in the morning to avoid exacerbating midday fatigue, and minimizing caffeine intake before bedtime to facilitate quality sleep. Understanding the timing and duration of caffeine's effects, as well as being mindful of its presence in various foods and drinks, can help individuals optimize their caffeine usage.

While caffeine can serve as a temporary aid in managing alertness, it should not substitute for adequate sleep or address underlying health issues. Proper planning and moderation are essential when using caffeine as an alertness management tool, particularly for safety-critical occupations like aviation. Additionally, individuals should be aware of alternative sources of caffeine, such as dark chocolate, and adjust their consumption accordingly.

Alcohol

Understanding the effects of alcohol on sleep, alertness, and performance is crucial for ensuring safety and well-being, particularly in safety-sensitive environments.

Alcohol Overview: Alcohol significantly impairs performance at moderate and high levels of intoxication, affecting response time, cognitive function, and environmental awareness. Many workplaces, including the aviation industry, enforce strict regulations regarding alcohol consumption to mitigate safety risks.

Effects of Alcohol: As a central nervous system depressant, alcohol induces relaxation and reduces inhibitions in small doses. However, higher doses lead to impairment, causing drowsiness, memory loss, and decreased consciousness. Alcohol intoxication poses significant risks, contributing to accidents and health issues such as alcoholism and cardiovascular disease.

Risk Factors and Consequences: Alcohol consumption increases the likelihood of accidents, with higher blood alcohol concentrations correlating with elevated accident risks. In Australia, alcohol is a major factor in various accidents, including road incidents and industrial mishaps. Understanding standard drink measurements and metabolization rates is essential for responsible alcohol consumption.

Australian Guidelines: Recent guidelines emphasize low-risk drinking habits, recommending limits for daily and single occasion alcohol consumption. Special considerations apply to children, pregnant women, and individuals planning pregnancy.

Alcohol and Performance: Alcohol consumption leads to reduced alertness and increased sleepiness, even after its effects wear off. Intoxication can result in overconfidence and performance errors, contributing to accidents, absenteeism, and decreased productivity in the workplace.

Persistent Effects: Even after blood alcohol levels return to zero, alcohol can continue to impair performance due to factors like dehydration and gastrointestinal disturbances. Studies have shown measurable performance deficits for up to 8 to 14 hours post-consumption, impacting psychomotor skills, cognitive function, and judgment, particularly relevant in aviation operations.

Nicotine

Nicotine, a stimulating compound naturally occurring in tobacco leaves, has been consumed through smoking or chewing for centuries. It triggers increased respiration and heart rate while suppressing appetite by activating specific nerve receptors sensitive to nicotine. In small doses, it acts as a stimulant, elevating alertness and inducing a sense of euphoria by stimulating the central nervous system.

Addictive Nature and Health Risks: Nicotine is highly addictive, with well-documented health hazards associated with tobacco use. Smoking cigarettes elevates the risks of various ailments, including heart disease, lung cancer, gum disease, and compromised circulation, among others. Smokers generally exhibit lower fitness levels compared to non-smokers.

Nicotine Content and Absorption: Cigarettes contain varying amounts of nicotine, ranging from 1 to 20 mg depending on brand and strength. Nicotine's effects typically diminish within an hour after consumption. It readily enters the body through various routes, including inhalation into the lungs, absorption through the skin via patches, and mucous membranes like gums and nasal linings.

Nicotine's Path in the Body: Nicotine primarily enters the body through the lungs, swiftly reaching the brain via the bloodstream, where it generates pleasurable sensations experienced by smokers. Maintaining consistent nicotine levels becomes a habit for smokers, with individual variability in metabolism rates and tolerance levels.

Nicotine Withdrawal: Withdrawal symptoms from nicotine can commence as early as a single night, disrupting sleep patterns and leading to distressing dreams, especially for heavy smokers. Symptoms include headaches, muscle aches, oral discomfort, impaired concentration, and fluctuations in blood pressure and heart rate, accompanied by feelings of stress, anxiety, depression, and irritability.

Managing Withdrawal: Avoiding nicotine intake in the evening and at bedtime may aid in improving sleep quality, particularly if withdrawal symptoms are manageable. Quitting smoking typically leads to better sleep patterns after around ten days, although withdrawal symptoms, which peak three to four days post-cessation, can persist for up to ten days.

Medications

Drugs enter the body through ingestion, injection, or inhalation, subsequently affecting brain function upon entering the bloodstream. Elimination from the body occurs primarily through the liver and kidneys, eventually excreted in urine. However, drug effects can vary significantly between individuals and even within the same individual due to factors such as time of day, mood, fatigue, and dietary intake. Age, gender, and body size also influence drug impact and recovery rates.

Prescription Medications: Certain prescription drugs can impair driving or heavy machinery operation and may interact with fatigue levels and other substances like alcohol, further compromising performance. Individuals in safety-sensitive roles should consult their healthcare provider regarding potential drug interactions and performance effects. It's essential to inform supervisors about prescribed medications and any recent anesthesia usage due to their potential impact on screening tests.

Over-the-Counter Drugs: Some over-the-counter medications for pain relief or colds and flu may cause drowsiness and fatigue-related symptoms. Individuals should carefully review usage instructions and labels and consult with pharmacists if unsure about potential side effects. Although some shift workers resort to over-the-counter sleep aids, it's crucial to use them judiciously, considering their potential to induce drowsiness the following day.

Stimulants and Alertness Aids: Certain over-the-counter stimulants like caffeine-based products or pseudoephedrine may enhance alertness but can also induce adverse effects such as increased anxiety, heart palpitations, or insomnia. These substances should be used sparingly and under medical supervision to mitigate safety and performance risks.

Sleeping Pills and Sedatives: Benzodiazepines, commonly prescribed for insomnia and anxiety, can produce a range of short-term effects, including relaxation, drowsiness, impaired memory, and motor coordination. Long-term usage can lead to tolerance, dependency, and withdrawal symptoms, affecting various aspects of physical and mental health. Benzodiazepines can impair fine motor skills, cognitive function, mood, alertness, and learning behaviour, making them unsuitable for safety-critical tasks like driving or operating machinery.

Performance Implications and Clearance Times: Benzodiazepine use has been associated with hangover-like symptoms and persistent impairment upon waking, potentially compromising work safety. Clearance times for benzodiazepines vary based on the specific drug and dosage, ranging from one to seven days. Chronic users or those who abuse benzodiazepines may experience extended clearance times, posing prolonged risks to safety and performance.

General Health and Well-being

Numerous studies have revealed health-related issues linked to unconventional work hours, with shift workers generally reporting more health complaints compared to those on traditional day shifts. Shift workers, particularly those on rotating schedules, tend to take more sick leave, visit workplace clinics more frequently, and exhibit lower scores on various health assessments.

Common complaints associated with non-traditional work hours include sleeping difficulties, fatigue, and irritability. These schedules can also impact physical systems such as the gastrointestinal, cardiovascular, and reproductive systems, influencing overall well-being beyond specific disorders.

Shift workers often report elevated stress levels, increased alcohol and drug use, and a general sense of weariness, which may be exacerbated by mental stress related to dissatisfaction in personal and social aspects of their lives.

Gastrointestinal Problems: Shift workers are significantly more likely to develop gastrointestinal disorders, including peptic ulcers, indigestion, heartburn, flatulence, and constipation. Irregularities in food intake due to changing work patterns can contribute to digestive issues. Adhering to regular meal times and adopting healthy eating habits can mitigate long-term gastrointestinal problems.

Cardiovascular Disease: Shift workers face a higher risk of cardiovascular diseases such as high blood pressure and heart attack compared to day workers. Family history, lifestyle factors like exercise, diet, and smoking, and insufficient sleep are significant contributors to cardiovascular health. Regular check-ups, maintaining a balanced diet, regular exercise, and avoiding smoking are essential for cardiovascular health.

Pregnancy and Reproductive Health: Female shift workers, especially those on night shifts, may experience irregular menstrual cycles and increased menstrual pain. Studies suggest associations between shift work and factors like fertility, spontaneous abortion risk, pre-term birth, and lower foetal growth and birth weight. While some observed differences between shift and non-shift workers are statistically small, considering work hours as a potential factor in reproductive health is advisable.

Well-being encompasses various aspects of an individual's personal, physical, material, mental, and spiritual state, contributing to their satisfaction, health, and sense of achievement across work, social connections, and leisure activities. In addition to challenges like loss, depression, anxiety, and stress, fatigue emerges as a significant threat to well-being in modern times.

Organizational Initiatives for Well-being: Many organizations have implemented programs aimed at enhancing employee well-being. These efforts may include equity and diversity policies, Occupational Health and Safety requirements, performance evaluation systems, flexible work arrangements, ample leave provisions, on-site fitness facilities, and access to support services such as chaplains, social workers, and psychologists. Such initiatives reflect the belief among senior management that employers bear a responsibility to foster the well-being of their workforce.

Individual Responsibility for Well-being: Regardless of their role within the organization, individuals hold a responsibility for their own well-being. Similar to fatigue management, maintaining staff well-being is a shared responsibility between supervisors and employees. However, individuals possess significant control over both their emotional and physical well-being.

Emotional Well-being: Strong emotional well-being is characterized by high self-esteem and positive relationships with family, friends, and colleagues. Individuals with robust emotional well-being exhibit resilience, maintain a balanced perspective on issues, and employ effective coping strategies. These strategies include thought management techniques, positive reinterpretation of events, relaxation methods, exercise, prioritization, seeking support, and acceptance of circumstances.

Physical Well-being: Individuals largely influence their physical well-being through factors such as exercise, diet, hydration, and sleep. Substance abuse, particularly alcohol and nicotine, can undermine physical well-being. Proper physical self-care results in increased energy levels, restful sleep, improved concentration, and a satisfying sense of health.

Material Well-being: Material well-being plays a significant role in overall well-being for many individuals and impacts their families as well. Financial stress is a prevalent modern-day stressor. Research suggests that while fair remuneration is expected, excessive pay can negatively affect work satisfaction. Beyond basic needs, people often seek non-material rewards such as recognition and meaningful work roles.

Spiritual Well-being: For some, spiritual well-being forms the cornerstone of their overall well-being. Spirituality encompasses intangible aspects that provide a sense of purpose or meaning in life, which may be associated with religious beliefs or personal philosophies. Studies indicate that individuals with well-developed spiritual beliefs tend to navigate challenges more effectively.

Striving for Balance: A balanced approach to life goals and activities is essential for fostering a strong sense of well-being. Models of life balance typically emphasize work, social connections, and leisure as core facets underpinning overall well-being.

Physical Exercise

Advantages of Physical Activity: Regular physical exercise brings a multitude of health benefits, including enhanced protection against heart disease, stroke, high blood pressure, type 2 diabetes, obesity, back pain, and osteoporosis. (It's important to note the increased prevalence of cardiovascular disease and other health issues among shift workers.)

While exercise has traditionally been linked primarily to physical health, it's now recognized for its holistic effects on the body, including the promotion of psychological well-being. Psychological benefits of regular exercise encompass improved mood, better stress management, heightened self-esteem, and an overall sense of well-being. Simply put, most individuals feel better after engaging in physical activity.

Exercise also plays a role in improving sleep quality. Studies indicate that exercising 30 to 180 minutes before bedtime can lead to increased deep (restorative) sleep. One study even found that evening exercise enhanced the perception of a good night's sleep and reduced daytime sleepiness. Additionally, being physically fit enhances stamina, thereby amplifying the enjoyment of leisure activities.

Specific Benefits of Physical Exercise: Physical exercise offers a wide array of benefits, including increased energy levels, reduced muscle tension and stress, improved muscle tone and strength, enhanced aerobic fitness, better flexibility, strengthened immune function, decreased body fat, improved bone density, enhanced circulation, better digestion, and overall healthier body functioning.

Establishing a Fitness Routine: Many individuals with non-traditional work hours struggle to establish regular exercise habits. On average, female shift workers carry 5 to 10 kg more weight than their non-shift working counterparts, while male shift workers carry 10 to 12 kg more.

To reap the maximum health benefits, experts recommend engaging in 20 to 30 minutes of aerobic activity three or more times weekly, along with muscle strengthening exercises and stretching at least twice weekly. However, if meeting this level of activity proves challenging, accumulating 30 minutes or more of moderate-intensity physical activity daily, three to four times weekly, can still yield significant health benefits. Moderate-intensity activities include everyday tasks like vacuuming, mowing, and walking, which require no special equipment and can be done at any time.

Prior to starting an exercise program, it's advisable to consult with a doctor, especially if you're overweight, over 30 years old, or new to exercise. For those who have been inactive, it's best to begin with less strenuous activities like walking, gentle cycling, or swimming at a comfortable pace, gradually increasing intensity to prevent injury.

RPAS Operations – Environmental or Operational Threats

Display and Control Challenges: The detachment between aircraft and operator in RPAS operations leads to a significant loss of sensory cues available to pilots of manned aircraft. Unlike pilots, RPAS operators rely solely on sensory information provided by onboard sensors via datalink, primarily limited to visual imagery with a restricted field-of-view. Consequently, RPAS operators experience relative "sensory isolation" from their controlled vehicle, lacking ambient visual input, kinaesthetic/vestibular feedback, and sound. Research is essential to understand how this sensory isolation affects operator performance and explore advanced display designs to compensate for the lack of direct sensory input.

Challenges of Data Link Bandwidth: The quality of visual sensor information available to RPAS operators is constrained by the bandwidth of the communications link between the vehicle and ground control station. Limited data link bandwidth imposes constraints on temporal and spatial resolution, colour capabilities, and field of view of visual displays, leading to transmission delays in response to operator inputs. Research is essential to address these challenges, exploring display designs to overcome bandwidth limitations and optimize trade-offs between display aspects.

Automation and System Failures: RPAS systems vary in the degree of flight control automation, ranging from manual control to fully automated flight. The optimal form of flight control depends on factors such as communication time delays and quality of sensory information. Research is needed to determine optimal control methods for different phases of flight and examine the interaction between human operators and automated systems. Additionally, research should focus on establishing and optimizing procedures for responding to system failures and loss of communication.

Crew Composition, Coordination, Selection, and Training: The composition, selection, and training of RPAS flight crews are critical factors in ensuring safe operations. Research is necessary to determine optimal crew size and structure for various mission categories and explore display designs and automation aids to reduce crew demands. Efforts are needed to facilitate crew communication, especially during control handovers, and establish standards for selecting and training RPAS operators.

Hazard and Risk Management: Effective risk management is crucial for RPAS operations, requiring pilots to be aware of available resources and maintain situational awareness. Techniques such as the Perceive, Process, Perform (3P) model and risk management checklists aid in making informed decisions and managing workload effectively. Moreover, understanding naturalistic decision-making and recognizing operational pitfalls can help mitigate risks associated with stress, workload, and distractions.

Addressing environmental and operational threats in RPAS operations necessitates a multifaceted approach encompassing advanced display designs, automation, crew coordination, hazard management, and effective decision-making strategies. Continued research and development efforts are crucial to enhancing RPAS safety and performance in diverse operational environments.

Operational Guidelines for RPAS - Addressing Link Loss Situations

When dealing with the possibility of losing control link connectivity, it's vital to establish effective practices to ensure flight continuity and safety. Control links are not infallible, and interruptions may occur, potentially jeopardizing the command-and-control relationship between the remote pilot and the RPAS (Remotely Piloted Aircraft Systems). To mitigate the impact of lost links, it's crucial to implement pre-programmed procedures that allow the RPAS to autonomously navigate until the link is reestablished.

Anecdotal evidence suggests that RPAS pilots must be prepared for each command to potentially be their last contact with the aircraft for a certain period if a link disruption happens. It's essential to exercise caution, especially when a single command could lead to unsafe flight conditions if not followed up promptly. For instance, directing the aircraft toward terrain without the ability to issue a subsequent command to steer away could be perilous.

Predictable behaviour during link loss situations is paramount for both the pilot and Air Traffic Control (ATC). This necessitates defining clear lost link procedures, including predetermined manoeuvres such as climbing or moving to a designated location. These procedures may need to adapt based on flight progress or specific operational requirements. Pilots and ATC must be well-informed about these procedures to avoid any surprises during lost link scenarios, emphasizing the importance of incorporating lost link programming details into the aircraft's flight plan.

Establishing best practices for managing lost link scenarios is essential, focusing on ensuring safe and predictable behaviour from the RPAS. Determining the duration of a link outage that triggers a lost link procedure is crucial but may vary based on operational factors such as flight phase or environment. Frequent interruptions may prompt pilots to employ workaround solutions, highlighting the need to strike a balance between flight predictability and maintaining control.

RPAS pilots face unique challenges due to limited sensory cues, relying primarily on visual feedback from onboard cameras. The absence of direct physical interaction with the aircraft complicates pre-flight checks, necessitating alternative approaches to ensure airworthiness. Additionally, RPAS pilots may encounter perceptual illusions and conflicts, underscoring the importance of evaluating their impact on flight safety and operations.

Vigilance and fatigue management are critical for RPAS pilots, especially during long-duration flights characterized by low workload. Strategies to maintain engagement and prevent monotony should be identified, balancing the need for rest breaks with operational demands. Handovers between control stations represent another area of concern, requiring clear protocols to ensure seamless transition and avoid communication breakdowns or mode management errors.

Flight planning for RPAS operations involves unique considerations, including ultra-long endurance flights, C2 link coverage, and contingency planning. Pilots must anticipate potential challenges such as adverse weather conditions or link disruptions, incorporating them into comprehensive flight plans to ensure mission success and safety.

In emergencies necessitating flight termination, RPAS pilots must weigh the risks to third parties against preserving the aircraft and payload. Decision-making may be complicated by limited sensory information and the absence of onboard occupants, emphasizing the need for clear protocols and real-time information to mitigate risks effectively.

Overall, RPAS operations require meticulous planning, effective communication, and adherence to safety protocols to ensure the safe and efficient conduct of missions.

Multirotor Remote Pilot Aircraft Systems Operations

By now, you've likely settled on the type of drone that suits your needs. The next step is ensuring a clear understanding of what functionalities you require from the system. Below are some straightforward inquiries you should address before purchasing accessories or finalizing your drone's design.

1. **Flight Time**: Determine how long you need the aircraft to remain airborne before requiring a battery change or refuelling.

2. **Battery Charge Time**: Consider the duration needed to charge the drone's batteries. While immediate charging is desirable, each battery will have a minimum charge time based on its specifications. Evaluate how long the aircraft needs to operate continuously and plan accordingly. For instance, if you require an hour of flight time but each battery provides only 10 minutes, multiple batteries will be necessary. If charging in the field is not feasible, additional battery sets will be needed to ensure continuous operation.

3. **Aircraft Dimensions**: Measure the approximate distance between diagonally opposite motors in multirotors or the wingspan in fixed-wing drones. Ensure that the dimensions align with transportation requirements, considering the vehicle that will carry it. Generally, larger aircraft offer longer flight durations but come at a higher cost.

4. **Payload**: Determine the cargo the aircraft needs to carry, whether it's a small

camera like a GoPro or a 30L tank of pesticide. Understand that payload requirements significantly impact cost.

5. **Ground Speed**: Assess the aircraft's speed relative to the ground, especially when mapping large areas within a limited battery time. Knowing the maximum speed and flight duration enables calculating the coverage area to avoid falling short during missions.

6. **Radio Link**: Understand the type and range of the drone's radio link. Radio frequency bands like 433MHz, 900MHz, 2.4GHz, or 5.8GHz offer varying ranges and data transmission capabilities. Choose the frequency based on your priorities, whether it's streaming video or covering long distances.

Regardless of your specific application, all drones should include the following essentials:

- Telemetry radio
- RC transmitter for manual control (required by some aviation authorities)
- Battery charger
- Ground station software (or physical ground station)
- Spare parts (batteries, props, etc.)
- Sensors tailored to your application (e.g., mapping camera, video camera with data link)

The Physics of Multirotor Drone Flight

When encountering a multirotor aircraft for the first time, observers often marvel at their ability to fly. A common inquiry arises: "How do these machines manage flight without traditional control surfaces?" This question warrants exploration into the underlying physics of multirotor flight.

Given the absence of conventional control surfaces, manoeuvring a typical multirotor relies solely on adjusting motor speeds. Consequently, altering the thrust output of the motors induces directional movements, steering the craft accordingly.

In any multirotor setup, a flight control board serves as an intermediary component between the radio receiver and the motor speed controllers. The flight controller assumes a dual role: Firstly, it interprets command signals from the radio receiver—pertaining to pitch, roll, yaw, and throttle—and translates them into throttle variations necessary for manoeuvring the craft. Secondly, in stability mode, it functions as a gyro stabilization module, ensuring the craft remains upright and level in the absence of explicit control inputs. Operating a multirotor aircraft without a flight controller board is exceedingly challenging, if not virtually impossible.

To aid in explaining the different flight modes, we will utilize a diagram depicting the top view of a Quad-X platform multirotor. This configuration is widely used in today's flight operations, making it highly relevant to our discussion on flight principles. As depicted in Figure 69, this illustration represents the quadcopter in a stable hover.

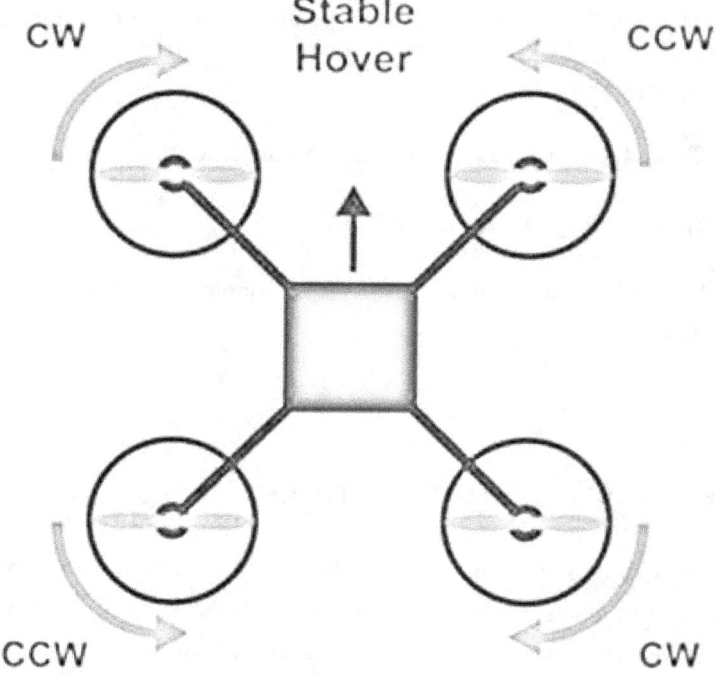

Figure 69: Quad in a stable hover.

The straight front arrow denotes the craft's front and the direction of forward motion. Surrounding each motor are curved arrows indicating the direction and velocity of propeller rotation. In this diagram, all four curved arrows are uniform in size, signifying that all motors are operating at the same speed, with the arrowheads indicating the propellers' rotation direction. Under these circumstances, each motor generates thrust equivalent to one-quarter of the airframe's weight. When the thrust from all four motors is combined, it balances the craft's weight, counteracting gravity's pull towards the ground. In the absence of other external forces, the craft will maintain level flight at a steady altitude.

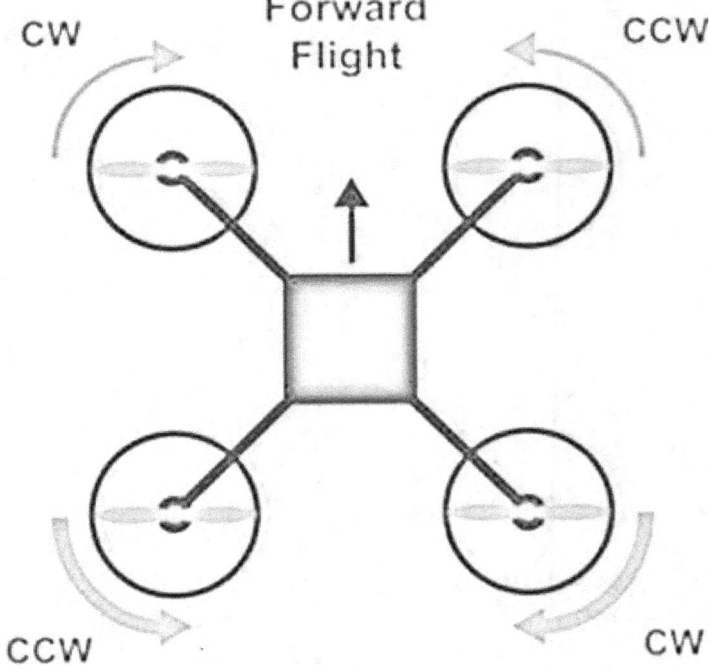

Figure 70: Quad moving forward.

To initiate movement in the quad, adjustments in motor speed are necessary, with some motors accelerating while others decelerate, contingent upon the intended outcome. Figure 70 illustrates the process when forward motion is desired. Both rear motors accelerate equally, denoted by the bolder curved arrows, while the front motors decelerate equally, indicated by the lighter curved arrows. This disparity in thrust results in the rear end of the craft lifting while the front end dips downward. Once the desired angle is attained, the motors revert to a slightly increased speed compared to their original hover speed, propelling the craft forward. As the craft tilts slightly, a portion of the lift force is directed forward, contributing to the craft's forward movement. However, a fraction of the lifting force is lost, necessitating a slight increase in motor speed to compensate. Conversely, to move backward, the opposite sequence occurs, with the front motors accelerating to tilt the craft backward, followed by all four motors returning to a consistent speed as the craft moves back toward the pilot. To revert to a stable hover, counteracting control inputs are applied briefly to arrest the craft's movement, followed by returning the controls to a neutral position once the craft stabilizes.

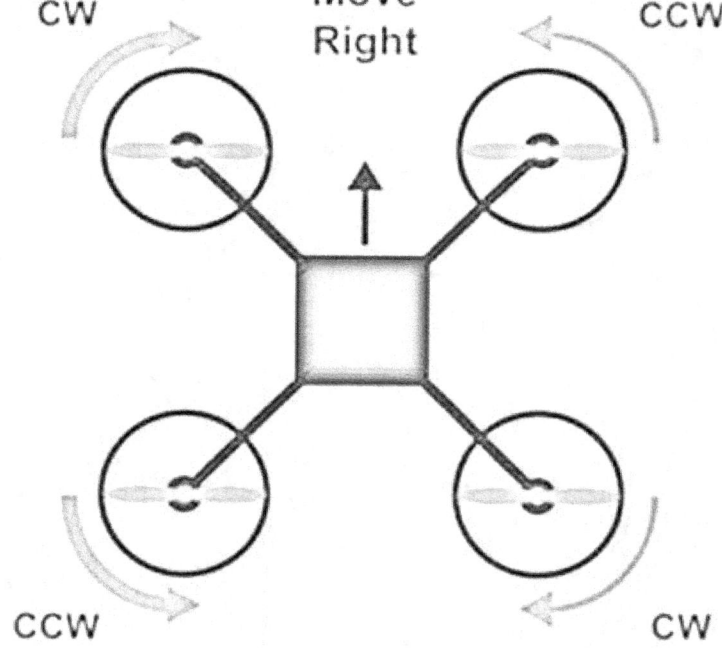

Figure 71: Moving control stick to the right.

To manoeuvre the Quad horizontally, a similar procedure is applied, albeit with different motors adjusting their speeds. In Figure 71, the depiction illustrates the outcome when shifting the control stick to the right. The two left motors accelerate while the two right motors decelerate. Once the craft achieves the desired angle, the motor speeds normalize, initiating movement to the right. Conversely, to veer left, the opposite occurs: the two right motors accelerate while the two left motors decelerate, prompting the craft to tilt leftward and commence leftward movement. As previously explained, to return to a stable hover, counteractive control inputs are briefly applied to halt the motion, followed by resetting the control stick to a neutral position.

When the craft is in a level hover and equipped with a flight controller incorporating accelerometers, the board can detect the force of gravity and determine the direction of "down." By aligning itself with gravity's force, the flight controller can automatically level the frame and maintain its position, even when disturbed by external forces like wind gusts.

The next control movement, particularly for novices to multirotors, often raises questions: How does a quad yaw or rotate left and right? In a quad configuration, as demonstrated in the preceding figures, two motors spin clockwise while the other two spin counterclockwise. This setup cancels out the natural torque tendencies of one motor pair with the opposing pair, preventing rotation. Examining Figure 72, to induce clockwise rotation, the two counterclockwise rotating motors accelerate while the two clockwise rotating motors decelerate by an equal amount. This maintains the overall lift generated, as the thrust gained by the faster motors equals the thrust lost by the slower ones. However, the torque moment produced by the counterclockwise motors increases while that of the clockwise motors decreases, resulting in a net torque increase that rotates the entire quad frame clockwise. Conversely, to yaw left, the two clockwise rotating motors accelerate while the two counterclockwise motors decelerate, creating a net torque difference that rotates the quad frame to the left.

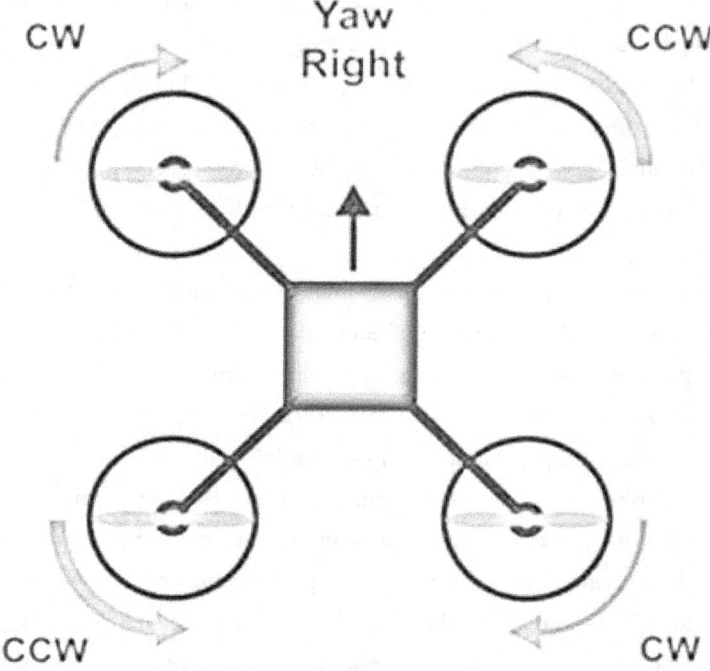

Figure 72: Quad clock-wise rotation.

The final aspect of flight to address is changes in altitude. As depicted in Figure 73, to ascend, all four motors increase in speed by an equal measure, resulting in a net thrust increase that lifts the quad upward. Conversely, to descend, the reverse occurs: all four motors decrease in speed by the same amount, leading to a net thrust decrease that allows the craft to descend under the influence of gravity.

All the manoeuvres discussed thus far essentially involve transitioning in and out of stable hover flight. If your multirotor's flight controller board includes an acrobatic mode without self-leveling capability, you can also perform manoeuvres like loops or rolls by sufficiently moving and holding the control stick. In a loop, the additional lift from the front motors continues to pull the front of the craft upward and over the top, eventually returning to level flight. Before attempting a loop in a quad, ensure you have ample altitude, as multirotor aircraft typically use fixed-pitch props, causing rapid descent when upside down. In a quad, quick loops can be executed by climbing up, followed by a flip at the apex. Alternatively, you can loop a quad from forward flight to achieve a smooth round loop, provided you maintain sufficient forward speed to counteract the force of gravity pulling the craft outward.

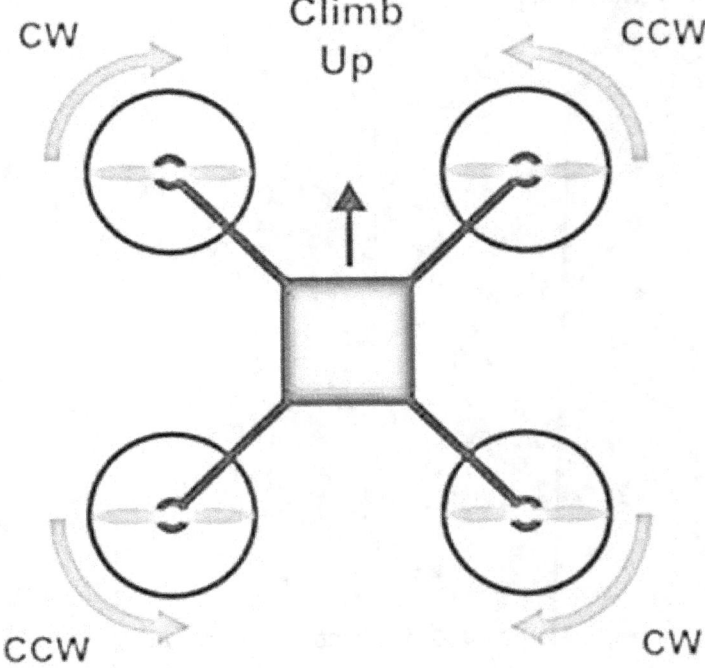

Figure 73: Changing altitude.

Performing flip rolls from a level hover is feasible, provided they are executed swiftly and from a sufficient altitude above the ground. Rolling a quad from forward flight resembles rolling a trainer aircraft with a flat-bottom airfoil. You must initiate the roll by pulling up slightly to establish a slight upward angle. The altitude lost during the roll naturally returns you to level flight upon completion or with a slight nose-down attitude, which can be adjusted with a slight pullback on the stick.

That essentially covers the fundamentals of how a multirotor craft manoeuvres without control surfaces and hopefully clarifies some of the underlying physics of these captivating models. Once you grasp the physics involved, operating a multirotor becomes far less mysterious.

Mastering the essential elements of piloting your new quadcopter involves grasping the concepts of Roll, Pitch, and Yaw. Once you have a solid understanding of these principles and their impact on your drone's flight, navigating your drone will become much smoother. Dedicate some time to acquaint yourself with how Roll, Pitch, and Yaw are incorporated into the design and behaviour of your drone. With consistent practice, you'll quickly elevate your piloting skills to professional levels!

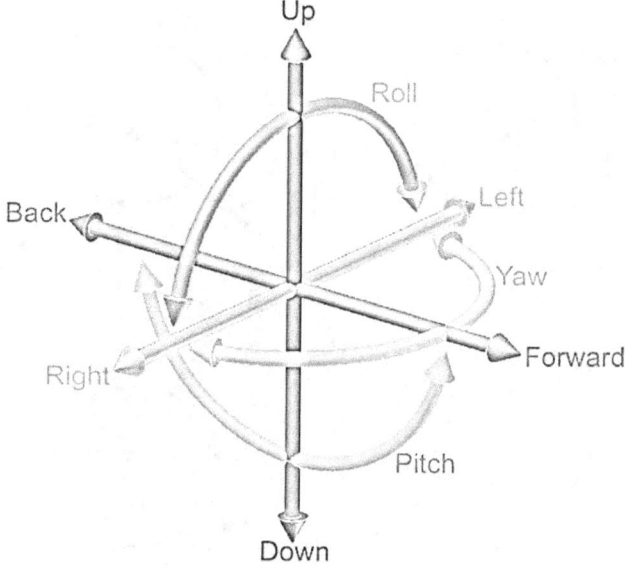

Figure 74: Drone control movements.

The transmitter for your drone plays a pivotal role in its operation, particularly concerning your quadcopter's flight dynamics. Equipped with two joysticks, the right joystick manages the "Pitch" and "Roll," while the left joystick handles the "Yaw." Roll denotes lateral movement, shifting the drone from side to side, while pitch governs forward and backward motion. Yaw dictates the clockwise or counterclockwise rotation of your UAV, and the throttle controls vertical ascent and descent. It's crucial to keep the throttle engaged while piloting your drone to maintain power and prevent it from descending once throttle input is reduced.

Figure 75 is a simple diagram that shows how the controls relate to Yaw, Pitch and Roll.

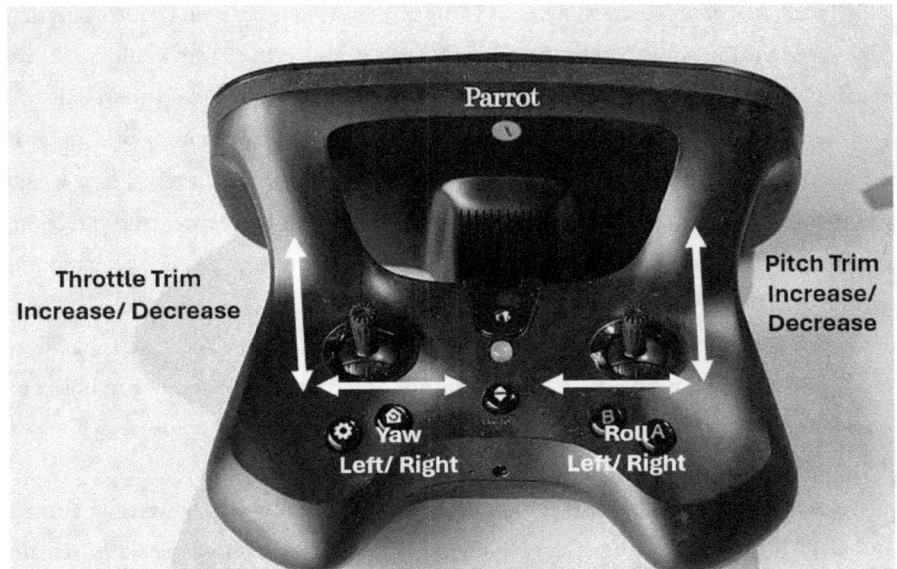

Figure 75: Controlling Yaw, Pitch and Roll. Back image: Parrot Bebop 2 Power Drone controller, Hunini, CC BY-SA 4.0, via Wikimedia Commons.

Unmanned Aerial Vehicles (UAVs) represent complex engineering achievements, demanding a profound comprehension of the underlying physics for their feasible design and construction. These aircraft must possess the capability to sense their position, velocity, acceleration, and various other parameters governing their motion. This discussion primarily centres on Vertical Take-off and Landing (VTOL) UAVs, exemplified in the following with the by the Draganflyer X6, yet the principles discussed extend to all airborne vehicles and UAVs.

Before delving into more intricate concepts such as airfoils and accelerometers, it is essential to grasp a few basic physical principles. These encompass force, mass, and acceleration. While a comprehensive explanation often necessitates calculus, we will adopt a purely algebraic approach.

Mass: Mass denotes a property determining how an object interacts within a gravitational field and influences phenomena like acceleration, momentum, and energy. Although mass is often conflated with weight, they are distinct concepts. Weight represents a force exerted on an object, while mass is an intrinsic property. The SI unit of mass is the Kilogram, distinct from pounds, which quantify force.

Velocity: Velocity, often synonymous with speed, distinguishes itself by incorporating both speed and direction. Unlike speed, which solely measures the rate of motion, velocity encapsulates direction, typically represented as an angle relative to a reference point.

Acceleration: Acceleration characterizes the rate of change in velocity over time. It can be calculated as the ratio of the change in velocity to the time interval over which the change occurs. Acceleration accounts for alterations in both speed and direction, rendering it a vector quantity. Accelerometers, electronic devices, gauge acceleration in various directions.

Force: Force, the product of mass and acceleration (Newton's Second Law), manifests as a "push" or "pull" on an object. The magnitude of force required to move an object or accelerate it correlates with its mass. Consequently, applying force to an object with mass induces acceleration.

These foundational concepts underpin the fundamental physics governing aircraft and UAV flight. While subsequent concepts build upon these principles, they remain fundamental to understanding flight dynamics.

UAV Flight Equilibrium

Equilibrium characterizes a state in which all forces acting upon an object precisely balance each other out, resulting in a net force of zero. Since any force applied to an object induces acceleration, an aircraft must experience balanced forces to maintain a stationary position. But how does this equilibrium occur?

Consider a hypothetical aircraft hovering in place. The primary forces acting on it include gravity, pulling downwards, and thrust from the motors, pushing upwards. For simplicity, we'll disregard airflow, torque from the propellers, and other lateral forces.

To hover without ascending or descending, the thrust generated by the motors must exactly counteract the force of gravity. Visually, this equilibrium is depicted with the green arrow representing gravitational force and the orange arrow depicting the lift force produced by the motors.

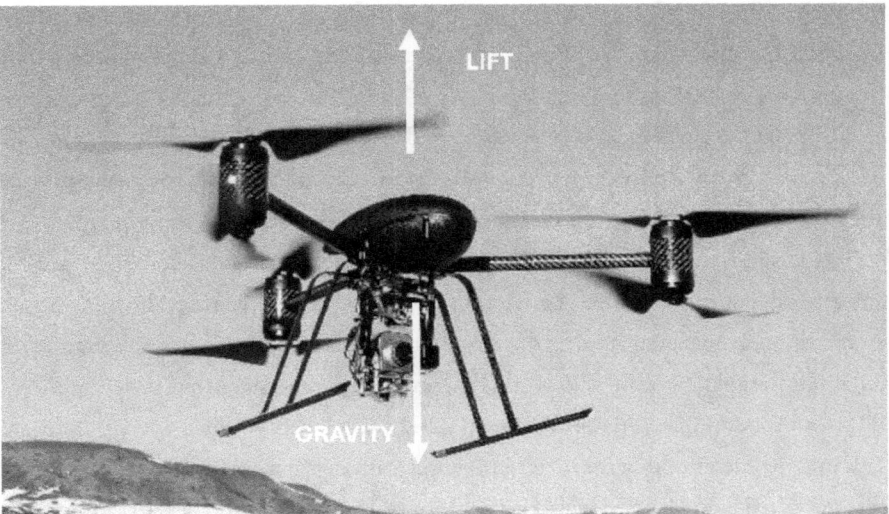

Figure 76: Lift and gravity forces acting on a drone. Back image: Draganflyer X6, Ian Burt, CC BY-SA 2.0, via Flikr.

This concept holds practical significance. For instance, in the case of the Draganflyer X6, weighing 1000 grams, the motors and propellers must provide precisely 1000 grams of thrust downwards to sustain the UAV in a hover.

However, equilibrium can be disrupted to induce specific manoeuvres. For instance, to initiate a turn with the Draganflyer X6, one set of propellers spins faster than the other two, creating an excess force on one side of the aircraft, resulting in acceleration. This acceleration facilitates the turn by tilting the aircraft. Once the aircraft is banked, the thrust from the motors is redirected away from the vertical direction, enabling movement relative to the ground. To halt the motion, the UAV banks in the opposite direction.

UAV Endurance

The main factors limiting drone operation are the range of your radio and the battery life. Typically, a standard 2.4GHz radio provides a range of up to 1km, extending to about 1.5km under ideal conditions. However, when using the drone in auto mission mode, you're not confined by the radio's range, although it's crucial to understand this feature thoroughly and ensure its legal compliance. Battery life varies depending on the drone model and equipment attached. Additionally, power consumption increases during high-speed flights, reducing flight time. Altitude above sea level also affects battery life, making it essential to test battery endurance under specific conditions and monitor battery levels closely during operation.

The maximum payload a drone can carry depends on various factors, including its design, motors, propellers, electronic speed controllers (ESC), batteries, and altitude above sea level. Refer to the specifications for each drone model for precise details.

The ideal location for drone flight is an open area where there's no risk to people, animals, or property. However, be cautious of strong RF interference, which may cause erratic drone behaviour. Starting on grass can mitigate damage in case of a crash, and obtaining permission from landowners is necessary for accessing private property.

Most drones utilize Lithium Polymer (LiPo) battery packs, which consist of several cells in series, determining the battery's voltage. Battery packs also vary in storage capacities measured in mAh, with higher capacities resulting in larger and heavier batteries.

While brushless motors on most Unmanned Aerial Systems (UAS) can operate in light rain, the flight controller, ESC, and other electronics should remain dry. Unless weather-rated, drones are not guaranteed to fly in rain.

If control is lost due to signal loss between the radio and the drone, the drone will enter Return To Land (RTL) mode and return to its take-off point if GPS lock was established. Similarly, activating this feature via a switch on the radio can bring the drone home in case of pilot error or visibility issues, provided it wasn't involved in a crash.

Flying a drone has become easier with stabilized flight controllers and GPS capabilities. Most people can take off and maintain flight, but advanced skills are needed for navigating obstacles and capturing specific shots, requiring practice and experience.

Many flight controllers support fully autonomous missions, from take-off to completing tasks like flying a grid and returning home. Monitoring can be done from the ground using ground control software or live video feeds.

Quadcopter Controls

Mastering the controls of a quadcopter is pivotal in your journey to becoming proficient in flying it. As you familiarize yourself with these controls, they will gradually become ingrained in your muscle memory, offering a seamless flying experience.

Each control operates independently, yet their synergy is what enables you to navigate the quadcopter effectively. By understanding how each control functions individually and their collective impact, you'll gain mastery over the quadcopter's movement dynamics.

It's important to note that the extent to which you manipulate the controls directly influences the quadcopter's response. During the initial learning phase, it's advisable to apply gentle pressure on the sticks, resulting in subtle quadcopter movements. With increased confidence and skill, you can progressively increase the intensity of your stick movements, enabling sharper and more precise maneuvers.

The four primary quadcopter controls include:

- Roll

- Pitch

- Yaw

- Throttle

Roll

Rolling is a control that shifts your quadcopter horizontally to the left or right. This action is executed by manipulating the right stick on your transmitter in either direction.

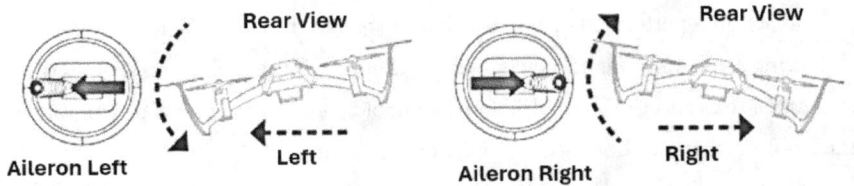

Figure 77: Quadcopter roll controls.

The term "roll" aptly describes this movement as it simulates the rolling motion of the quadcopter itself. For instance, when you push the right stick to the right, the quadcopter will incline diagonally downward to the right.

Figure 77 demonstrates a quadcopter executing left and right rolls. Take note of the quadcopter's tilt and the orientation of the propellers.

When rolling to the right, the underside of the propellers points leftward, directing airflow in that direction. Consequently, the quadcopter moves to the right. Conversely, when rolling to the left, the propellers angle to the right, causing airflow in that direction and resulting in leftward movement for the copter.

Pitch

To adjust the pitch of your quadcopter, use the right stick on your transmitter to move it either forward or backward. This action tilts the quadcopter, causing it to move either forward or backward accordingly.

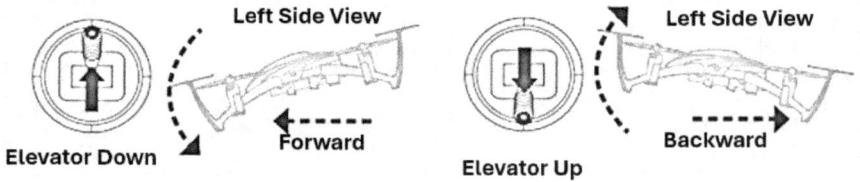

Figure 78: Quadcopter pitch controls.

Figure 78 shows an example of a quadcopter pitching forwards and backwards. Note that this view is from the left side.

Yaw

This action is performed by moving the left stick to the left or right.

During continuous flight, yaw is often combined with throttle. This enables the pilot to create circles and patterns. Moreover, it enables videographers and photographers to track objects that may be changing directions.

Throttle

Throttle provides the necessary power to the propellers of your quadcopter for take-off. During flight, you'll maintain constant throttle engagement.

To activate the throttle, push the left stick forward. To deactivate it, pull the stick backward.

Ensure not to deactivate it entirely until you're a few inches above the ground. Otherwise, there's a risk of damaging the quadcopter, potentially ending your training prematurely.

When the quadcopter is oriented towards you instead of facing away, the controls are reversed, which intuitively follows:

- Moving the right stick to the right causes the quadcopter to move right (roll).

- Moving the right stick forward results in the quadcopter moving forward (pitch).

- Moving the right stick backward leads to the quadcopter moving backward (pitch).

- And so forth.

Therefore, it's crucial to remain mindful of this adjustment as you manoeuvre the quadcopter. Focus on predicting the quadcopter's movements rather than its orientation relative to you.

Remote Control/Transmitter

A transmitter serves as a handheld controller enabling you to navigate your quadcopter and dictate its flight trajectory. Whenever you manipulate the sticks, it transmits corresponding signals to your copter, instructing it on the next action to take.

Various transmitters exist, differing in shape, size, and functionalities. However, certain components remain consistent across all transmitters.

Right Stick: Responsible for roll and pitch adjustments, the right stick manoeuvres your quadcopter left/right and backward/forward.

Left Stick: Managing yaw and throttle, the left stick rotates your quadcopter clockwise or counterclockwise and regulates its altitude during flight.

Trim Buttons: Each control possesses its own trim button for fine-tuning adjustments.

Upon initially engaging the throttle to lift your quadcopter, you might observe that the UAV tilts spontaneously and veers in one or multiple directions. This occurs due to imbalanced controls, necessitating the adjustment of specific controls for proper balance.

Pre-Flight Checklist

Performing a pre-flight checklist is crucial for ensuring the safety of both yourself and your quadcopter. It also helps prevent unnecessary delays by addressing any issues beforehand, allowing you to fully enjoy your flying experience. Here's a checklist to go through before each flight:

WEATHER AND SITE SAFETY CHECK

- Ensure precipitation chance is less than 10%
- Confirm wind speed is under 15 knots (less than 20 mph)
- Verify cloud base is at least 500 feet
- Ensure visibility is at least 3 statute miles (SM)
- Double-check civil twilight hours for dawn/dusk flights
- Establish take-off, landing, and emergency hover zones
- Check for potential electromagnetic interference
- Look out for towers, wires, buildings, trees, or other obstructions
- Watch for pedestrians and animals; set up safety perimeter if necessary
- Discuss flight mission with other crew members if present

VISUAL AIRCRAFT / SYSTEM INSPECTION

- Confirm registration number is displayed properly and is legible
- Check for abnormalities in aircraft frame, propellers, motors, undercarriage, etc.
- Inspect gimbal, camera, transmitter, payloads, etc., for abnormalities
- Remove gimbal clamp and lens caps
- Clean lens with microfiber cloth
- Attach propellers, battery/fuel source, and insert SD card/lens filters

POWERING UP

- Turn on transmitter/remote control and open relevant app

- Turn on aircraft

- Verify established connection between transmitter and aircraft

- Position antennas on transmitter toward the sky

- Ensure display panel/FPV screen is functioning properly

- Calibrate Inertial Measurement Unit (IMU) if needed

- Calibrate compass before every flight

- Verify battery/fuel levels on both transmitter and aircraft

- Confirm the UAS has acquired GPS location from at least six satellites

TAKING OFF

- Ascend to eye-level altitude for about 10-15 seconds

- Check for imbalances or irregularities

- Listen for abnormal sounds

- Test control response and sensitivity (pitch, roll, and yaw)

- Look out for electromagnetic interference or software warnings

- Conduct one final check to ensure the safety of the flight operations area

- Proceed with the flight mission

Getting Your Drone Off the Ground

To lift your quadcopter off the ground, focus solely on the throttle control. Gently push the throttle (left stick) upward to initiate propeller movement. Pause briefly, then repeat this action several times to familiarize yourself with the throttle's sensitivity.

Gradually increase the throttle input until the copter begins to ascend. Once airborne, smoothly lower the throttle back to zero and allow the quadcopter to descend and land.

Repeat this process 3-5 times, observing any unintended movements such as yaw rotation, lateral drifting (roll), or forward/backward motion (pitch). If you detect any undesired movements, utilize the corresponding trim button to correct them.

For instance, if the copter veers left when applying throttle, adjust the "roll" trim button located beside the right stick.

Continue adjusting the trims until you achieve a relatively stable hover by solely manipulating the throttle.

Quadcopter Propeller Design

Quadcopter propellers span a wide range of materials, sizes, and costs, from budget options to premium selections. Typically, less expensive propellers are subject to greater vibration due to less precise manufacturing, particularly evident in larger-sized propellers. However, this discrepancy diminishes for smaller craft. For those aiming for top-notch aerial photography or videography, investing in high-quality propellers is advisable. Additionally, regularly checking your quadcopter propellers with a quality prop balancer every few flights is recommended.

When selecting or designing propellers for your quadcopter, three key measurements should be considered:

1. Length (Diameter): The diameter of the spinning propeller disc, usually expressed in inches. Kv motor ratings influence the ideal prop size; higher Kv ratings necessitate smaller props for increased speed but reduced efficiency. Conversely, larger props, paired with lower Kv motors, offer easier control, consume less current, and can lift more weight. Consult manufacturer recommendations for optimal motor and propeller pairings when building a quadcopter.

2. Pitch: This measurement denotes the distance a propeller would advance forward through a solid in a single full revolution. For example, a propeller with a 7.0-inch pitch would move forward 7.0 inches in one revolution.

3. Bore: The bore measurement indicates the size of the hole in the centre of the propeller, which must match the shaft of your chosen motors. Adapters can resize a prop's bore, or some props feature a direct mounting system that securely attaches them to the motor head with screws.

Self-Locking Props

Most modern quadcopters utilize self-locking props. These props automatically secure themselves during flight by threading in the opposite direction of motor spin, preventing loosening mid-flight.

Considerations for Prop Size

The pitch of a propeller determines the thrust and required motor output. Multi-rotors typically employ props with pitches ranging from 3 to 5 inches, with lower pitches offering higher efficiency. Larger props or those with higher pitch lengths increase aircraft speed but also consume more power. Generally, props with smaller diameters or pitches can achieve higher RPMs with less motor effort, resulting in smoother operation and increased responsiveness to control inputs.

Clockwise (CW) and Counter-Clockwise (CCW) Propellers

Quadcopters utilize four propellers, with clockwise and counter-clockwise props featuring distinct designs. When purchasing propellers, you'll encounter terms like CW (clockwise) and CCW (counter-clockwise). Matching pairs of CW and CCW propellers are essential for generating thrust and counteracting opposing yaw motions during flight.

Quadcopter Propeller Materials

Quadcopter propellers are typically made from plastic or, in higher-end models, carbon fibre. Wood propellers are also available, commonly found in the model aircraft sector.

Hovering in Midair and Landing Your Drone

To achieve a stable hover, initiate take-off by gradually increasing the throttle until the quadcopter lifts off the ground. Once airborne, utilize slight adjustments of the right stick to maintain the quadcopter's position in the air. Additionally, minor corrections with the left stick (yaw) may be necessary to prevent unwanted rotation.

Gradually increase the throttle to elevate the quadcopter to a height of approximately one to one-and-a-half feet above the ground. Employ subtle movements of the right stick (and potentially the left stick) to ensure the quadcopter remains stationary in its hover.

When ready to land, gradually reduce the throttle. As the quadcopter descends and approaches a height of one to two inches above the ground, smoothly decrease the throttle entirely, allowing the UAV to gently descend and touch down.

Repeat this process until you feel comfortable maintaining a stable hover and executing smooth landings.

Flying Your Quadcopter Left/Right and Forward/Backward

To navigate a quadcopter in various directions such as left, right, forwards, and backwards, it's essential to maintain a steady throttle to sustain its flight. The right stick is then used to control the quadcopter's movement according to the desired direction.

Begin by achieving a stable hover with the quadcopter. Next, push the right stick forward to propel the copter a few feet ahead. To return it to its original position, pull the right stick back. Repeat this process to move the quadcopter backward a few feet before returning it to its initial hover position.

To shift the quadcopter to the left, push the right stick to the left to initiate lateral movement. Bring it back to its original position, then navigate it a few feet to the right by pushing the right stick to the right. If the quadcopter starts to rotate (yaw), adjust the left stick to the left or right to maintain its orientation.

During directional manoeuvres, it's common for the quadcopter to experience a drop in altitude. To counteract this, increase the throttle to provide additional power whenever you execute a turn or movement, ensuring the copter maintains a consistent altitude.

Flying a Square Pattern

You've successfully lifted off and mastered the basics of quadcopter navigation in the fundamental directions. Now, it's time to integrate these skills and advance to flying in defined patterns, enhancing your ability to coordinate multiple control inputs.

To execute a square pattern, maintain the quadcopter's orientation facing away from you throughout the manoeuvre. Begin by pushing the right stick forward (pitch) to propel the copter forward a few feet. Once you've reached the desired distance, return the right stick to its neutral position to hold the quadcopter in a stationary hover.

Next, shift the right stick to the right (roll) to guide the copter sideways to the right for a short distance. After reaching the designated point, stabilize the quadcopter in a hover for a brief pause, ensuring control and alignment.

Using Yaw Control to Rotate Your Quadcopter

To initiate rotation of your quadcopter, ensure it is airborne by adjusting the throttle accordingly. Upon achieving a stable hover, manipulate the left stick in either direction. This action induces rotational movement of the quadcopter while it remains in place.

Complete a full 360-degree rotation by continuously pushing the left stick in one direction. Then, reverse the direction of the left stick and repeat the process to execute another 360-degree rotation in the opposite direction.

Continue practicing this manoeuvre until you feel confident and comfortable with the rotation control.

Flying Continuously

Mastering continuous flight with a quadcopter involves coordinating rotations and directional changes simultaneously, which may require some adjustment. As the quadcopter changes orientation relative to your own, it's essential to closely monitor how each stick movement influences its flight path.

Begin by taking off and achieving a stable hover. Gradually rotate the copter to a slight angle using the yaw control. Utilize the right stick to navigate the copter left/right and forwards/backwards, familiarizing yourself with controlling the quadcopter while it faces various angles.

Continue practicing by rotating the copter to different angles and manoeuvring it accordingly with the right stick until you feel comfortable flying at different orientations. To maintain continuous flight, gradually push the right stick forward while simultaneously making slight adjustments to the left or right with the same stick.

Explore flying in different directions by adjusting the right stick forward (pitch) and modifying its lateral movements, while also using the left stick (yaw) to alter the copter's facing direction. Experiment with adjusting the copter's altitude by manipulating the left stick forward and backward (throttle) as you continue to refine your flying skills.

Different Milestones to Hit

Utilize these milestones to maintain organization throughout your learning journey. They serve as benchmarks to assess your progress and determine your next steps:

- Familiarize yourself with the four primary quadcopter controls – roll, pitch, yaw, and throttle – and grasp their effects on quadcopter movement.

- Understand the functionality of each component of your quadcopter.

- Establish and follow a pre-flight checklist before every take-off.

- Comprehend and adhere to safety protocols.

- Employ the throttle to initiate take-off and utilize trim buttons for necessary adjustments.

- Achieve comfort with hovering mid-air and executing gentle landings.

- Perform take-offs to a 3-foot altitude and land in the same position.

- Execute take-offs to a 3-foot altitude and perform a 180-degree spin with the UAV.

- Develop proficiency in manoeuvring the quadcopter left/right and forwards/backwards.

- Learn to navigate a quadcopter in a square pattern.

- Master quadcopter flight in circular patterns.

- Acquire the skill of rotating (yaw) a quadcopter.

- Learn to maintain continuous flight with a quadcopter.

- Execute all aforementioned tasks at an altitude of 25 feet.

Crash Avoidance

Experiencing the sight of your drone on the verge of nosediving into a tree or, worse, a lake can rank among the most distressing moments for any drone pilot. However, if your drone gets lodged in a tree, there's no need to panic as you have several retrieval options. Moreover, while drone crashes are a possibility, there are steps you can take to minimize the likelihood of such mishaps and mitigate potential damage to your drone.

First and foremost, it is imperative to read your drone's manual thoroughly. Many novice drone pilots make the mistake of bypassing this crucial step, only to encounter erratic behavior from their drone, colloquially known as a "fly away," resulting in the drone disappearing into the sunset, never to be recovered.

Additionally, before embarking on a drone flight, it's essential to check the weather conditions. Aside from avoiding fast-moving storms, it's crucial to assess wind speed and direction, especially when piloting lightweight drones like the Syma X5C, as strong winds can significantly impede flight control.

Furthermore, selecting an appropriate flying location is paramount. Opt for wide-open spaces with minimal or no trees and minimal foot traffic. This choice provides ample room for manoeuvring and ensures a clear line of sight with your aircraft throughout the flight.

Monitoring your flight time is another crucial aspect of safe drone piloting. Be mindful of your battery life and ensure you have sufficient charge remaining for the return trip. Consult your drone's manual to estimate battery life, and heed any advanced warnings indicating low battery levels.

Performing a thorough inspection of your drone before each flight is essential. Ensure that all propellers are securely fastened and free of damage or wear. Additionally, inspect the entire UAV for any damaged components, and promptly repair or replace any compromised parts before take-off.

To prevent drone flyaways, which can stem from hardware or software issues but are often the result of pilot error, prioritize pilot education and experience. Familiarize yourself with your drone's startup sequence, update firmware if applicable, and ensure proper calibration before each flight. Moreover, always use a fully charged battery, secure connections, and set GPS lock for added safety, reserving return-to-home functionality as a last resort. Following these guidelines can help minimize the risk of drone crashes and ensure a safer and more enjoyable flying experience.

Emergency procedures

The mission plan for Remotely Piloted Aircraft (RPA) should encompass detailed procedures and information pertaining to planned emergency flight protocols to be implemented in the event of a loss of data link with the RPA. Depending on system capabilities, these protocols may encompass:

- Automated transit of the RPA to a predetermined recovery zone followed by automated recovery.

- Automated transit of the RPA to a predetermined recovery zone followed by activation of a flight termination system.

In controlled airspace, specific abort and flight termination procedures must be briefed to Air Traffic Control (ATC). At a minimum, the briefing should include details regarding pre-programmed loss-of-link flight profiles, flight termination capabilities, and RPA performance under termination conditions. Continuous and automatic checking of the data link is essential, with real-time warnings displayed to the remote crew in case of failure.

In the event of a data link loss, excluding intermittent signal loss or programmed outages, immediate notification to ATC is imperative, followed by execution of recovery procedures. Parameters determining acceptable intermittent signal loss and total loss are predetermined by the manufacturer. An RPA experiencing a lost data link and executing a pre-programmed flight profile to termination or recovery should be given priority handling by ATC.

If communication between the RP (Remote Pilot) and ATC fails, the RP should select SSR (Secondary Surveillance Radar) code 7600, if applicable, and attempt to establish alternative communication channels. Pending re-establishment of communication with ATC, the RPA will adhere to the last acknowledged instruction or the conditions outlined in the Area Approval. If communication with ATC remains severed, the RPA sortie should be terminated.

The RPA mission plan should outline emergency procedures to be followed in the event of various contingencies, including engine failure, loss of data link, loss of control, failure of navigation equipment, and airframe damage. Emergency procedures may involve the utilization of recovery or fail-safe devices, such as parachutes, to mitigate risks to individuals or property. The deployment of such devices is encouraged where applicable to the RPA type. Additionally, in cases where an RPA is equipped with a recovery device like a ballistic parachute system, including a pyrotechnic charge, clear marking of the area or panel is essential for identification purposes.

Launch and Landing Zones

Launch Site Selection

When selecting a launch site for Remotely Piloted Aircraft (RPA), safety considerations take precedence. Launch site selection involves the following:

1. **Maintaining Adequate Buffer Zones**: RPSS personnel should ensure a buffer of at least 50 feet between aircraft operations and non-essential personnel. Observers, acting as safety supervisors, should monitor this buffer.

2. **Environmental Assessment**: No launches should proceed until all environmental assessments have been considered. Personnel have the authority to abort any launch if it poses hazards to the environment, themselves, or others in the area.

3. **Departure over Sparsely Populated Corridors**: The Pilot-in-Command (PIC) should endeavour to select a launch site that minimizes departures over populated areas. If flights over populated areas are necessary, each flight should be planned to minimize time spent in such areas.

Landing Site and Alternate Landing Sites

1. **Primary Landing Site**: Typically, the primary landing site is the same as the launch site. The PIC has the final authority over any approaches to the primary site and may abort any approach deemed unsafe.

2. **Alternate Landing Sites**: The PIC must designate at least one alternate landing site. In the event that a wave off is not possible and the primary landing site is deemed unsafe, procedures to utilize the secondary site will be activated.

3. **Mission Abort Sites**: Optionally, the PIC may designate an "abort site" where the aircraft may be safely "dumped" in an emergency situation. This site should minimize risk in the event of an emergency.

4. **Approaches over Populated Areas**: The PIC should make every effort to

select a landing site that minimizes approaches over populated areas.

5. **Landing Safety & Crowd Control**: All landing sites should be operated with the same safety standards as launch sites, maintaining a buffer of at least 50 feet between aircraft operations and non-essential personnel.

Flight Control/Ground Station Best Practices
Before Take Off:

1. Confirm transmitter antenna is fully extended.

2. Ensure transmitter trim settings are correct.

3. Confirm receiver antenna is fully extended.

4. Check take-off area for obstructions and clear it of people.

5. Review weather conditions and potential emergency landing areas.

6. Set flight timer alarm.

7. Announce "PREPARING TO TAKE OFF."

8. Launch aircraft.

In-Flight:

1. Climb to a safe altitude and check control systems.

2. Reset trims if necessary.

3. Maintain safe operating distance from people and buildings.

4. If flying over buildings or people, maintain a safe altitude.

5. Continually scan for potential hazards.

Landing:

1. Check control systems and set trims for emergency landing.

2. Scan landing area for obstructions and recheck weather conditions.

3. Announce "PREPARING TO LAND."

4. Always be prepared for a go-around.

5. Carefully land the aircraft away from obstructions and people.

Post-Flight:
1. Turn off aircraft power and/or disconnect batteries.

2. Turn off transmitter.

3. Power down photo equipment.

4. Visually inspect aircraft for damage.

5. Remove unused fuel if applicable.

6. Secure the aircraft.

The Circuit Pattern

You should acquaint yourself with the names of the four legs of the circuit.

The first leg after take-off is known as Upwind, though it's not often explicitly named. Upwind denotes the initial leg when flying a circuit, typically into the wind to utilize maximum runway length.

Next is the Crosswind leg, a brief segment where you attain cruising altitude post-take-off.

Downwind follows, a lengthy leg characterized by cruising with a tailwind. Ensure proper height and parallel alignment with the runway.

Base comes next, a brief crosswind leg preceding the final approach for landing.

Finally, the Final leg aligns with the runway for landing preparation. Maintain accurate positioning without cutting corners or making it too short.

Circuit training is a common practice at many airports, especially regional and general aviation aerodromes. Each airport establishes its own guidelines regarding the timing and frequency of circuit training, considering factors such as pilot demand, runway capacity, air traffic control services availability, and navigational equipment.

Given the varying facilities at different aerodromes, the frequency and timing of circuit training flights vary accordingly.

A training circuit encompasses five legs – take-off, crosswind, downwind, base, and final approach. Figure 79 illustrates a simplified representation of this circuit, with the take-off and final stages typically flown into the wind for safety. The direction of the circuit pattern depends on local terrain and runway positions. Aircraft symbols and dotted lines in Figure 1 suggest recommended entry points into the circuit pattern.

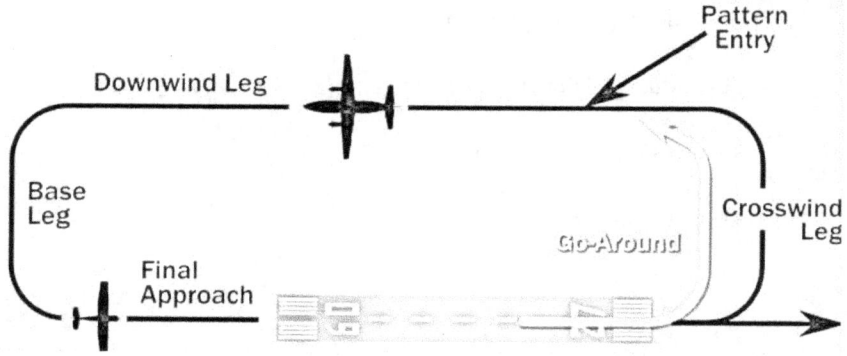

Figure 79: Circuit Pattern.

LEFT-HAND CIRCUITS

Figure 80 illustrates a left-hand circuit where the aircraft makes left turns after take-off, flying in an anticlockwise direction. This type of circuit operation is the most commonly used.

RIGHT-HAND CIRCUITS

In a right-hand circuit, the pilot executes right turns after take-off, following a clockwise circuit. This arrangement might be necessary due to high terrain limiting circuit operations to one side of the runway, irrespective of wind direction. Another scenario for using a right-hand circuit is at airports with parallel runways. During periods when air traffic control services are available, circuits can be conducted off both parallel runways simultaneously, allowing for concurrent left and right-hand circuits.

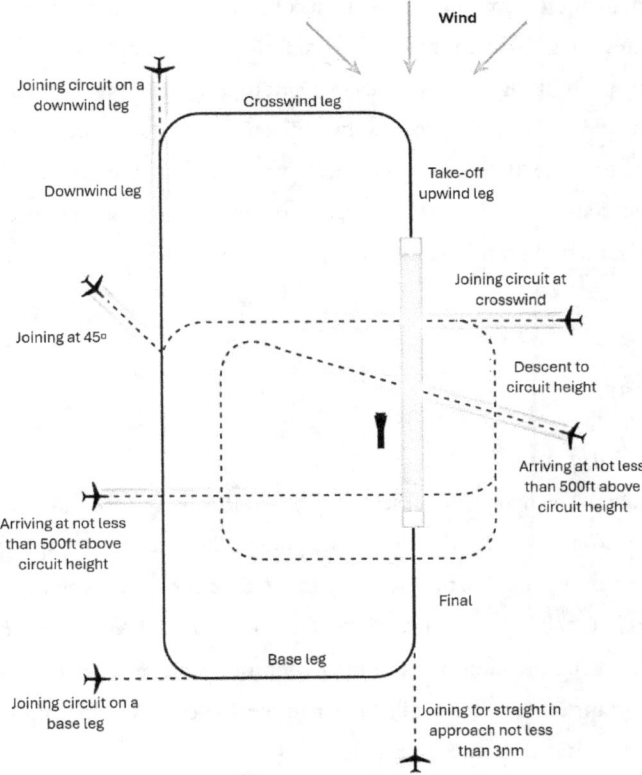

Figure 80: Left hand training circuit.

AIRCRAFT JOINING AND DEPARTING A CIRCUIT

At airports lacking a control tower, CASA regulations specify procedures for aircraft joining a circuit when approaching from outside the local area. This involves flying over the runway at least 500ft above the high-performance circuit or joining at the beginning, end, or partway along the downwind leg (at a 45o angle). If the circuit is clear, an arriving aircraft can join the final approach from three nautical miles out. Pilots at locations with an air traffic control tower must adhere to the tower's instructions regarding altitude and circuit entry/departure. Arrival paths in the circuit are designed to maximize visibility of other aircraft, with dotted lines in Figure 1 indicating approach paths. Aircraft departing the circuit can extend one of the legs but must only turn away when safely clear. Training aircraft at airports without a control tower should yield to commercial aircraft, extending a circuit leg if necessary to allow commercial landings.

AIRCRAFT NOISE IMPACTS

All aircraft, including training planes, must comply with international noise standards. While there are no regulated hours for circuit training, most airports set their own restrictions, typically prohibiting circuits from late night to early morning (for example, around 10pm to 7am). Many airports provide this information on their websites. The length of the circuit, and thus the area overflown, depends on factors like climb rate, weather conditions, air traffic, and pilot skill. Circuit size and location are regulated to ensure overall safety, sometimes resulting in training over populated areas near the aerodrome.

FPV Systems

FPV System Components

Flight Camera: The flight camera serves as your portal into the world of FPV, offering a remote view from the skies that immerses you in the multirotor experience. These cameras, which draw heavily from security camera technology, come in various types tailored for FPV use. They range from basic 600tvl standard definition models to those optimized for low-light conditions and high-definition cameras boasting 1080p resolution. It's important to note that while higher-resolution cameras offer more detail, they may introduce additional latency to the system.

Video Transmitters (VTx's): Video transmitters are responsible for broadcasting the video feed from your flight camera to your goggles or ground station. Available in different sizes, power levels, and configurations, VTx's enable the wireless transmission integral to the FPV system. They operate on multiple frequencies to suit different environments and accommodate numerous pilots simultaneously. Rated in milliwatts (mW), VTx's indicate their transmission range. Proper management of these transmitters is crucial for group flying and etiquette, as mishandling can lead to accidents and conflicts among pilots.

Goggles: FPV goggles provide the visual connection to your FPV multirotor, offering an immersive experience unmatched by ground stations and monitors. With various styles available, from DIY kits to feature-rich models with built-in DVR capabilities, goggles resemble virtual reality headsets, displaying the video feed directly in front of your eyes. The goggles incorporate a Video Receiver (VRx), available in different styles and capabilities, along with antennas that dictate the range of your FPV flight.

Figure 81: FPV pilot in Italy. Wearing FPV goggles and using a radio controller with a TBS Crossfire Micro TX transmitter. Mr.Oizo FPV, CC BY-SA 4.0, via Wikimedia Commons.

Figure 81: FPV pilot in Italy. Wearing FPV goggles and using a radio controller with a TBS Crossfire Micro TX transmitter. Mr.Oizo FPV, CC BY-SA 4.0, via Wikimedia Commons.

Power System Components: FPV Beginner Power Distribution Boards Power distribution boards simplify multirotor wiring by providing a centralized hub for power supply. Previously, complex wiring harnesses directly connected components, but power distribution boards streamlined this process. These boards connect to the battery via a connector and distribute power to all components. Some boards offer additional features like power filtering for cleaner, more reliable power and variable voltage outputs to optimize component performance.

Batteries: Batteries serve as the primary power source for multirotors, significantly impacting flight duration and overall performance. Typically, lithium polymer batteries, they consist of individual cells, each with a voltage rating of 3.7 volts. Adding more cells increases voltage, affecting motor speed. Choosing the right battery involves balancing weight and power, as heavier batteries shorten flight times and strain motors. Batteries are rated by voltage and amp hours, with higher amp hour ratings indicating longer-lasting charge under load.

FIXED WING REMOTE PILOT AIRCRAFT SYSTEMS OPERATIONS

S maller fixed-wing UAVs can be launched manually by the operator, who simply throws them into the air. Conversely, larger and heavier drones require more sophisticated methods of take-off, such as a catapult, runway, or launch from a larger aircraft.

Figure 82: Launch by hand on a small UAV. Bureau of Land Management Oregon and Washington from Portland, America, Public domain, via Wikimedia Commons.

Comparison: Fixed Wing UAV vs VTOL UAV Fixed-wing UAVs typically boast greater payload capacities and endurance for longer distances and flight durations compared to VTOL (Vertical Take-off and Landing) UAVs, all while consuming less power. This attribute makes them ideal for missions requiring extended endurance, such as mapping, surveillance, and defence operations. Additionally, fixed-wing UAVs may exhibit greater resilience to in-flight technical failures due to their ability to glide naturally in the event of propulsion loss.

However, fixed-wing UAVs may not be suitable for certain inspection tasks that demand precise positioning, such as capturing detailed images of specific structures or objects like pylon serial numbers or minute damages.

Figure 83: Examples of fixed wing drones. Vitaly V. Kuzmin, CC BY-SA 4.0, via Wikimedia Commons.

Fixed-wing drones find extensive application across industries like Construction, Agriculture, Mining, and Environmental sectors, primarily for large-scale mapping and surveying endeavours. Their versatility and capability to operate effectively in adverse weather conditions contribute to their increasing adoption across various industries. Flight plans can be meticulously designed to map extensive land areas, often employing continuous grid-like patterns with parallel flight lines. Subsequently, the photogrammetric images captured during these flights can be thoroughly analysed and monitored for various purposes.

Forces Acting on a Fixed Wing Aircraft

The following explanation offers a simplified overview aimed at providing a basic understanding of the forces that influence an aircraft's behaviour. It is designed to aid individuals new to aerodynamics in comprehending the fundamental principles at play. The four primary forces acting on an aircraft include:

1. Lift: Generated by air flowing over the surface of the aircraft's wings, lift increases with the speed of the airflow. The aircraft must attain a certain velocity for the wings to generate sufficient lift to enable take-off and sustained flight.

2. Weight: This force opposes the lift generated by the wings and is attributed to gravity. Gravity remains constant, perpetually drawing the aircraft back toward the ground. If the aircraft ceases forward motion, the wings no longer produce lift, causing the aircraft to descend due to the unopposed force of gravity.

3. Thrust: Typically provided by the aircraft's engine, thrust propels the aircraft forward, initiating airflow over the wings, which in turn generates lift.

4. Drag: As the aircraft moves through the air, it encounters resistance known as drag. Not all thrust generated by the engine contributes to forward speed; some of it is expended to counteract drag. Various types of drag exist, with profile drag being a prominent component. This drag arises from the aircraft's shape and its impact on aerodynamic efficiency. For instance, a bulky, boxy trainer aircraft will achieve lower speeds compared to a sleek, jet-shaped counterpart. While drag opposes thrust, there exists a threshold beyond which additional engine thrust fails to increase the aircraft's speed. The diagram below illustrates these four forces.

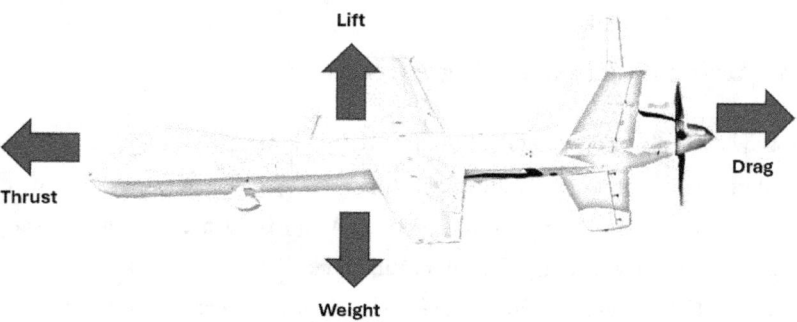

Figure 84: Forces acting on a fixed wing aircraft.

The wing generates lift to counteract the aircraft's weight, while the engine provides thrust to counterbalance the drag exerted by the airframe. Various configurations of this diagram exist throughout different phases of flight. For instance, if the engine fails to produce power, a portion of the lift vector compensates for the lack of thrust to overcome drag. However, gravity always exerts its force. In the absence of thrust, the aircraft will descend.

Control Surfaces

An aircraft's primary controls consist of the throttle, ailerons (one on each main wing), elevator, and rudder, essential for manoeuvring both on the ground and in the air.

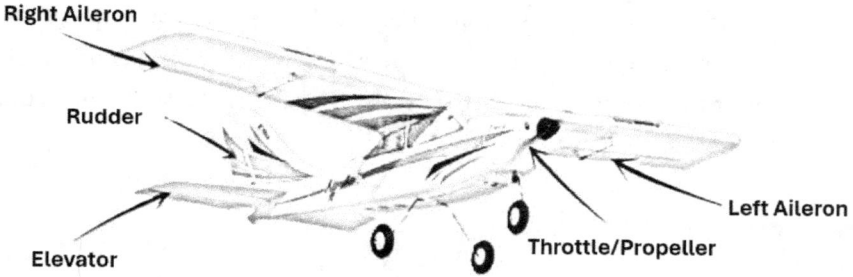

Figure 85: Fixed wing aircraft control surfaces.

The throttle manages engine power, increasing propeller speed as it's advanced, thereby generating thrust. Ailerons, positioned on the trailing edge of the wings, control roll around the aircraft's longitudinal axis. Elevators, situated on the horizontal tailplane, adjust pitch by moving the nose up or down, regulating both airspeed and attitude. The rudder, attached to the vertical fin, governs yawing movement, directing the nose left or right, although it primarily assists in balancing turns rather than initiating them.

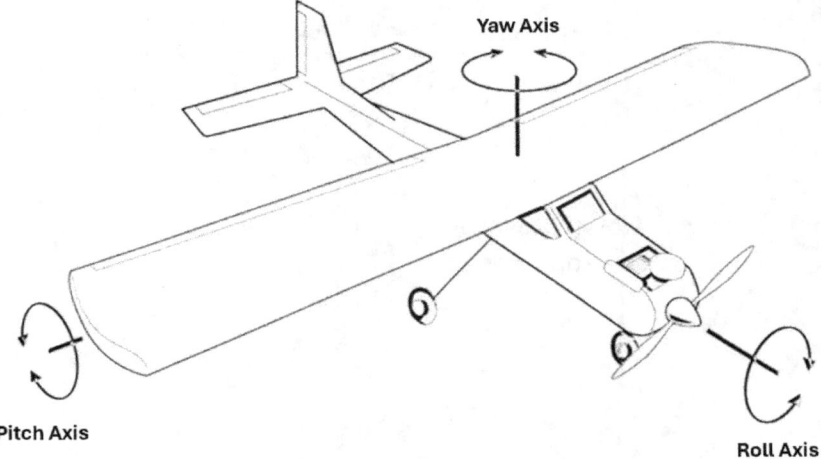

Figure 86: Fixed wing aircraft control axes.

When utilizing the elevator, pulling the stick back elevates the elevator, causing the aircraft's tail to descend, altering the aircraft's pitch and airspeed accordingly. Ailerons, meanwhile, control roll rate and bank angle. They operate inversely, with one rising as the other descends, initiating a roll to the respective side. Conversely, the rudder orchestrates yawing motion, essential for coordinated turns when coupled with aileron input.

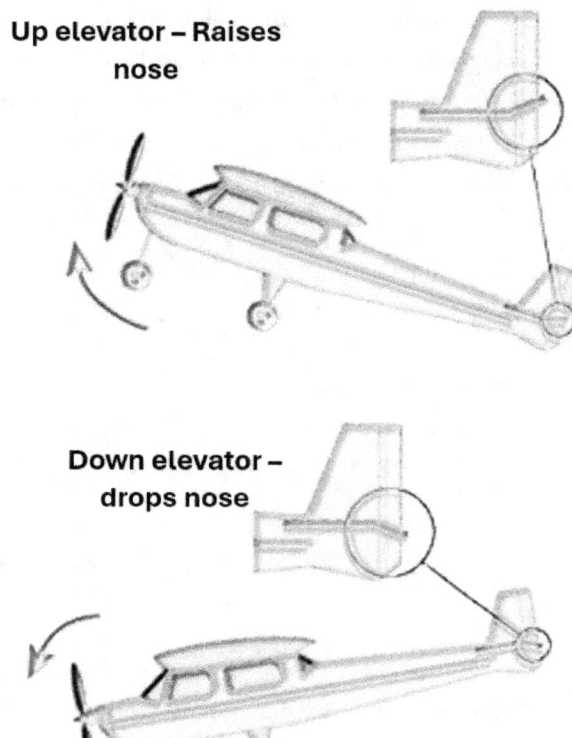

Figure 87: Elevator pitch control.

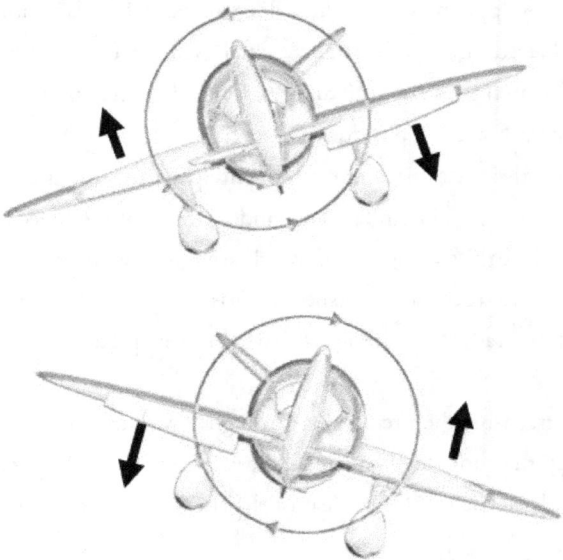

Figure 88: Aileron roll control.

Regarding throttle management, propeller revolutions regulate the rate of climb or descent. Advancing the throttle increases engine power, causing the aircraft to ascend, while reducing throttle induces descent. In landing scenarios, throttle adjustments affect the rate of descent, complementing elevator adjustments controlling airspeed.

In essence, understanding and proficiently manipulating these primary controls are fundamental to piloting a fixed wing drone effectively.

Taking Off, Turning, Climbing, Gliding, and Landing

TAKING OFF

The take-off phase is critical for any flight. Apply full power steadily but not abruptly. Use the rudder to steer while on the ground. As the propeller rotates, it generates a swirling vortex of air that can cause the aircraft to drift leftward. Be prepared for this and counteract it by applying some right rudder to maintain a straight path. Steering on the ground is achieved through the rudder, which is linked to either the nose wheel or a steerable tail wheel in the case of a tail dragger. Once airborne, the adverse turning effect diminishes, allowing for reduced rudder pressure.

To lift off, the aircraft must attain sufficient speed to generate the necessary lift. This occurs at a lower speed than cruising, and a safe climbing speed should always be maintained well above the stalling speed. Avoid excessive elevator input immediately after take-off, as it may cause a decrease in airspeed and risk exceeding the critical angle of attack, leading to a stall. Instead, allow the aircraft to gain speed gradually while maintaining a steady climb.

During take-off, ensure the aircraft remains aligned with the runway and does not veer left or right. Keep the wings level and avoid excessive pitch-up. Only reduce the throttle once a safe altitude is reached. Once clear of the runway, initiate a gentle turn onto the crosswind leg.

All take-offs should be conducted into the prevailing wind. Although the sequence remains similar for most fixed-wing aircraft, there are minor differences based on the type of undercarriage—tricycle or tail dragger. Regardless of the configuration, always utilize the entire runway to ensure ample room for recovery in case of engine failure.

Taking off - Sequence - Tricycle Undercarriage

- Position the aircraft at the centre of the runway, facing into the wind at the downwind end.

- Gradually increase throttle to maximum setting (full throttle), compensating for leftward motor pull with right rudder input.

- Maintain runway alignment using rudder control, while gradually applying up elevator to lift the nose and take off.

- Continue along the centreline with a slight nose-up attitude, ensuring the angle of attack does not exceed 20 degrees.

- Initiate the first turn of the circuit once sufficient speed and height are attained.

Taking off - Sequence - Tail Dragger
- Apply up elevator before starting the take-off to keep the tail wheel on the ground and allow initial rudder control.

- Gradually increase throttle to maximum setting, compensating for leftward motor pull with right rudder input.

- Control aircraft heading with rudder until near take-off speed, then release elevator input to allow the tail to rise.

- Apply a slight elevator input to raise the nose and lift off the ground.

- Maintain a slight nose-up attitude and ensure angle of attack remains below 20 degrees.

- Continue along the centreline until sufficient speed and height are achieved, then commence the first turn of the circuit.

Key Considerations:
- Ensure smooth throttle application to avoid engine spluttering.

- Anticipate leftward drift when increasing throttle and counteract with right rudder input.

- Maintain a climb angle below 20 degrees for a gradual ascent.

- Delay initiating the first turn until sufficient speed and height are attained.

- Some aircraft may require slight down elevator to prevent excessive angle of attack.

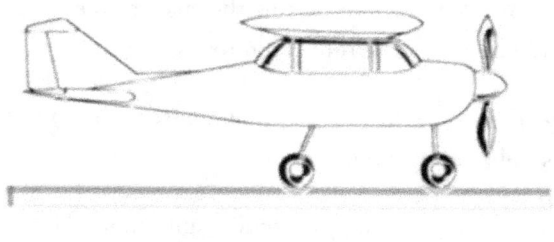

Tricycle Undercarriage

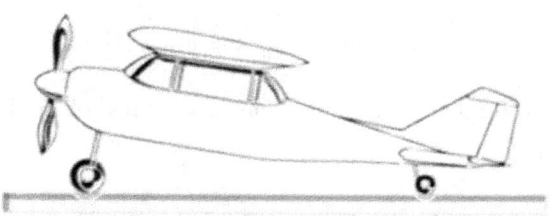

Tail Dragger

Figure 89: Tricycle undercarriage versus Tail Dragger.

Taking off - Tail Dragger Sequence

- Before initiating take-off, apply up elevator and maintain pressure to keep the tail wheel on the ground, enabling initial control of the aircraft's heading with the rudder.

- Begin the take-off by smoothly increasing throttle to maximum setting. Note that as throttle increases, the aircraft may tend to veer leftward due to motor torque. Compensate by applying right rudder input.

- Use the rudder to control the aircraft's heading until it reaches near take-off speed, then release elevator input to allow the tail to lift off the ground.

- Apply slight elevator input to raise the nose, facilitating lift-off.

- Maintain alignment along the centerline with a slightly raised nose, ensuring the angle of attack does not exceed 20 degrees to prevent stalling.

- Continue along the centreline until sufficient altitude and speed are attained, then initiate the first turn of the circuit.

Considerations:
- Ensure throttle application is smooth to prevent engine spluttering.

- Anticipate leftward veering during throttle increase and counteract with right rudder input.

- Keep the angle of attack below 20 degrees for a gradual climb.

- Delay the first circuit turn until the aircraft achieves adequate speed and height.

- Most aircraft require some elevator input for take-off, though some may need down elevator to prevent excessive angle of attack.

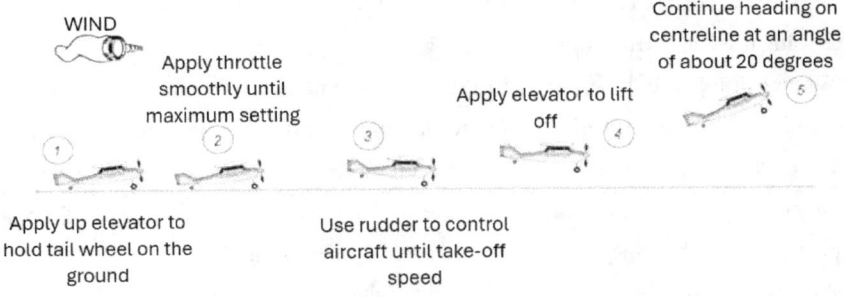

Figure 90: Tail dragger take-off sequence.

Turning: After mastering straight and level flight, turning becomes the next fundamental skill in aviation training. A well-executed turn involves smoothly changing direction at a consistent rate and airspeed, maintaining coordination without slip or skid, and without losing altitude. Strive to keep your turns gentle, with a moderate angle of bank, ideally around 30 degrees. If you increase the angle of bank for a sharper turn, you'll need to increase lift by pulling the elevator stick backward. However, be cautious of stalling.

Power Management: As angle of attack increases, so does drag, resulting in reduced airspeed. In steep turns, not only do we pull the stick back for increased lift, but we also require more power to counteract the added drag and prevent airspeed from dropping too low. However, pushing the turn to extreme limits can lead to a stall if the angle of attack nears the stalling angle, which is perilous. While full-sized aircraft have stall warning systems, it's crucial for model aircraft pilots to closely monitor speed and angle of attack to avoid stalling.

Climbing Turns: Climbing turns should be executed gently. To ascend, more thrust or power is necessary, with most of the engine's power allocated to provide this lift. If the nose is pitched too high without adequate power, speed may decrease, leading to a potential stall or spin.

LANDING

Control of our aircraft's nose attitude and speed is managed by adjusting the elevator stick, while the throttle regulates our rate of descent.

During the landing approach, it's crucial to maintain an appropriate speed and rate of descent to avoid overshooting or landing too long. Aim for a controlled descent with the aircraft's body angle slightly nose-down or level with the horizon.

The most successful landings typically result from meticulously flown rectangular circuits. Avoid cutting corners and reduce power gradually on the downwind leg, further decreasing it when turning onto the base leg.

When turning onto base, maintain a straight flight path with a square turn at the base position. Verbally announce "Landing" to alert others and adjust power as necessary.

On the final approach, execute a positive but moderate turn, keeping the nose level or slightly downward. Adjust your rate of descent with the throttle, adding power if needed to prevent undershooting or reducing it to avoid overshooting.

As you approach short final, be prepared for changes in pitch and speed due to headwind. Adjust power accordingly to prevent sinking too quickly and maintain a shallow descent.

During touchdown or if conditions are unfavourable, opt for a go-around. Apply full power, keep the wings level, and gradually climb straight ahead until at a safe altitude.

Remember, a successful landing begins with a well-executed downwind leg and precise positioning during turns onto base and final. Practice and patience are key to mastering this crucial skill, which is evaluated in all pilots, including handling dead stick and crosswind landings.

Landing Approach Sequence: Landing approaches entail aligning the aircraft with the runway in preparation for landing. The following steps outline the process:

- Maintain focus on the aircraft's altitude and airspeed while flying the circuit.

- During the downwind leg, reduce throttle to a speed suitable for the landing approach (above stall speed but not at full throttle), descending to an appropriate altitude (approximately 30 meters).

- Execute two 90-degree turns, ensuring the final turn aligns with the centreline of the runway, positioned approximately 50 to 100 meters short of the runway threshold. Limit banking to 30 to 40 degrees and adjust elevator to maintain level flight (avoid gaining or losing altitude). Utilize rudder to tighten the turn without increasing banking beyond 30 to 40 degrees. Aim to remain parallel to the centreline or slightly short of it. Make minor corrections if necessary to achieve alignment, using ailerons and rudder to control the rate of turn.

- Once aligned with the centreline, maintain level flight, ensuring the wings and nose remain parallel to the ground. Make subtle adjustments using ailerons and/or rudder to keep the aircraft centred on the runway.

- Repeat the landing approach until consistent alignment with the centre of the runway is achieved, without crossing the centreline.

- If the approach is not executed correctly, perform a fly-through (do not attempt to land) and try again.

Landing Sequence: Once the aircraft is aligned with the runway, maintaining straight and level flight (with wings and nose aligned), and at an appropriate altitude, the landing procedure can be initiated following this sequence:

- With the aircraft centred on the runway's centreline and throttle set to less than half (adjusted depending on aircraft type and wind conditions), initiate descent by slightly reducing throttle. As the aircraft slows down, the lift generated by the wings decreases, causing descent.

- Adjust throttle as necessary to control the rate of descent: increase throttle if the descent is too rapid, decrease throttle if it's too shallow. Avoid excessive nose-down attitude, as it may lead to both loss of altitude and increased speed. Remember, elevator controls pitch (nose position), while throttle regulates descent rate by altering lift.

- Employ subtle corrections to keep the aircraft aligned with the centreline and heading straight down the runway, maintaining level wings and aircraft orientation.

- Manage the descent to ensure the aircraft reaches the runway threshold at a height of approximately six to ten feet above ground level.

- Reduce throttle to idle as the aircraft approaches about 300mm above the runway, preparing to execute the flare manoeuvre.

- Execute the flare manoeuvre by gently pulling the aircraft's nose up and maintaining this attitude using elevator control. As the aircraft slows down, it will gradually lose lift and settle onto the runway smoothly, without bouncing.

- Upon touchdown, maintain directional control using the rudder to steer the aircraft along the runway.

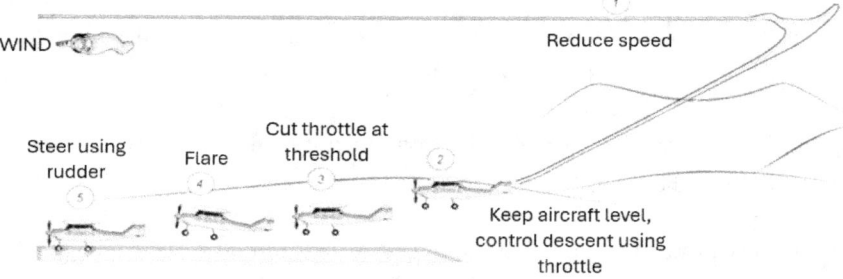

Figure 91: Landing sequence.

Here are some guidelines to improve landing proficiency:

- Understand the role of controls: Elevator adjusts pitch (nose position), while throttle regulates descent rate.

- Keep control inputs minimal: Ensure proper setup with level wings and correct aircraft heading, and make small adjustments only as needed.

- Maintain level orientation: Ensure the aircraft is neither pitched up nor down. Avoid habitually pointing the nose downward to lose altitude.

- Practice various landing approaches: Try high and low approaches, as well as short and long ones, from both ends of the runway.

- Communicate intentions: Announce "landing" on the downwind leg to alert other pilots.

- Focus on height and speed control: Maintain vigilance on altitude and airspeed throughout the circuit in preparation for landing.

- Align with the centreline: Execute final turn with approximately 30 degrees of bank to position the aircraft directly on or very close to the runway centreline.

- Land with power: Maintain some level of throttle, even if just above idle, during the landing approach.

- Reduce throttle at threshold: Cut throttle either on or just before reaching the runway threshold.

- Practice touch-and-go landings: Execute landings where the aircraft's main wheels lightly touch the runway before immediately taking off again.

- Practice landing from both directions: Ensure proficiency in landing approaches from both ends of the runway.

Learning to land can present several common challenges for pilots:

- One issue involves the downwind leg being positioned too close to the runway. This proximity leads to tight turns and overshooting the centreline during approach, making it difficult to align the aircraft properly for landing.

- Similarly, if the base wind leg is too close to the runway, pilots may find themselves making tight turns and struggling to maintain the appropriate altitude for a smooth landing. This can result in being either too high or too low during the approach phase.

- Excessive speed, either prior to or during the landing approach, poses another challenge. This can hinder the aircraft's ability to decelerate sufficiently to land safely on the runway, potentially leading to a runway overshoot.

- Proper alignment on the centreline of the runway is crucial for a successful landing. Inadequate setup for landing can result in difficulty maintaining alignment, affecting the accuracy of the approach.

- Approaching the runway at incorrect altitudes or distances presents additional hurdles. Pilots may struggle to adjust the rate of descent effectively, leading to unstable approaches and potentially unsafe landings.

- Another common mistake is nosing the aircraft down excessively in an attempt to lose altitude rapidly. However, this manoeuvre can inadvertently increase airspeed instead of slowing it down as intended, making it challenging to execute a smooth landing.

- Improper flare technique, or failing to flare altogether, can result in the aircraft touching down abruptly rather than smoothly transitioning to the runway. This can lead to harder landings and potential damage to the aircraft.

- Finally, pilots may encounter difficulties landing from both directions of the runway. Proficiency in executing landings from various directions is essential for well-rounded piloting skills and safe operations.

Landing Dead Stick

A dead stick landing is required when an aircraft's engine fails or loses power, leaving the pilot with no means of propulsion. This can happen due to various reasons such as mechanical failures, fuel exhaustion, or fuel system issues. In such situations, the pilot must rely solely on the aircraft's gliding capabilities to safely land the aircraft without engine power, hence the term "dead stick." Dead stick landings are a critical skill for pilots to master as they may encounter engine failures unexpectedly during flight.

Executing a dead-stick landing requires careful judgment and precise control. Once the aircraft's engine has ceased operation, the pilot must assess the glide distance while ensuring the aircraft remains above stall speed. There are no second chances in dead-stick landings; the pilot must execute a successful landing on the first attempt. Determining whether the aircraft can return to the runway depends on the pilot's judgment of altitude and airspeed. If feasible, the pilot may attempt to glide back to the runway; otherwise, they must select a suitable landing area in the outfield. Ideally, the chosen area should be flat and free of obstacles.

Maintaining control of the aircraft is crucial throughout the landing process. The pilot should keep the throttle stick pulled back, while ensuring the wings remain level and the nose slightly down to maintain glide speed. Avoiding sharp turns is essential, as they can rapidly decrease altitude. As the aircraft approaches the ground, whether on the runway or in the outfield, it should be kept level with a slight nose-up attitude until it slows down and eventually stalls, coming to rest on the ground.

During a runway landing, it's important to use the rudder to keep the aircraft centred on the runway. If landing in the outfield, take note of the landing spot and surrounding landmarks for retrieval purposes. After landing, the aircraft must be thoroughly inspected for any damage or structural issues, such as displaced firewalls or engine mounts. Additionally, the cause of the engine failure should be identified, whether it was due to fuel depletion, improper needle valve adjustment, or contaminated fuel.

To practice dead-stick landings, pilots can simulate engine failure by reducing throttle to idle during the downwind leg of the circuit. Adjusting the length of the downwind and base legs may be necessary to accommodate the shorter landing approach. Upon approach, align the aircraft with the runway centreline and execute a controlled landing, maintaining a level attitude with a slight nose-down pitch to retain some airspeed.

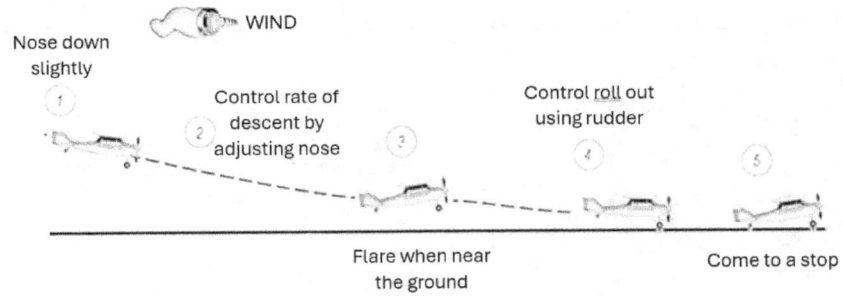

Figure 92: Dead stick landing sequence.

When conducting a crosswind landing, the main distinction from a normal landing is the influence of the wind, which attempts to divert the aircraft from its intended path. To stay aligned with the centerline of the runway, you'll need to angle your aircraft slightly into the wind's direction. This adjustment causes the aircraft to crab slightly, depending on the wind's force. The crucial aspect is ensuring the aircraft travels along the centerline, regardless of its actual orientation. Determining the appropriate amount of crabbing requires practice.

Prior to executing a crosswind landing, it's advisable to perform several approaches to gauge the correct crab angle. During the descent and touchdown, execute a flare maneuver, and upon wheel contact, use rudder input to align the aircraft's nose with the centerline of the runway. Adjustments in throttle and airspeed are often necessary, particularly in response to the wind's intensity.

Crosswinds can introduce additional challenges. Firstly, aircraft with substantial rudders and vertical stabilizers may experience weather cocking, where the aircraft tends to align its nose into the wind. This tendency can interfere with maintaining the desired crab angle. Secondly, strong winds can cause the aircraft to become susceptible to rolling, with the wind attempting to tip it onto its back. To counteract this effect, minimize control inputs and prioritize using the rudder to alter the aircraft's heading instead of the ailerons.

When navigating through windy conditions, remain vigilant of the wind's influence and maintain proximity to the runway, especially during the downwind leg, to ensure a safe return in the event of an engine failure. Additionally, be mindful that strong winds can swiftly carry the aircraft away from its intended path, so avoid straying too far from the runway's vicinity.

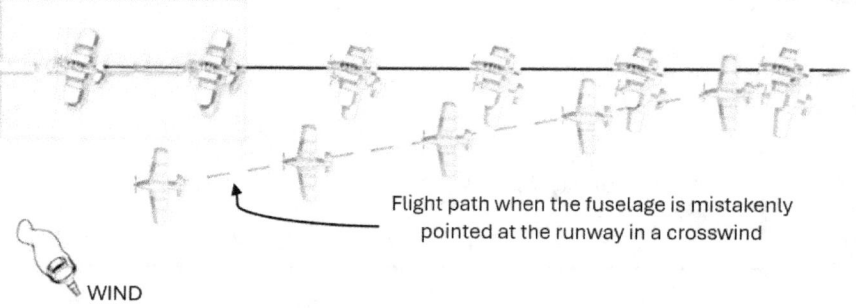

Figure 93: Crosswind landing.

Emergency procedures

Emergency procedures should be incorporated into the RPA mission plan, outlining actions to be taken in the event of a loss of data link with the RPA. Depending on system capabilities, these procedures could encompass various flight profiles, such as:

- Automated transit of the RPA to a pre-designated recovery area followed by automated recovery

- Automated transit of the RPA to a pre-designated recovery area followed by activation of a flight termination system

In controlled airspace, specific abort and flight termination procedures must be briefed to ATC. This includes providing information about pre-programmed loss-of-link flight profiles, flight termination capabilities, and RPA performance under termination conditions. Continuous automatic checks of the data link should occur, and real-time warnings should be displayed to the remote crew in case of failure. In the event of data link loss, excluding intermittent signal loss or during programmed outages, immediate notification to ATC and execution of recovery procedures are essential.

Parameters determining acceptable intermittent signal loss and total loss will be pre-determined by the manufacturer. An RPA experiencing a lost data link and executing a pre-programmed flight profile to termination or recovery should receive priority handling by ATC. If communication failure occurs between the RP and ATC, selecting SSR code 7600, if applicable, and attempting to establish alternative communications is necessary. Pending re-establishment of communications with ATC, the RPA will be controlled based on the last acknowledged instruction or conditions contained in the Area Approval. If communication with ATC remains unsuccessful, the RPA sortie should be aborted.

The RPA mission plan should outline emergency procedures for various scenarios, including engine failure, loss of data link, loss of control, failure of navigation equipment, and airframe damage. Additionally, the use of recovery or fail-safe devices, such as parachutes, to mitigate risks to people or property is encouraged where applicable to the RPA type. If an RPA is equipped with a recovery device like a ballistic parachute system, including a pyrotechnic charge, the area or panel should be clearly marked for easy identification.

Launch and Landing Zones

Launch site selection prioritizes safety above all else. Criteria for selecting launch sites include:

1. Ensuring Adequate Buffer Zones:

    - RPS personnel must maintain a buffer of at least 50 feet between aircraft operations and non-essential personnel.

- Observers, when not performing their duties, act as safety supervisors.

2. Environmental Considerations:

- No launches should occur until all environmental assessments have been evaluated.

- Personnel have the authority to abort any launch if it poses a hazard to the environment, themselves, or others nearby.

3. Departure Routes over Sparse Populated Areas:

- The Pilot in Command (PIC) should strive to choose launch sites that minimize departures over populated areas.

- If flights over populated areas are necessary, flight planning should aim to minimize time spent in these areas.

Regarding landing sites and alternate options:

1. Primary Landing Site:

- Typically, the primary landing site aligns with the launch site.

- The PIC has ultimate authority over approaches to the primary site and may abort any approach deemed unsafe.

2. Alternate Landing Sites:

- The PIC must designate at least one alternate landing site.

- If a wave-off is impossible and the primary landing site is unsafe, procedures for utilizing the alternate site will be followed.

3. Mission Abort Sites:

- Optionally, the PIC may designate an "abort site" for emergency situations.

- The abort site must be sufficiently distant to minimize risk if the aircraft needs to vacate airspace in an emergency.

4. Approaches over Populated Areas:

    - The PIC should endeavour to choose landing sites that minimize approaches over populated areas.

5. Landing Safety and Crowd Control:

    - All landing sites should be maintained and operated with the same safety standards as launch sites.

    - A buffer of at least 50 feet between aircraft operations and non-essential personnel should be maintained at all landing sites.

Flight Control/Ground station Best Practice

1. Prior to activating the transmitter, ensure that there are no frequency conflicts by utilizing a frequency scanner.

2. Verify that there are no identical NET ID's operating in the vicinity.

3. Before powering on any systems, ensure that all body parts, clothing, obstacles, and bystanders are clear of propellers or rotors and their arcs. Secure the aircraft to prevent unintended movement upon powering up the motor.

4. Audibly announce "CLEAR PROP."

5. Activate the transmitter, ensuring that displayed information such as aircraft memory and battery voltage is accurate.

6. Confirm that the throttle stick on the transmitter is in the power-off position.

7. Connect the battery and/or activate the power switch on the aircraft.

8. Follow the recommended range test procedures as specified in the radio transmitter/receiver owner's manual.

9. Verify proper operation of control surfaces.

10. Ensure all servos operate smoothly without abnormal noises or chatter during operation or at idle.

11. Test the motor/engine for proper functionality. Secure the aircraft and gradually adjust throttle from idle to full power and back down, checking for thrust, vibration, or anomalies. Confirm the motor stops completely when the throttle stick is in the off position.

12. Confirm the triggering device functions correctly.

Before Take-off:

1. Confirm the transmitter antenna is fully extended.

2. Ensure transmitter trim settings are correctly positioned.

3. Extend the receiver antenna fully.

4. Check the take-off area for obstructions and clear of people.

5. Review weather conditions and potential emergency landing areas.

6. Set the flight timer alarm.

7. Audibly announce "PREPARING TO TAKE OFF."

8. Launch the aircraft.

In-Flight:

1. Ascend to a safe altitude away from hazards and check control systems.

2. Adjust trims if necessary.

3. Maintain a safe operating distance from people and buildings.

4. If flying over buildings or people, maintain a safe altitude for recovery and minimize exposure.

5. Continuously scan flight and ground areas for potential hazards.

Landing:

1. Check control systems and adjust trims to ensure emergency abort landing capability if necessary.

2. Scan landing area for potential obstructions and reassess weather conditions.

3. Audibly announce "PREPARING TO LAND."

4. Always be prepared for a go-around.

5. Land the aircraft carefully away from obstructions and people.

Post-Flight:

1. Power off the aircraft and/or disconnect batteries.

2. Turn off the transmitter.

3. Power off photo equipment if applicable.

4. Visually inspect the aircraft for damage or excessive wear.

5. Remove unused fuel if necessary.

6. Secure the aircraft.

Flight Techniques

Managing a partial power loss after take-off in a single-engine aircraft

partial engine power loss occurs when the engine provides less power than commanded by the pilot but more than idle thrust. A partial engine power loss after take-off occurs when the aircraft is airborne and climbing immediately after take-off, typically below circuit height and in close proximity to the departure aerodrome. In this context, a total engine failure preceded by a partial power loss is treated as a partial power loss event if the pilot took action in response to the initial power reduction. Causes of engine power loss include mechanical issues within the engine, fuel or air flow restrictions, and mechanical blockages in engine controls like throttle cables. To effectively manage the situation:

1. Plan: Anticipating the possibility of a partial power loss and establishing re-

sponse strategies before flight provides an advantage. Planning ahead reduces mental workload, helps mitigate decision-making stress, and instils confidence in responding to emergencies.

2. Pre-flight checks: Many partial power loss incidents after take-off could have been detected and prevented during pre-flight checks. Physical inspections, engine run-ups, and on-take-off engine checks are crucial. Signs such as abnormal RPM drops during run-up checks or rough engine running during take-off can indicate fuel or spark plug issues.

3. Maintain aircraft control: If a partial power loss occurs, immediate response is essential. Inaction is not an option. Priority is given to maintaining control. Response options may include returning to the aerodrome or conducting an immediate forced landing. Factors like altitude, wind conditions, traffic, and terrain influence these decisions. Keeping glide speed and moderate bank angles helps maintain control, ensuring a safer landing with wings level and the aircraft level with the terrain, rather than risking a stall or spin.

Pre-flight planning and self-briefing

Pre-flight planning: When facing the possibility of a partial engine power loss after take-off, pilots must make critical decisions amidst stress, uncertainty, and high workload. Pre-flight planning plays a crucial role in preparing for such scenarios. Considering factors like wind direction, available landing options on and off the airfield, and surroundings in all directions during pre-flight planning can significantly reduce mental workload in the event of a partial engine power loss. Having a well-thought-out plan beforehand may also help mitigate the effects of decision-making under stress and boost confidence in executing emergency actions. Thus, it's essential to include the possibility of a partial engine power loss in your pre-flight planning as part of your threat and error management strategy.

Your pre-flight plan should encompass:

- Runway direction and optimal turn direction.

- Local wind speed and direction for the day.

- Terrain and obstacles along the flight path.

- Decision points considering aircraft altitude and performance, including options such as landing on the remaining runway or aerodrome, landing outside the aerodrome, or executing a turn back towards the aerodrome.

Pre-flight self-briefing: Similar to multi-engine aircraft pilots, all single-engine aircraft pilots should conduct a self-briefing before each take-off. The self-brief serves as a crucial reminder of planned actions in case of emergencies like partial power loss. Below details the role of pre-flight self-briefing.

Avoiding partial engine power loss

Pre-flight checks: The ATSB reported numerous occurrences where existing engine system abnormalities could have been detected or prevented before take-off. Prevention is key, and thorough pre-flight checks serve as a vital barrier to reducing the likelihood of a partial engine power loss after take-off.

Aircraft pre-flight - physical inspection: Instances of fuel starvation, exhaustion, or contamination resulting in partial power loss, often followed by complete engine failure, could have been prevented through rigorous physical inspections before flight. Conducting all relevant physical checks is crucial in minimizing the risk of partial or complete engine power loss. Even if the aircraft maintenance release is already signed for the day, a comprehensive pre-flight inspection, including engine and fuel system components, is essential.

Fuel-related partial power loss: Proper selection of the fuel tank before take-off, ensuring fuel drains are closed and not leaking, and securely closing fuel caps are factors that could have facilitated the detection or prevention of fuel-related partial power loss incidents. These events are often associated with engine surging, a particularly unpredictable form of partial power loss that can lead to complete engine failure.

Review of fuel-related occurrences suggests the following preventive measures:

- Drain fuel from all fuel drain points to check for water or contamination.

- Ensure fuel drain points are not leaking, especially bayonet-style fittings.

- Thoughtfully consider the fuel tank required for take-off.

- Confirm sufficient fuel quantity using multiple methods, such as crosschecking fuel gauge and tank dip.

Manage distractions: While these checks are routine for most pilots, distractions or time pressures may lead to incomplete inspections. All pilots should consider threat and error management during this phase of flight, planning for distractions and pressures. Minimizing distractions and ensuring thorough checks can prevent critical oversights.

Minimize aircraft fuel configuration changes: Cases suggest that residual fuel in fuel lines sustained the engine for take-off but was insufficient for sustained flight, leading to fuel starvation soon after rotation. Thorough engine run-up checks can diagnose abnormalities with both the engine and fuel system, preventing such occurrences.

Managing a partial engine power loss after take-off

Partial engine power loss can vary in severity, ranging from minimal power to nearly full power, with different levels of reliability in the remaining engine power. When confronted with a partial power loss, pilots must prioritize maintaining control of the aircraft over attempting to diagnose engine issues.

Maximize altitude or minimize distance: Climbing out at the manufacturer's recommended speeds for 'best rate' or 'best angle,' depending on the aircraft and location, will optimize options in the event of a partial power loss or engine failure. Adopting a 'cruise' climb setting prematurely may render the aircraft beyond the possibility of a glide return, even if above the 'turn-back' altitude specific to the aircraft.

Consider the following initial actions when responding to a partial loss in power:

- Lower the nose to maintain the aircraft's glide speed.

- Perform basic initial engine trouble checks as per the manufacturer's advice, but only if time allows.

- Monitor the aircraft's performance to assess whether it's maintaining, gaining, or losing altitude, which informs landing options.

- Navigate the aircraft for a landing based on its current altitude, performance, and pre-planned landing routes. Exercise caution when turning, as increased bank angles raise the stall speed. Maintain balance to minimize descent rate during turns.

- It's advisable to have a minimum planned turning altitude; CASA recommends at least 200 feet above ground level (AGL) for rolling wings level.

- Continuously reassess landing options and be prepared to adjust the plan accordingly.

- Execute the landing, ensuring to:

- Have a minimum planned altitude to roll wings level. CASA documentation suggests avoiding turns below 200 feet AGL, but this depends on factors like aircraft roll rate, airspeed, and pilot experience.

- Maintain glide speed until the flare point, ensuring adequate energy to arrest the vertical descent rate during flare.

As with a total power loss after take-off, during a partial power loss, avoiding attempts to diagnose the engine problem is crucial to maintaining control of the aircraft.

Stall Recovery

Stalls are a source of significant concern for student pilots and those unfamiliar with aviation, so let's delve into them here. As mentioned previously, an aircraft must achieve a certain speed to take off. During flight, it's crucial to maintain adequate airspeed to generate sufficient lift to support the aircraft without requiring an excessively steep angle of attack. When the angle of attack reaches a specific point, known as the critical angle of attack, the airflow over the wing can become disrupted or "burble" (refer to Figure 94), leading to a loss of lift (stall). The speed at which the wing can no longer support the aircraft without surpassing this critical angle of attack is termed the stalling speed. This speed may vary depending on changes in wing configuration, such as flap position. Additionally, abrupt manoeuvres, steep banking, and wind gusts can subject the aircraft to excessive load factors, causing it to exceed the critical angle of attack and stall at any airspeed and attitude. Maintaining speeds conducive to smooth airflow over the airfoil and control surfaces is essential for effective aircraft control.

Flying an aircraft, like any other skill, requires regular practice to maintain proficiency. Even professional pilots, including those from major airlines, military aviators, and flight instructors, undergo periodic classroom sessions to update their skills. It's incumbent upon all pilots to exercise sound judgment to ensure the safe and proficient operation of the aircraft they fly.

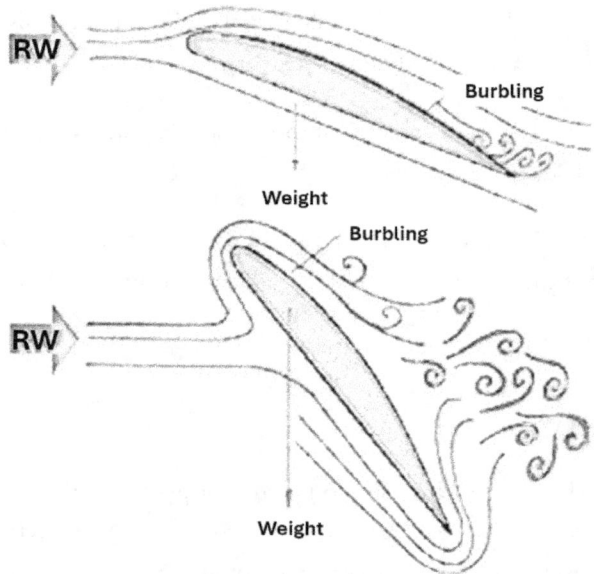

Figure 94: Airfoil approaching and entering a stall.

Stalls can be practiced with or without power to acquaint yourself with the specific stall characteristics of the aircraft without posing a potentially hazardous situation [65]. Various types of stalls are described below:

1. Departure Stalls (classified as power-on stalls) are practiced to simulate conditions during take-off and climb-out, including configuration. Many stall/spin accidents occur during these flight phases, particularly during overshoots. One contributing factor to such accidents is the pilot's inability to maintain positive pitch control, often due to a nose-high trim setting or premature flap retraction. Accidents have also been linked to failure in maintaining positive control during short field take-offs.

2. Arrival Stalls (classified as power-off stalls or reduced power stalls) are practiced to simulate typical approach-to-landing conditions and configuration. Simulations should also incorporate reduced power settings consistent with the approach requirements of the specific training aircraft. Numerous stall/spin accidents have been attributed to situations such as crossed control turns from base leg to final approach (resulting in a skidding or slipping turn), attempting

to recover from a high sink rate on final approach solely by increasing pitch attitude, and improper airspeed control on final approach or in other segments of the traffic pattern.

3. Accelerated Stalls can occur at airspeeds higher than normal due to abrupt and/or excessive control inputs. These stalls may manifest during steep turns, pull-ups, or other sudden changes in flight path. Accelerated stalls are typically more severe than unaccelerated stalls and often catch pilots off guard due to their unexpected nature.

The primary aspect in recovering from a stall involves reestablishing positive control of the aircraft by decreasing the angle of attack. Upon the initial indication of a stall, the angle of attack of the wing must be reduced to enable the wings to generate lift again. Each aircraft in normal flight may necessitate a distinct amount of forward pressure to restore lift. It's important to note that excessive forward pressure could impede recovery by applying a negative load on the wing.

Subsequently, in the stall recovery process, smoothly applying maximum allowable power is essential to augment airspeed and minimize altitude loss. As the airspeed increases and recovery progresses, power should be adjusted to return the aircraft to the desired flight condition. Once recovery is underway, establishing straight and level flight should be prioritized, employing full coordination of the controls.

Throughout the recovery procedure, it's imperative to ensure that neither the airspeed indicator nor the tachometer, if present, reaches their high-speed red lines at any point during a practice stall.

Secondary Stalls

If the recovery from a stall is not executed correctly, it may result in a secondary stall or even a spin. A secondary stall arises from attempting to expedite the stall recovery before the aircraft has regained adequate flying speed. When this situation occurs, the elevator back pressure should be released once again, akin to a standard stall recovery. Upon attaining sufficient airspeed, the aircraft can be maneuvered back to straight-and-level flight.

Cross-Control Stalls

Flight students are instructed to avoid sharply banked turns at low altitudes. When overshooting the extended centreline on a turn from base to final, there's a tendency to compensate by applying inside rudder to increase the turn rate, necessitating opposite aileron to maintain the bank angle. This skidding turn inclination can cause the nose to drop, requiring back pressure on the control column. In extreme cases, this can lead to a full aft control column with full opposite aileron and full inside rudder, resulting in an incipient spin—termed an "under the bottom stall."

A top-rudder stall or "over the top stall" can occur when the aircraft is slipping. To counter this, the aircraft should roll toward the higher wing at the stall point.

Slow Flight

Demonstrating skill and control is particularly evident at slow speeds. Just as skating or biking at slower speeds requires greater skill, flying at reduced speeds showcases a pilot's proficiency. Most V_{s1} slow flight manoeuvres can be executed within a ten-degree bank angle. Additional rudder should be applied to the right with opposite aileron. Overstepping the 10-degree limit risks a cross-control stall. Introducing some power enables a 30-degree bank, increasing the possibility of stall spins. Slow flight near the stall is termed minimum controllable. The rudder's effectiveness in controlling the stall and yaw is best illustrated during this exercise. Proper rudder application is confirmed when the stall break occurs straight ahead without any wing drop. Any aileron application would counterproductively exacerbate the stall and lead to a more abrupt wing drop.

Aircraft Stall Factors

Wilbur Wright coined the term "stall" in 1904 to describe how Orville allowed the aircraft to pitch up excessively and stall during a turn. The potential for an aircraft to stall or spin is inherent in its design. A pilot's ability to detect and respond to this potential is a testament to their flying skill. When an aircraft is flown at an angle surpassing the critical angle of attack, it stalls. In deliberate training stalls, airspeed is decreased, and abusive control inputs causing unusual attitude stalls are avoided. Low speed is not the cause of the stall; rather, it's the angle of attack.

The elevator controls, and the pressures exerted on them, dictate whether the wing will achieve an angle of attack adequate to stall. When the angular disparity between the aircraft's direction and its actual path exceeds approximately 11 degrees to the wing's chord line, a stall occurs—known as the critical angle of attack. Exceeding this angle with elevator inputs causes the airflow to separate from the upper wing surface, reducing the lift coefficient, increasing the drag coefficient, and conveying various aerodynamic, mechanical, and physiological cues to the pilot.

Stall warnings provide a ten-knot alert of imminent stalls as typically performed. Inadvertent stalls I've encountered coincided with the sound of the warning horn. Stall speeds are affected by weight, with a 20% weight increase resulting in a 10% higher stall speed, and vice versa. Weight is a critical factor in stall speeds, and aircraft manual figures are based on gross weights to provide a safety margin. This margin can be adjusted if the actual weight is lower than the gross weight, allowing for a reduced approach speed.

Stall speeds are set at the most critical centre of gravity (CG) condition, resulting in the highest stall speed. The aircraft's behaviour during entry, progression, and recovery from a stall determines its stall characteristics, which are typically assessed at the aft CG position when the stall speed is at its lowest.

Clearing Turns

Certain protocols apply to all training stalls. Prior to initiating any stall, it is imperative to perform precise 90-degree clearing turns to the left and right. These manoeuvres should mirror the stall process in terms of turn duration, bank angle, altitude, and heading. A well-executed practice stall typically results in an initial altitude loss of 100 feet. Stalls may be categorized as incipient, partial, full, or aggravated based on their severity. Prolonging an aggravated stall leads to a further decrease in airspeed, necessitating either additional power or altitude for recovery.

Recovery from a stall always involves applying full power, retracting flaps (if extended), climbing, and maintaining the best rate of climb speed, typically set at 65 knots. While an old FAA guideline recommended gaining 300 feet during recovery, practical considerations often limit this in various scenarios. Trim adjustments should be made for a positive climb.

Stall Avoidance

Stall Avoidance Practice at Slow Airspeeds (PTS)

　1. Maintain heading and altitude while reducing power and adjusting trim.

　2. Maintain heading and altitude while activating the stall warning.

　3. Demonstrate elevator trim adjustment from neutral to full up.

　4. Observe the aircraft's left turning tendency and assess rudder effectiveness.

　5. Demonstrate the use of right rudder as required.

　6. Illustrate the effect of rudder input by releasing and reapplying.

　7. Execute turns to the right and left without using rudder to demonstrate yaw.

8. Perform slow flight manoeuvres including climbs, descents, and turns.

9. Demonstrate flap extension and retraction at slow speeds to avoid stalling.

10. Manage distractions effectively.

11. Monitor altitude loss and note airspeed changes during transition phases.

Stall Recognition: The occurrence of a stall is primarily due to the angle of attack, rather than airspeed or aircraft attitude. a. Indications may include mushy controls. b. Changes in exterior airflow pitch. c. Sensations such as buffet, vibration, pitching, and sounds. d. Activation of the stall warning system. e. Physical sensations experienced by the pilot.

Natural Stall Warning: Certain older aircraft lack stall warning systems, relying instead on the initial buffeting felt on the horizontal tail surfaces. Modern stall warning systems typically provide alerts up to 10 knots before the stall, as mandated by FAR 23.207, although no specific warning point is defined.

Generic Stall Recovery: Upon stall recognition, promptly reduce the angle of attack. The speed of control inputs should correspond to the severity of the stall. Smoothly apply power and establish straight-and-level flight or initiate a climb as necessary. Incorrect control inputs during a stall may lead to an incipient spin. Effective stall and spin recoveries require intellectual rather than instinctive actions.

Secondary Stall: A secondary stall is considered a "failure" during any flight evaluation. It occurs when the pilot over-controls the recovery from an initial stall, resulting in an abrupt and violent stall recurrence due to reduced stick forces at low speeds.

Stalls Down Low: Ground proximity and low altitude turns can predispose aircraft to stalls due to factors such as increased turbulence, steep bank angles, lack of coordination, and reduced airspeed. Proper recovery may be hindered by the pilot's reluctance to lower the nose, leading to potential loss of control.

Deep Stall: A deep stall may occur when the aircraft is in a high angle-of-attack and high drag configuration, such as during minimum controllable airspeed. Recovery from a deep stall may necessitate adjusting the aircraft's centre of gravity. Stalls should be avoided if the status of the aircraft's centre of gravity is uncertain.

Stall Recoveries: Effective stall recoveries minimize altitude loss and avoid secondary stalls. Excessive forward elevator input may result in an excessive counteraction and potential secondary stall. Misuse of ailerons can induce a sideslip, potentially leading to a spin. Recovery actions should be carefully coordinated with power and speed adjustments to prevent further complications.

Spins

A spin can be described as an exacerbated stall resulting in what's known as "autorotation," where the aircraft descends in a corkscrew motion. During autorotation, the aircraft rotates around a vertical axis, causing the rising wing to be less stalled than the descending wing, inducing a combination of rolling, yawing, and pitching motions. Essentially, the aircraft is compelled downward by gravity, exhibiting rolling, yawing, and pitching movements in a spiral trajectory.

This autorotation phenomenon stems from an unequal angle of attack on the wings. The rising wing experiences a decreasing angle of attack, leading to increased relative lift and reduced drag, thus being less stalled. Conversely, the descending wing encounters an increasing angle of attack beyond the wing's critical angle of attack (stall), resulting in decreased relative lift and increased drag.

A spin is triggered when the aircraft's wing surpasses its critical angle of attack (stall) while experiencing a sideslip or yaw, either at or beyond the actual stall point. During this uncoordinated manoeuvre, a pilot may not immediately realize that the critical angle of attack has been exceeded until the aircraft starts yawing uncontrollably toward the descending wing. Failure to initiate stall recovery promptly may result in the aircraft entering a spin.

If a stall occurs while the aircraft is in a slipping or skidding turn, it can lead to a spin entry and rotation in the direction opposite to the turn, irrespective of which wingtip is raised. While some aircraft need deliberate effort to initiate a spin, others may inadvertently enter a spin due to mishandling of controls during turns, stalls, and flight at minimum controllable airspeeds. This underscores the importance of practicing stalls until the skill to recognize and recover from them is honed.

At the onset of a stall, it's common for one wing to drop. In such instances, the nose tends to yaw towards the lower wing. Here, proper use of the rudder is crucial. Applying the correct amount of opposite rudder prevents the nose from yawing towards the low wing. By maintaining directional control and preventing the nose from yawing before initiating stall recovery, a spin can be avoided. Allowing the nose to yaw during the stall causes the aircraft to slip in the direction of the lowered wing, leading to a spin entry.

The stall angle of attack refers to the critical angle at which the airflow over an aircraft's wing separates from its surface, transitioning from smooth to turbulent flow. At this critical angle, lift generation decreases rapidly, leading to a stall. Pilots typically associate a specific indicated airspeed with the stall angle for a given weight and configuration of the aircraft. However, this stall speed varies depending on factors such as aircraft weight and configuration, making airspeed an indirect measure of an approaching stall.

Quoted stall speeds usually represent the 1G straight-and-level speed at a standard aircraft weight. Increasing aircraft weight or entering a turn increases the stall speed. For example, a steep 60-degree banked turn subjects the aircraft to a 2G load, resulting in an increased stall speed proportional to the square root of that load. Therefore, pilots should focus on angle of attack rather than airspeed when evaluating proximity to a stall. The elevator position, indicating how far back the control column is held, serves as a better indicator of stall proximity.

During a balanced, wings-level stall with the ball in the middle, both wings maintain the same angle of attack. While aerodynamic forces may attempt to pitch the nose forward at the stall, no overall rolling or yawing should occur.

However, if the aircraft yaws, a roll develops in the direction of the yaw due to differential lift on the wings. The outer wing, experiencing increased speed, generates more lift, while the inner wing, with an increased angle of attack, may stall, reducing lift. This asymmetric lift causes the aircraft to roll further in the direction of the initial yaw, leading to an accelerating roll rate.

Changing angles of attack also influence drag. The down-going wing experiences increased drag, while the up-going wing encounters reduced drag, further exacerbating the yaw towards the down-going wing.

As the aircraft yaws and stalls, it enters autorotation, simultaneously rolling about the longitudinal axis due to differential lift and yawing about the vertical axis due to differential drag. This combined motion creates a spin axis, causing the aircraft to enter a self-sustaining spin until opposing forces intervene.

Various factors can cause yaw, including out-of-balance flight, wing drop at the stall, aileron application inducing drag, gyroscopic effect from the propeller, gusts, uneven lift production due to ice or wing damage, and asymmetric power on twin-engine aircraft. The most common cause of unintentional spins is yaw at the stall resulting from out-of-balance flight.

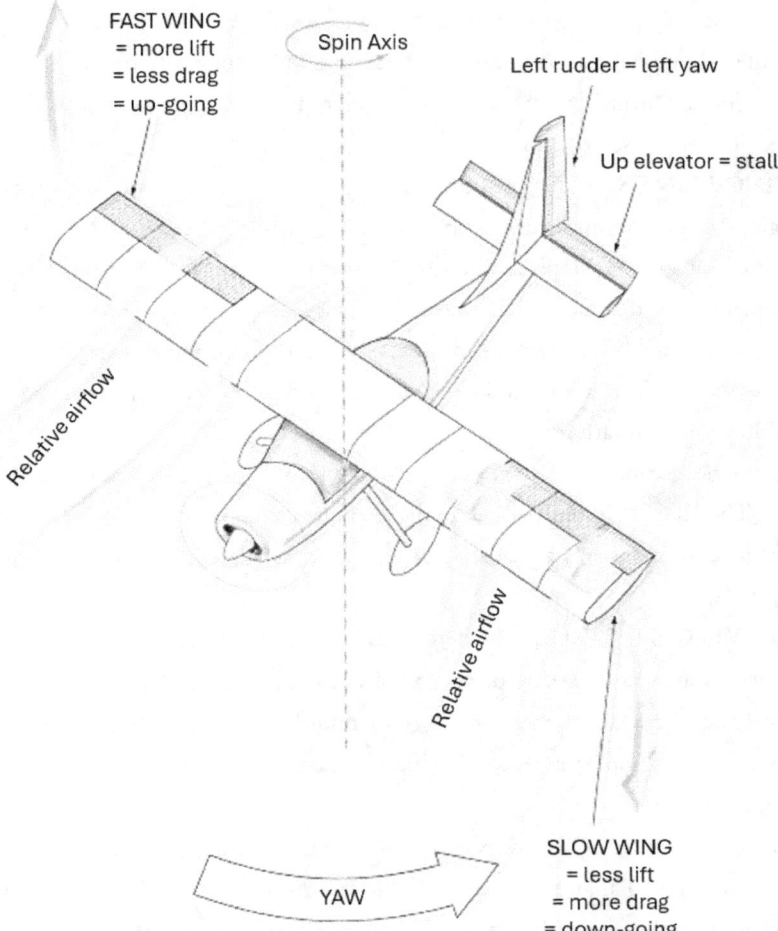

Figure 95: Stall and yaw combine to produce a new axis, the spin axis.

To trigger a spin, an aircraft must first be stalled. Therefore, consistent practice in stalls aids the pilot in swiftly and instinctively identifying the signs of an impending spin. Developing the ability to promptly apply corrective measures whenever spin conditions are detected is crucial. In situations where avoiding a spin becomes impossible, pilots should promptly initiate spin recovery procedures.

There are four stages of a spin: entry, incipient, developed, and recovery.

ENTRY STAGE: During the entry stage, the pilot initiates the spin, either intentionally or unintentionally. The procedure for entering a spin is similar to that of a power-off stall. As the aircraft nears the stall, the power is gradually reduced to idle while simultaneously pitching the nose up to induce a stall. At the point of stall, full rudder input in the desired spin direction is applied smoothly, along with full back (up) elevator to its limit. Throughout this process, the ailerons remain in a neutral position unless specified otherwise by the AFM/POH.

INCIPIENT STAGE: The incipient stage begins as the aircraft stalls and rotation begins, continuing until the spin fully develops, which typically takes up to two turns for most aircraft. In this phase, the aerodynamic and inertial forces are not yet in balance. Incipient spins that are not allowed to progress into a steady-state spin are commonly utilized for initial spin training and recovery practice. During this stage, the indicated airspeed is usually near or below the stall speed, and the turn-and-slip indicator indicates the direction of rotation.

Initiation of incipient spin recovery should occur before completing a full 360° rotation. The pilot applies full rudder in the opposite direction of rotation. If unsure of the spin direction, referencing the turn-and-slip indicator will reveal deflection in the rotation direction.

DEVELOPED STAGE: The developed stage occurs when the aircraft's rotational, airspeed, and vertical speed stabilize, typically in a nearly vertical flightpath. Here, aerodynamic and inertial forces reach equilibrium, resulting in constant or repetitive attitudes, angles, and rotational motions about the vertical axis. The spin remains in equilibrium during this phase.

RECOVERY STAGE: The recovery stage begins as the wings' angle of attack decreases below the critical angle, causing autorotation to slow down. Consequently, the nose pitches upward, and rotation ceases. This phase can last from a quarter to several turns.

To initiate recovery, control inputs are enacted to disrupt the spin equilibrium and halt both rotation and stall. Following the manufacturer's recommended spin recovery procedures is crucial. In their absence, the following steps are suggested:

Step 1: REDUCE THE POWER (THROTTLE) TO IDLE. Power can exacerbate spin characteristics, resulting in a flatter spin attitude and increased rotation rates.

Step 2: POSITION THE AILERONS TO NEUTRAL. Ailerons may adversely affect spin recovery; hence, ensuring neutral ailerons is optimal to prevent exacerbating the situation.

Step 3: APPLY FULL OPPOSITE RUDDER AGAINST THE ROTATION. Ensure full opposite rudder input to counteract the spin rotation.

Step 4: APPLY A POSITIVE AND BRISK, STRAIGHT FORWARD MOVEMENT OF THE ELEVATOR CONTROL FORWARD OF THE NEUTRAL TO BREAK THE STALL. Promptly after full rudder application, a forceful elevator movement decreases the angle of attack, breaking the stall.

Step 5: AFTER SPIN ROTATION STOPS, NEUTRALIZE THE RUDDER. Failure to do so may induce yawing or skidding due to increased airspeed acting on a deflected rudder.

Step 6: BEGIN APPLYING BACK-ELEVATOR PRESSURE TO RAISE THE NOSE TO LEVEL FLIGHT. Caution must be exercised to avoid excessive back-elevator pressure, which could lead to a secondary stall.

These recovery procedures should only be used when the manufacturer's procedures are unavailable. Pilots must be thoroughly acquainted with manufacturer-provided spin recovery procedures before attempting spin training.

Confusion regarding spin direction and distinguishing between a spin and a spiral is a common issue. In a spiral, airspeed increases, indicating the airplane is no longer stalled. It is crucial for the pilot to promptly recognize the spin, its direction, and execute the recovery procedure correctly within a short timeframe, typically around three seconds. The minimum altitude loss for a textbook recovery ranges from 1000 to 1500 feet.

Direction of Spin: Difficulty in discerning spin direction may arise when the pilot's focus is on roll direction. The correct spin direction is indicated by the turn needle, which responds solely to rotation in the yawing plane. While the turn coordinator may provide valid readings in an upright spin, it may be unreliable in an inverted spin. The ball's reliability is compromised due to centrifugal forces and its position relative to the aircraft's centre of gravity.

PARES Spin Recovery

Power: Ensure that the throttle is fully closed. This action reduces the propeller's forces that could maintain the nose up, potentially flattening the spin and obstructing the elevator. Additionally, it prevents engine overspeeding during later recovery stages.

Ailerons: Avoid using aileron to roll out of a spin, as it could exacerbate the spin, making it flatter, faster, and more stable. In most standard light aircraft, maintaining neutral aileron position is the most suitable for recovery from an unintentional spin.

Rudder: Correctly identifying the opposite rudder to the spin direction is crucial. Use the turn needle for accurate guidance, as it reliably indicates the direction of yaw (and hence the spin). Avoid relying on the artificial horizon, heading indicator, or ball for this purpose. Changing your field of vision to sight straight down the aircraft's nose allows you to focus solely on the yaw component of the spin. Forcefully apply rudder in the direction indicated by the ground movement observed beyond the nose. For example, in a left spin where the ground appears to blur to the right, apply right rudder for recovery. Sensing the resistance of the rudder pedals and pressing the heavier one fully to the control stop is another method. While challenging, consciously relaxing your feet enhances your feel and reduces the tendency to oppose full opposite rudder application.

Elevator: Gradually move the stick or control column forward until the spin ceases to reduce the angle of attack and unstall the aircraft.

Stops: After the spin ends, centre the rudder and ailerons, and smoothly recover from the dive.

ON GROUND CONTROL

Airports encompass any land or water area utilized or intended for aircraft take-off or landing. This includes various specialized facilities like seaplane bases, heliports, and those accommodating tilt rotor aircraft [45]. Furthermore, an airport comprises not only the actual landing and take-off zones but also adjacent structures, amenities, and associated rights of way.

As a US example, airports are broadly categorized into towered and non-towered types. These classifications further branch into:

- Civil Airports: Open to the general public.

- Military/Federal Government Airports: Operated by military entities, NASA, or other federal agencies.

- Private Airports: Reserved for private or restricted use, not accessible to the general public.

A towered airport operates with an active control tower, where air traffic control (ATC) ensures the safe and efficient flow of air traffic, particularly in areas with significant flight operations or high traffic volumes [45].

In contrast, a non-towered airport lacks an operational control tower. Although two-way radio communication isn't mandatory, it's recommended for pilots to monitor aircraft activity on the designated frequency to enhance situational awareness. The Common Traffic Advisory Frequency (CTAF) facilitates this practice, serving as a platform for airport advisory communications at non-towered airports. The CTAF may utilize various frequencies like UNICOM, MULTICOM, FSS, or tower frequencies, as indicated in aeronautical publications [45].

At non-towered airports, traffic patterns are always entered at pattern altitude, with entry methods contingent upon the arrival direction. A common approach from the downwind side involves aligning with the pattern at a 45-degree angle to the downwind leg and entering at midfield.

Airport data is crucial for remote pilots operating near airports, offering insights into communication frequencies, available services, runway closures, and ongoing construction. Three primary sources provide this information:

1. **Chart Supplement U.S. (formerly Airport/Facility Directory):** This publication offers comprehensive details about airports, heliports, and seaplane bases accessible to the public. Published in seven regional books updated every 56 days, it's available digitally and serves as a valuable resource for pilots.

2. **Notices to Airmen (NOTAMs):** NOTAMs disseminate time-sensitive aeronautical information, crucial for flight planning. Covering temporary changes like runway closures, construction, and navigational aid status, pilots must review NOTAMs before every flight to ensure informed decision-making.

3. **Automated Terminal Information Service (ATIS):** ATIS broadcasts local weather conditions and operational details like active runways and ATC procedures. Updated hourly (or more frequently as needed), pilots rely on ATIS to stay informed about current conditions impacting their operations.

Remote pilots should exercise prudence by consulting these sources before each flight to mitigate risks associated with airport operations.

Additionally, aeronautical charts serve as essential navigation aids for pilots, providing detailed information about operating areas. Two primary charts used for visual flight rules (VFR) operations are [45]:

Sectional Charts: Widely utilized by pilots, sectional charts offer detailed information with a scale of 1:500,000. These charts cover airport data, navigational aids, airspace, and topography, facilitating comprehensive flight planning.

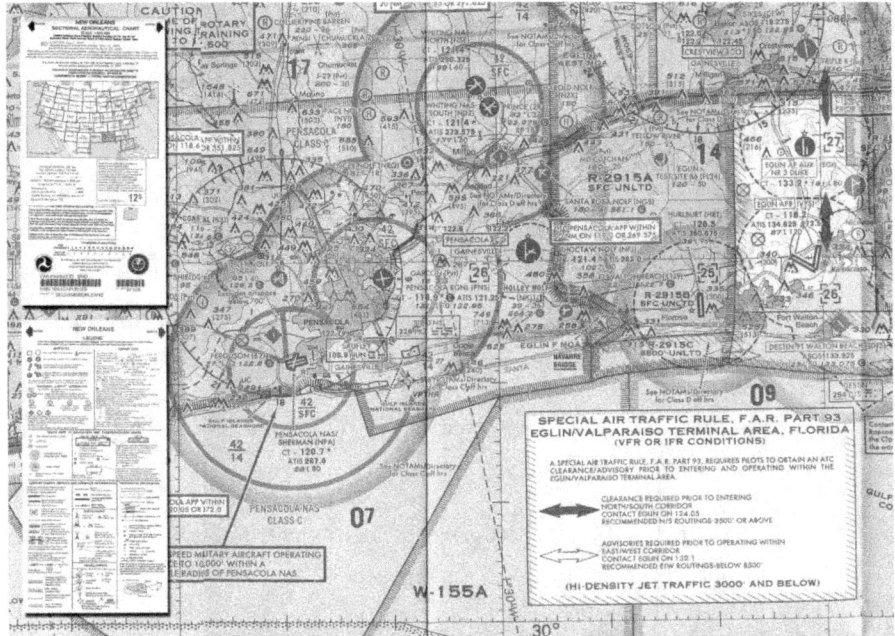

Figure 96: Example sectional chart.

VFR Terminal Area Charts: VFR Terminal Area Charts offer valuable assistance for navigating within or around Class B airspace. With a scale of 1:250,000 (1 inch = 3.43 NM or roughly 4 SM), these charts present a more intricate depiction of topographic features. Typically updated semi-annually, though some Alaskan and Caribbean charts may follow different revision schedules.

Remote pilots can access a catalogue of aeronautical charts and related publications through the Aeronautical Navigation Products website for detailed ordering instructions.

Using Longitude and Latitude as Reference Points

Latitude and longitude are geographical coordinates used to pinpoint specific locations on the Earth's surface.

Latitude:
- Latitude lines are parallel circles running east and west around the Earth.
- They measure the distance north or south of the equator, which is designated

as 0° latitude.

- Each degree of latitude is approximately 69 miles (111 kilometres) apart.

- Examples:

    - In the USA, the latitude ranges from approximately 25° N to 49° N, covering states like Florida and Washington.

    - In Europe, latitudes span from around 35° N to 70° N, encompassing countries like Spain and Sweden.

    - In Australia, latitudes vary from about 10° S to 45° S, including cities such as Sydney and Melbourne.

    - In Southeast Asia, latitudes extend from roughly 5° N to 20° N, covering regions like Thailand and Vietnam.

Longitude:
- Longitude lines, also known as meridians, run from the North Pole to the South Pole and intersect the equator at right angles.

- The Prime Meridian, passing through Greenwich, England, is the reference line for measuring east and west, with 0° longitude.

- Each degree of longitude is widest at the equator (approximately 69 miles or 111 kilometres) and converges at the poles.

- Examples:

    - In the USA, longitudes range from about 67° W to 125° W, covering states like California and New York.

    - In Europe, longitudes span from around 10° W to 40° E, encompassing countries like Portugal and Russia.

    - In Australia, longitudes vary from approximately 115° E to 155° E, including cities such as Perth and Brisbane.

    - In Southeast Asia, longitudes extend from roughly 95° E to 125° E, covering regions like Indonesia and the Philippines.

Variation:
- Variation refers to the angle between true north (TN) and magnetic north (MN).

- It can be east or west, depending on whether MN is to the east or west of TN.

- Isogonic lines on aeronautical charts connect points with equal magnetic variation, while the agonic line indicates where there is no variation.

- Examples:
  - In the USA, the magnetic north pole is located close to 71° N latitude and 96° W longitude, causing variations in different regions.
  - Similar variations occur in Europe, Australia, and Southeast Asia due to differing magnetic forces and geological conditions.

Planning your aerodrome Operation

Adequate planning is crucial for safe taxi operations, requiring as much attention as other flight phases. Here's how to plan your aerodrome operation effectively:
- Foresee your taxi route by gathering information from sources like ATIS, NOTAMs, ERSA, recent experiences, and aerodrome charts.

- Familiarize yourself with the layout of departure and arrival aerodromes.

- Keep an aerodrome chart or diagram accessible for reference during both planning and taxiing.

- Verify the expected taxi route against the aerodrome chart or ERSA, paying close attention to complex intersections.

- Determine when to focus on the taxi route, especially during complex intersections and runway crossings.

- Confirm your assigned route if you're uncertain about the instructions received from ATC.

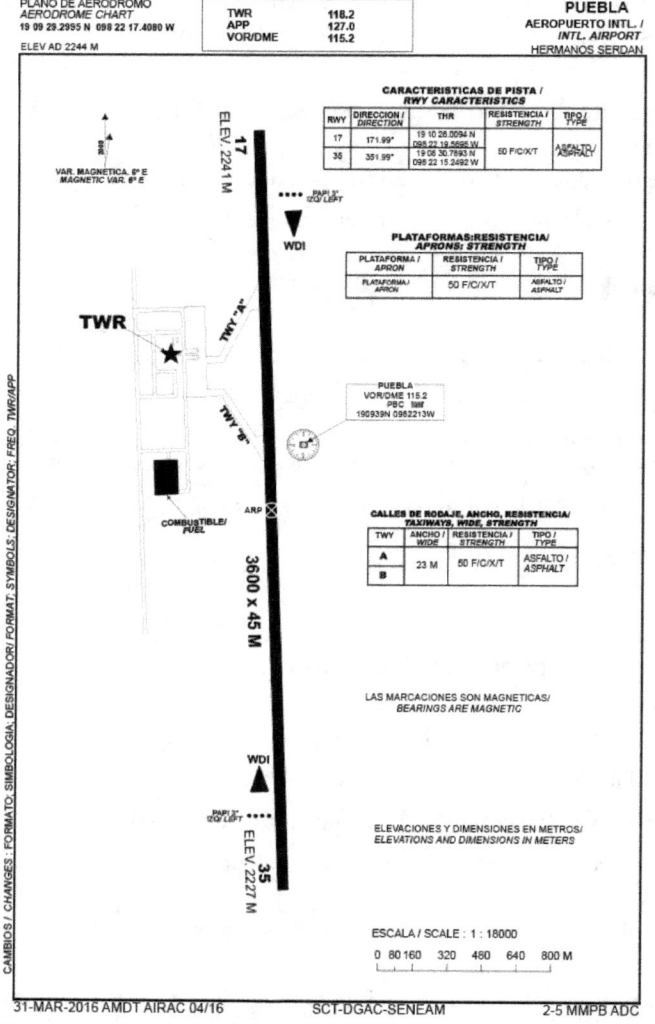

Figure 97: Sample Aerodrome Chart. SICT - AFAC - SENEAM, CC BY-SA 4.0, via Wikimedia Commons.

Responsibility for collision avoidance on the ground is often misunderstood. While ATC manages movement on the aerodrome, avoiding collisions is a shared responsibility among the pilot in command, airside driver, and ground personnel. ATC provides information on other aircraft/vehicles, but maintaining vigilance is crucial.

Runway confusion, particularly common at aerodromes with parallel runways, can lead to incorrect runway entry, take-off, or landing. To prevent this:

- Pay close attention to runway clearances.

- Always read back the assigned runway in full.

- During approach briefings, agree on how to positively identify the correct runway.

- Visually confirm the correct runway before entering or landing on it, using signage, orientation, and markings for identification.

- Note that runway lighting differs from taxiway lighting, aiding in distinguishing between them.

- Ensure your communication calls are directed to the correct aerodrome control frequency, especially at aerodromes with parallel runway operations.

Exercise extreme caution when flying below 2,000 feet above ground level (AGL) due to the presence of numerous antenna towers, including radio and television towers. These structures often exceed 1,000 feet AGL, with some reaching heights greater than 2,000 feet AGL. Most of these towers are supported by guy wires, which can be challenging to spot, especially in good weather conditions, and may become completely invisible during dusk or periods of reduced visibility. These guy wires can extend horizontally for approximately 1,500 feet from the structure. Therefore, it is advisable to maintain a horizontal distance of at least 2,000 feet from all antenna towers. Furthermore, be aware that new towers may not be depicted on your current chart, as the information may not have been received prior to the chart's printing.

In Australia, Aerodrome Charts offer detailed information about the layout and names of runways and taxiways, as well as the locations of major facilities. These charts can be obtained from various sources, including:

- En Route Supplement Australia (ERSA)

- Departure and Approach Procedures (DAP)

- Visual Terminal Charts (VTC)

ERSA and DAP charts are accessible on the Airservices website.

For all aircraft, the designated taxi clearance limit is typically the holding point for the runway, unless otherwise specified by air traffic control (ATC), such as an intermediate point like the holding (run-up) bay. If the holding bay is not designated as an intermediate clearance limit, an aircraft cleared to the runway holding point may proceed to an en route holding bay and subsequently depart from the holding bay to reach the runway holding point, ensuring to yield to other aircraft on the taxiway. However, a specific ATC clearance is necessary to cross any runway intersecting the taxi route.

It's crucial for pilots to accurately read back the term "holding point" if it's included in a taxi clearance, as failure to do so is a common readback error.

Taxi Procedures

Implementing sound operating procedures during taxiing enhances aerodrome operations' safety. This section highlights some key tasks to integrate into your taxi procedures.

ATC Instructions: Whenever feasible, obtain your airways clearance before requesting your taxi clearance. Once you receive taxi instructions, remember to:

- Jot down taxi instructions, particularly if they are complex, to minimize the risk of forgetting any part of the instruction.

- Monitor ATC instructions/clearances issued to other aircraft to enhance situational awareness.

- Exercise extra vigilance if another aircraft has a similar-sounding call sign.

- Listen attentively to avoid responding to an instruction/clearance meant for someone else.

- Seek clarification immediately if you are uncertain about any ATC instruction or clearance.

- Read back all required instructions/clearances with your aircraft call sign, adhering to the Aeronautical Information Publication (AIP) requirements.

- Note that an ATC taxi instruction does not authorize crossing a runway holding point, illuminated stopbar, or entering/taxiing on ANY runway unless specifically cleared to do so.

- Inform ATC promptly if you anticipate a delay or are unable to comply with their instructions.

- Be alert for light signals from the tower in case of suspected radio problems.

ATC will designate the crossing points for an aircraft when instructing a runway crossing. A typical instruction might be: 'Alpha Bravo Charlie on Taxiway November cross Runway One Seven' Your readback should be: 'On November, crossing runway One Seven, Alpha Bravo Charlie'

Some Australian airports are equipped with the Advanced Surface Movement Guidance Control System (A-SMGCS), enabling precise tracking of aircraft and vehicles on the airport surface in all visibility conditions. To cooperate with A-SMGCS, pilots should operate their transponders following AIP Australia ENR 1.6. A-SMGCS does not involve a 'squawk ident' procedure, as all tracking is automatic. If A-SMGCS is unavailable, ATC may halt or restrict low visibility operations.

Readback Instructions for Runway Entry or Hold Short If instructed to hold short of a runway, refrain from crossing the marked runway holding point. Always read back any clearance or instruction to hold short of, enter, land on, conditionally line up on, take-off on, and cross or backtrack on any runway. Avoid merely acknowledging these clearances or instructions with 'Roger' or 'Wilco' or your call sign.

Is the Tower Active? To avoid confusion regarding whether the Tower is active or if CTAF procedures apply, listen to the ATIS. If the tower is inactive, the ATIS will be identified as information ZULU and will include the activation time and the CTAF frequency.

Situational Awareness

Maintaining a 'sterile' cockpit is crucial to remain focused on your duties without distractions such as conversing with passengers or using mobile phones.

During taxiing, it's vital to be aware of your location, its relation to your intended taxi route, and other aircraft and vehicles present on the aerodrome. This awareness, known as 'situational awareness,' can be maintained by:

- Understanding and adhering to ATC instructions and clearances.

- Utilizing current aerodrome charts/diagrams.

- Familiarizing yourself with visual aids on the aerodrome, like markings, signs, and lights.

- Monitoring the radio and using the aerodrome chart to locate other aircraft and vehicles.

- Avoiding distractions and minimizing 'heads down' activities while the aircraft is in motion.

TIP: If uncertain about your location on the aerodrome, ensure clearance from any runway and halt the aircraft. Notify ATC and request progressive taxi instructions if needed.

Non-Controlled Aerodromes

At non-controlled aerodromes, where ATC's safety net is absent, 'alerted' see-and-avoid principles become crucial. In addition to guidance in this booklet, monitor the aerodrome frequency and broadcast intentions to maintain situational awareness for yourself and others. While standard broadcasts are outlined in AIP, supplement with additional broadcasts if necessary to mitigate collision risks.

Some non-controlled aerodromes may offer an aerodrome frequency response unit (AFRU) to confirm the correct frequency and radio functionality.

While Taxiing

Exercise extra caution when instructed to taxi on a runway, especially at night or in reduced visibility conditions. Utilize available resources to stay on your assigned taxi route, including aerodrome charts, markings, signs, lights, and heading indicators.

Ensure you request, receive, and comply with hold short or crossing instructions when approaching intersecting runways.

Activate rotating beacon and taxi lights.

Before entering or crossing any runway, thoroughly scan left, ahead, above, and right to ensure the runway and its approaches are clear.

When issued a 'line up and wait' instruction by ATC, pay close attention, especially at night or in low visibility. Before entering the runway, scan its full length, check for approaching or landing aircraft, and activate strobe lights if equipped.

When holding position at night, consider lining up slightly off the centreline to differentiate your aircraft from runway lights and markings.

After Landing

Exercise caution after landing on a runway intersecting with another runway, particularly at aerodromes with parallel runway systems. You require specific ATC clearance to cross or enter any runway.

Do not hold on the active runway unless authorized by ATC.

Avoid exiting onto another runway without ATC clearance.

Do not accept last-minute turn-off instructions from the tower unless you fully understand and can comply.

Refrain from non-essential communications or actions until safely off and clear of the runway.

Remember, a clearance to land includes clearance to cross any other runway during landing. However, exiting the landing runway onto another runway requires a specific clearance.

Aircraft Lights

During both day and night operations, exterior aircraft lights serve crucial functions to enhance visibility and communicate important information to other pilots and ground personnel on an aerodrome. Let's delve into the specifics of their use:

1. **Engines Running:**

    - When the aircraft's engines are running, it's standard practice to turn on the rotating beacon. This beacon emits a flashing light to indicate that the aircraft's engines are operational, alerting others to the presence of an active aircraft.

2. **Taxiing:**

    - Before initiating taxi manoeuvres, pilots should activate several exterior lights to increase visibility. These typically include the rotating beacon, navigation lights, taxi lights, and if available, logo lights. These lights help other pilots and ground personnel identify the moving aircraft and discern its direction of travel.

3. **Crossing a Runway:**

    - When crossing a runway, it's essential to illuminate all exterior lights on the aircraft. However, pilots must consider potential safety hazards posed by the forward-facing lights, which could impair the vision of other pilots or ground personnel during runway crossings. Therefore, caution is necessary to balance visibility with potential glare.

4. Entering the Departure Runway (Line Up and Wait):

- Upon receiving instructions to line up and wait on the departure runway, pilots should activate all exterior lights to enhance the aircraft's visibility. This is particularly important for alerting aircraft on final approach and ensuring visibility to air traffic control (ATC) personnel. Depending on the circumstances, pilots may also choose to activate landing lights to further increase their aircraft's conspicuousness.

5. Take-Off:

- When cleared for take-off or when initiating the take-off roll at an aerodrome without an operating control tower, pilots should activate the landing lights. These powerful lights enhance the aircraft's visibility to other aircraft in the vicinity and aid in collision avoidance during critical phases of flight.

The strategic use of exterior aircraft lights during different phases of operation plays a vital role in promoting safety and situational awareness on the aerodrome, both during daylight hours and at night. These lights not only make the aircraft more conspicuous but also communicate the pilot's intentions effectively to other stakeholders in the aviation environment.

Aerodrome Markings, Signs and Lights

Taxiway Marking Patterns

When taxiway markings comprise a combination of solid and dashed lines, typically seen at runway holding positions:

- Crossing from the dashed side to the solid side is permitted without restrictions.

- However, obtaining ATC clearance is mandatory before crossing from the solid side to the dashed side, especially at aerodromes with an operational control tower.

- In case of instructions to "hold short," halt before reaching the initial solid line of the runway holding point marking, as illustrated below.

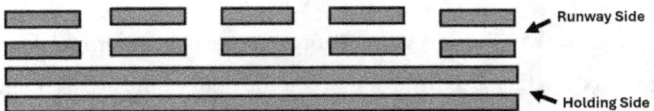

Figure 98: Holding position markings pattern ahead of a crossing runway.

Intermediate Holding Positions

Intermediate holding position markings indicate a holding point situated between taxiways. You are required to stop at these positions if directed by ATC to hold short of a specific taxiway.

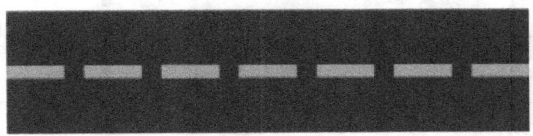

Figure 99: Intermediate holding position marking.

Aerodrome Signs

In addition to aerodrome markings and lights, aerodrome signs play a crucial role in guiding aircraft safely around the aerodrome.

Understanding the colour codes and meanings of these five types of signs is essential for safe taxiing:

1. Location sign: These signs identify the current taxiway. They feature yellow inscriptions on a black background.

2. Mandatory instruction sign: These signs mark the entrance to runways or critical areas and areas off-limits for aircraft. They display white inscriptions on a red background. Clearance from ATC is required before proceeding past this point.

3. Direction sign: Placed before intersections, these signs indicate the taxiway designations leading out of the intersection and the direction of turn required to align the aircraft. They have black inscriptions on a yellow background.

4. Destination sign: These signs use arrows to indicate directions to specific destinations on the airfield, such as runways, terminals, or airport services. They also feature black inscriptions on a yellow background.

Sign arrays: Arrays of direction signs are organized clockwise from left to right, with left turn signs on the left and right turn signs on the right of the location sign.

Taxi-holding point sign: Found adjacent to yellow runway holding point markings on taxiways intersecting runways, these signs provide information about the taxiway and the associated runway. For example, a sign may indicate that you are at Taxiway Alpha's Holding Point for Runway 15-33, with the thresholds for Runway 15 to the left and Runway 33 to the right.

Figure 100: Example Taxi holding point sign.

Runway Stop Bars and Aerodrome Lighting

Runway stop bars are critical safety features designed to prevent runway incursions, which are incidents where aircraft inadvertently enter a runway without proper clearance. These incidents are common and can lead to serious accidents. Stop bars serve as visual alerts to pilots, signalling them to stop and hold at designated points on the taxiway.

In Australia, stop bars have been implemented at several airports and are considered essential for preventing runway incursions. However, their use is not limited to Australia; they are deployed at airports worldwide to enhance safety during ground operations.

Stop bars are simple yet effective. They consist of a series of lights embedded in the pavement, forming a solid line perpendicular to the taxiway and runway. When illuminated, these lights create a visual barrier, signalling to pilots that they must stop and await further instructions from air traffic control (ATC).

Crossing a stop bar is strictly prohibited without explicit clearance from ATC. Pilots must wait until the stop bar lights are turned off and ATC instructs them to cross. This protocol ensures that aircraft movements on the ground are coordinated and safe.

Aerodrome lighting plays a crucial role in ensuring safe ground operations, especially in low visibility conditions. Different lighting configurations are used to delineate runways, taxiways, and other critical areas. Here are some key aspects of aerodrome lighting:

- Runway edge lights: These lights mark the edges of the runway and are typically white. In some cases, such as on runways equipped with high-intensity lighting, the edge lights within 600 meters from the end of the runway may be yellow.

- Taxiway edge lights: These lights or reflectors are blue and guide aircraft along taxiways.

- High-intensity approach lighting (HIAL): Used to assist aircraft during approach and landing, HIAL systems typically feature red and white lights.

- Taxiway centreline lights: These lights or reflectors are green and help pilots maintain alignment while taxiing.

Pilots must be vigilant and adhere to specific lighting configurations. For example, illuminated red lights across a taxiway indicate a stop bar, and pilots must not proceed until instructed by ATC. Flashing yellow lights, known as runway guard lights, highlight holding points and serve as additional visual cues for pilots.

The implementation of stop bars and proper understanding of aerodrome lighting contribute significantly to the overall safety of aircraft operations, mitigating the risk of runway incursions and ensuring efficient ground movements at airports worldwide.

RPAS Ground Operations

Integrating Remotely Piloted Aircraft Systems (RPAS) into airspace shared with manned aircraft demands meticulous attention to unique procedures to ensure safety and seamless integration. These procedures ideally align with those developed for manned aircraft to uphold consistency and enhance safety standards.

Key considerations in the integration of RPAS flights encompass:

a) Flight Planning:

Establishing distinctive RPAS type designators and formulating appropriate communication phraseology for interactions with Air Traffic Control (ATC).

b) VFR Flight:

Defining separation standards and establishing right-of-way rules to govern visual flight operations.

c) IFR Flight:

Establishing separation standards and delineating right-of-way rules for instrument flight operations.

d) Contingency and Emergency Procedures:

Addressing potential scenarios such as Command and Control (C2) link failure, establishing protocols for ATC communication failure with remote pilots, and outlining intercept procedures while ensuring compliance with air defence protocols.

Regarding flight planning, until official RPAS type designators are established, placeholders like "ZZZZ" are recommended on flight plan forms. Additionally, Air Navigation Service Providers (ANSPs) must devise methods to convey unique information related to RPAS flights, particularly regarding lost C2 link procedures.

Unique characteristics of RPAS that influence aerodrome operations include their capability to detect aerodrome signs, avoid collisions, and adhere to ATC instructions. Consideration must also be given to implications for aerodrome certification requirements, infrastructure needs, and their integration with manned aircraft.

Within controlled aerodrome environments, RPAS operations should mimic those of manned aircraft, necessitating effective communication and manoeuvring procedures. Remote pilots must maintain communication with ATC, acknowledge instructions, and adhere to aerodrome markings and signals for safe operations.

For RPAS operations at uncontrolled aerodromes under the Aerodrome Flight Information Service (AFIS), effective communication with AFIS officers is vital to exchange safety-related traffic information. Compliance with aerodrome markings, signage, and manoeuvring protocols among other aircraft is imperative.

States may opt to establish dedicated aerodromes exclusively for RPAS operations, requiring the formulation of specific protocols and procedures to govern such operations.

Comprehensive emergency response plans must be in place at aerodromes to coordinate actions during emergencies occurring on-site or in the immediate vicinity.

Aerodrome operators may need to enhance their safety management systems to effectively accommodate RPAS operations, incorporating additional requirements and protocols specific to RPAS activities.

DRONE OPERATIONS

NAVIGATING REMOTE PILOT SYSTEMS

Depending on the severity of low-visibility conditions, various navigation methods may be necessary for piloting your drone. For mild conditions such as light fog or haze, visual navigation utilizing eyesight and camera observation is sufficient. In moderate conditions like moderate fog or rain, GPS navigation utilizing a GPS sensor and mobile device to track position on a map is recommended. In severe conditions such as heavy fog or snow, where GPS signals or visual contact may be compromised, inertial navigation relying on a gyroscope and compass to measure speed, acceleration, and heading becomes essential. Adjusting navigation methods based on the level of visibility ensures safe and effective drone operation in diverse weather conditions.

As a general overview of where drones can be operated, in the United States, drones, also known as Unmanned Aircraft Systems (UAS), can operate in various airspace categories, subject to specific regulations and restrictions imposed by the Federal Aviation Administration (FAA). Here are the primary categories where drones can operate:

1. Class G Airspace: Also known as uncontrolled airspace, Class G airspace is available for drone operations without the need for special permissions or clearances from air traffic control. However, drone pilots must still adhere to FAA regulations, including maintaining visual line of sight with the drone and flying below 400 feet above ground level.

2. Class B, C, D, and E Airspace: Drones can operate in controlled airspace with the appropriate authorization from the FAA and coordination with air traffic control. This typically involves obtaining approval through the FAA's Low Altitude Authorization and Notification Capability (LAANC) system or by

filing for a Part 107 waiver.

3. Restricted and Prohibited Areas: Certain airspace areas, such as around airports, military installations, and other sensitive locations, have restrictions or prohibitions on drone operations. Pilots must be aware of these areas and obtain the necessary permissions or avoid flying in restricted airspace.

4. Temporary Flight Restrictions (TFRs): TFRs may be established by the FAA for events, emergencies, or other temporary reasons. Drone operations are typically prohibited within TFR areas without specific authorization from the FAA.

5. Special Use Airspace (SUA): SUA includes areas designated for specific military or government activities, such as restricted areas, military operations areas (MOAs), and warning areas. Drone operations may be restricted or prohibited in these areas.

6. National Parks and Wilderness Areas: While drone operations are generally permitted in national parks and wilderness areas, they are subject to restrictions imposed by the National Park Service and other federal agencies. Pilots must comply with regulations specific to each park or wilderness area.

It's essential for drone operators to familiarize themselves with the airspace classifications, regulations, and restrictions applicable to their intended operating areas. Additionally, adherence to FAA guidelines, such as those outlined in Part 107 of the Federal Aviation Regulations, is necessary to ensure safe and legal drone operations in the United States.

In Australia, drone operations are regulated by the Civil Aviation Safety Authority (CASA), and drones, known as Remotely Piloted Aircraft (RPA) or Unmanned Aircraft Systems (UAS), can operate in various airspace categories, subject to specific regulations and restrictions. Here are the primary areas where drones can operate:

1. Non-Controlled Airspace (Class G): Similar to the United States, Class G airspace in Australia is uncontrolled airspace where drone operations are generally permitted without the need for special permissions or clearances from air traffic control. However, operators must still comply with CASA regulations, including maintaining visual line of sight with the drone and flying below certain altitude limits.

2. Controlled Airspace (Class C, D, E, and CTAF): Drone operations in controlled airspace require approval from CASA and coordination with air traffic control. This involves obtaining permission through CASA's online platform, known as "Can I Fly There?" or by applying for specific airspace approvals.

3. Restricted and Prohibited Areas: Certain areas in Australia, such as around airports, military installations, and other sensitive locations, have restrictions or prohibitions on drone operations. Operators must be aware of these areas and obtain the necessary permissions or avoid flying in restricted airspace.

4. Danger Areas and Military Operations Areas (MOAs): Danger areas and MOAs are designated for military training and exercises. Drone operations may be restricted or prohibited in these areas when they are active.

5. National Parks and Protected Areas: While drone operations are generally permitted in national parks and protected areas, operators must comply with regulations specific to each park or reserve. This may include restrictions on flying near wildlife, cultural sites, or other sensitive areas.

6. Urban and Built-Up Areas: Drone operations in urban and built-up areas are subject to additional regulations and considerations, including privacy concerns, safety considerations, and local government regulations.

7. Special Events and Temporary Restrictions: Temporary restrictions may be imposed for special events, emergencies, or other reasons. Operators must adhere to any temporary flight restrictions (TFRs) issued by CASA or other authorities.

It's essential for drone operators in Australia to familiarize themselves with CASA regulations, airspace classifications, and any local restrictions or requirements specific to their intended operating areas. Adherence to safety guidelines and responsible flying practices is crucial to ensuring safe and legal drone operations in Australia.

In Europe, drone operations are regulated by the European Union Aviation Safety Agency (EASA) and individual national aviation authorities within the European Union (EU) and European Free Trade Association (EFTA) member states. Here are the primary areas where drones can operate:

1. Open Category: The Open category is divided into subcategories based on the level of risk associated with the operation and the specific requirements for

drone pilots. Depending on the subcategory and the drone's characteristics, operations may be permitted in different types of airspace, including rural, suburban, and urban areas.

2. Specific Category: The Specific category allows for more complex drone operations that do not fit within the limitations of the Open category. Operators must obtain an operational authorization from the relevant aviation authority and conduct risk assessments for their specific operations. This category includes operations in controlled airspace and other areas with specific requirements.

3. Certified Category: The Certified category is for drones that have been certified for operations in controlled airspace and other complex environments. These drones must meet stringent safety and reliability standards, similar to manned aircraft, and undergo certification by EASA or national aviation authorities.

4. Controlled Airspace: Similar to other regions, drone operations in controlled airspace require coordination with air traffic control and may require specific permissions or approvals from the relevant aviation authority. Operators must adhere to procedures for obtaining airspace authorizations and ensuring safe integration with manned aircraft.

5. Restricted and Prohibited Areas: Certain areas in Europe, such as around airports, military installations, and other sensitive locations, have restrictions or prohibitions on drone operations. Operators must be aware of these areas and comply with regulations to avoid flying in restricted airspace.

6. National Parks and Protected Areas: Drone operations in national parks and protected areas are subject to regulations specific to each country. Operators must comply with any restrictions on flying near wildlife, cultural sites, or other sensitive areas.

7. Urban and Built-Up Areas: Drone operations in urban and built-up areas are subject to additional regulations and considerations, including privacy concerns, safety considerations, and local government regulations.

8. Temporary Restrictions: Temporary restrictions may be imposed for special events, emergencies, or other reasons. Operators must adhere to any temporary

flight restrictions (TFRs) issued by the relevant aviation authorities.

It's essential for drone operators in Europe to familiarize themselves with EASA regulations, national aviation regulations, airspace classifications, and any local restrictions or requirements specific to their intended operating areas. Adherence to safety guidelines and responsible flying practices is crucial to ensuring safe and legal drone operations in Europe.

In the UK, drone operations are regulated by the Civil Aviation Authority (CAA). Here are the primary areas where drones can operate:

1. Open Category: The Open category is divided into subcategories based on the level of risk associated with the operation and the specific requirements for drone pilots. Depending on the subcategory and the drone's characteristics, operations may be permitted in different types of airspace, including rural, suburban, and urban areas.

2. Specific Category: The Specific category allows for more complex drone operations that do not fit within the limitations of the Open category. Operators must obtain an operational authorization from the CAA and conduct risk assessments for their specific operations. This category includes operations in controlled airspace and other areas with specific requirements.

3. Certified Category: The Certified category is for drones that have been certified for operations in controlled airspace and other complex environments. These drones must meet stringent safety and reliability standards, similar to manned aircraft, and undergo certification by the CAA.

4. Controlled Airspace: Drone operations in controlled airspace require coordination with air traffic control and may require specific permissions or approvals from the CAA. Operators must adhere to procedures for obtaining airspace authorizations and ensuring safe integration with manned aircraft.

5. Restricted and Prohibited Areas: Certain areas in the UK, such as around airports, military installations, and other sensitive locations, have restrictions or prohibitions on drone operations. Operators must be aware of these areas and comply with regulations to avoid flying in restricted airspace.

6. National Parks and Protected Areas: Drone operations in national parks and

protected areas are subject to regulations specific to each country. In the UK, operators must comply with restrictions on flying near wildlife, cultural sites, or other sensitive areas.

7. Urban and Built-Up Areas: Drone operations in urban and built-up areas are subject to additional regulations and considerations, including privacy concerns, safety considerations, and local government regulations.

8. Temporary Restrictions: Temporary restrictions may be imposed for special events, emergencies, or other reasons. Operators must adhere to any temporary flight restrictions (TFRs) issued by the CAA.

It's essential for drone operators in the UK to familiarize themselves with CAA regulations, airspace classifications, and any local restrictions or requirements specific to their intended operating areas. Adherence to safety guidelines and responsible flying practices is crucial to ensuring safe and legal drone operations in the UK.

In South East Asia, drone operations are regulated by individual countries, each with its own set of rules and regulations. While specific regulations may vary from one country to another, there are common areas where drones can typically operate across the region:

1. Open Areas: Drones can often operate in open areas such as rural or sparsely populated areas where there are minimal risks to people, property, and other aircraft. These areas are usually away from congested airspace and populated areas.

2. Designated Flying Sites: Some countries designate specific areas or flying sites for recreational or commercial drone operations. These sites may have facilities for drone pilots, such as landing pads, charging stations, and safety equipment.

3. Agricultural Areas: Drones are frequently used for agricultural purposes such as crop monitoring, spraying, and mapping in rural agricultural areas. However, operators must comply with any regulations related to agricultural activities and airspace restrictions.

4. Industrial Zones: In industrial areas or zones, drones may be used for inspection, surveillance, and monitoring of infrastructure such as pipelines, power lines, and industrial facilities. Operators must obtain any necessary permissions and adhere to safety guidelines.

5. Construction Sites: Drones are commonly used for aerial surveying, mapping, and progress monitoring at construction sites. However, operators must ensure compliance with any regulations related to construction activities and airspace restrictions.

6. Tourist Attractions: Drones are often used to capture aerial footage and photographs at tourist attractions such as beaches, landmarks, and natural landscapes. However, operators must respect privacy concerns, adhere to local regulations, and obtain any necessary permits or permissions.

7. Protected Areas: Drones may operate in protected areas such as national parks, wildlife reserves, and conservation areas for environmental monitoring, research, and surveillance purposes. However, operators must obtain permits and comply with regulations to protect sensitive ecosystems and wildlife.

8. Urban Areas: In some cases, drones may be permitted to operate in urban areas for specific purposes such as aerial photography, videography, and surveillance. However, operators must comply with strict regulations regarding safety, privacy, and airspace restrictions.

9. Emergency Response: Drones may be used for emergency response activities such as search and rescue operations, disaster assessment, and delivery of medical supplies in disaster-affected areas. Operators must coordinate with local authorities and adhere to regulations governing emergency operations.

It's important for drone operators in South East Asia to familiarize themselves with the regulations and requirements of the specific country where they intend to operate. This includes obtaining any necessary permits or licenses, adhering to safety guidelines, and respecting local customs and regulations. Additionally, operators should stay informed about any updates or changes to regulations to ensure compliance with the law.

To provide a more specific in depth example, drone operations in Australian airspaces are considered in the following.

Maps, aeronautical charts, and weather briefings are crucial components of flight planning for drone operations. Here's a detailed breakdown of where drones can operate, airspace considerations, and classes of airspace:

Permissible Drone Operations:

- Drones can operate where there is no unreasonable risk of injury to persons or damage to property.

- Altitude is limited to 400 feet (121 meters) above ground level (AGL).

- Operations must be more than 3 nautical miles (5.5 kilometres) from an aerodrome or Helicopter Landing Site (HLS).

- Operation outside restricted or prohibited airspace, such as Amberley Military Zone.

- Conducted in good weather conditions (Visual Meteorological Conditions - VMC).

- Maintain a distance of 30 meters from people or property not involved in the operation.

Restricted Drone Operations:
- Drones cannot operate over populated areas unless risks can be mitigated.

- Risk mitigation strategies may include notifying residents, adjusting timing, or erecting signage and safety cones.

Airspace Considerations:
- Cowboy operators may disregard regulations, posing safety risks.

- Three key airspace considerations:
  - No-fly zone within 3 nautical miles (5.5 kilometres) around aerodromes like Brisbane, Archerfield, and Gold Coast.
  - Helicopter Landing Sites (HLS) require special attention, particularly in areas like Brisbane CBD with multiple HLS at hospitals.
  - Restricted airspace, e.g., Amberley Military Zone, imposes additional limitations.

Classes of Airspace:
- Airspace administration in Australia adheres to International Civil Aviation

Organization (ICAO) standards.

- Classes of airspace in Australia's Flight Information Regions (FIRs) include:
  - Class A to G airspace, each with specific characteristics regarding separation, services provided, speed limitations, and radio communication requirements.

These regulations and considerations help ensure safe drone operations within Australia's airspace, promoting both aviation safety and regulatory compliance.

VFR Altimetry: Transition Layer, Altitude, and Level

In Australia, the altimetry system incorporates a transition layer between the transition altitude, always set at 10,000 feet, and the transition level of FL110. This system aims to differentiate aircraft using QNH from those employing 1013.2 hPa as a reference datum. For operations at or below the transition altitude:

- The altimeter reference is either the current local QNH of a station within 100 nautical miles of the aircraft's route or the current area forecast QNH if the local QNH is unavailable.

- While cruising in the standard pressure region, the altimeter reference must be set to 1013.2 hPa.

Transition between QNH and 1013.2 hPa should occur in the standard pressure region on climb after passing 10,000 feet and before leveling off, or on descent to a level in the Altimeter Setting Region before entering the Transition Layer.

QNH information is obtainable from reporting stations, ATIS, TAF, ARFOR, AERIS, or from ATS. Cruising within the transition layer is prohibited.

Regarding altimetry at specific flight levels:

- FL125 is not available when the area QNH falls below 963 hPa.

- FL120 is not available when the area QNH falls below 980 hPa.

- FL115 is not available when the area QNH falls below 997 hPa.

- FL110 is not available when the area QNH falls below 1013 hPa.

Area QNH, forecasted and valid for three hours, must meet specific standards regarding accuracy and consistency across adjoining areas.

For altimeter phraseology:

- Altitudes measured from QNH or area QNH datum are expressed in full (e.g., 3000 feet as 'three thousand').

- Expressions of heights measured from the 1013.2 hPa datum must always include the term 'flight level.'

Preflight altimeter checks involve verifying altitude accuracy using accurate QNH and known elevations like tarmac, threshold, or airfield reference point elevation.
For VFR altimeters:

- With accurate QNH set, VFR altimeters should read site elevation within specified tolerances to be considered serviceable by the pilot.

- VFR altimeters are not permitted for aeroplane operations above FL200.

Accurate QNH is provided by ATIS, a tower, or an automatic remote-reporting aerodrome sensor, while site elevation data is sourced from aerodrome survey data.

VFR flight under specific regulations mandates adherence to visual meteorological conditions, speed restrictions, and operational limitations, including restrictions on night VFR and special VFR clearances.

Determination of flight visibility and aerodrome meteorological minima are responsibilities assigned to the pilot in command, subject to regulations outlined by CASA.

ATS Surveillance Services: Operating Requirements for ADS-B Transmitters

In Australia, pilots of aircraft equipped with a functional ADS-B transmitter suitable for receiving ATS surveillance services are required to activate the transmitter throughout the duration of flight.

Some ADS-B installations may share controls with the SSR transponder, preventing independent operation of the two systems. If compliance with a particular instruction is not possible, pilots must promptly inform ATC and request alternative instructions.

Aircraft equipped with ADS-B featuring an aircraft identification feature must transmit the specified aircraft identification as indicated in the flight notification or, in the absence of a filed flight notification, the aircraft registration.

Operation of Transponders: ATS typically assigns a temporary discrete code for each flight operating in controlled airspace or participating in Surveillance Information Service (SIS), except as noted below.

Unless otherwise instructed by ATC, pilots of Mode 3A or Mode S transponder-equipped aircraft in Australian airspace must activate their transponders, simultaneously activating Mode C capability if available.

Pilots must ensure that both transponders and ADS-B transmitters are activated, with the altitude function selected, as primary radar coverage is limited within 50 nm of major airports, relying on SSR transponder and ADS-B transmitter data. TCAS also relies on transponder data for collision avoidance functions.

When operating in Australian airspace, aircraft must select and use codes based on specific criteria, including flight type, airspace class, and military or civil operations.

Pilots are responsible for selecting the appropriate code prior to requesting SIS or clearance into controlled airspace, if a discrete code has already been coordinated.

The identification function (SPI) should only be operated when requested by ATC.

During departure from a radar-controlled aerodrome, pilots must keep the transponder in Standby mode until reaching the departure runway. Upon arrival, the transponder should be switched to Standby or Off as soon as practical after landing.

Transponder Emergency Codes: In the event of an emergency during flight, excluding loss of two-way communications, pilots should select code 7700 unless they have a specific reason to maintain the currently assigned code.

For aircraft experiencing a loss of two-way communications, the transponder should be set to code 7600.

If a radar controller observes a 7600 code, they will request the pilot to operate the identification (SPI) function. Control of the aircraft will continue using the identification transmission to acknowledge instructions if the identification signal is received. If not, the aircraft must maintain the transponder on code 7600 and follow radio failure procedures.

Radio Communications Procedures: Pilots seeking ATS surveillance services should direct their request to the ATS unit they are communicating with. If an area approach Control Centre (AACC) is not established, pilots will be informed of the time or location to transfer to a control frequency. In the presence of an AACC, procedural and ATS surveillance services may be provided on a common frequency, with the callsign indicating the service being provided.

Identification Procedures: Before providing an ATS surveillance service, positive identification of the aircraft is required. However, control services will not be provided until the aircraft enters controlled airspace.

Vectoring Procedures: Upon receiving heading instructions, pilots must immediately commence a rate 1 turn, or the standard rate of turn for the aircraft type, and maintain the given heading unless instructed otherwise. Aircraft will typically be vectored along routes where the pilot can monitor navigation.

Special VFR flights cannot be vectored by ATC unless there is an emergency. When an aircraft is vectored off an established route, the pilot will be informed of the reason for the vectoring, if not self-evident. If an aircraft reports unreliable directional instruments, the pilot will be asked to make all turns at an agreed rate before receiving manoeuvring instructions.

Controllers assign altitudes to vectored aircraft to ensure terrain clearance, but in visual meteorological conditions (VMC) during the day, pilots may be allowed to arrange their own terrain clearance, with instructions provided accordingly.

Pilots being vectored will routinely receive position information to aid pilot navigation in the event of radio or ATS surveillance system failure. ATC maintains short intervals between transmissions to enable prompt recognition of communication failure, especially when aircraft are on headings that could infringe terrain clearance or separation standards.

Before take-off, ATC may assign a heading for the departing aircraft to follow after take-off, with frequency change instructions if needed. Arriving aircraft may be vectored to establish for a radar or visual approach, avoid hazardous weather, or expedite traffic flow.

Time

UTC (Coordinated Universal Time) is widely used in aviation worldwide, serving as the standard time reference for international air traffic control and management. Virtually all countries utilize UTC or UTC-derived time for aviation operations to ensure consistency and coordination across global airspace. Some countries also use their own local time zones in conjunction with UTC for specific purposes, such as flight planning and scheduling. Therefore, while all countries may not exclusively operate solely on UTC time, it is a fundamental component of aviation timekeeping and coordination globally.

The term "Zulu" is employed in ATC procedures to denote Coordinated Universal Time (UTC). For instance:

- 0920 UTC is vocalized as "zero nine two zero zulu"

- 0115 UTC is vocalized as "zero one one five zulu" When converting from Standard Time to UTC:

- Eastern Standard Time requires subtracting 10 hours

- Central Standard Time necessitates subtracting 9.5 hours

- Western Standard Time entails subtracting 8 hours Note: Daylight saving time is not uniformly implemented across Australia and is not detailed in the Aeronautical Information Publication (AIP). Refer to AIP SUP and NOTAM Daylight Saving for specifics. Radiotelephone transmissions adopt the 24-hour clock system. The hour is represented by the first two digits and the minutes by the last two digits. For instance:

- 0001 is articulated as "zero zero zero one"

- 1920 is articulated as "one nine two zero" Time may be conveyed in minutes only (two digits) in radiotelephone communications when ambiguity is improbable. The current time at a station is conveyed to the nearest minute to aid pilots in time checks. Control towers provide time to the nearest half-minute when granting a taxi clearance to departing aircraft. For example:

- 0925:10 is articulated as "time, two five"

- 0932:20 is articulated as "time, three two and a half"

- 2145:50 is articulated as "time, four six" Time format: Date and time are represented in a combination of the date and time in a single six-figure group. However, a 10-figure group, comprising the year, month, date, hours, and minutes, is utilized for NOTAMs and SUPs. This is condensed to an eight-figure group (omitting the year) for a Specific Pre-flight Information Bulletin (SPFIB). The format is yymmddhhmm. For instance:

- 1215 hours UTC on 23 March 2010 would be written as 1003231215

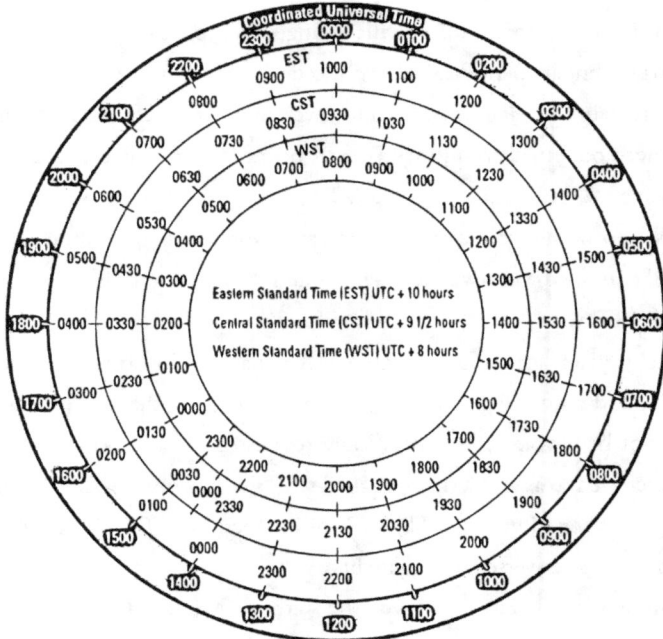

Figure 101: Coordinated Universal Time.

Pre-operations information and NOTAM

Accessing and reviewing current NOTAMs plays a crucial role in your flight preparation process. They serve as an effective tool for informing pilots about changing conditions at specific locations, including the time frame, areas, and altitudes affected by these changes.

Obtaining the latest NOTAMs holds equal importance for both controlled and non-controlled aerodromes. For instance, events like major racing meets at venues such as Bathurst, Louth, and Birdsville draw a significant number of visiting aircraft, often requiring adherence to special procedures.

A compelling illustration of the significance of reviewing current NOTAMs is exemplified at William Creek, situated in remote South Australia. Unprecedented rainfall in Queensland's Channel Country in recent years has led to flooding across central Australia, transforming the historically dry salt bed of Lake Eyre North & South into a vast inland sea. This spectacle has attracted sightseers by air, leading to a notable increase in air traffic.

Notably, in the William Creek entry in the En Route Supplement Australia (ERSA), under "Additional Information," specific changes to broadcast procedures and/or frequency management are periodically introduced to accommodate sightseeing flights and increased activity in the Lake Eyre area. However, many transient pilots remain unaware of these changes, potentially resulting in unsafe operations, such as continuing to operate on the published CTAF frequency, 126.7MHz.

The safest approach involves broadcasting and monitoring the temporary frequency, 127.8, and, if equipped with two radios, maintaining vigilant monitoring on 126.7MHz as published in ERSA.

Additionally, when accessing the National Aeronautical Information Processing System (NAIPS) and requesting forecasts, it's essential to note that Melbourne FIR NOTAMs will not be visible unless specifically requested via a Sub-FIR NOTAM code (commonly referred to as a "7 series"), aligned with the appropriate Area Forecast. These codes, although buried in the Pre-Flight Planning section of ERSA, provide vital local information on areas traversed during flights.

Furthermore, it's imperative to check the status of Military Restricted Areas (RAs) along and near your planned route, as straying into these areas without clearance during active periods can pose significant hazards. RAs are marked on visual charts, and their status can be verified through NOTAMs.

Conditional RA Status designations indicate the likelihood of obtaining clearance to transit restricted airspace, offering guidance on flight planning. However, in cases of declared emergencies, efforts will be made to secure approval for transit, regardless of conditional status.

To obtain clearance for restricted areas, a similar procedure to accessing civil class C airspace clearance is followed, including contacting the appropriate frequency as per ERSA. If in doubt regarding the status of restricted airspace, assuming RA3 and avoiding the area is recommended.

If uncertain about the status of any airspace along your planned route, it's advisable to seek clarification. Additionally, conducting a thorough pre-flight briefing, including retrieving all relevant NOTAMs, ensures comprehensive flight preparation.

RPA Hazards

RPA may encounter various hazards, as outlined in the Global Air Traffic Management Operational Concept (Doc 9854), which emphasizes the importance of mitigating collision risks to an acceptable level. These hazards encompass other aircraft, terrain, weather phenomena, wake turbulence, incompatible airspace activities, and, when grounded, surface vehicles and other obstacles in apron and manoeuvring areas. According to Doc 9854, a hazard is defined as an object or condition with the potential to cause an accident or incident.

It's crucial to acknowledge that while the risk severity of a hazard may be minor for an RPA, it may differ significantly for manned aircraft facing the same hazard in the same airspace, and vice versa. Therefore, separate risk analyses may be necessary for manned and unmanned aircraft encountering the same hazard. Mitigation strategies tailored to RPAS are essential for their full integration into non-segregated airspace and aerodromes. While air traffic management assists in mitigating certain hazards for RPAS, such as incompatible airspace activity, additional measures, like DAA capabilities or operational procedures, are required to address hazards such as conflicting traffic, terrain, adverse weather conditions, ground operations, and other airborne risks like wake turbulence, wind shear, birds, or volcanic ash.

RPAS must adhere to airspace regulations, procedures, and safety standards established by the State and/or ANSP. Depending on the specific operating environment and flight conditions, one or more DAA capabilities may be necessary to mitigate hazards effectively. For instance, if an RPA operates in segregated airspace or only during fair weather conditions, certain DAA capabilities may not be required. However, if RPAS are susceptible to encountering these hazards, appropriate systems and procedures must be in place to provide adequate DAA capabilities for each specific hazard.

Furthermore, RPAS can detect hazards, including conflicting traffic, using both optical and non-optical technologies. Optical techniques, such as video, LIDAR, and thermal imaging, rely on visible and near-visible electromagnetic radiation, whereas non-optical techniques, like primary radar, SSR, ADS-B, and multilateration, primarily use radio-frequency electromagnetic radiation and are less dependent on meteorological conditions.

Vectors and the wind triangle

Dead reckoning entails navigating based solely on calculations derived from time, airspeed, distance, and direction. Except for oceanic flights, dead reckoning is typically used in conjunction with pilotage for cross-country flying. The heading and ground speed, initially computed before the flight, are continuously monitored and adjusted based on pilotage observations at checkpoints.

The Impact of Wind: Wind's influence on our journey is a critical aspect of navigation. Wind, a moving mass of air over the Earth's surface, affects aircraft movement similarly to how it affects other objects in our daily lives, such as trees, dust, balloons, and clouds. Since much of aviation navigation is adapted from maritime navigation, understanding wind's impact on air travel can be illustrated by comparing it to sea travel.

Imagine a boat departing from point A and heading towards point B. If the water current flows from left to right, the boat will drift to the right, potentially leading it to reach point C instead of point B.

In aviation, wind plays a similar role, causing aircraft to deviate from their intended path. When the wind blows from the side (crosswind), it affects the aircraft's track, causing it to drift. Even if the aircraft is pointed directly towards its destination (heading), it may still travel off course (track) due to the wind.

Wind can also be head-on (headwind) or from behind (tailwind). For instance, if an aircraft is flying north with a True Airspeed of 120 Knots and encounters a headwind of 20 knots, its Ground Speed will decrease to 100 knots. Conversely, on the return leg southbound, with the same wind speed and direction, the aircraft will experience a tailwind, resulting in an increased Ground Speed of 140 knots.

Understanding Drift: Drift refers to the deviation between an aircraft's heading and the track it follows, caused by wind. If the wind pushes the aircraft's track to the right of its heading, there is right drift, and vice versa. An easy way to determine the drift direction is by comparing the track to the heading: if the track is to the right of the heading, there is right drift, and if it's to the left, there is left drift.

Vectors and the wind triangle play a crucial role in understanding aircraft navigation and the effects of wind on flight paths. Let's delve into the detailed explanation:

Velocity Vectors: When an aircraft is in flight, its motion is influenced by both its own velocity and the velocity of the wind. Both of these velocities are vector quantities, meaning they have both magnitude (speed) and direction. By adding these velocities together, we can determine the resultant vector representing the aircraft's groundspeed and its track over the ground. This is commonly represented using scaled, arrowed lines to depict each vector quantity. The lengths of these lines represent the magnitude (speed) of each vector, and their placements indicate the application points and directions of motion. The resultant vector represents the aircraft's track over the ground and its groundspeed.

For example, if an aircraft departs from waypoint Alpha to waypoint Beta while maintaining a certain heading, the wind velocity at the cruise altitude will affect its position relative to the intended path. The resultant drift from the intended path is determined by considering both the aircraft's velocity and the wind velocity.

The Wind Triangle: To accurately navigate from one point to another while compensating for wind, we need to calculate both the expected wind velocity and the heading required to counteract its effects. In the wind triangle, we have three vectors: the wind vector, the air (or heading) vector, and the ground vector. However, we often only know the wind vector and part of either the air vector or the ground vector.

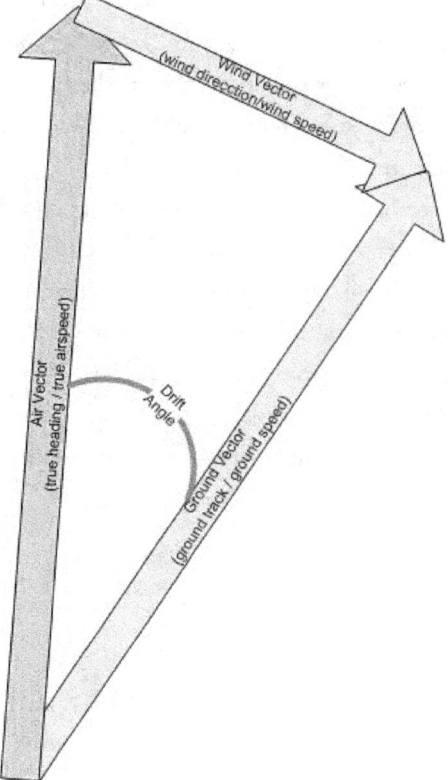

Figure 102: Vector diagram of the wind triangle, showing relationship among air vector, wind vector, and ground vector. Aarky~commonswiki, Public domain, via Wikimedia Commons.

To determine the heading and ground speed, we can plot scaled vectors on paper. This involves marking waypoints, using protractors to measure bearings, ruling lines to represent wind direction and magnitude, and using dividers or rulers to measure distances. By connecting these vectors, we can find the heading and ground speed required for the aircraft to reach its destination.

Additionally, we can estimate these values using the 1-in-60 rule or tables, which provide shortcuts for mental arithmetic. These methods involve approximating the wind correction angle and ground speed based on the wind's relative angle to the track and the aircraft's true airspeed.

Trigonometrical Relationships: Understanding trigonometric relationships such as sine and cosine helps in estimating crosswind and headwind/tailwind components of the wind velocity. By applying these relationships, we can approximate the effects of wind on the aircraft's motion without the need for complex calculations.

Navigation Calculators: Circular slide rules and E-6B calculators are tools used for flight planning and navigation calculations. These instruments provide solutions for the wind triangle problem, allowing pilots to determine headings, ground speeds, and wind correction angles. While traditional circular slide rules offer a tangible solution, modern electronic versions provide convenience and accuracy in a compact form.

Navigating through the wind involves understanding the interplay between wind velocity and aircraft motion. The Wind Triangle method allows pilots to calculate the necessary adjustments to heading and ground speed to compensate for wind effects. Here's a detailed explanation of how to perform these calculations:

1. **Understand the Wind Triangle:** The Wind Triangle is a graphical representation used to solve navigation problems involving wind. It consists of three vectors:

    - Wind Vector: Represents the velocity and direction of the wind.

    - Air (or Heading) Vector: Represents the aircraft's velocity and direction relative to the air mass.

    - Ground Vector: Represents the aircraft's velocity and direction relative to the ground.

2. **Gather Information:** Before plotting the Wind Triangle, you need to gather information about the wind velocity and the aircraft's true airspeed. This information is typically obtained from weather forecasts and aircraft performance charts.

3. **Plot Scaled Vectors:** To begin plotting the Wind Triangle, mark the waypoints of the flight path on a piece of paper. Use a protractor to measure the bearings between waypoints. Then, draw lines to represent the wind direction and magnitude relative to the waypoints.

4. **Wind Vector:** Start by plotting the wind vector using the given wind direction and speed. Use arrows to indicate the wind direction and scale the length of the

vector according to the wind speed.

5. **Air Vector:** If the true airspeed (TAS) is known, use dividers or rulers to measure the distance representing the TAS along the intended track from the starting point. Mark this point as the air vector's endpoint.

6. **Connect Vectors:** Connect the endpoints of the wind vector and the air vector with a straight line. This line represents the aircraft's groundspeed and direction relative to the ground.

7. **Determine Heading and Ground Speed:** The heading required to counteract the wind effect is the angle between the air vector and the ground vector. Measure this angle using a protractor, and this gives the heading needed to reach the destination. The length of the ground vector represents the groundspeed required to reach the destination.

8. **Alternative Methods:** If you prefer quicker estimations, you can use the 1-in-60 rule or tables. These methods involve approximating the wind correction angle (WCA) and groundspeed based on the wind's relative angle to the track and the aircraft's true airspeed. The 1-in-60 rule is especially useful for mental arithmetic, providing a rough estimate of WCA based on the wind's angle relative to the track.

Mastering the Wind Triangle method allows pilots to accurately navigate through varying wind conditions by calculating the necessary adjustments to heading and ground speed. Whether plotting vectors on paper or using shortcut methods like the 1-in-60 rule, understanding the Wind Triangle is essential for safe and efficient flight navigation.

Typically, pilots don't draw the wind triangle to scale on graph paper but utilize an analogue navigation computer for solving it. However, the Navigation Computer essentially generates a scaled drawing of the Triangle of Velocities. Considering a practical scale for speed representation is essential if not using the navigation computer, as it allows for drawing the triangle on a manageable piece of paper. The chosen scale can vary; for instance, one inch could represent one knot or one centimetre could equal one knot.

Let's suppose we're flying with a True Airspeed (TAS) of 100 knots and heading north (000 degrees). The observed wind is coming from 240 degrees with a speed of 30 knots. Utilizing the wind triangle, we can determine our track and ground speed [66].

Step 1: On a piece of paper, preferably graph paper, draw the Air Vector. It should have a direction of 000 degrees and a vector length equivalent to 100 knots (let's say, 100 mm).

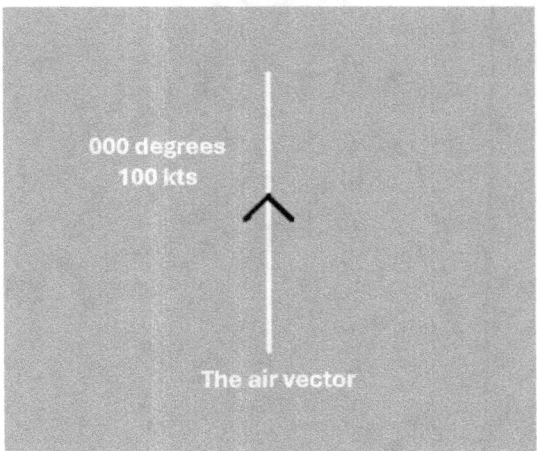

Figure 103: Air vector.

Step 2: Draw the wind vector. The wind direction is from 240 degrees. Using the same units as proportionate to 100 knots TAS (100 mm), draw the length of the wind vector (30 mm).

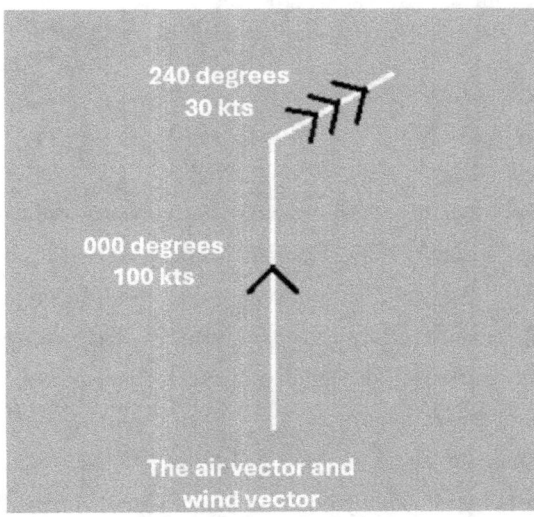

Figure 104: Air and wind vectors.

Step 3: Connect the air vector and the wind vector to obtain the ground vector, which will provide the resultant track and ground speed.

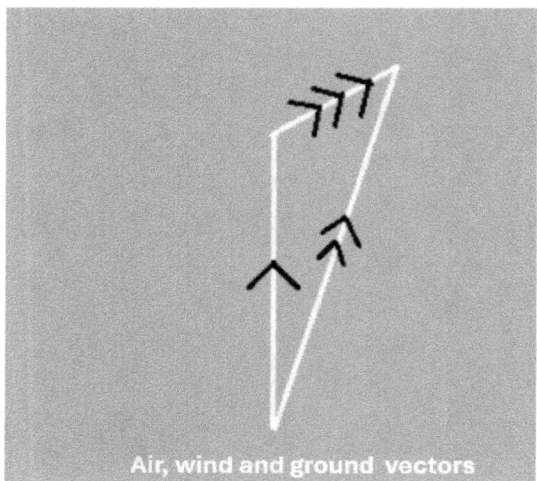

Figure 105: Air, wind and ground vectors.

When this is done on your graph paper, measuring the track with a protractor will yield approximately 012°, and measuring the length of the ground vector will give a length equivalent to approximately 118 knots (118 mm).

Drone Navigation

Mastering the various flight modes offered by your drone is a crucial aspect of navigation. Typically, drones feature multiple flight modes, including GPS, sport, and manual modes. GPS mode utilizes GPS to maintain position and altitude, making it ideal for novice pilots. Sport mode enhances agility and speed, while manual mode grants full control over the drone's movements. Understanding the distinctions between these modes and knowing when to apply each is essential.

For beginners, maintaining visual contact with the drone is invaluable. This involves ensuring the drone remains within your direct line of sight throughout the flight, facilitating better control and risk avoidance. Furthermore, being mindful of weather conditions is vital. Strong winds, rain, or snow can adversely affect the stability and performance of the drone, necessitating caution during flight.

Drones navigate through a combination of different technologies and methods, depending on their level of sophistication and the requirements of their mission.

1. **Visual Tracking**: For basic drones without automation, pilots rely on visual tracking to determine the drone's position and orientation. This can be done visually from the ground, with the pilot's relative position serving as a reference point. Drones equipped with onboard cameras relay visual data to the pilot's screen, aiding in navigation.

2. **GPS/GNSS Receivers**: Advanced drones utilize GPS (Global Positioning System) or GNSS (Global Navigation Satellite System) receivers for more intelligent navigation features. These features include:

    - **Position Hold**: Allowing the drone to maintain a fixed location at a set altitude.

    - **Return-to-Home Navigation**: The drone automatically returns to its take-off location at the press of a button.

    - **Autonomous Flight**: Flight paths are predetermined based on GPS/GNSS waypoints, which the drone follows using autopilot functions.

3. **Satellite Navigation (GNSS)**: GNSS encompasses multiple satellite constellations, including GPS, GLONASS, Galileo, and BeiDou. By receiving timing information from orbiting satellites, a GNSS receiver can calculate positions on the Earth's surface, enabling real-time drone navigation.

4. **Inertial Navigation**: In environments where satellite signals may be obstructed, such as valleys or urban areas with tall buildings, inertial navigation comes into play. Inertial Measurement Units (IMU), consisting of gyroscopes, accelerometers, and sometimes MEMS (Micro Electrochemical Sensors), provide data on linear acceleration and measurements of pitch, roll, and yaw. The onboard flight controller utilizes this data to provide navigational information and ensure smooth flight capabilities. However, inertial sensors accumulate errors over time. To address this, integrated satellite/inertial navigation systems use data fusion algorithms like the Kalman Filter to combine inertial measurements with satellite system position estimates for more accurate navigation over time.

Navigating a drone involves several steps and considerations, depending on factors such as the drone's capabilities, the mission requirements, and the environment in which it operates. Here's a general guide on how to navigate a drone effectively:

- **Pre-Flight Planning**:

  - **Mission Objectives**: Clearly define the purpose of the drone flight, including tasks such as aerial photography, surveillance, mapping, or inspection.

  - **Flight Area Assessment**: Evaluate the airspace and terrain where the drone will operate. Identify any potential hazards, obstacles, or restricted areas.

  - **Weather Check**: Review weather conditions, including wind speed and direction, temperature, precipitation, and visibility. Ensure that weather conditions are suitable for safe drone operations.

- **Preparation**:

  - **Check Drone Systems**: Inspect the drone, including the airframe, propellers, motors, batteries, and sensors, to ensure that all components are functioning properly.

  - **Battery Management**: Charge drone batteries fully and carry spare batteries if needed to extend flight time.

  - **Flight Equipment**: Prepare necessary equipment such as remote controller, smartphone or tablet for FPV (First Person View), and any additional accessories like landing pads or propeller guards.

- **Navigation Methods**:

  - **Manual Control**: For drones without autonomous navigation features, manually control the drone using the remote controller, adjusting throttle, pitch, roll, and yaw to manoeuvre the aircraft.

  - **Autonomous Navigation**: Utilize GPS/GNSS-based features such as position hold, return-to-home, or waypoint navigation for automated flight paths. Program the waypoints or flight parameters before take-off using the drone's software or app.

- **Flight Execution**:

    - **Take-off**: Launch the drone from a flat, clear area away from obstacles and people. Ascend to a safe altitude before proceeding with the mission.

    - **Navigation Monitoring**: Continuously monitor the drone's position, orientation, and flight parameters during the mission. Use visual observation and telemetry data from the remote controller or onboard sensors.

    - **Obstacle Avoidance**: Maintain situational awareness to avoid collisions with obstacles, buildings, or other aircraft. If equipped, utilize obstacle avoidance sensors or features to detect and navigate around obstacles.

    - **Real-Time Adjustments**: Make necessary adjustments to the drone's flight path, altitude, speed, or heading based on changing environmental conditions or mission requirements.

- **Post-Flight Procedures**:

    - **Landing**: Guide the drone safely back to the ground at the designated landing zone. Use manual or automated landing procedures, depending on the drone's capabilities.

    - **Data Retrieval**: Retrieve any data or footage captured during the flight, if applicable. Transfer data from onboard storage or memory cards to a computer or storage device for analysis or further processing.

    - **Drone Maintenance**: Perform post-flight checks and maintenance tasks, such as battery removal and storage, propeller inspection, and cleaning, to ensure the drone is ready for future flights.

Manual control of a drone involves piloting the aircraft using a remote controller (also known as a transmitter) without relying on autonomous navigation features. Here's a detailed explanation of how to manually control a drone:

1. **Understanding the Remote Controller**:

    - Familiarize yourself with the layout and functions of the remote controller. It typically consists of two control sticks, buttons, switches, and possibly a screen for telemetry data.

- The control sticks are usually spring-loaded and return to a centred position when released. They control the drone's movement along different axes.

2. **Throttle Control**:

- The throttle stick, usually located on the left side of the controller, controls the drone's altitude or vertical movement.
- Pushing the throttle stick upward increases the drone's throttle, causing it to ascend. Pulling the stick downward decreases throttle, causing the drone to descend.
- Gradually adjust the throttle to achieve smooth ascents and descents, avoiding sudden changes in altitude.

3. **Pitch and Roll Control**:

- The right control stick, often located to the right of the throttle stick, controls the drone's forward/backward (pitch) and sideways (roll) movement.
- Pushing the right stick forward tilts the drone forward, causing it to move forward. Pulling the stick backward tilts the drone backward, causing it to move backward.
- Similarly, pushing the stick to the left or right tilts the drone left or right, respectively, causing it to roll in that direction.

4. **Yaw Control**:

- Yaw control refers to the rotation of the drone around its vertical axis, allowing it to turn left or right.
- Typically controlled by rotating the left control stick (often referred to as the yaw stick) to the left or right.
- Rotating the stick counterclockwise (to the left) causes the drone to yaw left, while rotating it clockwise (to the right) causes the drone to yaw right.

5. **Coordinate Movements**:

    - Coordinate throttle, pitch, roll, and yaw inputs to achieve desired flight manoeuvres.

    - For example, to perform a smooth ascent while moving forward, simultaneously increase throttle and push the right stick forward to pitch the drone forward.

6. **Practice and Precision**:

    - Practice flying the drone in open areas with ample space to manoeuvre safely.

    - Start with basic movements such as hovering, ascending, descending, forward/backward flight, and turns.

    - Gradually increase the complexity of manoeuvres as you become more comfortable with the controls.

7. **Safety Considerations**:

    - Always maintain line of sight with the drone and avoid flying near people, buildings, or other obstacles.

    - Be mindful of weather conditions, especially wind speed and direction, which can affect the drone's stability and control.

Autonomous navigation allows drones to fly predetermined routes or perform specific tasks without continuous manual control from the operator. This is achieved through GPS/GNSS-based features and flight modes provided by the drone's software or app. Here's a detailed explanation of how to utilize autonomous navigation features:

1. **Understanding GPS/GNSS**:

    - Global Positioning System (GPS) or Global Navigation Satellite System (GNSS) provides accurate positioning information by receiving signals from satellites orbiting the Earth.

    - Drones equipped with GPS/GNSS receivers use this data to determine their precise location, altitude, and speed.

2. **Available Autonomous Features**:

    ○ **Position Hold**: Allows the drone to maintain a fixed position in space by continuously adjusting its flight controls based on GPS data.

    ○ **Return-to-Home (RTH)**: Automatically directs the drone to fly back to its take-off point or designated home location when triggered by the pilot or under certain conditions such as low battery or loss of signal.

    ○ **Waypoint Navigation**: Enables the drone to follow a pre-defined sequence of GPS coordinates (waypoints) to execute a specific flight path autonomously.

3. **Preparing for Autonomous Flight**:

    ○ Ensure the drone's GPS/GNSS system is activated and has acquired a sufficient number of satellite signals for accurate positioning.

    ○ Use the drone's software or app to access autonomous navigation features and configure flight parameters.

4. **Programming Waypoints**:

    ○ Select the desired waypoints on the map displayed in the drone's software or app.

    ○ Define the altitude, speed, and other parameters for each waypoint, specifying any necessary actions or manoeuvres.

    ○ Review the planned flight path to ensure it avoids obstacles, restricted areas, and other potential hazards.

5. **Activating Autonomous Mode**:

    ○ Once the flight plan is programmed and verified, activate the autonomous mode or flight mode on the drone's controller or app.

    ○ Depending on the drone model, this may involve selecting the specific autonomous feature (e.g., position hold, return-to-home, or waypoint navigation) from a menu or switching to an autonomous flight mode.

6. **Monitoring Flight Progress**:

    - Monitor the drone's flight status, position, and telemetry data displayed on the controller or app.

    - Stay alert for any unexpected changes or warnings, and be prepared to intervene manually if necessary.

7. **Post-Flight Analysis**:

    - After completing the autonomous flight mission, review the recorded flight data and analyse any issues or deviations from the planned route.

    - Make any necessary adjustments to improve future autonomous flights, such as refining waypoint locations or adjusting flight parameters.

Utilizing maps for drone navigation is a critical aspect of ensuring safe and efficient flight operations. The process involves several meticulous steps aimed at maximizing situational awareness and planning. Here's a detailed breakdown of how to effectively use maps for drone navigation:

Firstly, selecting a suitable mapping application lays the foundation for successful navigation. It's essential to opt for a reliable application or software that offers detailed maps, satellite imagery, and features tailored for drone navigation. Popular options include Google Maps, DroneDeploy, and DJI Fly, each providing unique functionalities to support drone operations.

Pre-flight planning is a crucial phase where the flight route is meticulously mapped out using the chosen application. Operators must identify key points of interest, strategically place waypoints, and assess potential obstacles or hazards along the intended route. Factors such as airspace restrictions, terrain elevation, weather conditions, and nearby structures must be carefully considered to ensure a safe and efficient flight.

Accessing map data is imperative for real-time navigation. Operators should open the selected mapping application on a compatible device, such as a smartphone or tablet, ensuring a stable internet connection or pre-downloading map data for offline use, especially in remote areas with limited connectivity.

Exploring different map layers available in the application provides operators with comprehensive insights into the flight environment and terrain features. From street maps to satellite imagery, topographic maps, and terrain elevation models, adjusting map layers as needed enhances situational awareness and facilitates effective route planning.

Setting waypoints along the intended flight path guides the drone along the desired route, ensuring sufficient coverage of the area of interest. Operators use the mapping application to strategically place waypoints, taking into account factors such as terrain features, landmarks, and mission objectives.

Reviewing airspace information provided by the mapping application is crucial to identify restricted zones, no-fly zones, or airspace regulations in the vicinity. Operators must ensure compliance with local aviation authorities' regulations and obtain any necessary permissions or authorizations for drone operations in controlled airspace.

Utilizing navigation tools available in the mapping application, such as distance measuring tools, compass, and GPS coordinates, enhances navigation accuracy and aids in estimating distances and maintaining orientation during flight.

During flight, operators use the mapping application for real-time monitoring of the drone's position, altitude, speed, and telemetry data. Staying vigilant for any deviations from the planned route, unexpected obstacles, or changes in weather conditions ensures safe and successful flight operations.

After completing the flight mission, operators conduct a post-flight analysis using recorded flight data, including flight logs and GPS tracks, within the mapping application. Analysing flight performance, assessing the accuracy of the planned route, and identifying areas for improvement in future flights contribute to continuous refinement of drone navigation techniques and procedures.

Global Navigation Satellite Systems (GNSS)

Global Navigation Satellite System (GNSS) plays a vital role in enabling drone pilots to navigate their unmanned aerial vehicles (UAVs) accurately and efficiently. Here's how drone pilots utilize GNSS for navigation:

1. Position Fixing: GNSS provides precise three-dimensional positioning information to drone pilots by receiving signals from satellites orbiting the Earth. This allows pilots to determine the exact latitude, longitude, and altitude of their

drone's location, enabling them to establish its position on a map.

2. Waypoint Navigation: Drone pilots can program specific GPS coordinates, known as waypoints, into their UAV's flight control system before take-off. By using GNSS, the drone can autonomously navigate along predefined flight paths, visiting each programmed waypoint in sequence. This feature is particularly useful for conducting aerial surveys, mapping missions, or surveillance operations.

3. Automated Flight Modes: Many modern drones are equipped with autonomous flight modes enabled by GNSS technology. These modes include features such as position hold, return-to-home, and follow-me. In position hold mode, the drone uses GNSS to maintain its position relative to a fixed point, allowing for stable hovering even in windy conditions. Return-to-home mode automatically guides the drone back to its take-off point if it loses connection with the remote controller or encounters low battery levels.

4. Obstacle Avoidance: Some advanced drones utilize GNSS data in conjunction with onboard sensors to detect and avoid obstacles during flight. By correlating GNSS position data with terrain maps or obstacle databases, these drones can adjust their flight paths to avoid collisions with buildings, trees, or other objects in their vicinity.

5. Real-Time Tracking and Monitoring: GNSS enables drone pilots to monitor their UAV's position and trajectory in real-time using ground control station software or mobile apps. Pilots can visualize the drone's flight path on a map, track its speed, altitude, and battery life, and make adjustments as necessary to ensure safe and efficient operation.

6. Precision Landing: GNSS can facilitate precision landing for drones equipped with this capability. By leveraging accurate positioning data provided by GNSS satellites, drones can execute controlled descents and land precisely at predefined landing zones or docking stations, even in challenging environments.

GNSS, encompassing systems like GPS, GLONASS, Beidou, and Galileo, is a global term for satellite navigation systems. Navigation typically involves three main steps: establishing the desired track or flight plan, determining the current position relative to the flight plan, and executing corrective actions if there are any deviations.

Various types of navigation systems exist:

- Pilotage relies on visual ground references.

- Astronavigation involves angular measurements between celestial bodies and the visible horizon.

- Dead reckoning utilizes visual checkpoints along with time, speed, and heading measures to estimate distance travelled.

- Inertial navigation uses on-board computers to process speed, attitude, and information from motion sensors like accelerometers, gyroscopes, and magnetometers to determine the current location from a known starting point.

- Radio navigation applies radio frequencies to determine current position, utilizing aids like GNSS, VOR, DME, and ADF.

GNSS navigation involves determining timing, position, and velocity using multiple GNSS subsystems. It calculates position on Earth's surface by measuring pseudo-distances from at least three known position satellites, with a fourth satellite enabling altitude calculation. Satellite navigation receivers mitigate errors by combining signals from multiple satellites and employing strategies like Kalman filtering to merge noisy data and estimate position, time (UTC), and speed.

GNSS system elements include:

- A constellation of satellites and ground auxiliary systems for maintenance.

- The platform's GNSS receiver.

- Augmentation Systems:

    ◦ ABAS (Air-Based Augmentation Systems), which use on-board devices and special algorithms to check integrity by processing GNSS signals. RAIM is a widely used system within ABAS, employing redundant GNSS signals for integrity and fault detection.

    ◦ SBAS (Satellite-Based Augmentation System), which utilizes accurately located reference stations to detect errors, transferring them to a computing centre and broadcasting corrections via geostationary satellites. Systems like EGNOS (Europe) and WAAS (USA) compensate for GNSS limitations in accuracy, integrity, continuity, and availability.

- GBAS (Ground-Based Augmentation System), which broadcasts signals from ground stations using VHF and UHF bands, primarily used in airports for traffic control and final approach (LAAS). DGPS and RTK are considered types of GBAS.

Operating without GPS

Drones can operate without GPS through a combination of advanced sensors, offering a range of benefits across various industries.

To navigate without GPS, drones utilize high-tech sensors onboard. Optical sensors serve as the drone's eyes, stabilizing it during flight. These sensors provide data on altitude, attitude, and location, enabling the drone to hover and manoeuvre accurately, even in the absence of GPS signals.

Additionally, LiDAR sensors may be employed to establish real-time spatial location using SLAM technology, enabling stable flight and the creation of 3D maps during operation. Combining visual and LiDAR sensors, drones like Flyability's Elios 3 can generate detailed 2D or 3D maps while flying, particularly beneficial for inspections in confined spaces.

LiDAR, short for Light Detection and Ranging, functions by emitting laser pulses toward an object, creating a 3D image upon their reflection. This technology, similar to a fish finder in concept, is capable of penetrating foliage and debris, making it ideal for search and rescue missions and various other applications.

While drones without GPS were initially challenging to operate, advancements in sensor technology have made them indispensable in certain scenarios. In environments where GPS signals are unreliable or unavailable, GPS-denied drones excel, offering precise navigation and data collection capabilities.

Industries such as oil & gas, power generation, and mining heavily rely on GPS-denied drones for inspections in challenging environments. Notably, these drones are crucial for indoor inspections of large assets like boilers and storage tanks, where GPS signals cannot penetrate.

In scenarios like bridge inspections, wind turbine maintenance, and maritime inspections, where metal structures or dense materials obstruct GPS signals, GPS-denied drones ensure stable and accurate flight operations.

Moreover, GPS-denied drones are invaluable in search and rescue missions, where GPS signal loss could be life-threatening. By eliminating the reliance on GPS, these drones provide uninterrupted service, even in densely wooded areas or disaster sites with obstructed GPS signals.

The benefits of using GPS-denied drones are manifold. They can operate in any environment, offering detailed inspections through advanced sensor technology. Furthermore, they enhance safety by removing humans from hazardous environments and reducing downtime for critical infrastructure.

As sensor technology continues to evolve, GPS-denied drones will find even broader applications across industries, offering unparalleled precision and efficiency in various operational scenarios.

Managing Remote Pilot Aircraft Systems Energy Source Requirements

Drones primarily rely on batteries as their power source, with lithium polymer (LiPo) batteries being the most common due to their high energy density and lightweight properties. These batteries provide the necessary electrical energy to power the drone's motors, flight controller, cameras, and other onboard electronics.

Apart from batteries, some larger drones may incorporate alternative power sources or hybrid systems for extended flight times or specific applications:

1. Fuel-powered engines: Some drones, particularly those designed for long-endurance flights or heavy payloads, may use internal combustion engines powered by gasoline or other fuels. These engines offer longer flight times compared to batteries but are generally heavier and more complex.

2. Solar panels: Solar-powered drones utilize photovoltaic cells mounted on the aircraft's wings or fuselage to convert sunlight into electrical energy. While solar panels can help extend flight times, they are typically used in conjunction with batteries to provide continuous power during both daytime and nighttime flights.

3. Tethered power systems: Tethered drones are connected to a ground-based power source via a cable, allowing them to remain airborne indefinitely. These systems are commonly used for surveillance, monitoring, and telecommunica-

tions applications where continuous aerial coverage is required.

4. Hydrogen fuel cells: Some experimental drones may incorporate hydrogen fuel cell technology as an alternative to batteries. Fuel cells generate electricity by combining hydrogen and oxygen, producing water vapor as a byproduct. While still in the early stages of development, hydrogen fuel cells offer the potential for longer flight times and reduced environmental impact compared to traditional batteries.

Overall, while batteries remain the primary power source for most drones, ongoing advancements in alternative power technologies may offer new possibilities for future drone applications.

Battery operated drones typically use lithium polymer (LiPo) batteries due to their high energy density and lightweight properties, which are crucial for flight. LiPo batteries provide the necessary power to drive the drone's motors, electronics, and other components. These batteries come in various shapes, sizes, and configurations to suit different drone models and requirements.

The capacity of drone batteries is measured in milliampere-hours (mAh), indicating how much charge the battery can hold. Higher capacity batteries generally provide longer flight times, but they may also be larger and heavier, affecting the drone's overall weight and flight performance.

Additionally, some drones may use specialized batteries with features such as smart battery management systems (BMS) or intelligent flight battery technology. These features help optimize battery performance, monitor cell voltage and temperature, and provide safety mechanisms to prevent overcharging, over-discharging, and short circuits.

Overall, LiPo batteries remain the preferred choice for drones, offering a balance between energy density, weight, and performance to meet the demands of aerial operations.

Lithium Polymer Batteries

LiPo batteries, short for Lithium Polymer, have revolutionized the electric drone world, particularly for planes, helicopters, and multi-rotor aircraft, making electric flight a highly viable alternative to fuel-powered models.

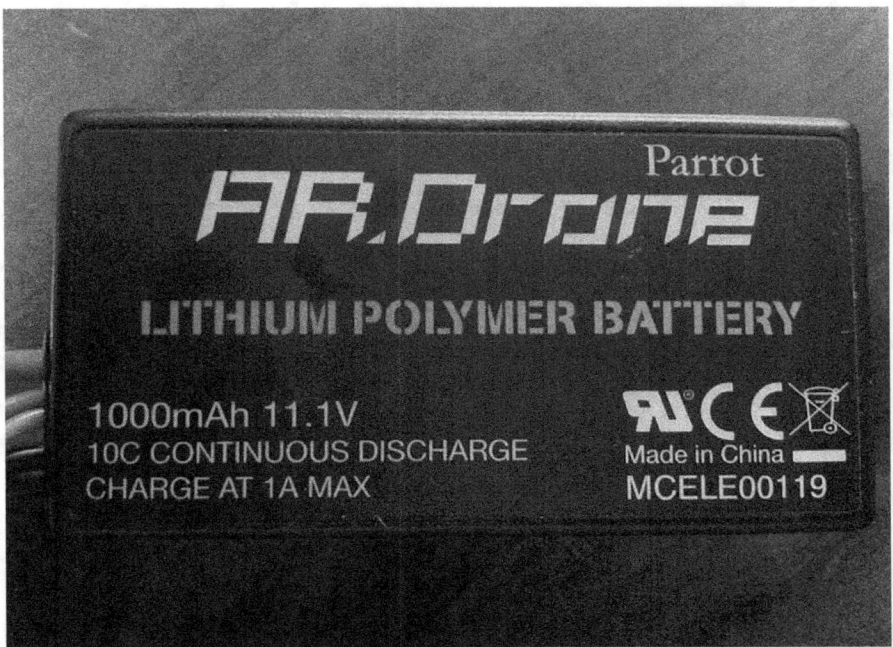

Figure 106: Standard LiPo battery for AR Drone. Rhorton4549, CC BY-SA 3.0, via Wikimedia Commons.

The advantages of LiPo batteries over traditional rechargeable battery types like NiCad or NiMH are significant and contribute to their popularity in drone aviation:

1. Lightweight and versatile: LiPo batteries are lightweight and can be manufactured in various shapes and sizes, offering flexibility in design and installation.

2. High energy density: These batteries boast large capacities, meaning they can store a substantial amount of energy in a compact package.

3. High discharge rates: LiPo batteries can deliver power rapidly, making them ideal for powering demanding electric motors commonly used in drone aircraft.

In essence, LiPo batteries provide exceptional energy storage relative to their weight, support fast discharges, and are available in a wide range of configurations.

These benefits have propelled the popularity of electric flight, surpassing traditional fuel-powered models in terms of power-to-weight ratios. Electric cars and boats have been around for decades, but the advent of LiPo battery technology has facilitated the rise of electric planes, helicopters, and multi-rotor aircraft.

However, LiPo batteries also have some drawbacks to consider:

1. Cost: While prices are gradually decreasing, LiPo batteries are still more expensive than NiCad or NiMH batteries.

2. Limited lifespan: Despite improvements, LiPo batteries typically endure only 300-500 charge cycles, with proper care. Neglect or mishandling can significantly reduce their lifespan.

3. Safety concerns: Due to their high energy density and volatile electrolytes, LiPo batteries can pose safety risks, including swelling, bursting, or catching fire if mistreated.

4. Maintenance requirements: LiPo batteries demand specialized care to prolong their lifespan. Factors such as charging, discharging, storage conditions, and temperature management all influence battery longevity, emphasizing the importance of proper handling.

Understanding LiPo Batteries:

LiPo batteries power the electronics and motors of drones, offering high energy density compared to other battery types. Unlike conventional batteries, LiPo batteries utilize Lithium Polymer chemistry, enabling them to store a significant amount of energy relative to their weight.

While older battery technologies like NiCad or NiMH are heavier and less efficient, LiPo batteries are constructed from individual cells connected in series or parallel configurations to achieve desired voltage and capacity levels.

Key specifications to consider when selecting a LiPo battery include:

- Number of cells: Determines the battery's voltage, with each cell typically providing 3.6V. Increasing the number of cells in series boosts voltage, while parallel connections increase capacity.

- Voltage range: Nominal voltage per cell is 3.6V, with a safe operating range of 3.0V to 4.2V per cell to prevent instability or damage.

- Capacity: Measured in milliampere-hours (mAh), represents the battery's energy storage capacity and determines how long it can power devices.

- Discharge rate: Expressed as the battery's C rating, indicates the rate at which energy can be drawn from the battery without damage. Higher discharge rates support more demanding applications.

- Burst discharge rate: Specifies the additional discharge capability for short bursts, typically lasting 15-30 seconds.

LiPo batteries offer high energy density, compact size, and rapid energy delivery, making them ideal for powering drones. However, users must adhere to safety guidelines and proper maintenance practices to maximize battery performance and longevity.

Lithium Polymer (LiPo) batteries dominate the landscape. However, it's worth mentioning Lithium Ion (Li-Ion) batteries, as they are utilized in some high-end radios. While both Li-Ion and LiPo batteries share a similar chemical composition, relying on lithium ion exchange between the cathode and anode, there are key differences in their packaging and electrolyte composition.

Li-Ion Batteries: Li-Ion batteries employ a flammable solvent-based organic liquid as the electrolyte. Encased within a hard metal can, similar to traditional batteries, Li-Ion batteries keep the electrodes tightly wound against a separator sheet, limiting options in terms of shape and size.

LiPo Batteries: In contrast, true LiPo batteries utilize a dry electrolyte polymer separator sheet, resembling a thin plastic film, instead of a liquid electrolyte. This separator, laminated between the anode and cathode, facilitates lithium ion exchange, hence the name "lithium polymer." This design allows for a diverse range of cell shapes and sizes.

However, a drawback of true LiPo cell construction is the slow lithium ion exchange through the dry electrolyte polymer, which hampers discharge and charging rates. While heating the battery can expedite this process, it's not practical for most applications.

If this challenge could be addressed, the safety risks associated with lithium batteries would diminish significantly. With the growing emphasis on electric vehicles and energy storage, significant advancements in lightweight and safe LiPo technology are anticipated in the near future. The potential for flexible LiPo batteries, akin to fabric, opens up exciting possibilities.

LiPo Hybrids: Presently, all LiPo batteries are actually hybrids known as lithium-ion polymer batteries. Although they're colloquially referred to as LiPo batteries, they don't strictly adhere to the dry LiPo battery type. By introducing a gelled organic/solvent-based electrolyte to saturate the polymer separator, the lithium ion exchange rate is significantly improved. However, LiPo hybrids, like Li-Ion batteries, still carry the risk of bursting into flames if mishandled.

Initially, LiPo batteries were more costly to manufacture compared to Li-Ion batteries, but their prices have since dropped considerably due to their widespread adoption in electric-powered aircraft and portable communication/entertainment devices.

LiPo hybrids maintain the flat cell structure of their dry counterparts, offering flexibility in sizes and shapes. Pouch cells, utilized in most LiPo batteries, eliminate wasted air spaces found in round celled battery packs, resulting in a lightweight and efficient power source ideal for weight-conscious applications like drones.

LiPo Battery Ratings

LiPo (Lithium Polymer) battery ratings encompass several key specifications that define their performance and suitability for various applications. Understanding these ratings is essential for selecting the right battery for your needs:

1. Voltage (V): This represents the electrical potential difference between the positive and negative terminals of the battery. LiPo batteries have a nominal voltage of 3.7 volts per cell. The total voltage of a LiPo battery pack is determined by the number of cells connected in series. For example, a 3-cell LiPo battery pack has a nominal voltage of 11.1 volts (3 cells × 3.7 volts/cell).

2. Capacity (mAh or Ah): Capacity refers to the amount of electric charge a battery can store and is measured in milliampere-hours (mAh) or ampere-hours (Ah). It indicates how long the battery can provide power to a device before requiring recharging. Higher capacity batteries can power devices for longer durations. For instance, a 2200mAh battery can supply a current of 2200 milliamps for one hour.

3. Discharge Rate (C Rating): The discharge rate, often denoted as the C rating, indicates how quickly the battery can deliver its stored energy. It is expressed as a multiple of the battery's capacity. For example, a 25C battery with a capacity of 2200mAh can discharge at a rate of 25 times its capacity, or 55 amps (25 × 2.2A). Higher C ratings signify faster discharge rates and are suitable for high-performance applications that demand more power.

4. Charge Rate: This specifies how quickly the battery can be recharged. It is typically expressed as a multiple of the battery's capacity, similar to the discharge rate. Charging a battery at a rate higher than its specified charge rate can reduce its lifespan and pose safety risks.

5. Cell Configuration: LiPo batteries consist of individual cells connected in series or parallel configurations to achieve the desired voltage and capacity. The cell configuration affects the overall voltage, capacity, and discharge rate of the battery pack. Common configurations include 2S (2 cells in series), 3S (3 cells in series), and 3S2P (3 cells in series and 2 sets of parallel cells).

Understanding these ratings enables users to select LiPo batteries that meet the voltage, capacity, and performance requirements of their devices while ensuring safe and efficient operation.

Figure 107: LiPo Battery Ratings. Back Image: Lipo battery, CC BY-SA 3.0, via Wikimedia Commons.

VOLTAGE: In contrast to traditional NiCad or NiMH battery cells, which typically have a nominal voltage of 1.2 volts per cell, LiPo battery cells boast a nominal voltage of 3.7 volts per cell. This characteristic allows for fewer cells to be employed in constructing a battery pack. For instance, in smaller-scale RC aircraft like toy helicopters or hobby-grade micros such as the Blade mCX2 or Nano QX, a single 3.7-volt LiPo cell suffices to power the model.

Except for the smallest electric models, LiPo battery packs typically consist of two or more cells connected in series to provide higher voltages. For larger models, this cell count can escalate to six cells or even more for larger birds or applications requiring high voltage (HV). Below is a breakdown of LiPo battery pack voltages according to cell counts. The numbers in parentheses, such as 1-12S, denote how many cells are connected in series (S) within the battery pack:

- 3.7-volt battery = 1 cell × 3.7 volts (1S)
- 7.4-volt battery = 2 cells × 3.7 volts (2S)
- 11.1-volt battery = 3 cells × 3.7 volts (3S)
- 14.8-volt battery = 4 cells × 3.7 volts (4S)
- 18.5-volt battery = 5 cells × 3.7 volts (5S)
- 22.2-volt battery = 6 cells × 3.7 volts (6S)
- 29.6-volt battery = 8 cells × 3.7 volts (8S)
- 37.0-volt battery = 10 cells × 3.7 volts (10S)
- 44.4-volt battery = 12 cells × 3.7 volts (12S)

It's worth noting that packs or cells may be connected in parallel to increase capacity, indicated by a number followed by a "P". For example, 2S2P signifies two two-celled series packs connected in parallel to double the capacity. This configuration is commonly seen in high-capacity LiPo receiver packs.

Understanding these voltages is crucial, as each model, or more precisely, the motor/speed controller combination, specifies the required voltage for proper operation and RPM. Deviating from this requirement could necessitate changes in gearing or motor KV rating.

A brief note on motor ratings: Some newcomers to electric flight may find brushless electric motor ratings confusing, particularly the kv rating. Contrary to what one might think, kv does not represent kilo-volts. Instead, it denotes how many RPM the motor turns per volt. For instance, a 1000kv motor with a voltage range of 10-25 volts would rotate at approximately 10,000 RPM at 10 volts and up to around 25,000 RPM at 25 volts. While delving into motor ratings isn't necessary here, it's worth mentioning, as it's a common point of confusion among beginners.

CAPACITY: Capacity represents the amount of power or energy that the battery pack can store, measured in milliampere-hours (mAh). Essentially, it indicates how much current load or drain, measured in milliamps, the battery can sustain for one hour until it is fully depleted.

For instance, if an LiPo battery is rated at 1000mAh, it would discharge completely in one hour under a 1000 milliamp load. If the same battery were subjected to a 500 milliamp load, it would last for two hours before being depleted. However, with a higher load, such as the common 15-amp drain in a 3S-powered 450-sized helicopter during hovering, the battery would drain in only about 4 minutes.

In scenarios where high current draw is involved, opting for a larger capacity battery pack, like a 2000mAh pack, can significantly extend flight time. With a 15-amp draw, for example, doubling the battery capacity would extend flight time to approximately 8 minutes until depletion.

The key takeaway here is that increasing battery capacity enhances flight time. Unlike voltage, capacity can be adjusted to achieve longer or shorter flight durations. However, it's important to consider size and weight constraints, as higher capacity batteries tend to be larger and heavier. Increasing the capacity of an LiPo battery is akin to installing a larger fuel tank in a vehicle.

MAXIMUM CHARGE RATE: This denotes the manufacturer's specified highest safe charge current for the battery. It's important to note that charging the battery at its maximum rate can reduce its overall lifespan, as elaborated upon later on this page in the LiPo charging calculation section. Essentially, this figure represents a safe maximum, not an optimal choice for maximizing battery longevity.

DISCHARGE RATE: Recall the third figure I mentioned earlier when you're shopping for LiPo batteries? Yes, that's the discharge rate. This aspect is perhaps the most overrated and misunderstood of all battery ratings. The discharge rate essentially indicates how rapidly a battery can be safely discharged. Remember that ion exchange process we discussed earlier on this page? Well, the speed at which ions can move from anode to cathode in a battery determines the discharge rate. In the LiPo battery realm, this is referred to as the "C" rating.

If a battery has a discharge rating of 10C, it means you can safely discharge it at a rate ten times higher than its capacity. Similarly, a 15C pack allows for discharge at fifteen times the capacity, and a 20C pack permits discharge at twenty times the capacity, and so forth.

For instance, consider our 1000 mAh battery with a 20C discharge rating. This implies that you could draw a sustained load of up to 20,000 milliamps or 20 amps from the battery. To put it into perspective, this equates to approximately 333 mAh of draw per minute. Therefore, the 1000 mAh pack would be completely drained in about 3 minutes if exposed to the maximum rated 20C discharge rate continuously. Here's the calculation: 20,000 mA divided by 60 minutes equals 333 mAh, which is then divided into the 1000 mAh capacity of the pack, giving us 3.00 minutes.

Most LiPo battery packs display both the continuous C rating and a maximum burst C rating. The burst rating indicates the battery's discharge rate for brief bursts, typically lasting a few seconds at most. For example, you might see something like "Discharge rate = 25C Continuous/50C Bursts".

Generally, higher C ratings result in more expensive and slightly heavier batteries. While opting for an extremely high discharge-rated pack may not be necessary, selecting too low a discharge C rating can damage your battery and possibly your electronic speed control (ESC).

Choosing the appropriate C rating depends on your specific needs and budget. For beginners or those engaging in lighter flying activities, opting for lower C rated packs initially can be a cost-effective approach. Similarly, for multi/quad-rotors that draw less current, lower C rated packs are often sufficient. As a rough guideline, 25C to 30C discharge rated packs are suitable for most 250-450 size electric helicopters engaged in general or light sport flying. Larger models may require packs rated between 30C to 35C, while more aggressive flying styles may necessitate 40C and higher discharge rated packs.

As technology advances, LiPo packs are becoming more affordable. If you find a higher discharge rated pack at a comparable price to a lower rated one, opting for the former can offer benefits such as cooler operation and longer lifespan. However, it's important to avoid pushing a LiPo pack to its limits, as this can significantly reduce its overall lifespan. With proper care, a pack with a discharge rating at least double the maximum intended usage can typically withstand around 400 charge and discharge cycles with average degradation.

Regarding high voltage (HV) electric aircraft, which use LiPo packs over 8S, they often operate at reduced current levels. Consequently, lower discharge ratings may suffice for these applications. However, it's worth noting that enthusiasts operating HV models at their limits may still require high discharge rated packs. Nonetheless, the higher voltage offered by HV setups can provide advantages such as reduced current and heat generation.

Lastly, monitoring the temperature of your packs after use provides another effective means to assess if you're utilizing a sufficient C rating. Unfortunately, despite a pack being labelled as 30C, its real-world performance may not necessarily align with this specification. In practical terms, C ratings lack verifiability, rendering them somewhat arbitrary. Moreover, as packs age, their internal resistance tends to increase, resulting in lower C ratings and elevated temperatures during operation.

As a general guideline, if you find yourself unable to comfortably grip a LiPo pack tightly after usage, it's likely too warm.

Furthermore, leaving packs inside a vehicle on a hot, sunny day can substantially elevate their temperature, potentially exceeding 40C. Whether heat originates internally or externally, both scenarios have detrimental effects on LiPo performance and longevity. In hot climates, it may be prudent to store fully charged LiPo packs in a cooler if they will be kept in a closed vehicle for any duration.

Overcharging

Over discharging is undoubtedly the primary culprit for damaging LiPo batteries irreversibly and rapidly raising their temperature. Pushing a LiPo pack down to or below 3.0 volts per cell under load can result in significant heat generation and drastically reduce its lifespan.

To prevent such damage, adhering to the "80% rule" is highly recommended. This rule advises against discharging a LiPo pack beyond 80% of its capacity to ensure its safety. For instance, if you possess a 2000 mAh LiPo pack, limiting the draw to no more than 1600 mAh (80% of 2000 mAh) is prudent. However, it's essential to consider that as packs age, their capacity diminishes.

Utilizing computerized chargers proves invaluable in adhering to this rule, as they provide insights into the battery's capacity, enabling adjustments to flight times accordingly. Alternatively, measuring the open circuit voltage immediately after a flight can also indicate an 80% discharge, with a discharged LiPo cell typically showing around 3.74 to 3.75 volts.

Implementing LiPo battery monitors post-flight facilitates adherence to the 80% rule by assessing the state of charge accurately. These monitors offer a quick overview of individual cell voltages and the overall pack voltage, aiding in determining if the pack has been discharged within safe limits.

However, it's crucial to verify the accuracy of these monitors against calibrated digital volt meters or computerized chargers, as cheaper monitors may lack precision. Additionally, relying on timing flight durations offers a practical approach, particularly when considering the limitations of low voltage monitors or telemetry voltage warnings.

Nevertheless, aggressive or hard flying necessitates caution, as the 80% rule may be overly conservative. In such scenarios, limiting the discharge to 70% or even 60% may be more appropriate to maximize LiPo lifespan.

Internal resistance emerges as another critical parameter in assessing LiPo battery health. Typically ranging from 2 to 6 milliohms for higher capacity and discharge-rated cells when new, this resistance increases with age, leading to elevated temperatures and capacity loss. Good-quality computerized chargers support measuring internal resistance, allowing users to track battery condition accurately over time.

Charging LiPo Batteries

Charging LiPo batteries requires careful attention due to their distinct characteristics compared to conventional rechargeable battery types. Using a charger specifically designed for lithium chemistry batteries is crucial for both battery lifespan and safety.

One critical aspect to consider is the maximum charge voltage and current. A 3.7-volt LiPo battery cell is fully charged at 4.2 volts, and charging it beyond that can significantly shorten its lifespan. Studies indicate that charging to 4.1V can yield over 2000 cycles, while charging to 4.2V provides about 500 cycles. Charging beyond 4.2V drastically reduces cycle life. Some enthusiasts suggest a termination voltage of 4.15 volts per cell for optimal performance and cycle life. Additionally, new "high voltage" LiPo cells capable of handling up to 4.35 volts while maintaining a 500-cycle life are emerging.

Using a charger specified for LiPo batteries and selecting the correct voltage or cell count is vital. Failure to do so can lead to battery damage or even fire hazards. LiPo battery chargers typically employ the constant current/constant voltage (cc/cv) charging method, gradually reducing the charge current as the battery voltage approaches 100%.

When selecting the charging current, adhering to the "1C rule" is essential—never charge a LiPo pack at a rate greater than its capacity. While some experts advocate for charging at rates up to 2C or 3C on high-quality packs with low internal resistance, doing so can reduce battery life. Charging above 1C increases the risk of thermal runaway and puffing, particularly in high ambient temperatures.

Seven main factors contribute to shortening LiPo battery life, including heat, leaving the battery fully charged for extended periods, over-discharging, overcharging, inadequate balancing, improper storage voltage, and physical damage.

Balancing multi-cell LiPo battery packs is critical to ensure all cells maintain uniform voltage levels. Balancing prevents overcharging or discharging of individual cells, which can damage the battery or pose safety risks. While single-cell LiPo batteries do not require balancing, multi-cell packs must be balanced regularly. This can be achieved during charging through the balance plug using a balancing charger, with a standalone balancer connected during charging, or after charging with a standalone balancer. Alternatively, using a computerized charger with built-in balance circuitry is the safest and most efficient method, ensuring each cell is properly balanced and charged to extend battery lifespan.

Charging LiPo batteries on a concrete floor can be a safe practice when done with proper precautions. Here's a breakdown of the safety tips mentioned:

1. Charge on the Concrete Floor: Charging larger multi-celled LiPo batteries directly on the concrete floor in a workshop, away from combustible materials, is a common practice. Concrete is non-flammable and can help contain any potential fire.

2. Cool Down Before Charging: Allow at least 15 minutes for a LiPo battery to cool down after use before charging it. Charging a hot battery can cause overheating and damage.

3. Never Leave Unattended: It's crucial never to leave LiPo batteries charging unattended. While it may not always be practical to stay in the same room, never leave the house while batteries are charging.

4. Storage in Metal Containers: Storing LiPo batteries in metal tool chests or ammo boxes can help contain any potential fire. These containers offer superior protection compared to LiPo sacks or bags.

5. Smoke Detector and Fire Extinguisher: Installing a smoke detector above the charging area and having a fire extinguisher nearby adds an extra layer of safety. In case of a fire, these measures can help detect it early and suppress it.

These safety precautions aim to mitigate the risks associated with LiPo batteries, such as fire hazards. While LiPo batteries are generally safe if handled correctly, following safety guidelines and being prepared for emergencies is essential for responsible use.

Storage

How you store your LiPo batteries between uses significantly impacts their lifespan. As mentioned earlier, a LiPo cell that falls below 3 volts under load (approximately 3.6V open circuit voltage) is usually irreversibly damaged, resulting in reduced capacity or the inability to hold a charge due to cell oxidation. Storing batteries close to this critical voltage threshold poses the risk of irreversible damage.

Over time, batteries naturally self-discharge, although LiPo batteries do so at a slower rate compared to other rechargeable battery types, losing about 1% of their capacity per month. However, leaving them in a near-fully discharged state for extended periods can lead to irreversible damage as the cells oxidize.

It's essential to store LiPo batteries in a charged state, but not fully charged, as this can also degrade the cell matrix. Fully charged LiPo batteries should be used promptly, akin to F1 cars waiting on the grid. The rate at which LiPo packs age during storage depends on both storage temperature and state of charge.

For optimal battery life, it's recommended to store RC LiPo batteries in a cool room, which slows down the chemical reaction, at around 40-60% charged state, equivalent to approximately 3.85 volts per cell. Storing batteries within this range helps maintain stability. Storing batteries in the fridge, close to 0 degrees Celsius, can extend their storage time by slowing down the chemical reaction that oxidizes the cathode in the cells. This method is particularly useful for smaller packs used in micros.

To ensure longevity and safety, adhere to best practices for storing LiPo batteries:

1. Maintain a charge of 3.8V per cell (40-50% charge).

2. Store batteries in a fireproof location or use a LiPo Safe bag made from fire-resistant material.

3. Ensure batteries are stored at room temperature.

4. If storing fully charged LiPo batteries in the fridge, pack them in a zip-lock freezer bag and remove air to prevent condensation. Allow the battery pack to warm up to room temperature before use, especially for larger packs.

By following these guidelines, you can maximize the lifespan of your LiPo batteries and ensure safe and efficient use.

From a chemical perspective, the swelling of a LiPo battery can be attributed to three primary causes, along with an exacerbating factor that worsens the situation universally. While these issues also affect hard-shell lithium-ion batteries, the hard shell can endure significant pressure before expanding.

Water Contamination: Water, along with other substances containing oxygen that can be released by electrolysis or heat, acts as a contaminant in LiPo batteries, leading to lithium oxidation and subsequent cell swelling. The presence of water inside the battery leads to the production of free oxygen and hydrogen, contributing to instability. Over-discharge or over-charge conditions exacerbate this situation, resulting in the formation of lithium hydroxide.

Formula Degradation from Over-charge/Over-discharge: Overcharging or rapid charging of lithium batteries causes an accumulation of excess free lithium on the anode, leading to metallic lithium plating. This process results in the formation of lithium oxide on the anode, which consumes oxygen atoms and releases free oxygen. Similarly, over-discharging leads to the formation of lithium oxide on the cathode, albeit at a slower rate. This abuse causes corrosion on both poles of the battery, significantly impacting its performance and lifespan.

Poor Separator Construction: Some low-quality LiPo batteries suffer from poor separator formulation, resulting in a dry separator with high internal resistance. Over time, a higher percentage of the LiPo becomes lithium oxide, causing the internal resistance to increase further. Additionally, inconsistencies in anode or cathode chemistry within battery batches contribute to performance discrepancies and potential swelling.

Exacerbating Factor of Heat: Heat accelerates the degradation of LiPo batteries and exacerbates swelling. While operating LiPo batteries at higher temperatures enhances performance, excessive heat during charging or discharging leads to significant metallic lithium generation, a major cause of puffing and cell destruction. The permissible voltage per cell decreases with rising temperatures, and excessive heat can break chemical bonds, releasing lithium to bond with oxygen and create lithium oxide.

Battery Selection

To achieve optimal flight duration and performance, it's crucial to understand how to select the right LiPo battery for your drone. Like other components in a drone system, batteries are interconnected, and choosing the correct one depends on factors such as the drone's size and the type and quantity of motors utilized. This guide aims to outline the steps to ensure compatibility between your battery and drone system before making a purchase.

Determining the Battery Size Needed: To maximize flight times, it's advisable to use the largest battery in terms of capacity that fits within your drone's maximum take-off weight. Additionally, consider the physical dimensions of the battery to ensure it fits your drone's designated space.

Assessing Battery Discharge Rate and Capacity: One of the most critical yet often overlooked factors is checking the battery's discharge C rating to ensure it's optimal for your drone. Using a discharge rate that's too low can damage the battery and lead to underperformance, while a rating that's too high adds unnecessary weight, reducing flight time.

Calculating Maximum Continuous Current Output: To determine the total current draw of your drone system, use the formula: Max Continuous Amp Draw (A) = Battery Capacity (Ah) x Discharge Rate (C) For instance, for a 5100mAh 3-cell LiPo battery with a 10C rating, the maximum continuous amp draw would be (5.1Ah x 10) = 51A.

Finding the Optimal C Rating: By examining the specifications of your motors, particularly the thrust data tables, you can identify the maximum current draw. For example, if each motor draws 10A at maximum thrust, and you have four motors, the total current draw would be 4 x 10A = 40A. Accounting for other equipment, such as autopilots and FPV gear, add an additional margin, such as 1A, to the total current draw.

Determining Capacity Requirements: Choose a battery with a capacity and C rating that meet the required current draw while keeping the drone's weight at around 50-70% of the maximum motor thrust. Aim for the highest possible capacity battery within this weight limit.

Considering Battery Voltage (Cell Count): Battery voltage affects motor power output, with higher voltages allowing for more power. However, higher voltage batteries are heavier due to containing more cells. Consult motor thrust data tables to compare efficiency and power with different cell counts.

Selecting Battery Connectors: Choose a battery connector that suits your preference and stick with it for ease of use and compatibility across different drones. Common connectors include Deans/Tplug, XT60, and EC3.

Number of Batteries: The decision to use one or more batteries depends on factors such as safety, charging time, cost, and complexity. Multiple batteries offer redundancy and faster charging but may be more complex to mount and wire. Consider your specific drone setup and personal preference when deciding on the number of batteries to use.

Calculating Flight Time of LiPo Battery

Before determining flight time, it's essential to ascertain the quadcopter's average amperage consumption. Once we have this figure, we can proceed to calculate flight duration.

To calculate flight time, begin by dividing the battery's capacity in ampere-hours by the quadcopter's average amp draw. Then, multiply the result by 60 to obtain the flight time in minutes.

For instance, consider an 11.1-volt 30C 3000mAh LiPo battery used in a Scout. If the calculated average amp draw of the Scout is approximately 20 amps, the resulting flight time would be 9 minutes.

Here are six strategies to prolong your battery life:

1. Camera Consideration: Unless you're heavily invested in aerial photography or videography, consider removing the camera from your quadcopter. Cameras not only add weight to the drone but also consume its battery at a faster rate, making flight time shorter.

2. Upgrade Battery Capacity: Opt for a battery with a higher milliampere-hour (mAh) rating to achieve longer flight times. However, be mindful of weight, as heavier batteries may counteract the extended power benefits.

3. Experiment with Propeller Sizes: Propeller size can impact power consumption. Larger propellers may be suitable if you're attaching a camera, while smaller

ones could suffice otherwise. Experiment with different sizes to find the optimal balance for your flight time.

4. Fly in Favourable Conditions: Choose ideal weather conditions for flying to maximize battery life. Avoid windy or rainy conditions, as they can make flight more challenging and drain the battery faster. Opt for fair weather with light breezes for optimal performance.

5. Follow the 40-80 Rule: Instead of fully draining and recharging your lithium-ion battery, aim to keep it between 40% and 80% charge. Avoid overcharging or completely draining the battery, as this can degrade its overall lifespan. Additionally, charge the battery in a cool environment to maintain its capacity.

6. Charge Strategically: Charge your battery a few hours before flying rather than days in advance. Rechargeable batteries lose charge gradually when left off the charger, so timing your charges closer to flight time can help maximize battery performance.

While these tips can enhance flight duration, it's important to temper expectations. Significant increases in flight time may not be achievable, so it's wise to have spare batteries on hand.

CONDUCTING AERIAL SEARCH USING REMOTE PILOTED AIRCRAFT

Search and rescue drones, also known as unmanned aircraft, are essential tools utilized by emergency responders, including law enforcement, firefighters, and volunteer rescue teams. These drones are particularly valuable for conducting searches across expansive areas to locate missing individuals or victims in need of assistance in various environments.

Unmanned aerial vehicles (UAVs) play a crucial role in providing real-time visual information and data, especially in the aftermath of natural disasters such as earthquakes or hurricanes. They serve as aerial surveillance systems, aiding in the search for lost individuals, even in rugged terrains like mountains.

During emergencies where lives are at risk, timely information and live imagery are vital for decision-making by emergency personnel. UAVs offer situational awareness over vast areas rapidly, minimizing the time and manpower required to locate and rescue injured or lost individuals. This efficiency significantly reduces the costs and risks associated with search and rescue missions, thereby enhancing public safety.

Search and Rescue (SAR) operations involve locating and providing lifesaving assistance to individuals in distress and facing imminent danger. SAR efforts can complement other emergency services, particularly in challenging environments such as remote areas or at sea, where traditional emergency services may face limitations.

UAS deployed in SAR operations have versatile applications, including:
- Terrorism search and rescue

- Assisting emergency communication networks

- Monitoring various catastrophes such as nuclear accidents, fires, collisions, and accidents

- Surveillance of natural disasters like landslides, wildfires, floods, and storms

- Locating missing persons

- Conducting post-disaster relief operations

Figure 108: An FAA certified drone operator is tied in with rope and looks up at the edge of the canyon. Grand Canyon National Park, CC BY 2.0, via Wikimedia Commons.

Drones play a vital role in search and rescue (SAR) operations by providing valuable capabilities that enhance the effectiveness and efficiency of search efforts. Here's how drones are used in search and rescue:

1. Aerial Surveillance: Drones are equipped with cameras and sensors that provide real-time aerial imagery and video footage. This allows search teams to cover large areas quickly and efficiently, scanning difficult-to-access terrain such as

forests, mountains, or disaster-stricken areas.

2. Rapid Deployment: Drones can be deployed rapidly, allowing search teams to begin operations immediately after receiving a distress call or when an emergency occurs. This quick response time can be critical in situations where every minute counts, such as locating missing persons or assessing the extent of a natural disaster.

3. Remote Sensing: Drones can carry specialized sensors such as thermal imaging cameras or multispectral cameras, which can detect heat signatures, body heat, or other anomalies that may indicate the presence of survivors or individuals in distress, even in low-light conditions or dense foliage.

4. Search Pattern Optimization: Drones can be programmed to fly predetermined search patterns, covering designated areas systematically and thoroughly. This helps search teams to avoid duplication of efforts and ensures that no areas are overlooked during the search operation.

5. Access to Inaccessible Areas: Drones can access areas that are difficult or dangerous for human search teams to reach, such as steep cliffs, dense forests, or areas affected by natural disasters. This capability allows drones to search areas that would otherwise be inaccessible, increasing the chances of locating missing persons or survivors.

6. Situational Awareness: Drones provide search teams with real-time situational awareness, allowing them to assess the conditions on the ground, identify potential hazards, and coordinate rescue efforts more effectively. This information helps decision-makers prioritize resources and allocate them where they are needed most.

7. Communication Relay: Drones equipped with communication equipment can serve as a relay between search teams on the ground and command centres, providing a reliable communication link in remote or disaster-affected areas where traditional communication infrastructure may be disrupted.

Overall, drones are valuable tools in search and rescue operations, providing search teams with enhanced capabilities, improved situational awareness, and increased efficiency, ultimately helping to save lives in emergencies and disasters.

SAR Communications

The use of frequencies in search and rescue (SAR) operations is critical for effective communication and coordination during emergencies. Distress traffic encompasses all messages related to immediate assistance required by individuals, aircraft, or marine craft in distress. This includes SAR communications and on-scene communications.

Distress calls take absolute priority over all other transmissions. Upon receiving a distress call, all other transmissions on the frequency must immediately cease to prevent interference with the distress call [67]. Certain frequencies are designated as protected, meaning they are exclusively reserved for distress and safety communications. SAR personnel must be vigilant not to cause interference and should cooperate with authorities to report and halt any unauthorized transmissions.

SAR communications must facilitate several key functions:

1. Rapid transmission of distress messages: It is essential for distress messages to be quickly transmitted to alert rescue authorities and initiate response efforts.

2. Rapid communication of distress information: Once a distress message is received, it must be promptly communicated to relevant rescue authorities to ensure swift action.

3. Coordination of SAR units: Effective coordination among SAR units is necessary to optimize search and rescue efforts and ensure resources are deployed efficiently.

4. Liaison between controlling/coordinating authorities and SAR units: Clear communication channels are needed to facilitate collaboration between controlling or coordinating authorities and SAR units on the ground or in the field.

Priority calls, known as radiotelephony priority calls, are commonly used to raise alarms and indicate the severity of the situation. These priority calls are categorized into three progressive levels [67]:

1. Distress (MAYDAY): Indicates a situation where immediate assistance is required to prevent loss of life or serious injury.

2. Urgency (PAN PAN): Indicates a situation that is urgent but not immediately life-threatening, such as a mechanical failure or medical emergency requiring assistance.

3. Safety (SECURITE): Indicates a message related to safety, such as navigational hazards or weather warnings, to alert other vessels or aircraft in the vicinity.

Emergency Signalling Devices

In situations of distress at sea or in remote areas, individuals may resort to various methods to alert potential rescuers. These emergency signalling devices range from sophisticated emergency radio beacons to simple reflective mirrors.

Daylight Devices

Reflective mirrors serve as effective daylight signalling devices, allowing survivors to redirect sunlight towards search and rescue (SAR) units. Mirrors have been observed from distances of up to 45 miles and altitudes of 10,000 feet, although the average detection range is around 10 miles. Additionally, fluorescent material, such as retro-reflective tape, enhances visibility and has been detected from distances of up to five miles, with an average of 3.5 miles. Another daylight signalling tool is the fluorescent sea dye marker, which colors the water green or red, visible from distances of up to 10 miles, though it may not be visible when searching against sunlight glare. Orange smoke generating signals have been sighted at distances of up to 12 miles, with an average of eight miles, but their effectiveness diminishes in windy conditions. Pyrotechnic flares, while usable during daylight, have a detectable range of only about 10 percent compared to nighttime.

Night-time Devices

In nighttime scenarios, fires are highly effective signals, visible from distances of up to 50 miles, depending on fire size and surrounding light conditions. Flashing strobe lights serve as compact and efficient night signalling devices, detectable from distances of up to 20 miles, with an average range of 3.5 miles. However, incandescent lights found on some life jackets have a significantly smaller detectable range, typically around 0.5 mile. Flares, star shells, and rockets can be detected from distances of up to 35 miles, with an average of 25 miles. Furthermore, with the aid of Night Vision Goggles (NVG), even faint light sources such as mobile phone screens can be seen from considerable distances, while larger light sources like fires, torches, and strobe lights are visible from even farther away.

RADAR/IFF/SSR

Beyond using RADAR to detect distressed craft, Identification Friend or Foe (IFF) systems can be utilized to enhance RADAR detectability. IFF comprises an interrogator and a transponder, with the interrogator sending electronic challenges and the transponder responding with pulses. These responses, displayed slightly beyond the RADAR target, can be detected at greater ranges than the craft itself. Additionally, Secondary Surveillance RADAR (SSR) systems, used by Airservices Australia and civil aircraft, function similarly and are compatible with emergency protocols.

Radio and Distress Beacons

Standard radio communication and various emergency equipment, including handheld VHF transmitters, distress beacons (GMDSS approved), AIS-SARTs, and 9 GHz SAR Transponders, aid survivors in transmitting distress signals and messages. These devices are crucial for alerting and coordinating SAR efforts across different types of incidents, including maritime, aviation, and land-based emergencies.

Types of SAR Incidents

Search and rescue (SAR) operations encompass a wide array of incidents that necessitate swift evaluation and resolution. These incidents can be categorized based on the type of craft involved, the environment, and the specific challenges individuals are facing. Generally, a SAR incident is deemed imminent or actual when it becomes evident that individuals are in distress or when a call for assistance is made.

In the maritime domain, SAR incidents arise under various circumstances. These include instances where a surface vessel or craft explicitly requests aid, transmits a distress signal, or exhibits signs of distress such as sinking or being overdue. Additionally, SAR incidents may involve situations where the crew is abandoning ship or facing imminent peril due to impaired craft operation. Moreover, activation of distress beacons or the need for medical evacuation (MEDEVAC) also constitute maritime SAR incidents.

Aviation SAR incidents are similarly categorized based on specific triggers. These triggers encompass scenarios where aircraft fail to adhere to communication protocols, such as reporting schedules, or where flight notification procedures are incomplete. Imminent or actual aviation SAR incidents may involve aircraft that do not report arrival, fail to adhere to air traffic control instructions, or exhibit signs of distress like forced landings or crashes. Activation of distress beacons, including Emergency Locator Transmitters (ELT) or Personal Locator Beacons (PLB), further signify aviation SAR incidents.

On land, SAR incidents involve diverse scenarios requiring assistance. These may include situations where requests for aid are received, vehicles or individuals are reported overdue, or distress beacons are activated. Imminent or actual land SAR incidents also encompass instances where individuals or vehicles are in visible distress or where medical evacuation is warranted.

Overall, SAR incidents across maritime, aviation, and land domains demand prompt and coordinated responses to ensure the safety and well-being of those in distress. By categorizing incidents based on specific triggers and conditions, SAR teams can effectively prioritize and deploy resources to mitigate risks and facilitate timely rescues.

SAR Incident Information

The success or failure of any search and rescue (SAR) operation hinges greatly on the availability and quality of information. This information must fulfill three key criteria: it must be accurate, current, and relevant. Given the often time-sensitive nature of SAR operations, it is imperative to initiate the search as promptly as possible once the situation permits. However, search operations invariably encounter a challenge wherein the urgency imposed by the circumstances conflicts with the initial delay necessitated by the need to gather and assess as much pertinent information as feasible.

An in-depth understanding of the information gathering process is fundamental for the Search Commander and Search Management Coordinator (SMC). The information process comprises four distinct stages: collection, collation, evaluation, and dissemination. In the collection phase, information pertinent to the search is swiftly gathered from diverse sources, including unexpected ones. This information encompasses details about the missing person(s), vessel, or aircraft, as well as environmental factors such as sea conditions, terrain, and weather. Subsequently, in the collation phase, collected information is organized into relevant categories, facilitating its accessibility for command and control elements. The evaluation stage involves scrutinizing the amassed information to discern its accuracy, reliability, and timeliness, discarding any irrelevant or outdated data. Finally, in the dissemination phase, specific information is relayed to searchers in the field, relevant authorities, and concerned family members and media outlets, ensuring that it remains current, accurate, and pertinent to maintain confidence in the search efforts.

Information gathering within SAR operations entails three primary aspects: determining the type of information required, ensuring access to and availability of information, and evaluating the acquired information. Key information to be obtained from the distressed craft or individual reporting the emergency includes details such as their name, contact information, position of the emergency, nature of the emergency, time of occurrence, and details about the craft or individuals involved. Additionally, information about weather and sea conditions, navigation capabilities, survival equipment, and potential route deviations is crucial for effective search planning and execution. Other sources, including friends, relatives, associates, yacht clubs, and aero clubs, may also provide valuable supplementary information to aid in SAR operations.

Aviation and Maritime Search Planning

The wellbeing of survivors in search and rescue (SAR) operations hinges critically on swift location and support. Upon becoming aware of an incident, SAR authorities must promptly initiate procedures for a rapid search of the most probable area of distress. Typically, the initial SAR response involves employing simple techniques to swiftly cover the likely area of distress. This initial search area is typically delineated in basic shapes such as circles, squares, or rectangles, tailored to the nature of the distressed craft's operation. It encompasses all plausible alternative tracks of the craft and incorporates areas highlighted by intelligence data. This preliminary strategy precedes more intricate calculations that yield a more precise search area, forming the basis for a formally planned and executed action if the initial search yields no success. This first stage of search allows for swift allocation and briefing of the necessary resources.

The process of search planning encompasses several key steps. Firstly, evaluating the situation includes assessing the outcomes of any previous search efforts. Next, estimating the distress incident location and survivors' potential post-distress movements are crucial. These estimates are then used to determine the most probable location of survivors and the associated uncertainty. Subsequently, the optimal allocation of available search assets is determined to maximize the likelihood of locating the survivors. This involves defining search sub-areas and patterns for assignment to specific search assets. Finally, a comprehensive search plan is formulated, detailing the current situation, search objectives, responsibilities of search facilities, coordination instructions, and reporting requirements. These steps are iterated until either the survivors are found or further searching is deemed futile based on the situation evaluation.

Every SAR mission necessitates a search plan, ranging from concise plans for individual units to intricate plans involving numerous units. Regardless of complexity, the Search Management Coordinator (SMC) is responsible for developing the plan, recognizing that lives may be at stake. The search plan includes crucial elements such as a detailed description of the search target, the search area encompassing weather conditions and potential risks, the optimal search pattern, and appropriate track spacing. While additional detailed information may be provided by the SMC to the first search unit, these four factors constitute the minimum required for conducting a search. The SMC crafts the initial or optimal search plan with the assumption of sufficient and suitable search units being available, thereafter making every effort to secure the necessary resources.

Air Search Patterns

Air search patterns are systematic methods used by aircraft to search for objects or individuals over vast areas. These patterns are designed to cover designated search areas efficiently, maximizing the chances of locating the target while minimizing the time and resources expended. Several types of air search patterns exist, each suited to different scenarios and environmental conditions. Commonly employed air search patterns include:

Trackline Pattern: A trackline pattern search, also known simply as a trackline search, is a methodical aerial search pattern used to cover large areas of terrain or water systematically. In this search pattern, the aircraft flies along predetermined parallel tracks spaced apart by a specified distance, similar to the lines on a grid. The objective is to ensure comprehensive coverage of the search area while maintaining a structured and efficient search process.

Here's how a trackline pattern search typically works:
1. Planning: Before initiating the search, search planners analyze available information, such as the last known location of the target, prevailing weather conditions, and any other relevant intelligence. Based on this information, they determine the boundaries of the search area and establish the spacing and orientation

of the tracklines.

2. Trackline Setup: The search area is divided into parallel tracklines, with each trackline spaced apart at a predetermined interval. The spacing between tracklines depends on factors such as the search area's size, the aircraft's speed, and the desired overlap between adjacent search paths.

3. Execution: Once the tracklines are established, the aircraft flies along each trackline, systematically covering the search area. Typically, the aircraft follows a straight path along each trackline, making coordinated turns at the end of each leg to transition to the next trackline. Pilots may use navigation aids, such as GPS systems, to ensure precise navigation along the tracklines.

4. Observation: During the flight along each trackline, crew members onboard the aircraft continuously scan the terrain or water below for signs of the target. They maintain visual and/or electronic observation, looking for any objects or indicators that may indicate the presence of the target.

5. Adjustments: Search planners may adjust the trackline spacing or orientation based on real-time observations, changing environmental conditions, or new information received during the search. These adjustments help optimize the search effort and increase the likelihood of locating the target.

6. Completion: The aircraft continues flying along the tracklines until the entire search area is covered or until the target is located. Once the search is complete, search planners assess the effectiveness of the search effort and determine any follow-up actions required, such as refining the search area or initiating additional search patterns.

Trackline pattern searches are commonly used in various search and rescue operations, including locating missing persons, downed aircraft, or vessels in distress. By following a structured and methodical approach, trackline searches help search teams conduct thorough and efficient searches, maximizing the chances of locating and rescuing the target.

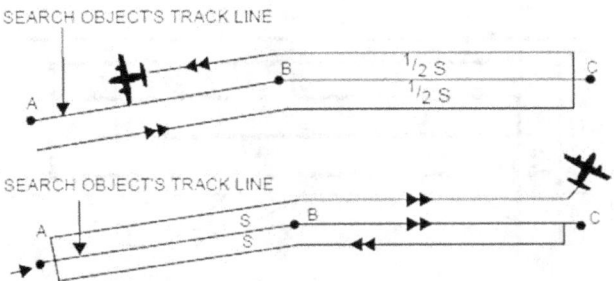

Figure 109: Trackline search pattern.

Expanding Square Pattern: In this pattern, the aircraft flies along a series of straight legs, each increasing in length, forming a square-shaped search area. After completing each leg, the aircraft makes a 90-degree turn to cover the next leg. This pattern is suitable for searching large areas with a high probability of the target being within the search area.

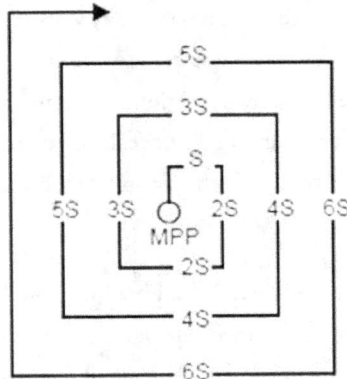

Figure 110: Square search pattern.

Parallel Track Search Pattern: Also known as the track line or track crawl pattern, this involves flying parallel tracks spaced apart by a predetermined distance. The aircraft flies along one track, turns around at the end, and flies back along the adjacent track. This pattern is effective for systematic coverage of linear search areas, such as coastlines or roads.

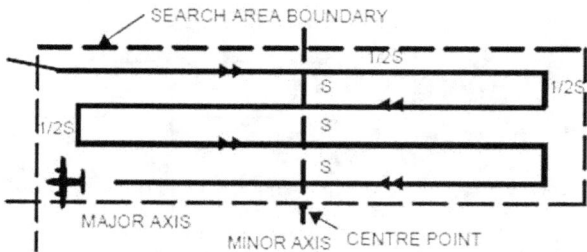

Figure 111: Parallel track search pattern.

A parallel track pattern search is a systematic method employed in aerial search and rescue operations to cover large areas of terrain or water efficiently. In this search pattern, aircraft fly along parallel tracks spaced apart by a certain distance, similar to the lines on a grid. The primary objective is to ensure comprehensive coverage of the search area while maintaining a structured and coordinated search effort.

Here's how a parallel track pattern search typically works:

1. Planning: Before initiating the search, search planners analyse available information, such as the last known location of the target, prevailing weather conditions, and any other relevant intelligence. Based on this information, they determine the boundaries of the search area and establish the spacing and orientation of the parallel tracks.

2. Track Setup: The search area is divided into parallel tracks, with each track spaced apart at a predetermined interval. The spacing between tracks depends on factors such as the size of the search area, the speed of the aircraft, and the desired overlap between adjacent search paths.

3. Execution: Once the parallel tracks are established, the aircraft flies along each track, systematically covering the search area. Pilots follow a predetermined flight path along each track, making coordinated turns at the end of each leg to transition to the next parallel track. Navigation aids, such as GPS systems, may be used to ensure precise navigation along the tracks.

4. Observation: During the flight along each track, crew members onboard the aircraft continuously scan the terrain or water below for signs of the target. They maintain visual and/or electronic observation, looking for any objects or

indicators that may indicate the presence of the target.

5. Adjustments: Search planners may adjust the track spacing or orientation based on real-time observations, changing environmental conditions, or new information received during the search. These adjustments help optimize the search effort and increase the likelihood of locating the target.

6. Completion: The aircraft continues flying along the parallel tracks until the entire search area is covered or until the target is located. Once the search is complete, search planners assess the effectiveness of the search effort and determine any follow-up actions required.

Parallel track pattern searches are commonly used in various search and rescue operations, including locating missing persons, downed aircraft, or vessels in distress. By following a structured and methodical approach, parallel track searches help search teams conduct thorough and efficient searches, maximizing the chances of locating and rescuing the target.

Sector Search Pattern: In a sector search, the search area is divided into sectors, typically pie-shaped wedges radiating outward from a central point. The aircraft flies along each sector boundary, making coordinated turns at the end of each leg to cover the entire area. This pattern is suitable for searching sectors of interest identified based on intelligence or likelihood of finding the target.

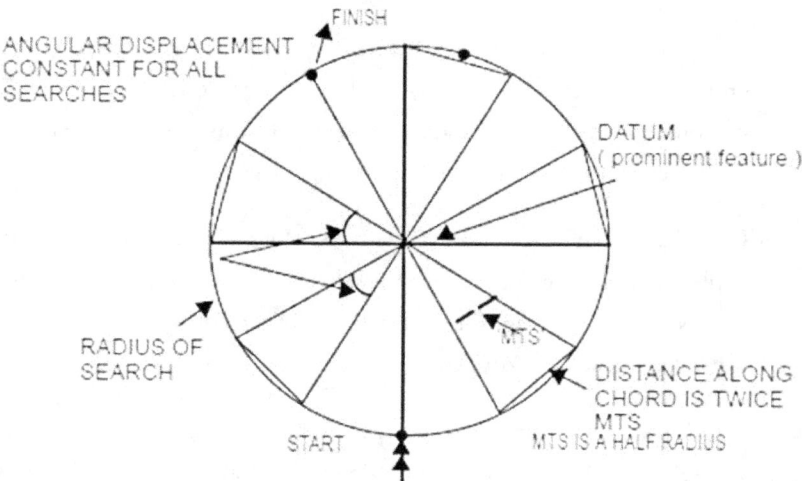

Figure 112: Sector search pattern.

A sector search pattern, also known as a sector sweep or sector scan, is a systematic method used in aerial search and rescue operations to cover a defined area of terrain or water. This method involves dividing the search area into pie-shaped sectors, with each sector assigned to an aircraft or search asset. The primary objective is to ensure comprehensive coverage of the search area while minimizing overlap and maximizing efficiency.

Here's how a sector search pattern typically works:

1. Planning: Search planners analyse available information, such as the last known location of the target, prevailing weather conditions, and any other relevant intelligence. Based on this information, they determine the boundaries of the search area and divide it into sectors.

2. Sector Assignment: Each sector is assigned to a specific aircraft or search asset responsible for searching that area. The number of sectors and the size of each sector depend on factors such as the size of the search area, the number of available search assets, and the desired search coverage.

3. Execution: Aircraft or search assets begin their search by flying along the perimeter of their assigned sector, following a predetermined flight path. The aircraft typically fly along the outer edge of the sector, gradually converging

toward the center while maintaining a constant radius from a designated point. This flight path creates a sweeping motion across the sector, covering the entire area systematically.

4. Observation: Crew members onboard the aircraft continuously scan the terrain or water below for signs of the target. They maintain visual and/or electronic observation, looking for any objects or indicators that may indicate the presence of the target. Observers may use binoculars, cameras, or other specialized equipment to enhance their search capabilities.

5. Overlap: In some cases, adjacent sectors may overlap slightly to ensure complete coverage and eliminate gaps between search areas. This overlap helps minimize the risk of missing the target due to uncertainties in the search area's boundaries or the target's location.

6. Communication: Search teams maintain communication with each other and with the coordination center to provide updates on their progress, share information, and coordinate search efforts. This communication ensures that search assets work together effectively and avoid duplication of effort.

7. Completion: Once all sectors are searched, search planners assess the effectiveness of the search effort and determine any follow-up actions required. If the target is not located, search planners may adjust the search strategy, expand the search area, or deploy additional search assets based on new information or developments.

Sector search patterns are commonly used in various search and rescue operations, including locating missing persons, downed aircraft, or vessels in distress. By dividing the search area into manageable sectors and assigning specific search assets to each sector, sector searches help search teams conduct thorough and efficient searches, increasing the likelihood of locating and rescuing the target.

Creeping Line Search Pattern: In this pattern, the aircraft flies along a straight line at a low altitude, typically following a terrain feature or reference point. The aircraft maintains a slow ground speed, allowing for thorough observation of the search area below. This pattern is often used in areas with complex terrain or dense vegetation.

Spiral Search Pattern: In a spiral search, the aircraft circles outward from a central point while gradually expanding the radius of the circle. This pattern provides comprehensive coverage of a circular search area, with the aircraft spiralling outward until the entire area is searched. Spiral searches are useful for locating targets with an uncertain location or for conducting wide-area reconnaissance.

Similarly, a contour search pattern, also known as a contour flight or contour search, is a search technique used in aerial search and rescue operations. In this method, aircraft fly along the contour lines of terrain features, such as mountainsides or coastlines, to systematically cover an area of interest. The goal of a contour search pattern is to ensure comprehensive coverage of the search area while maximizing the chances of spotting the target.

Here's how a contour search pattern typically works:

1. Terrain Analysis: Search planners analyse the topography and terrain features of the search area to identify prominent contour lines, such as ridges, valleys, or shorelines. These natural features serve as reference points for the contour search pattern.

2. Flight Planning: Based on the terrain analysis, flight planners develop a flight path that follows the contour lines of the terrain. The aircraft fly parallel to these contour lines, maintaining a consistent altitude and distance from the terrain while covering the designated search area.

3. Altitude Control: Pilots carefully control the altitude of the aircraft to ensure that it remains at a safe distance from the terrain features below. This typically involves flying at a constant altitude above the highest elevation within the search area to avoid obstacles and maintain a clear line of sight.

4. Speed and Heading: Aircraft maintain a steady speed and heading throughout the search, adjusting as necessary to follow the contours of the terrain. Pilots may use navigational instruments or visual references to ensure accurate navigation along the planned flight path.

5. Observation: Crew members onboard the aircraft continuously scan the terrain below for signs of the target. They maintain visual and/or electronic observation, looking for any objects or indicators that may indicate the presence of the target. Observers may use binoculars, cameras, or other specialized equipment

to enhance their search capabilities.

6. Communication: Search teams maintain communication with each other and with the coordination centre to provide updates on their progress, share information, and coordinate search efforts. This communication ensures that search assets work together effectively and avoid duplication of effort.

7. Completion: Once the designated search area is covered, search planners assess the effectiveness of the search effort and determine any follow-up actions required. If the target is not located, search planners may adjust the search strategy, expand the search area, or deploy additional search assets based on new information or developments.

Contour search patterns are particularly effective in mountainous or rugged terrain where traditional search patterns may be impractical or unsafe. By following the natural contours of the terrain, search aircraft can systematically cover large areas while minimizing the risk of missing the target. This method allows search teams to conduct thorough and efficient searches, increasing the likelihood of locating and rescuing the target.

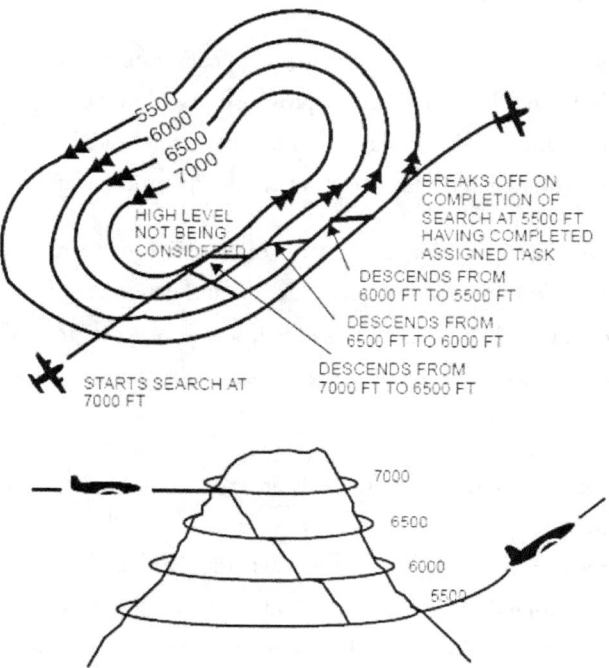

Figure 113: Contour search pattern.

Grid Search Pattern: In a grid search, the search area is divided into a series of equally sized grids or rectangles. The aircraft flies along each grid line, making coordinated turns at the end of each leg to cover the entire area. Grid searches are highly systematic and suitable for thoroughly searching large, open areas with uniform terrain.

Electronic Search Pattern: An electronic search pattern, also known as an electronic surveillance pattern or electronic reconnaissance pattern, is a method used in search and rescue (SAR) operations to detect and locate electronic signals emitted by distress beacons, emergency locator transmitters (ELTs), personal locator beacons (PLBs), and other electronic distress signalling devices.

Here's how an electronic search pattern typically works:

1. Signal Detection: Search teams use specialized electronic equipment, such as direction-finding (DF) antennas or radio receivers, to detect signals transmitted by distress beacons or other electronic distress signalling devices. These signals may include emergency locator transmitter (ELT) signals from downed aircraft, personal locator beacon (PLB) signals from individuals in distress, or other

distress signals on designated frequencies.

2. Frequency Monitoring: Search teams monitor specific frequencies allocated for distress and emergency communications, such as the international distress frequencies (121.5 MHz and 406 MHz) for aviation and maritime distress. They may also monitor additional frequencies used by specific types of distress beacons or devices.

3. Direction Finding: Using direction-finding equipment, search teams determine the direction from which the detected signals are emanating. This information helps narrow down the search area and provides guidance for subsequent search efforts.

4. Triangulation: By taking multiple bearings on the signal from different locations, search teams can triangulate the position of the distress beacon or transmitter more accurately. This triangulation process helps refine the search area and improves the chances of pinpointing the exact location of the distress signal.

5. Search Area Adjustment: Based on the detected signals and triangulated positions, search teams adjust their search area and focus their efforts on areas where the signals are strongest or most consistent. They may also consider factors such as terrain, weather conditions, and other relevant information to prioritize search areas.

6. Grid Search: In some cases, search teams may conduct a grid search or systematic sweep of the search area to ensure comprehensive coverage and identify any additional signals or distress indicators. This may involve flying predetermined search patterns or grids while continuously monitoring for distress signals.

7. Confirmation and Response: Once a distress signal is confirmed and its location determined, search teams coordinate with rescue authorities to initiate a response. This may involve deploying ground or air assets to the location of the distress signal for further investigation, rescue, or assistance.

Electronic search patterns rely on specialized equipment and techniques to detect and locate distress signals quickly and accurately. By leveraging electronic surveillance capabilities, search teams can enhance their effectiveness in locating and assisting individuals or aircraft in distress, thereby improving overall search and rescue outcomes.

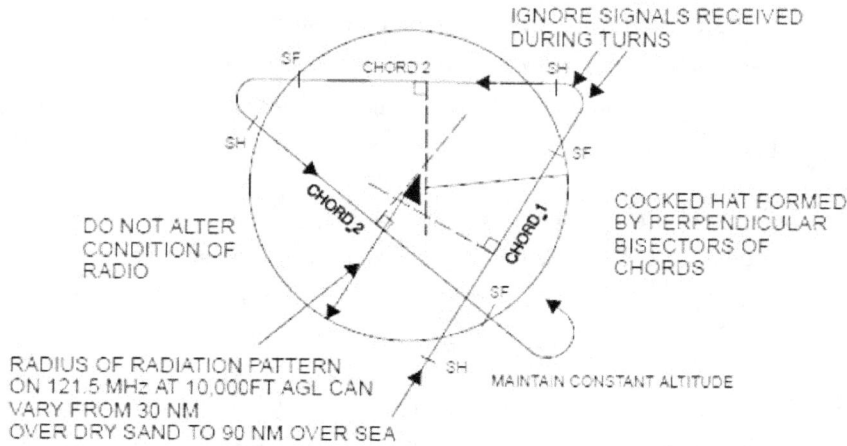

Figure 114: Electronic search pattern. automatically generated

Each air search pattern has its advantages and limitations, and the choice of pattern depends on factors such as the size and shape of the search area, environmental conditions, available resources, and intelligence regarding the target's probable location. By employing these patterns effectively, search and rescue teams can conduct systematic and thorough searches, increasing the likelihood of locating and rescuing the target efficiently.

SAR Crew Briefing

Briefing and de-briefing search crews thoroughly is a crucial aspect of search planning. These processes, although time-consuming, are essential for ensuring the effectiveness of search operations. Preparation for briefings must begin early and preferably well before departure. It is important to recognize that many personnel involved in search operations may lack training or experience in this role. Therefore, field SAR personnel should be given ample opportunity to familiarize themselves with all pertinent details of the distress situation. All instructions pertaining to the SAR operation must be conveyed clearly and precisely.

The individual assigned to conduct the briefing must have a comprehensive understanding of the overall plan and the tasks assigned to each search unit.

Comprehensive briefing of search units is essential for the success of any search operation. The Search and Rescue Mission Coordinator (SMC) should ensure that briefings are meticulously prepared, and if group briefings are conducted, the venue should be suitable for the purpose. While briefings for marine units will cover similar topics as those for air and land units, there may be limited opportunities for face-to-face interaction. Briefing Officers should be mindful of the challenges associated with indirect briefings and the increased potential for misunderstanding. Similar arrangements should be made for debriefing SAR units.

Various methods can be employed to describe search patterns and delineate the boundaries of search areas. When selecting a method, RCC staff must consider the SAR knowledge of the recipients and the mode of transmission of the information.

Geographical coordinates are commonly used to designate an area, with the corners of a search area defined by latitude and longitude. However, this method may be prone to error in measurement and transmission.

The Universal Grid Reference, overprinted on JOG series charts and many larger scale maps, provides another method for referencing locations. This grid consists of numbered blue lines spaced 1000 meters apart, vertically and horizontally. Instructions for its use are typically provided on the margins of each sheet.

Another grid system, based on a military 1000-yard grid, may be found on earlier editions of certain map series. This grid is overprinted in black and operates similarly to the Universal Grid Reference. It is important to specify the map used by name and edition number when using grid references. Additionally, some maps may display both grid systems.

Track Line: A track line search can be specified by indicating relevant points along the track along with the width of coverage. For example: "Fly a track extending 4 nautical miles on each side of a line connecting coordinates 16° 20' S 135° 15' E and 17° 50' S 137° 28' E."

Landmarks: Describing a search area using natural or man-made boundaries is particularly effective, especially in mountainous regions. Precision is essential in providing descriptions. Vague statements like "7 nautical miles SSW of..." should be avoided. Instead, directions should be given using positive bearing and distance. For instance, "bearing 202° (True) from Dixon Island at a distance of 7 nautical miles."

Commercial and Industrial Applications

In recent years, there has been a significant surge in the commercial utilization of drones, driven by an increasing number of industries recognizing the myriad benefits offered by unmanned aerial vehicles (UAVs). These applications traverse various sectors and encompass a multitude of functions, heralding transformative changes in traditional practices while enhancing efficiency across diverse domains.

One significant application lies in infrastructure inspection and maintenance, where commercial drones have gained traction due to their capability to access otherwise inaccessible locations in a cost-effective manner. By leveraging drones, industries can detect structural issues in bridges, buildings, and energy facilities, facilitating timely repairs and ensuring safety protocols are upheld.

In the realm of search and rescue operations, drones have become indispensable tools, facilitating swift and efficient location of missing persons. Equipped with advanced imaging technologies, drones cover vast areas quickly, detecting heat signatures or signs of human presence, thereby significantly enhancing the likelihood of successful rescues.

Moreover, the agricultural sector has embraced drones for precision farming, revolutionizing crop management practices. By collecting and analysing data on soil conditions, irrigation, and plant health, drones empower farmers to identify issues early, optimize resource usage, and improve yields.

Law enforcement agencies leverage drones to enhance public safety and operational efficiency. Drones provide real-time intelligence in critical situations, aid in accident investigations, and support routine patrols, thereby augmenting law enforcement efforts.

In addition, drones are utilized extensively in aerial photography and LiDAR surveys, offering unique perspectives and detailed data on landscapes and structures. They enable the capture of high-resolution imagery and surveys, facilitating various applications across industries.

Figure 115: Inspection of rock slope stability in marble quarries by using images from drone. Riccardo.salvini, CC BY 4.0, via Wikimedia Commons.

Furthermore, drones have revolutionized mapping and surveying practices, offering a faster, more accurate, and cost-effective alternative to traditional methods. They cover large areas quickly, capturing high-resolution imagery, and supporting professionals in construction, mining, and environmental management.

Drones play a vital role in environmental monitoring and conservation efforts, providing valuable data and insights for sustainable resource management. They track ecosystem health, wildlife populations, and the impact of human activities on the environment, aiding in conservation initiatives.

In emergency response and disaster management scenarios, drones facilitate rapid deployment, real-time data collection, and enhanced situational awareness. They aid in damage assessment, victim location, and supply delivery, contributing to effective disaster response and recovery efforts.

Furthermore, drones are employed for inspecting and maintaining telecommunications infrastructure and power lines, enabling efficient identification of issues and reducing service disruptions.

Lastly, while still in nascent stages, drone delivery holds promise for revolutionizing transportation, particularly in remote or inaccessible areas. Drones facilitate the swift and efficient transport of medical supplies, medications, and cargo, potentially saving lives and minimizing logistical challenges.

In essence, the commercial utilization of drones spans a wide spectrum of applications, offering transformative solutions across industries and sectors. As technological advancements continue, the potential for innovation and integration of drones into various workflows is expected to expand further, ushering in a new era of efficiency, safety, and sustainability.

Drones are increasingly being employed for infrastructure inspection and maintenance due to their ability to access inaccessible locations and conduct inspections cost-effectively. This adoption has gained traction across various industries, including civil engineering, construction, and energy. By leveraging drones, industries can efficiently detect structural issues in critical infrastructure such as bridges, buildings, and energy facilities, thereby facilitating timely repairs and ensuring safety standards are met.

One example of drone usage in infrastructure inspection is in the inspection of bridges. Traditional bridge inspections often involve manual methods or expensive equipment such as scaffolding or cherry pickers, which can be time-consuming and pose safety risks to workers. Drones equipped with high-resolution cameras and sensors can fly close to the structure, capturing detailed images and data. This allows inspectors to assess the condition of the bridge deck, supports, and other components without the need for physical access. Drones can detect signs of corrosion, cracks, or other defects, enabling engineers to identify maintenance needs promptly.

Figure 116: A view of Fernbridge by drone. Fernbridge crosses the Eel River on highway 211 in Humboldt County, California. California Department of Transportation, Public domain, via Wikimedia Commons.

Similarly, drones are utilized in the inspection of buildings, especially in urban areas where accessing certain parts of a structure can be challenging. Drones equipped with cameras and sensors can fly around buildings, capturing images and videos of the exterior and interior. This aerial perspective provides inspectors with valuable insights into the condition of the building's facade, roof, and other elements. For example, drones can detect facade damage, leaks, or structural weaknesses, allowing building owners to address maintenance issues proactively.

In the energy sector, drones are employed for the inspection of various facilities, including power plants, wind turbines, and oil rigs. These structures often span large areas and are located in remote or hazardous environments, making traditional inspection methods impractical or unsafe. Drones equipped with specialized sensors, such as thermal cameras or LiDAR, can identify issues such as equipment malfunctions, leaks, or structural damage. For instance, drones equipped with thermal cameras can detect hotspots on power lines or solar panels, indicating potential faults or inefficiencies. By conducting routine inspections using drones, energy companies can minimize downtime, reduce maintenance costs, and ensure operational safety.

Overall, the adoption of commercial drones for infrastructure inspection and maintenance offers numerous benefits, including improved efficiency, cost savings, and enhanced safety. By leveraging drone technology, industries can conduct comprehensive inspections of critical infrastructure, identify maintenance needs promptly, and implement proactive measures to ensure the integrity and reliability of vital assets.

Drones have become indispensable tools in agriculture, particularly in precision farming, where they have revolutionized crop management practices. By collecting and analysing data on various aspects of crop growth and field conditions, drones empower farmers to make informed decisions that optimize resource usage, enhance productivity, and minimize environmental impact.

One significant application of drones in agriculture is soil mapping and analysis. Drones equipped with sensors, such as multispectral or hyperspectral cameras, can capture high-resolution images of fields from above. These images are then processed using specialized software to generate detailed maps of soil properties, including moisture levels, pH levels, and nutrient content. For example, drones can identify areas of soil compaction, nutrient deficiencies, or excessive moisture, allowing farmers to implement targeted soil management strategies such as precision fertilization or drainage improvements.

Another key use of drones in agriculture is crop monitoring and health assessment. By regularly surveying crops from the air, drones can detect early signs of stress, disease, or pest infestation. For instance, multispectral cameras mounted on drones can capture spectral signatures indicative of plant health, allowing farmers to identify areas of the field that require attention. Drones can also monitor crop growth patterns, assess canopy coverage, and track vegetation indices such as NDVI (Normalized Difference Vegetation Index), which provides insights into plant health and Vigor.

In addition to soil and crop monitoring, drones are used for precision irrigation management. By analysing aerial imagery and sensor data, drones can identify areas of the field that require more or less water, allowing farmers to adjust irrigation schedules and optimize water usage. For example, drones can detect areas of drought stress or overwatering, enabling farmers to apply water precisely where it is needed most. This targeted approach to irrigation not only conserves water but also improves crop health and yields.

Furthermore, drones are employed for crop scouting and pest management. By surveying fields regularly, drones can identify signs of pest infestation or weed growth early, allowing farmers to take timely corrective action. For instance, drones equipped with thermal cameras can detect temperature differentials caused by pest activity, while drones with RGB cameras can capture detailed images of weed distribution. This early detection enables farmers to implement integrated pest management strategies, such as targeted pesticide application or mechanical weed control, minimizing crop damage and reducing reliance on chemical inputs.

The use of drones in agriculture and precision farming offers numerous benefits, including improved crop yields, reduced input costs, and more sustainable farming practices. By harnessing the power of drone technology, farmers can gain valuable insights into their fields, optimize resource management practices, and ultimately increase profitability while minimizing environmental impact.

The utilization of drones across various sectors of the economy is experiencing rapid growth, with a particularly significant surge observed in the agricultural industry. Projections suggest that the agricultural drone market, valued at $1.2 billion (USD) in 2019, is poised to expand to $4.8 billion by end 2024 [68]. Over the coming years, drone deployment in agriculture is expected to become increasingly prevalent, spanning activities ranging from scouting to security across farms of all sizes.

Drones play a pivotal role in the agricultural landscape, contributing to what is commonly referred to as 'precision agriculture.' These unmanned aerial vehicles gather crucial data that aids farmers in making informed agronomic decisions. This data, obtained through drone surveillance of fields, serves as a foundation for optimizing planting schedules and treatment strategies, ultimately aiming to maximize crop yields.

In many regions, drones have already cemented their status as indispensable tools in large-scale precision farming endeavours. By meticulously documenting field conditions, drones provide farmers with actionable insights to fine-tune their agricultural practices. Reports suggest that the implementation of precision farming systems has the potential to boost yields by up to 5%, a significant improvement in an industry known for its narrow profit margins [68].

Scouting/Monitoring Plant Health

The utilization of drone imagery for monitoring plant health has emerged as a highly successful application in agricultural practices. Drones equipped with specialized imaging equipment, such as the Normalized Difference Vegetation Index (NDVI), employ detailed color information to assess plant health. This enables farmers to conduct real-time monitoring of crop growth, facilitating prompt intervention to address any emerging issues and ensure the well-being of plants. Additionally, drones equipped with standard cameras offer a cost-effective alternative for crop health monitoring, surpassing the limitations of satellite imagery in terms of proximity and precision. By capturing close-range images, drones provide accurate data on crop conditions, allowing for timely interventions to rectify any anomalies, such as stand gaps or pest infestations.

Monitoring Field Conditions

In addition to plant health monitoring, drones play a crucial role in monitoring field conditions and soil health. Through precise field mapping, including elevation data, drones enable growers to identify irregularities within fields, aiding in the detection of drainage patterns and areas of varying moisture levels. This information proves invaluable in implementing efficient irrigation strategies and optimizing watering techniques. Furthermore, some agricultural drone services offer nitrogen level monitoring in soil, facilitating precise fertilizer application and contributing to long-term soil health improvement.

Planting and Seeding

A nascent yet promising application of drones in agriculture is the utilization of automated drone seeders for planting seeds, primarily observed in the forestry sector. Automated drone seeders offer the advantage of reaching inaccessible areas without endangering workers' safety. With the capability of planting seeds more efficiently, a team of operators overseeing multiple drones can achieve remarkable daily planting rates, significantly enhancing reforestation efforts.

Spray Application

Drone technology is widely employed for spray application treatments in regions like southeast Asia, where drones account for a substantial portion of agriculture spraying operations. Drone sprayers navigate challenging terrains, reaching areas inaccessible to traditional equipment and reducing the need for manual labour-intensive methods. These sprayers deliver precise spray applications, optimizing chemical usage and minimizing environmental impact. However, regulatory frameworks governing drone sprayer usage vary across countries, with ongoing considerations regarding safety and environmental implications.

Figure 117: Drone spray application. Diuliano.web, CC BY-SA 4.0, via Wikimedia Commons.

Security

Drone technology extends its utility to farm security, offering efficient monitoring of vast agricultural landscapes and hard-to-reach areas. Drones equipped with cameras provide real-time surveillance, enabling proactive security measures and swift response to potential threats. Moreover, drones aid in asset tracking and monitoring of livestock, enhancing farm management practices and safeguarding valuable resources.

Drone Pollination

Innovations in drone technology include the development of pollinating drones, offering a potential solution to address pollination challenges in agriculture. Researchers in various regions are exploring the feasibility of small drones capable of pollinating plants autonomously, potentially revolutionizing crop pollination methods and contributing to sustainable agricultural practices.

Drone AI

Advancements in drone technology encompass the integration of machine learning algorithms to enhance artificial intelligence capabilities. The development of AI-powered drones aims to improve crop monitoring accuracy, particularly in diverse planting patterns and lesser-known crops. By training AI systems to recognize various crops and planting patterns, drones can offer more effective monitoring solutions tailored to the needs of diverse agricultural landscapes.

Drone Irrigation

Research endeavours are exploring the utilization of drones equipped with microwave sensing technology for efficient irrigation management [68]. By capturing precise soil health data, including moisture levels, drones facilitate targeted irrigation strategies, conserving water resources and mitigating the impact of climate change-induced drought conditions.

Drones have further emerged as indispensable tools for law enforcement agencies, offering a myriad of applications to enhance public safety and operational efficiency. Through the deployment of drones, law enforcement agencies can access real-time intelligence, conduct efficient accident investigations, and bolster routine patrols, thereby augmenting their overall effectiveness in maintaining law and order.

Drones for Real-Time Intelligence: Law enforcement agencies utilize drones to gather real-time intelligence in critical situations, providing valuable situational awareness to officers on the ground. For example, during active shooter incidents or hostage situations, drones equipped with high-resolution cameras can provide aerial views of the scene, enabling tactical teams to assess the situation and formulate appropriate response strategies. By providing live video feeds and aerial perspectives, drones offer invaluable support in decision-making processes, enhancing the safety of both law enforcement personnel and civilians.

Drones for Accident Investigations: Drones play a pivotal role in accident investigations, offering aerial perspectives and detailed imagery of accident scenes. Law enforcement agencies deploy drones equipped with high-resolution cameras to capture images and footage of accident sites, facilitating comprehensive analysis and reconstruction of events. For instance, in traffic accidents or crime scenes, drones enable investigators to document evidence, map out the scene, and gather critical data, expediting the investigative process and ensuring accurate documentation for legal proceedings.

Drones for Routine Patrols: Routine patrols are essential for maintaining public safety and deterring criminal activities. Law enforcement agencies leverage drones for aerial surveillance during routine patrols, enabling officers to monitor large areas efficiently and identify potential security threats. Drones equipped with thermal imaging cameras and night vision capabilities enhance visibility in low-light conditions, allowing for effective surveillance during nighttime operations. Moreover, drones can access remote or hard-to-reach areas, complementing ground patrols and enhancing overall patrol coverage.

Figure 118: Queensland (Australia) Police Service drone, Remotely Piloted Aircraft Systems (RPAS). Queensland Police Service, CC BY 4.0, via Wikimedia Commons.

Example: In a metropolitan area prone to traffic accidents and congestion, the local police department integrates drones into their traffic management operations. When responding to major traffic incidents, such as accidents or road closures, the department deploys drones equipped with high-resolution cameras to assess the scene from above. The aerial footage captured by the drones provides real-time intelligence to traffic management personnel, allowing them to divert traffic, allocate resources effectively, and coordinate emergency response efforts. Additionally, drones aid in documenting accident scenes, capturing critical evidence for subsequent investigations and legal proceedings. By leveraging drones for traffic management and accident investigations, the police department enhances public safety, minimizes traffic disruptions, and improves operational efficiency.

The utilization of drones for aerial photography and LiDAR (Light Detection and Ranging) surveys has experienced significant growth, presenting innovative opportunities for capturing detailed data and unique perspectives on landscapes and structures. Drones, equipped with advanced imaging systems and LiDAR sensors, enable the acquisition of high-resolution imagery and precise elevation data, fostering a wide range of applications across industries.

Drones for Aerial Photography: Drones equipped with high-quality cameras are employed for aerial photography, enabling the capture of stunning imagery from unique vantage points. These drones are capable of capturing high-resolution photos and videos of landscapes, buildings, and infrastructure with exceptional detail and clarity. For example, in the real estate industry, drones are utilized to capture aerial photographs and videos of properties, providing prospective buyers with immersive views and detailed insights into the surrounding environment. Similarly, in the tourism sector, drones are employed to capture breathtaking aerial footage of scenic destinations, enhancing marketing campaigns and promotional materials.

Figure 119: LIDAR survey being performed with a Yellowscan LIDAR on the OnyxStar FOX-C8 HD. Cargyrak, CC BY-SA 4.0, via Wikimedia Commons.

Drones for LiDAR Surveys: LiDAR-equipped drones are utilized for conducting surveys to generate precise elevation models and three-dimensional maps of terrain and structures. LiDAR technology utilizes laser pulses to measure distances and create highly accurate digital elevation models (DEMs) and point clouds. These surveys are invaluable for various applications, including urban planning, environmental monitoring, and infrastructure development. For instance, in urban planning projects, LiDAR surveys conducted by drones provide detailed topographic data and facilitate the design and development of infrastructure projects, such as roads, bridges, and drainage systems. Additionally, in forestry management, LiDAR surveys enable the assessment of tree canopy heights and forest structure, aiding in resource management and conservation efforts.

Example: A construction company undertaking a large-scale infrastructure project integrates drones equipped with both high-resolution cameras and LiDAR sensors into their surveying and monitoring operations. Prior to the commencement of construction, the company conducts aerial surveys using drones to capture detailed imagery and LiDAR data of the project site. The drones capture high-resolution aerial photographs and videos, providing comprehensive visual documentation of the site conditions and surrounding terrain. Simultaneously, LiDAR-equipped drones collect precise elevation data, generating accurate digital elevation models and point clouds of the area. This combined dataset enables engineers and project managers to analyse the site's topography, identify potential obstacles or challenges, and optimize the project's design and planning phase. Throughout the construction process, drones are deployed for periodic aerial inspections and progress monitoring, ensuring adherence to project timelines and quality standards. By leveraging drones for aerial photography and LiDAR surveys, the construction company enhances project management efficiency, minimizes costs, and improves overall project outcomes.

Drones have transformed mapping and surveying processes by providing a more efficient, accurate, and economical alternative to conventional methods. These unmanned aerial vehicles offer several advantages, including rapid coverage of vast areas and the capture of high-resolution imagery. This technology has significantly benefited various industries, including construction, mining, and environmental management.

In construction, drones are used to create detailed maps of construction sites, monitor progress, and assess the topography of the terrain. By capturing aerial imagery, drones enable project managers to plan and coordinate construction activities more effectively, leading to improved project outcomes and cost savings.

Similarly, in the mining industry, drones are employed to survey mining sites, track changes in land formations, and measure stockpiles of materials. The ability of drones to collect accurate data quickly allows mining companies to optimize their operations, identify potential hazards, and comply with regulatory requirements.

Environmental management also benefits from drone technology, as drones are used to monitor ecosystems, track changes in land use, and assess the impact of human activities on natural habitats. Conservation organizations utilize drones to survey wildlife populations, monitor deforestation, and identify areas in need of protection. By providing detailed aerial data, drones assist in making informed decisions to preserve biodiversity and manage natural resources sustainably.

Overall, drones have revolutionized mapping and surveying practices across various industries, offering a versatile tool for gathering spatial data and informing decision-making processes. Their ability to cover large areas efficiently and capture detailed imagery makes them invaluable assets for professionals involved in construction, mining, environmental management, and beyond.

Drones have become indispensable tools in environmental monitoring and conservation efforts, playing a crucial role in providing valuable data and insights for sustainable resource management. These unmanned aerial vehicles enable the tracking of ecosystem health, wildlife populations, and the impact of human activities on the environment, thereby facilitating conservation initiatives.

One specific example of how drones are used in environmental monitoring is in the assessment of ecosystem health. By capturing high-resolution imagery of forests, wetlands, and other natural habitats, drones can provide detailed insights into vegetation cover, biodiversity, and habitat fragmentation. This information is essential for identifying areas of conservation concern and implementing targeted management strategies to preserve ecosystems.

Drones are also instrumental in monitoring wildlife populations, particularly in remote or inaccessible areas. Conservation biologists use drones to conduct aerial surveys of endangered species, such as orangutans in Borneo or elephants in Africa, to estimate population sizes, track movements, and identify potential threats. This data helps inform conservation efforts, such as habitat restoration and anti-poaching initiatives, aimed at protecting vulnerable species from extinction.

Furthermore, drones are valuable tools for assessing the impact of human activities on the environment, such as deforestation, habitat destruction, and pollution. By collecting aerial data, drones can document land-use changes, illegal logging activities, and pollution hotspots, providing evidence for enforcement agencies and advocacy groups to take action against environmental degradation.

Figure 120: USGS Team Flies Drones for Oregon BLM Forestry Research. Bureau of Land Management Oregon and Washington from Portland, America, Public domain, via Wikimedia Commons.

Drones have become essential tools in emergency response and disaster management scenarios, providing invaluable support in various critical tasks. One primary use of drones in this context is their role in rapid deployment, allowing emergency responders to quickly assess the situation and plan their response strategies. For example, during natural disasters such as earthquakes or hurricanes, drones can be deployed to survey affected areas, identify hazards, and assess the extent of damage to infrastructure and communities.

In addition to rapid deployment, drones play a crucial role in real-time data collection and enhanced situational awareness. Equipped with high-resolution cameras and sensors, drones can capture detailed imagery and gather vital information from disaster zones, allowing emergency responders to make informed decisions and prioritize their actions effectively. For instance, drones can provide aerial views of flooded areas to identify trapped individuals or assess the structural integrity of buildings.

Moreover, drones aid in damage assessment and victim location, significantly improving the efficiency and effectiveness of search and rescue operations. By conducting aerial surveys and thermal imaging, drones can help locate survivors in disaster-stricken areas, guiding rescue teams to their exact locations and potentially saving lives. Furthermore, drones can be utilized to deliver essential supplies, such as food, water, or medical equipment, to inaccessible or hard-to-reach areas, ensuring timely assistance to those in need.

Drones are increasingly being utilized for inspecting and maintaining critical infrastructure, particularly in the telecommunications and power sectors. One of the primary applications of drones in this domain is the inspection of telecommunications infrastructure, including cell towers, antennas, and communication networks. Equipped with high-resolution cameras and sensors, drones can capture detailed imagery of these structures, allowing engineers to identify potential issues, such as damaged components or structural defects, without the need for manual inspections.

Similarly, drones are employed for inspecting power lines and electrical infrastructure, enabling efficient identification of faults and reducing the risk of service disruptions. By conducting aerial surveys of power lines, drones can detect signs of wear and tear, vegetation encroachment, or other hazards that may pose a risk to the reliability and safety of electrical networks. This proactive approach to maintenance helps utility companies prevent outages and minimize downtime, ultimately improving service reliability for consumers.

Furthermore, drones equipped with specialized sensors, such as LiDAR (Light Detection and Ranging), can capture detailed data on terrain elevation and vegetation density, providing valuable insights for planning and optimizing infrastructure expansion or upgrades. By leveraging drone technology for infrastructure inspection, telecommunications and power companies can enhance maintenance practices, reduce operational costs, and improve overall system reliability.

While still in the early stages of implementation, drone delivery holds significant promise for revolutionizing transportation, especially in remote or inaccessible areas where traditional delivery methods may be impractical or costly. One key application of drones in this context is the swift and efficient transport of medical supplies, medications, and other critical items to remote communities or disaster-affected areas.

For example, drones can be used to deliver emergency medical supplies, such as defibrillators, first aid kits, or blood samples, to remote clinics or accident sites, enabling faster response times and potentially saving lives in emergency situations. Similarly, drones equipped with thermal imaging cameras can transport medical samples, vaccines, or organs for transplantation, maintaining their integrity and temperature control during transit.

In addition to medical delivery, drones hold promise for transporting cargo and goods to remote or underserved regions, facilitating economic development and improving access to essential supplies. For instance, drones can deliver food, water, or agricultural products to rural communities, overcoming logistical challenges such as poor infrastructure or impassable terrain. By reducing the time and cost of transportation, drone delivery systems have the potential to enhance supply chain efficiency and promote economic growth in remote areas.

Overall, while drone delivery is still in its infancy, ongoing advancements in technology and regulatory frameworks are expected to drive its adoption and integration into mainstream transportation systems, offering new opportunities for efficient and accessible delivery services in various sectors.

REFERENCES

1. Pu, C., et al., *A Stochastic Packet Forwarding Algorithm in Flying Ad Hoc Networks: Design, Analysis, and Evaluation.* Ieee Access, 2021.
2. Poljak, M. and A. Šterbenc, *Use of Drones in Clinical Microbiology and Infectious Diseases: Current Status, Challenges and Barriers.* Clinical Microbiology and Infection, 2020.
3. Khan, M.A., et al., *An Efficient and Conditional Privacy-Preserving Heterogeneous Signcryption Scheme for the Internet of Drones.* Sensors, 2023.
4. Araar, O., K. Benjdia, and I. Vitanov, *Hardware-Free Collision Detection and Braking for Securing Drone Propellers.* Aircraft Engineering and Aerospace Technology, 2021.
5. Rosser, J.C., et al., *Surgical and Medical Applications of Drones: A Comprehensive Review.* JSLS Journal of the Society of Laparoscopic & Robotic Surgeons, 2018.
6. Jeyabalan, V., et al., *Context-Specific Challenges, Opportunities, and Ethics of Drones for Healthcare Delivery in the Eyes of Program Managers and Field Staff: A Multi-Site Qualitative Study.* Drones, 2020.
7. Boutilier, J.J., et al., *Optimizing a Drone Network to Deliver Automated External Defibrillators.* Circulation, 2017.
8. Schierbeck, S., et al., *National Coverage of Out-of-Hospital Cardiac Arrests Using Automated External Defibrillator-Equipped Drones — A Geographical Information System Analysis.* Resuscitation, 2021.
9. Lin, Y.-F., et al., *Research on the Transformation of Historic Patterns of Cultural Landscape Using Aerial Photogrammetry and Geo-Database: A Case Study of Kuliang in*

Fuzhou, China. *The International Archives of the Photogrammetry Remote Sensing and Spatial Information Sciences*, 2021.

10. Wane, P., *Michael J. Boyle, the Drone Age: How Drone Technology Will Change War and Peace*. Prometheus, 2022.
11. Brunton, E., et al., *Fright or Flight? Behavioural Responses of Kangaroos to Drone-Based Monitoring*. Drones, 2019.
12. Banik, D., et al., *A Decision Support Model for Selecting Unmanned Aerial Vehicle for Medical Supplies: Context of COVID-19 Pandemic*. The International Journal of Logistics Management, 2022.
13. Bevan, E., et al., *Measuring Behavioral Responses of Sea Turtles, Saltwater Crocodiles, and Crested Terns to Drone Disturbance to Define Ethical Operating Thresholds*. Plos One, 2018.
14. Silalahi, S., T. Ahmad, and H. Studiawan, *Transformer-Based Named Entity Recognition on Drone Flight Logs to Support Forensic Investigation*. Ieee Access, 2023.
15. Egan, C.C., et al., *Testing a Key Assumption of Using Drones as Frightening Devices: Do Birds Perceive Drones as Risky?* Ornithological Applications, 2020.
16. Bezas, K., et al., *Coverage Path Planning and Point-of-Interest Detection Using Autonomous Drone Swarms*. Sensors, 2022.
17. Schäffer, B., et al., *Drone Noise Emission Characteristics and Noise Effects on Humans—A Systematic Review*. International Journal of Environmental Research and Public Health, 2021.
18. Chun, C., *Drone maker Zipline, on track for 1 million deliveries, adds vitamins, pizzas and prescriptions to cargo*. 2023, CNBC.
19. Shahid, N., et al., *Path Planning in Unmanned Aerial Vehicles: An Optimistic Overview*. International Journal of Communication Systems, 2022.
20. Zhang, B., et al., *Overview of Propulsion Systems for Unmanned Aerial Vehicles*. Energies, 2022.
21. Shakhatreh, H., et al., *Unmanned Aerial Vehicles (UAVs): A Survey on Civil Applications and Key Research Challenges*. Ieee Access, 2019.
22. Feng, Q., J. Liu, and J. Gong, *UAV Remote Sensing for Urban Vegetation Mapping Using Random Forest and Texture Analysis*. Remote Sensing, 2015.
23. Yinka-Banjo, C. and O. Ajayi, *Sky-Farmers: Applications of Unmanned Aerial Vehicles (UAV) in Agriculture*. 2020.

24. Elmeseiry, N., N. Alshaer, and T. Ismail, *A Detailed Survey and Future Directions of Unmanned Aerial Vehicles (UAVs) With Potential Applications.* Aerospace, 2021.
25. Nemer, I.A., et al., *RF-Based UAV Detection and Identification Using Hierarchical Learning Approach.* Sensors, 2021.
26. Medaiyese, O.O., et al., *Hierarchical Learning Framework for UAV Detection and Identification.* 2021.
27. Wang, H., et al., *Survey on Unmanned Aerial Vehicle Networks: A Cyber Physical System Perspective.* Ieee Communications Surveys & Tutorials, 2020.
28. Shrestha, R., et al., *Machine-Learning-Enabled Intrusion Detection System for Cellular Connected UAV Networks.* Electronics, 2021.
29. JoUAV, *Different Types of Drones and Uses (2024 Full Guide).* 2024.
30. PennState College of Earth and Mineral Sciences. *Classification of the Unmanned Aerial Systems.* 2024 [cited 2024 22/4/2024]; Available from: https://www.e-education.psu.edu/geog892/node/5.
31. AviAssist. *Which Drone type training suits your needs?* 2024 [cited 2024 22/4/2024]; Available from: https://aviassist.com.au/which-drone-type-suits/.
32. AVPL International, *Drones categorized by inclusive weight, per Drone Rules 2021.* 2023, Medium.
33. García, I.Q., et al., *A Quickly Deployed and UAS-Based Logistics Network for Delivery of Critical Medical Goods During Healthcare System Stress Periods: A Real Use Case in Valencia (Spain).* Drones, 2021.
34. Filho, F.H.I., et al., *Drones: Innovative Technology for Use in Precision Pest Management.* Journal of Economic Entomology, 2019.
35. Schootman, M., et al., *Emerging Technologies to Measure Neighborhood Conditions in Public Health: Implications for Interventions and Next Steps.* International Journal of Health Geographics, 2016.
36. Ayamga, M. and B. Tekinerdoğan, *Exploring the Challenges Posed by Regulations for the Use of Drones in Agriculture in the African Context.* Land, 2021.
37. Ayamga, M., B. Tekinerdoğan, and G. Rambaldi, *Developing a Policy Framework for Adoption and Management of Drones for Agriculture in Africa.* Technology Analysis and Strategic Management, 2020.
38. Yıldızel, S.A. and G. Calış, *Unmanned Aerial Vehicles for Civil Engineering: Current Practises and Regulations.* European Journal of Science and Technology, 2019.

39. Yıldız, S., S. Kıvrak, and G. Arslan, *Using Drone Technologies for Construction Project Management: A Narrative Review.* Journal of Construction Engineering Management & Innovation, 2021.
40. Stöcker, C., et al., *Review of the Current State of UAV Regulations.* Remote Sensing, 2017.
41. Macpherson, E., *Is the World Ready for Drones?* Air and Space Law, 2018.
42. UAVCoach. *Drone Laws in the United States of America.* 2024 [cited 2024 22/4/2024]; Available from: https://uavcoach.com/drone-laws-in-united-states-of-america/.
43. Federal Aviation Administration. *Recreational Flyers & Community-Based Organizations.* 2023 [cited 2024 22/4/2024]; Available from: https://www.faa.gov/uas/recreational_flyers.
44. Wawrzyn, D., *Commercial Drone Laws and Regulations in the US, Australia, and Europe: What You Need to Know.* 2024.
45. Federal Aviation Administration, *Remote Pilot – Small Unmanned Aircraft Systems Study Guide.* 2016, Flight Standards Service Washington DC: Federal Aviation Administration.
46. Civil Aviation Safety Authority. *Drone rules.* 2024 [cited 2024 22/4/2024]; Available from: https://www.casa.gov.au/knowyourdrone/drone-rules.
47. Wilson, H., *Navigating Legislation in Australia to Utilise Drones for your Spatial Company.* 2024.
48. Williams, T. and E. Grinbergs, *Drone Laws: New Registration and Mandatory Reporting Scheme* 2021, Holman Webb Lawyers.
49. Leslie, J., *Drone Laws UK 2024 & Regulations.* 2024.
50. Drone Site Surveys. *Drone Laws UK 2024.* 2024 [cited 2024 22/4/2024]; Available from: https://dronesitesurveys.co.uk/drone-laws-uk/.
51. Wiegert, H., *The 2024 EU Drone Regulations: What You Need to Know.* 2023, Drone Nomad.
52. Drone Laws, *The Open Category of Drones in Europe.* 2024.
53. UAVCoach. *Drone Laws in India.* 2024 [cited 2024 23/4/2024]; Available from: https://uavcoach.com/drone-laws-in-india/.
54. Bennett University. *Drone Regulations in India: Navigating the Legal and Regulatory Landscape.* 2024 [cited 2024 23/4/2024]; Available

from: https://www.bennett.edu.in/media-center/blog/drone-regulations-in-india-navigating-the-legal-and-regulatory-landscape/.

55. IAS Vision. *Drone Rules 2022: Amendment and Classification*. 2024 [cited 2024 23/4/2024]; Available from: https://iasvision.com/drone-rules-2022/.
56. Tennyson, E., *Aeronautical Charts: Scale is key difference between VFR aeronautical chart types*. 2024, AOPA.
57. Pilot Institute. *How to Read A Sectional Chart: An Easy to Understand Guide*. 2020 [cited 2024 23/4/2024]; Available from: https://pilotinstitute.com/sectional-chart/.
58. Pachpute, S. *How do drones fly in air? Which drone is more popular?* 2024 [cited 2024 24/4/2024]; Available from: https://cfdflowengineering.com/working-principle-and-components-of-drone/.
59. Gateway Data Systems. *Pre and Post Flight Checklists – DJI Phantom 3 Professional*. 2016 [cited 2024 24/4/2024]; Available from: https://gatewaydatasystems.com/2016/01/12/pre-and-post-flight-checklists-dji-phantom-3-professional/.
60. Carnes, T., *A Low Cost Implementation of Autonomous Takeoff and Landing for a Fixed Wing UAV*. 2014, Virginia Commonwealth University: Richmond, Virginia.
61. Experimental Aircraft Info. *Taking Off Into The Wind*. 2024 [cited 2024 24/4/2024]; Available from: https://www.experimentalaircraft.info/flight-planning/aircraft-performance-4.php.
62. Green, D. *Tailwind Takeoffs and Landings*. 2024 [cited 2024 24/4/2024]; Available from: https://www.challengers101.com/Tailwind.html.
63. Newcome, L., *UVS Info*. 2013.
64. Ofcom, *Spectrum for Unmanned Aircraft Systems (UAS) licence: Licensing guidance document for licensed equipment on drones*. 2023.
65. Pilotfriend. *Stalls*. 2024 [cited 2024 26/4/2024]; Available from: http://www.pilotfriend.com/training/flight_training/fxd_wing/stalls.htm.
66. Aviators Guide. *Wind Triangle*. 2020 [cited 2024 26/4/2024]; Available from: https://aviatorsguide.wordpress.com/2020/08/11/wind-triangle/.
67. Splash Marine, *Assist in Search and Rescue*. 2005.
68. Croptracker, *Drone Technology In Agriculture*. 2024.

INDEX

A

Accelerometer, 343, 347, 449, 458

Aerial, 9–11, 14, 16–19, 22–23, 25–27, 29–30, 32–33, 35–39, 42, 44, 51, 57–58, 63, 66, 70, 78, 89, 93, 106, 112, 125, 203, 205, 236, 265, 356, 432, 450, 456–457, 462, 477, 479–480, 487, 490, 492, 494, 517–519

Aerial view, 18

Agriculture, 16, 22–24, 52, 148, 518–519, 521

Aileron, 220, 229, 261, 377

Airspace, 10–12, 27, 29, 51–54, 56–65, 67–68, 73, 78–80, 103–104, 106, 111, 113, 115–119, 123, 126–129, 132, 134–135, 138–143, 147, 160–162, 235, 237, 239, 362, 410, 423, 426–437, 440–441, 450, 455–456

Altitude, 12, 51, 54, 56, 58–61, 63, 65, 71, 73–74, 76, 78, 80–81, 84, 89, 95–96, 103, 107–108, 111, 113, 118–119, 121–123, 125, 128, 135, 138–140, 142, 162–163, 205, 207–208, 216–217, 219, 221–222, 239, 243–245, 251–253, 255–257, 260, 266, 341, 344–345, 350, 353, 355, 358–360, 364–365, 367, 410, 427, 434–437, 439, 443, 448–449, 451–454, 456–459, 483, 493–494

Antenna, 209, 248, 262–263, 355, 364, 368, 415, 496, 515

Architecture, 207, 296

Asia, 412–413

Australia, 18, 52–53, 70–72, 76, 78–80, 204, 412–413, 415, 417, 422, 510, 520

Authorization, 56, 58–59, 103, 106, 426–427, 429–430, 456

Autonomous, 16, 19, 21, 235–237, 251–252, 350, 449–451, 453–455, 457, 518, 521

Axes, 228, 375

B

Battery, 71, 124, 205–206, 208, 210, 215–219, 240, 246–247, 249, 262, 338–339, 349–350, 361, 365, 369–370, 450–451, 454, 457, 461–478

Battery management, 462

Best practices, 10, 12, 56, 474

C

CAA, 11, 83–85, 87–90, 94, 98–101

Camera, 24, 75, 78, 107–108, 123, 136–137, 205, 208, 232, 234, 241–242, 246, 248–250, 339, 354, 368, 426, 477

Cameras, 14, 22, 24–25, 36, 49, 51, 54, 75, 205, 234, 368, 449, 461, 480–481, 493–494

CASA, 70–78, 203–204, 520

Charging, 216, 338, 431, 464–465, 469, 472–475, 477

Chassis, 204

Civil aviation, 70, 72, 74, 79–80, 83, 85, 87–89, 94, 98–101, 110, 112, 116, 121, 146, 204, 520

Clouds, 73, 152–154, 157–158, 184, 442

Collaboration, 100, 482

Collision detection, 517

Combustible, 473

Communication, 60, 80, 120–121, 123, 125, 128, 141, 143, 159–162, 237, 239–240, 263, 278, 293, 311, 335, 337, 362, 409–410, 415, 419, 423–424, 434, 436–438, 480–482, 484, 493, 495, 497, 518–519

Communication protocols, 484

Compass, 355, 426, 456

Compliance, 10, 12, 52, 55, 61, 71, 74–77, 79–81, 103–104, 108, 119–121, 135, 139, 161, 235, 349, 424, 432, 434–435, 456

Components, 121, 145, 151, 203–207, 223, 229, 239, 293, 353, 361, 368–369, 432, 445, 450, 462, 476, 521

Construction, 30, 223, 225, 265, 347, 410, 432, 465, 520

Control, 13, 15, 22, 58–60, 63–65, 70, 72–73, 79, 100, 115, 117, 119, 130–132, 134, 136–137, 141–142, 145, 148, 160–162, 203, 205–209, 213, 215–231, 235–237, 241–244, 246–247, 250–253, 260–261, 263, 266–267, 294, 296, 339–340, 342–346, 350–362, 364–367, 374–377, 399, 409, 415–416, 420, 422, 426–430, 435–437, 448, 450–454, 457, 459, 470, 484–485, 494

Controller, 78, 114, 137, 146–148, 205, 207–209, 235–237, 242, 251, 262, 340, 343–344, 347, 350, 353, 369, 436, 449–452, 454–455, 457, 461, 468

Crop monitoring, 431

D

Data, 11, 17, 22–23, 25, 27, 29–30, 51–52, 54–55, 57, 68, 79, 84, 101, 114, 126–127, 129, 133, 145, 147–148, 152, 154, 159–160, 173, 177, 189, 191–192, 205, 236–237, 339, 362, 410, 435–436, 449, 451–459, 476–477, 479, 521

Decision-making, 25–26, 29, 233, 251, 261, 268–269

Documentation, 81, 120–121, 127

E

Elevator, 220, 229, 376

Emergency procedures, 138, 144, 160–161, 361–362

Emergency services, 162

Emerging technologies, 519

Endurance, 251, 349–350

Environmental monitoring, 17, 26, 30, 432

F

FAA, 52, 56–58, 62–63, 66, 130–131, 480, 520

Fixed Wing, 34–35, 260, 371–375, 521

Flight, 26, 53, 67–68, 163, 197, 199, 243, 314, 338–339, 348, 353, 394, 400, 427, 434, 440, 449–451, 455, 457, 477, 518, 520–521

Frame, 204, 206–207, 211, 343, 354, 439

Frequency, 67, 294, 339, 365–366, 368

Fronts, 150, 185–187

Fuselage, 207

G

Gimbal, 208, 354

GPS, 243, 449, 453, 459

Ground station, 117, 137, 145, 241, 243, 368, 459

Guidelines, 27, 29, 51, 53, 56, 58, 71, 86, 88, 95, 100–101, 106–107, 113, 117, 215, 243, 361, 365, 427–428, 430–432, 465, 474–475

Gyroscope, 206, 426, 449, 458

H

Hardware, 361, 517

Hovering, 212, 214, 220, 222, 227, 255, 263, 348, 360, 453, 457, 469

Human factors, 275, 309–310

Hybrid, 39–40, 461, 465–466

I

Imaging, 17, 21–22, 25, 441, 481

India, 110–116, 520–521

Industrial, 84, 89, 98–99, 105, 431, 501

Infrared, 25

Infrastructure inspection, 112

Innovation, 18, 21, 24–25, 104, 111, 264, 520

Inspection, 12, 26, 58, 76, 106, 112, 119–121, 123, 361, 431, 450–451, 459–460, 502

Integration, 29, 52, 94, 99, 148, 429–430, 441

L

Landing, 67, 72, 79, 100, 121–123, 136, 144, 160, 215, 222, 226, 231, 234–235, 238, 241, 251–261, 265–267, 354, 357–358, 360, 363–365, 367, 384, 387–388, 418, 431, 436, 450–451, 457, 484, 521

Landing gear, 136, 222, 241, 260

Law enforcement, 57, 479

Lessons learned, 139, 142

Licensing, 51, 54, 79, 146, 203, 521

LiDAR, 30, 511

Lidar, 30, 511

LiPo, 461–477

Lithium, 370, 461–462, 464–466, 472, 475–476

Load factors, 195

M

Magnetometer, 458

Maintenance, 10–11, 82, 152, 223, 233, 264, 310, 451, 458, 460, 465

Manoeuvrability, 204, 211, 226, 229

Mapping, 26, 126–128, 141, 339, 431–432, 450, 455–457, 518

Memory card, 232, 451

METAR, 151

Meteorology, 146

Mission, 13, 16–17, 21, 25, 75, 125, 128, 143, 160, 232, 240, 243–244, 264, 335, 337, 339, 349–350, 354–355, 362–363, 449–451, 455–457, 459–460, 479, 487

Monitoring, 14–17, 23–26, 30, 73, 76, 89, 106, 120, 147–148, 160, 431–432, 440, 455–456, 461, 471, 497, 506–507, 518

Motors, 204–207, 210, 217, 219, 233, 235, 250, 252, 263, 338, 340–344, 348–350, 354, 356, 370, 450, 461–464, 476

Multirotor, 36–37, 214, 338–340, 343–345, 368–370

N

Nano, 118

Navigation, 19, 62, 64–66, 68, 79–81, 121, 126–129, 145, 358, 362, 426, 437, 442, 445–446, 448–451, 453–459

NOTAM, 410, 439

O

Objective, 51

Obstacle avoidance, 451

Operator, 9–12, 51–52, 54–56, 58, 61–62, 68, 70–71, 73, 76–79, 97, 103, 105–108, 110–112, 115–116, 118, 122, 125, 127–129, 139, 146, 160–162, 203, 208, 231, 240, 248, 251, 335, 424, 427–428, 430–433, 453, 456, 480

Operator fatigue, 251

P

Path, 67, 73–74, 111, 119, 125, 127, 133, 138, 140, 142, 161, 196, 206, 235, 237, 245, 266, 359, 367, 442–443, 445, 449–451, 454, 456–457, 488, 490, 493–494, 518

Payload, 51, 54, 75, 111, 206, 208, 223, 232, 339, 350, 354, 461

Performance, 125, 137–139, 143, 146, 160, 171, 204–206, 215, 223–228, 236, 240, 251, 253, 255–256, 311–312, 316, 319, 321–322, 328–332, 336, 362, 370, 445, 448, 456

Permits, 11, 51, 54, 63, 74, 120, 260, 432, 470

Pest control, 22

Photogrammetry, 75, 517–518

Photography, 16–18, 27, 75–76, 105, 112, 205, 356, 432, 450, 477

Pilot, 9, 11, 13–14, 16, 27–29, 53, 56–60, 62, 64, 66, 68, 75–76, 78, 80–82, 106–108, 110, 113–114, 120–123, 128–130, 132–133, 135–136, 144–151, 154–155, 158–159, 199, 203–204, 222, 226, 228, 230, 234, 239, 241, 253–256, 258–267, 309, 312, 338, 342, 350, 352, 360–361, 365–366, 368–369, 371, 409–411, 414, 416–417, 419–420, 422–424, 426, 429–431, 435–440, 445–446, 448–449, 454, 456–457, 461, 520–521

Pitch, 206–208, 211–212, 216–220, 227–229, 266–267, 340, 346–347, 352–353, 355–357, 360, 376, 449–450, 452–453

Polymer, 370, 461–462, 464–466

Power consumption, 349, 477

Procedures, 10–11, 26, 54, 60–61, 79–80, 106, 120–121, 128, 138–139, 142, 144, 160–162, 216, 218, 233, 235–237, 361–363, 367, 416–417, 423–424, 429–430, 436–437, 439–441, 451, 456, 484, 486

Processing, 205, 451, 458

Propellers, 136, 204–208, 210–212, 214, 231, 233, 241, 248, 262, 264, 341, 348–352, 354, 356–357, 361, 450, 477, 517

Propulsion, 204, 223, 518

Q

Quadcopter, 211, 213, 221, 340, 345–346, 350–353, 355–360

R

Radar, 58, 67–68, 122, 127, 147, 150, 237, 295, 298, 300, 436–437, 441, 484

Radio, 59–60, 77–78, 80, 128, 130, 137, 147, 149–150, 205, 208, 231, 251, 262, 292, 302, 339–340, 349–350, 369, 409, 415, 417–418, 434, 436–437, 440–441, 458, 465, 483–484, 496

Range, 14, 17, 20, 24, 29, 46, 83, 105, 124, 134, 145–147, 149, 151, 224, 228, 240, 243–244, 262, 339, 349, 356, 368, 459, 463–465, 468, 474, 483–484, 511

Real estate, 16, 18, 57

Real-time monitoring, 23, 456

Receiver, 136–137, 205, 209, 241, 243, 262, 340, 364, 449, 453, 458, 468

Reconnaissance, 13, 16–17, 22, 25, 75, 264, 496

Regulations, 16, 27, 29, 51–57, 61–62, 66, 68, 70–72, 74–77, 79–81, 83–85, 87, 89–90, 93, 95, 97–106, 110–113, 117–118, 121–122, 127, 135, 140, 147, 162, 204, 235, 253, 367, 426–435, 441, 456, 519–521

Remote, 15, 21, 56–59, 62, 71, 75–76, 81–82, 88, 90–93, 98, 106, 108, 119–121, 129, 145, 203, 205, 208–209, 215–216, 218–219, 251, 263, 309, 312, 336, 338, 353, 362, 368, 371, 410, 424, 426, 435, 439, 450–451, 455, 457, 461, 479, 481, 483, 518, 520

Remote Control, 15, 205, 208–209, 215–216, 218–219, 263, 353

Remote control, 15, 205, 208–209, 215–216, 218–219, 263, 353

Remote Pilot, 56–59, 76, 81–82, 106, 108, 120, 129, 203, 309, 338, 371, 410, 424, 426, 461, 520

Repairs, 233

Reporting, 68, 77, 151, 434–435, 484, 486–487, 520

Resolution, 22, 24–25, 127–128

Restricted zones, 29, 72, 456

Risk assessment, 10, 76, 103–104

Roll, 206–208, 211–212, 216–220, 227–229, 340, 344–345, 347, 351, 353, 355–356, 360, 377, 420, 449–450, 452–453

Rotors, 9, 167, 207–208, 211, 220

Route, 26, 65, 67–68, 80, 99, 121–122, 125, 127–128, 136, 138, 143–144, 146, 148–149, 159–161, 240, 413–414, 416–418, 434, 437, 440, 453, 455–456, 486

RPAS, 203–204, 423, 510

Rudder, 220, 229

S

Safety protocols, 10, 139, 161–162, 360

Search and rescue, 21–22, 25, 72, 432, 459–460, 479–480, 482–486, 488, 490–494, 496, 498, 521

Sensors, 9, 14, 21–22, 25–26, 51, 54, 151, 189, 205, 234, 251, 335, 449–451, 457–459, 480–481, 517–519

Signal, 71, 117, 160–161, 208–209, 237, 243–244, 260, 262–263, 340, 350, 353, 362, 426, 436, 449, 453–454, 456, 458–460, 483–484, 496–497

Single rotor, 207, 266

Situational awareness, 74, 276, 417–418, 420, 451, 455–456, 479, 481–482

Skills, 10–11, 78, 346, 350, 358–359

Software, 339, 350, 355, 361, 450, 453–455, 457

Stability, 194, 196, 204, 208, 210, 215, 217, 223–229, 340, 448, 453, 474, 502

Surveillance, 9–10, 14, 16, 24–25, 52, 57, 112, 431–432, 435–437, 450, 457, 461

Surveying, 106, 112, 125, 432

T

Take-off, 252, 254, 257, 381, 393, 396

Task, 9, 15, 234, 251, 260, 266, 350, 360, 416, 498

Telemetry, 123, 238, 339, 451–452, 455–456, 472

Thermal imaging, 17, 22, 25, 441, 481

Thunderstorms, 145, 156–158, 160

Tracking, 16, 25, 51, 231, 237, 252

Training, 51, 54, 65–68, 76, 88, 92–95, 98, 106–108, 110, 113, 126, 136, 162, 203, 251, 253, 265, 352, 365–368, 428, 498, 508, 519, 521

Transmission, 208–209, 293, 310, 335, 339, 368, 436–438, 482, 499

Transmitter, 124, 136–137, 205, 208, 216–219, 234, 240–244, 339, 346, 351–355, 364–365, 368–369, 435–436, 451, 484, 496

U

UAV, 9, 14, 24, 32, 38, 40, 44, 51, 70, 76–78, 123, 203, 348–349, 371, 518–521

UK, 21, 83–88, 92–99, 337, 520

Unmanned Aerial Vehicle, 9, 14, 19, 22, 37, 51, 57, 70, 78, 203, 456, 518–519

Urban planning, 17, 29–30

USA, 52, 56–57, 69

V

Video, 16, 18, 27, 55, 76, 101, 123, 136–137, 239, 241–242, 339, 350, 368, 441

Visibility, 52, 86, 107, 350, 354, 367, 426, 435, 450

W

Waypoints, 444–445, 449–450, 454–457

Weather, 67–68, 71, 117, 163–164, 166–167, 169–170, 174, 177–178, 182–183, 186–187, 189, 191–192, 215, 361, 364, 368, 426, 432–433, 437, 441, 445, 448, 450, 453, 455–456, 478, 483, 486–487, 490, 492, 497

Weather conditions, 71, 117, 167, 183, 186–187, 189, 191, 215, 361, 364, 368, 426, 433, 441, 448, 450, 453, 455–456, 478, 487, 492, 497

Weight, 43, 54, 114, 171, 193, 196, 200, 206, 208, 210, 213, 225–226, 228–230, 246, 341, 347, 356, 370, 462–464, 469, 476–477, 519

Wind resistance, 208

Wind shear, 170, 176–177, 441

Wireless, 368

Y

Yaw, 206, 208, 211, 216–220, 227–229, 340, 343, 347, 352–353, 356–357, 359–360, 405, 449–450, 452–453

www.ingramcontent.com/pod-product-compliance
Lightning Source LLC
Chambersburg PA
CBHW072142070526
44585CB00015B/986